W9-BHP-882

JUN 11 1998

According to Jean O'Brien, Indians did not simply disappear from colonial Natick, Massachusetts, as the English extended their domination. Rather, the Indians creatively resisted colonialism, defended their lands, and rebuilt kin networks and community through the strategic use of English cultural practices and institutions. In the late eighteenth century, Natick Indians experienced a process of "dispossession by degrees" that rendered them invisible within the larger context of the colonial social order, and enabled the construction of the myth of Indian extinction.

Dispossession by degrees

CAMBRIDGE STUDIES IN NORTH AMERICAN INDIAN HISTORY

Editors
Frederick E. Hoxie, *The Newberry Library*
Neal Salisbury, *Smith College*

Also in the series

Richard White, *The Middle Ground: Indians, Empires, and Republics in the Great Lakes Region, 1650–1815*

Sidney L. Harring, *Crow Dog's Case: American Indian Sovereignty, Tribal Law, and United States Law in the Nineteenth Century*

Colin G. Calloway, *The American Revolution in Indian Country: Crisis and Diversity in Native American Communities*

Frederick E. Hoxie, *Parading Through History: The Making of the Crow Nation in America, 1805–1935*

Dispossession by degrees

Indian land and identity in
Natick, Massachusetts, 1650–1790

JEAN M. O'BRIEN

CAMBRIDGE
UNIVERSITY PRESS

PUBLISHED BY THE PRESS SYNDICATE OF THE UNIVERSITY OF CAMBRIDGE
The Pitt Building, Trumpington Street, Cambridge CB2 IRP, United Kingdom

CAMBRIDGE UNIVERSITY PRESS
The Edinburgh Building, Cambridge CB2 IRP, United Kingdom
40 West 20th Street, New York, NY 10011-4211, USA
10 Stamford Road, Oakleigh, Melbourne 3166, Australia

© Jean M. O'Brien 1997

This book is copyright. Subject to statutory exception
and to the provisions of relevant collective licensing agreements,
no reproduction of any part may take place without
the written permission of Cambridge University Press.

First published 1997

Printed in the United States of America

Typeset in Ehrhardt

Library of Congress Cataloguing-in-Publication Data

O'Brien, Jean M.
Dispossession by degrees : Indian land and identity in Natick,
Massachusetts / Jean M. O'Brien.
p.   cm. – (Cambridge studies in North American Indian history)
ISBN 0-521-56172-8 (hardback)
1. Indians of North America – Massachusetts – Natick – Land Tenure.
2. Indians of North America – Massachusetts – Natick – Kinship.
3. Indians of North America – Massachusetts – Natick – Cultural
assimilation. 4. Massachusetts – History – Colonial period. ca.
1600–1775.   I. Title. II. Series.
E78.M4027 1997   96-22551
974.4'4 – dc20   CIP

A catalog record for this book is available from
the British Library

ISBN 0-521-561728 hardback

For my parents, Gene and Mae O'Brien,
and our extended family

CHEYNEY COMMUNITY COLLEGE
ELAINE NICPON MARIEB LIBRARY

Contents

List of illustrations

Figures

Tables

Acknowledgments

I have accumulated many debts in completing this book, and am solely responsible for any errors that may remain in it. It grew out of my first seminar with Ted Cook in colonial American social history, a field then importantly shaped by community studies, at the University of Chicago. When settling on a research topic I thought: why not study an Indian community? Natick, so prominent in the literature as a missionary "experiment," seemed a logical choice. When the time came to choose a dissertation topic, I decided to continue my investigation beyond King Philip's War because there seemed to be so little existing literature that did so. As I struggled to pull together materials that could tell Natick's story, I came to understand why it might be the case that its post-1676 history had been left largely untold. At Chicago, Kathy Conzen and Ray Fogelson joined Ted Cook on my dissertation committee, and generously encouraged my work. I am deeply grateful to all three of my mentors, who at Chicago and ever since have been supportive, generous, and unstintingly helpful.

As I struggled to make my dissertation a book, I incurred additional debts. At the University of Minnesota, I have had the great fortune of many generous colleagues who offered welcome assistance in reading and critiquing various drafts of chapters as well as stimulating conversations that importantly shaped my work. The Colonial History Workshop, especially Rus Menard, Lucy Simler, John Howe, Jen Spear, Brett Mizelle, Matt Mulcahy, Jean Russo, Wendel Cox, David Rayson, Ginny Jelatis, and Anne Enke read many chapters and offered sound advice. My American Studies writing group also counseled me often and well. For their helpful contributions I thank David Noble, Lary May, Elaine Tyler May, Carol Miller, John Wright, David Roediger, Leola Johnson, Riv Ellen Prell, and Angela Dillard. Lisa Disch, Jennifer Pierce, and Lisa Bower, colleagues in a newer writing group, provided intensive, insightful readings of every chapter, crucial prose suggestions, and good-humored encouragement. Ann Waltner and Mary Jo Maynes generously read the entire manuscript at two important stages, and put me on track with lightning-fast, sage advice that is deeply appreciated. I also thank my research assistants Sheri Brown, Margaret Rodgers, and especially Anne Enke. For my illustrations and maps I thank Amy Alving, who taught me Excel, and Allan Willis and Mark Lindberg at the University of Minnesota Cartographic Laboratory, who put all the maps and figures into their present form. Others at the University of Minnesota who supplied gratefully acknowledged assistance include Barbara Hanawalt, Stuart Schwartz, Allan Isaacman, Sara Evans, Byron Marshall, Dennis Valdez, and Janet Spector. Jim Merrell, a fellow Minnesotan and (fortunately for us) recurrent visitor to the University, has provided indispensable guidance for years. Elsewhere, I want to thank Thomas Doughton, Colin Calloway, Barry O'Connell, Ann Plane, Ruth Herndon, Kathy Brown, Bill Hart, James Axtell, Nancy Shoemaker, Fredricka Teute, who offered insightful readings and advice, and Gerald Schnabel, Earl Nyholm, Kent Smith, Melissa Meyer, Brenda Child, Pat Albers, Carol Karlsen, Peter Wood, and Bea Medicine for their support.

I have been greatly assisted over the years by financial assistance and intellectual stimulation from institutions that made the dissertation and its transformation into a book possible. Two year-long dissertation fellowships from the University of Chicago, the Harry Barnard Dissertation Year Fellowship and CBS Bicentennial Narrators Scholarship, freed me from my day jobs to do research and write. A Newberry Library Pre-doctoral dissertation fellowship gave me not just a year in residence at that astounding research center, but full-time access to a terrific group of fellows and staff, especially Fred Hoxie, Colin Calloway, and the inimitable John Aubrey. The D'Arcy McNickle Center also made room for me with a carrel throughout my years in graduate school in Chicago, which expanded my intellectual community north of Hyde Park. A Kate B. and Hall J. Peterson two-month fellowship at the American Antiquarian Society gave me access to another great institution and community, as did a Society of the Cincinnati Fellowship from the Massachusetts Historical Society. At these institutions I would like especially to acknowledge John Hench, Peter Drummey, and Louis Tucker, and thank both institutions for permission to cite from their manuscript collections. Thanks also to Martha Jones at the Morse Institute Library, for assistance and permission to cite from their collections, and staff members at the Massachusetts Archives, Middlesex County Court House, and Boston Public Library. The cover illustration, "The Basket Seller" by Cornelius Kreighoff, c. 1850 (oil on board, 24.8 x 18.9 cm, gift of The Fund of the T. Eaton Co. Ltd. for Canadian Works of Art), is owned by and reproduced with permission from the Art Gallery of Ontario. I also gratefully acknowledge the University of Minnesota for fellowship support: two graduate school grants-in-aid, a summer research fellowship, and a McKnight-Land Grant Professorship.

I have had the good fortune to work with Frank Smith, Andrea Caserta, and Jeff Hoffman at Cambridge University Press, who have all been wonderful and cheerful about my questions. To the series editors, Fred Hoxie and Neal Salisbury, I offer my deepest gratitude for their fabulous guidance.

Much of this book is about families, and it is my privilege to acknowledge the love and support of my family, which matter to me in incalculable ways. My parents, Gene and Mae O'Brien, my brothers Mark and Mike, my twin sister Julie Johnson, and her husband and children Jay, Laura, and Thomas, and my other twin sisters Maggie Palmisano, her husband and children Peter, Jack, and Sam, and Nan Wambheim, and her husband and children Dave, Joe, and Sarah compose this large and often noisy lot. Words can't express what this is all about, but they know.

Finally, I want to thank my husband, Timothy J. Kehoe, whose own family has to my good fortune become my own. Tim has also offered feedback on my work, an abundance of enthusiasm in everyday matters, and astounding connections to people and places. His presence in my life insures that there will never be a dull moment.

Crafting this book according to varying rhythms over the past fourteen years evoked strong resonance with me because, as I came to learn, Natick's history paralleled crucial aspects of my own family's history. In researching and writing this book, I have had frequent occasion to remember my maternal grandmother, Caroline Edna Wright Tonneson, who understood my halting Ojibwe when I came home to visit from college but chose monolingual English for her children. My grandmother and her extended family, very few of whom survived to perpetuate their lineages, witnessed the implementation of the federal government's allotment and assimilation policies first-hand. Like most Ojibwe people on the White Earth Reservation in northwestern Minnesota, they lost all of their land.

Prologue

"My land"

Natick and the narrative of Indian extinction

The button-wood trees, in front of the south tavern, were set out in 1783 . . . Their being planted on the Indian burying ground gave offence to some of the few remaining individuals of the tribe; and one poor girl, with a mixture of grief and anger, endeavoured to uproot them; but they resisted her efforts, as they have many a violent storm, are still in a thriving condition, and measure 17 feet in circumference, at the height of two feet from the ground.[1]

A. *The narrative construction*

This passage by William Biglow, from the section on "Remarkable Trees" in the first published history of Natick, Massachusetts (1830), describes a scene rich with symbolism. In planting buttonwood trees in front of a tavern and on the Indian burying ground, the relatively recently arrived English residents of the once all-Indian community engaged in a colonial act. In "grief and anger," an offended Indian girl defiantly resisted this deed of desecration and erasure, presumably hoping to defend the graves and memory of her people. By the 1780s, the Indian burying ground constituted one of the last places within the town that Indians could claim as their own.[2]

These were not the only Natick trees Biglow found remarkable. The others he wrote about served to mark the Indian-mission origin of the town. He noted two oaks that grew upon the place English Calvinist missionary John Eliot preached to the Indians (between 1650 and 1690). He also noted the elms Indians had planted in front of the houses of their two eighteenth-century English ministers, Oliver Peabody (from 1722 until 1752) and Stephen Badger (from 1753 until 1799) as "trees of friendship."[3] In contrast to the buttonwood trees,

---

[1] William Biglow, *History of the Town of Natick, Massachusetts From the Days of the Apostolic Eliot, 1650, to the Present Time, 1830* (Boston: Marsh, Capen, and Lyon, 1830), 11–2.

[2] For an argument that focuses on the ways in which New England Indian identity was maintained by a shifting ideological connection to a mythic, then historic, landscape using the Native concept "manit" (power), see Constance A. Crosby, "From Myth to History, or Why King Philip's Ghost Walks Abroad," in *The Recovery of Meaning: Historical Archaeology in the Eastern United States,* ed. Mark P. Leone and Parker B. Potter (Washington: Smithsonian Insitution Press, 1988), 183–209; and for a study of the connection between memory and place, see Kent C. Ryden, *Mapping the Invisible Landscape: Folklore, Writing, and the Sense of Place* (Iowa City: University of Iowa Press, 1993).

[3] Biglow, *History of Natick*, 10–1.

these plantings symbolized cooperation between two peoples and reflected cultural changes Indians had made in order to survive.

Like the buttonwood trees and unlike the displaced Indians, English residents were firmly rooted in Natick by the end of the eighteenth century. The condition of the other trees Biglow surveyed paralleled the historical legacy of the Indian community in telling ways. The oaks that had grown at the inception of the Indian mission community had decayed for forty years. The elms planted for Peabody had died in the early nineteenth century. Badger's vigorous elms stood "in front of the house now occupied by Mr. Oliver Bacon," who was neither a minister nor a friend, but a Euro-American whose relatives had bought land from Indian and English sellers in the last half of the eighteenth century. Land acquisition was a Bacon family tradition. Eight Bacons bought land from Indians in Natick. At least six more got Natick land from relatives who had bought land from other English sellers in the speculative frenzy of late eighteenth-century Natick.[4]

The planting of the buttonwood trees by English people who dispossessed Indians of their land mocked the dramatic transformation of Natick as an Indian place. Founded as a missionary experiment in 1650, Natick had endured as a largely autonomous Indian community well into the eighteenth century. But beginning in the 1740s, half a century before the Eliot oaks began to decay, so too did Indian ownership of Natick land start to erode.

Biglow's history resembled many other nineteenth-century accounts of New England towns in its minute description of the landscape, its recounting of the "glorious acts" of remarkable residents, the implanting of English institutions, and its laments about "the fate of the tribe of Aborigines."[5] The "advertise-

---

[4] Middlesex County Court, Grantee and Grantor Records (hereafter cited as MCG), Cambridge, MA, 65:503, to Oliver Bacon from Oliver Peabody, 1758/1765, 69 1/2 acres. Indian purchases: MCG 92:217, John Ephraim to Asa Bacon and Oliver Bacon Jr., 1784/1786, 17 acres; MCG 53:450, John Peegun to Daniel Bacon, 1755/1756, 4 acres; MCG 65:505, Daniel Thomas to Ephraim Bacon, 1759/1765, 7 acres; MCG 56:82, Isaac and Mary Ephraim to John Bacon, 1754/1757, 9 3/4 acres; MCG 65:502, Joseph Comecho to Oliver Bacon, 1752/1765, 9 acres; MCG 41:226, John Wamsquan to Stephen Bacon, 1740/1740, 20 acres; MCG 40:238, Joseph Ephraim to Timothy Bacon, 1739/1739, 6 acres; MCG 66:630, Jacob Chalcom to William Bacon, 1757/1767, 7 acres. From relatives or other English sellers, see: MCG 87:280, John Bacon to David Bacon, 1784/1784, 10 acres; MCG 56:638, Stephen Bacon Jr. to Elijah Bacon, 1760/1760, 12 acres; MCG 56:135, Stephen Bacon to Henry Bacon, 1740/1758, 100 acres; MCG 105:338, William Bacon to Joseph Bacon, 1791/1791, 30 acres; MCG 85:75, Ephraim Bacon to Josiah Bacon, 1783/1783, 10 acres; MCG 49:267, Matthew Hastings to Michael Bacon, 1749/1750, 20 acres and buildings; MCG 96:225, Oliver Bacon to Oliver Bacon Jr. 1782/1787, 23 and 10 acres. The first date refers to the year the deed was consummated, and the second, to the year the deed was registered with the county court.

[5] Biglow, *History of Natick*, 84. This may have been the same Oliver Bacon who wrote his own history of Natick in which he declared Natick Indians extinct, "except this one poor Indian girl, the orphan daughter of a departed race." Oliver N. Bacon, *A History of Natick From Its First Settlement in 1651 to The Present Time; with Notices of the First White Families* (Boston: Damrell G. Moore, Printers, 1856), 17.

ment" for the book called attention to the present "excitement . . . respecting the rights of the Indians and the treatment, which they ought to receive," an allusion to the crisis over Andrew Jackson's Indian policy that aimed at (and partially accomplished) the forced removal of eastern Indian nations to "Indian territory" west of the Mississippi River. Removal proponents used stories of tragic decline to justify dispossessing eastern Indians. They lamented that whenever Indians and Europeans came together, Indians absorbed the vices rather than the virtues of Europeans. Their vision of Indian decline provided Euro-Americans with ideological justification for forcibly removing Indians from Native homelands to protect them from frontiersmen they refused to restrain who lawlessly encroached on Native lands and jeopardized Indian survival. Pushed well beyond the "frontier," Indians could take their time adopting the trappings of "civilization" or continue to reject them if they wished.[6] By referring to the removal debate, Biglow claimed a connection between Natick's history and the "Cherokee crisis" and promised to reveal "the circumstances which accompanied the gradual decrease and final extinction of the first tribe, that was brought into a state of civilization and christianity, by a protestant missionary." Still, in telling the story about the Indian girl and her companions, he contradicted his claim about extinction and undermined the simplistic narrative of decline.

In fact, Natick's remarkable history as an Indian place reveals a complicated story of conquest and Indian resistance that serves as a counterpoint to stories of extinction that fueled the emerging myth of the "vanishing Indian" in which Biglow's narrative participated. Nineteenth-century local histories in New England and elsewhere claimed formerly Indian places as Euro-American by making heroic claims about conquest and "settlement." In the process, they erased Indians from the landscape by foreclosing the possibility of Indian futures. Recurrent stories within local histories about "the last full-blooded Indian" gestured toward Indian disappearance by making precise claims about the end of Indian lineages.[7] By writing about Indians in this voice, local historians betrayed their assumptions about racial purity, their wishful thinking about

---

[6] See, for example, Robert F. Berkhofer Jr., *The White Man's Indian: Images of the American Indian from Columbus to the Present* (New York: Vintage Books, 1978); Brian W. Dippie, *The Vanishing American: White Attitudes and U.S. Indian Policy* (Lawrence, KS: University of Kansas Press, 1982); Francis Paul Prucha, *The Great Father: The United States Government and the American Indian* (Lincoln: University of Nebraska Press, 1984); Ronald N. Satz, *American Indian Policy in the Jacksonian Era* (Lincoln: University of Nebraska Press, 1975); Anthony F. C. Wallace, *The Long, Bitter Trail: Andrew Jackson and the Indians* (New York: Hill and Wang, 1993); Bernard W. Sheehan, *Seeds of Extinction: Jeffersonian Philanthropy and the American Indian* (New York: Norton, 1973); and Joshua David Bellin, "Apostle of Removal: John Eliot in the Nineteenth Century," *New England Quarterly* (hereafter cited as *NEQ*) 69 (1996): 3–32.

[7] William Simmons, *Spirit of the New England Tribes: Indian History and Folklore, 1620–1984* (Hanover: University Press of New England, 1986), 3–4. See also Russell G. Handsman, "Illuminating History's Silences in the 'Pioneer Valley'" *Artifacts* 19 (1991): 14–25.

Indian erasure, and their inability to grasp the complicated mosaic of Indian survival in New England.

B. *An alternative narrative: expropriation and survival*

These self-serving narratives of Indian extinction are false. Contrary evidence can be found in other remarkable histories: of the Mashpee and Gay Head Wampanoag and the Nipmuck in Massachusetts, the Mashantucket Pequot and Mohegan in Connecticut, the Narragansett in Rhode Island, the Abenaki in Vermont and western Maine, and the Passamaquoddy and Penobscot in Maine, among others, who are all still there. This fact successively confronted the states of Maine, Massachusetts, Rhode Island, Connecticut, and Vermont as legal problems beginning in the 1970s when Indian peoples there pressed their claims for recognition and restitution and often succeeded.[8] In other words, Indian "disappearance" occurred in Euro-American imaginations, or rather in their failure to imagine how Indians struggled and survived, and how cultural change *is* persistence.[9] The history of Natick Indians is somewhat different in that no identifiably separate group "Natick Indians" survives into the present. But, as this book will argue, that does not mean Natick Indians became extinct.

Rich scholarship that has appeared in recent years recognizes that survival into the present, not extinction in the remote and distant past, is the appropriate narrative for New England Indian history. The path-breaking work of William S. Simmons reminds us of an elaborate southeastern New England Indian spirituality still in existence, which includes stories about the landscape as well as larger patterns of Indian religious belief that changed over time and in conjunction with Christian religious belief.[10] Other scholars, Native and non-Native (updating the insights of Frank Speck's field work of the 1940s)

---

[8] See, for example, Jack Campisi, *The Mashpee Indians: Tribe on Trial* (Syracuse: Syracuse University Press, 1991); James Clifford, "Identity in Mashpee," in *The Predicament of Culture: Twentieth-Century Ethnography, Literature, and Art* (Cambridge: Harvard University Press, 1988), 277–346; Paul Brodeur, *Restitution: The Land Claims of the Mashpee, Passamaquoddy, and Penobscot Indians of New England* (Boston: Northeastern University Press, 1985); and Jack Campisi, "The Trade and Intercourse Acts: Land Claims on the Eastern Seaboard," in *Irredeemable America: The Indians' Estate and Land Claims*, ed. Imre Sutton (Albuquerque: University of New Mexico Press, 1985).

[9] On the invisibility of Indians in current historical scholarship, see James H. Merrell, "Some Thoughts on Colonial Historians and American Indians," *William and Mary Quarterly* (hereafter cited as *WMQ*), 3d ser., 46 (1989): 94–119.

[10] See especially Simmons, *Spirit of the New England Tribes*; Simmons, *Cautantowwit's House: An Indian Burial Ground on the Island of Conanicut in Narragansett Bay* (Providence: Brown University Press, 1970); Simmons, "Southern New England Shamanism: An Ethnographic Reconstruction," in *Papers of the Seventh Algonquian Conference*, ed. William Cowan (Ottawa: Carleton University, 1976), 217–56; and Simmons, "The Great Awakening and Indian Conversion in Southern New England," in *Papers of the Tenth Algonquian Conference*, ed. William Cowan (Ottawa: Carleton University, 1979), 25–36.

have connected the histories of the Wampanoag, Narragansett, Pequot, Nip-muck, Abenaki, and others from the past into the present.[11] Still more have built a solid bedrock of scholarly work on the colonial histories of New England Indians.[12] This growing scholarship resists the extinction myth that has so powerfully informed the paradigm of New England Indian history and edu-cates a broader audience about something that Native people of New England knew all along: that they are still Indian and that they are still there.

How is it, then, that nineteenth-century Euro-Americans were so sure that New England Indians were about to vanish? The colonial history of New England Indians provided plenty of material for constructing such a narrative. Epi-demics preceded permanent English invasion, and they continued to wreak havoc among Indian populations. The unidentified scourge of 1616–19 raged twenty to thirty miles inland from Massachusetts Bay, reducing the Native pop-ulation by fifty percent to ninety percent. Smallpox, which appeared by 1633, ripped through Native populations, including those that had been spared from the mysterious 1616–19 outbreak.[13]

[11] See, for example, Frank G. Speck, "Reflections Upon the Past and Present of the Massachu-setts Indians," *Bulletin of the Massachusetts Archaeological Society* 4 (1943): 33–8; Frank G. Speck, "A Note on the Hassanamisco Band of Nipmuc," Ibid., 4 (1943): 49–56; Laurie Wein-stein, "'We're Still Living on Our Traditional Homeland': The Wampagnoag Legacy in New England," in *Strategies for Survival: American Indians in the Eastern United States*, ed. Frank W. Porter III (Westport, CT: Greenwood Press, 1986), 85–112; Laurie Weinstein, ed., *Endur-ing Traditions: The Native Peoples of New England* (Westport, CT: Bergin & Garvey, 1994); Laurence M. Hauptman and James D. Wherry, eds., *The Pequots in Southern New England: The Fall and Rise of an American Indian Nation* (Norman: University of Oklahoma Press, 1990); Ethel Boissevain, "The Detribalization of the Narragansett Indians: A Case Study," *Ethnohistory* 3 (1956): 225–45; Ethel Boissevain, "Narragansett Survival: A Study of Group Persistence through Adopted Traits," *Ethnohistory* 6 (1959): 347–62; and Peter Benes, ed., *Algonkians of New England: Past and Present*, The Dublin Seminar for New England Folklife Annual Proceedings (Boston: Boston University, 1993).

[12] See footnote 20 for treatments of Natick's history. Published treatments of colonial New England Indian history include Francis Jennings, *The Invasion of America: Indians, Colo-nialism, and the Cant of Conquest* (New York: Norton, 1976); Neal Salisbury, *Manitou and Providence: Indians, Europeans, and the Making of New England, 1500–1643* (New York: Oxford University Press, 1982); William Cronon, *Changes in the Land: Indians, Colonists, and the Ecology of New England* (New York: Hill and Wang, 1983); James Axtell, *The Euro-pean and the Indian: Essays in the Ethnohistory of Colonial North America* (New York: Oxford University Press, 1981); Axtell, *After Colombus: Essays in the Ethnohistory of Colo-nial North America* (New York: Oxford University Press, 1988); Dean R. Snow, *The Archaeology of New England* (New York: Harcourt Brace Jovanovich, 1980); Colin G. Cal-loway, *The Western Abenakis of Vermont, 1600–1800: War, Migration, and the Survival of a People* (Norman: University of Oklahoma Press, 1990); David L. Ghere, "The 'Disap-pearance' of the Abenaki in Western Maine: Political Organization and Ethnocentric Assumptions," *American Indian Quarterly* 17 (1993): 193–207; Paul R. Campbell and Glenn W. La Fantasie, "Scattered to the Winds of Heaven – Narragansett Indians 1676–1880," *Rhode Island History* 37 (1978): 67–83; and Robert S. Grumet, ed., *North-eastern Indian Lives, 1632–1816* (Amherst: University of Massachusetts Press, 1996).

[13] See, for example, John Duffy, *Epidemics in Colonial America* (Baton Rouge: Louisiana State University Press, 1953); S. F. Cook, *The Indian Population of New England in the Seven-*

Devastation of Indian populations facilitated English invasion and paved the way for other forms of encroachment. English colonization fundamentally altered Indian economies; cattle trampled their corn fields, and the short-lived fur trade and the English presence itself undermined hunting and fishing by fundamentally altering ecosystems and threatening species. The war of conquest against the Pequot in 1637 jeopardized their survival and provided cautionary tales for other Indians who considered military resistance. The 1676 Indian resistance movement, known as King Philip's War, ended in Indian defeat, enslavement in the West Indies, and thoroughgoing retribution for those who participated. From then on, New England Indians persisted through peaceful coexistence within their drastically reduced homelands, living in small clusters that barely entered English fields of vision.[14]

For a century before the English plantation at Plymouth in 1620 announced that colonists intended to stay, Europeans and Indians engaged in relations of exchange that transformed both peoples. During the sixteenth century, European manufactured items such as metal kettles, knives, glass items, and cloth traveled through elaborate existing Native trade networks in exchange for furs. Indians incorporated new items of material culture selectively and in Indian ways. Native notions about reciprocity and gift-giving, central to Native ways of relating to the natural, supernatural, and human world, regulated intergroup relations, alliance building, social interactions, marriage, and ritual performance as well as the exchange of uniquely available resources. These ideas governed the emergence of trade and diplomacy between Indians and Europeans. By the early seventeenth century, systematic fur trade relations replaced more sporadic exchange. Indian economies shifted in emphasis toward hunting as they became enmeshed in trade relations with Europeans, which diminished Indian autonomy and upset the balance implicit in Indian notions of reciprocity. The new trade, in combination with the devastating epidemics, altered power relations among Indian groups and even communities as Indian survivors formed villages with relatives.[15]

---

teenth Century (Berkeley: University of California Press, 1976); Alfred W. Crosby, "Virgin Soil Epidemics as a Factor in the Aboriginal Depopulation in America," *WMQ*, 3d ser., 33 (1976): 289–99; and Timothy L. Bratton, "The Identity of the New England Indian Epidemic of 1616–19," *Bulletin of the History of Medicine* 62 (1988): 351–83.

[14] See, for example, Jennings, *Invasion of America*; Salisbury, *Manitou and Providence*; Salisbury, "Social Relationships on a Moving Frontier: Natives and Settlers in Southern New England, 1638–1675," *Man in the Northeast* 33 (1987): 89–99; Peter A. Thomas, "Contrastive Subsistence Strategies and Land Use as Factors for Understanding Indian-White Relations in New England," *Ethnohistory* 23 (1976): 1–18; Cronon, *Changes in the Land*; Axtell, *European and the Indian*; and Axtell, *After Columbus*.

[15] See Snow, *Archaeology of New England*, especially 44–99; Salisbury, *Manitou and Providence*, especially chapters 1–3; Cronon, *Changes in the Land*, Chapter 5; Peter A. Thomas, "In the Maelstrom of Change: The Indian Trade and Cultural Process in the Middle Connecticut River Valley, 1635–1665" (Ph.D. diss., University of Massachusetts, 1979); Elise M. Brenner, "Sociopolitical Implications of Mortuary Ritual Remains in Seventeenth-

As Indians struggled to survive, English colonists multiplied rapidly. Twenty-one thousand colonists arrived in Massachusetts Bay in the "great migration" of the 1630s, and for two centuries their numbers doubled every generation. A relatively homogeneous group mostly from southeastern England, they came principally in families. In New England they married young and lived long, producing many children. During the 1630s, disputes over religion, as well as desire for land and participation in the fur trade, propelled colonists outward to the Connecticut River Valley and what would become Rhode Island and Connecticut. By the 1670s, English towns dotted most of the eastern third of Massachusetts Bay, stretching throughout Narragansett Bay, and much of the Connecticut River Valley and Long Island Sound.[16]

As they became surrounded by English people who seized their lands, Indians in southeastern New England could no longer sustain their mobile economy, which integrated agriculture, fishing, hunting, gathering of wild plant foods and shellfish, and provided them with abundance for what looked to the English like little labor. English expansion thrust surviving Indians onto marginal lands where they wrested their living from an altered and less abundant environment and continued to survive as Indian people even though "an earlier Indian way of life had become impossible."[17] Those Indians who still owned land modified their economic pursuits and adopted aspects of English land use, including livestock raising as a replacement for hunting and the use of plows and fences. Over the course of the colonial period, they also engaged in wage labor and the emerging whaling industry, sold baskets and brooms, and became indentured servants.[18] Indians persisted mostly in small clusters throughout southeastern New England, as indeed they did elsewhere throughout the eastern seaboard.[19]

Century Native Southern New England," in *The Recovery of Meaning*, ed. Leone and Potter, 147–82; and Virginia DeJohn Anderson, "King Philip's Herds: Indians, Colonists, and the Problem of Livestock in Early New England," *WMQ*, 3d ser., 51 (1994): 601–24.

[16] For overviews, see Jack P. Greene, *Pursuits of Happiness: The Social Development of Early Modern British Colonies and the Formation of American Culture* (Chapel Hill: University of North Carolina Press, 1988); David Hackett Fisher, *Albion's Seed: Four British Folkways in America* (New York: Oxford University Press, 1989); Bernard Bailyn, *The Peopling of British North America: An Introduction* (New York: Vintage Books, 1986); and Douglas McManis, *Colonial New England: A Historical Geography* (New York: Oxford University Press, 1975).

[17] Cronon, *Changes in the Land*, 164.

[18] Cronon, *Changes in the Land*, especially chapters 7–8; Anderson, "King Philip's Herds"; Richard R. Johnson, "The Search for a Usable Indian: An Aspect of the Defense of Colonial New England," *Journal of American History* 64 (1977): 623–51; Daniel Vickers, "The First Whalemen of Nantucket," *WMQ*, 3d ser., 40 (1983): 560–83; John A. Sainsbury, "Indian Labor in Early Rhode Island," *NEQ* 48 (1975): 378–93; Joshua Micah Marshall, "'A Melancholy People': Anglo-Indian Relations in Early Warwick, Rhode Island, 1642–1675," *NEQ* 68 (1995): 402–28; and Ruth Wallis Herndon, personal communication.

[19] See, for example, Cronon, *Changes in the Land*, 159, 162–5; Porter, *Strategies for Survival*; Weinstein, *Enduring Traditions*; Benes, *Algonkians of New England*; Karen Blu, *The Lumbee*

Natick, the community whose history is the focus of this study, was one of these places of Indian persistence.[20] Natick's history, though tragic in its own way, nevertheless belies the simplistic myth of Indian decline through disease, warfare, and extinction that Biglow and other historians purveyed. Instead, its story is one of slow but steady displacement of Indian by English landowners primarily through the workings of the market economy. While English chicanery plays its part in this story, English displacement of Indians within the

Problem: The Making of an American Indian People (New York: Cambridge University Press, 1980); Gerald M. Sider, *Lumbee Indian History: Race, Ethnicity, and Indian Identity* (New York: Cambridge University Press, 1993); C. A. Weslager, *The Nanticoke Indians: Past and Present* (Newark: University of Delaware Press, 1983); and David Stephen Cohen, *The Ramapo Mountain People* (New Brunswick, NJ: Rutgers University Press, 1988).

[20] Other examinations of Natick's history include Neal Salisbury, "'Conquest of the Savage': Puritans, Puritan Missionaries, and Indians, 1620–1680" (Ph.D. diss., UCLA, 1972); Michael Crawford, "Indians, Yankees, and the Meetinghouse Dispute of Natick, Massachusetts, 1743–1800," *New England Historical and Genealogical Register* 132 (1978): 278–92; Dane Morrison, "'A Praying People': The Transition from Remnant to Convert Among the Indians of the Massachusetts Bay Colony" (Ph.D. diss., Tufts University, 1983); Elise Melanie Brenner, "Strategies for Autonomy: An Analysis of Ethnic Mobilization in Seventeenth-Century Southern New England" (Ph.D. diss., University of Massachusetts, 1984); Harold W. Van Lonkhuyzen, "A Reappraisal of the Praying Indians: Acculturation, Conversion, and Identity at Natick, Massachusetts, 1646–1730," *NEQ* 63 (1990): 396–428; Daniel Mandell, "'To Live More Like my Christian English Neighbors': Natick Indians in the Eighteenth Century," *WMQ*, 3d ser., 48 (1991): 552–79; and Mandell, "Standing by His Father: Thomas Waban of Natick, circa 1630–1722," in *Northeastern Indian Lives, 1632–1816*, ed. Robert S. Grumet (Amherst: University of Massachusetts Press, 1996), 166–92. Other works that contain extensive discussions of Natick as part of broader studies include Alden Vaughan, *New England Frontier: Puritans and Indians, 1620–1675* (Boston: Little, Brown and Co., 1965); Susan L. MacCulloch, "A Tri-Partite Political System Among Christian Indians of Early Massachusetts," *Kroeber Anthropological Society Papers* 34 (1966): 63–73; Kenneth Morrison, "'That Art of Coyning Christians': John Eliot and the Praying Indians of Massachusetts," *Ethnohistory* 21 (1974): 77–92; Salisbury, "Red Puritans: The 'Praying Indians' of Massachusetts Bay and John Eliot," *WMQ*, 3d ser., 32 (1975): 27–54; Jennings, *Invasion of America*; William Burton, "Hellish Fiends and Brutish Men: Amerindian-Euroamerican Interaction in Southern New England" (Ph.D. diss., Kent State University, 1976); Kathleen J. Bragdon, "Probate Records as a Source for Algonquian Ethnohistory," in *Papers of the Tenth Algonquian Conference*, ed. William Cowan (Ottawa: Carleton University, 1979); Elise M. Brenner, "To Pray or To Be Prey: That is the Question[:] Strategies for Cultural Autonomy of Massachusetts Praying Towns," *Ethnohistory* 27 (1980): 135–52; Henry Warner Bowden, *American Indians and Christian Missions* (Chicago: University of Chicago Press, 1981); Kathleen J. Bragdon, "Crime and Punishment among the Indians of Massachusetts," *Ethnohistory* 28 (1981): 23–32; Bragdon, "'Another Tongue Brought In': An Ethnohistorical Study of Native Writings in Massachusett" (Ph.D. diss., Brown University, 1981); James Axtell, *The Invasion Within: The Contest of Cultures in Colonial North America* (New York: Oxford University Press, 1985); James Holstun, *A Rational Millennium: Puritan Utopias of Seventeenth-Century England and America* (New York: Oxford University Press, 1987); James Naeher, "Dialogue in the Wilderness: John Eliot and the Indians' Exploration of Puritanism as a Source of Meaning, Comfort, and Ethnic Survival," *NEQ* 62 (1989): 346–68; and Daniel Mandell, "Behind the Frontier: Indian Communities in Eighteenth-Century Massachusetts" (Ph.D. diss., University of Virginia, 1992).

bounded place called Natick occurred principally through the excruciating workings of business as usual.

In seeking to tell the intricate history of Natick as an Indian place, I use narratives about how it was bounded as a missionary experiment, and pull together the traces Natick Indians left in vital records, probate dockets, commonwealth political proceedings, and especially hundreds of land deeds and other documents regarding Indian landownership as well as the frustratingly few records Indians produced themselves. The identifiably Indian surnames of Natick families, such as Waban and Awassamug, plus geographical and racial labels included in some records, made it possible to link together scattered intriguing etches Indians made in the documentary record of colonial Massachusetts. In constructing this narrative, I draw upon evidence from these disparate sources to compile life histories and genealogies, to flesh out social relations within the community and the commonwealth more generally, and to reconstruct the land market that gradually transformed Natick from an Indian to an English place.

In addition to this transformation, Natick's history illuminates a protracted struggle over the place of Indians in Massachusetts and New England more broadly. Like Indians throughout the eastern seaboard, Native people in New England struggled within a "New World" that transformed relationships between peoples, within groups and their cultures, and altered their relationship to the land.[21] As elsewhere, Indians negotiated about whose customs would govern the country in day-to-day, face-to-face encounters that represented and evoked "creative adaptations" in a colonial context.[22] In Natick, Indians resisted erasure. They defended their lands, rebuilt kin connections and community, and retained their "Indianness" within the extraordinary constraints posed by English colonialism. By looking closely at Natick, we can come to understand how Biglow and others could conclude by the early nineteenth century that Indians were about to disappear, and how they could be wrong. The problem was with Euro-American eyesight, that is, their assumptions about what constituted Indianness and the place of Indians in society. These assumptions were not monolithic, and they changed over the course of the colonial period.[23]

At the center of this story of survival and transformation is land: struggles

---

[21] James H. Merrell, *The Indians' New World: Catawbas and their Neighbors from European Contact through the Era of Removal* (New York: Norton, 1989).

[22] James H. Merrell, "'The Customes of Our Countrey': Indians and Colonists in Early America," in *Strangers within the Realm: Cultural Margins of the First British Empire*, ed. Bernard Bailyn and Philip D. Morgan (Chapel Hill: University of North Carolina Press, 1991), 117–56; T. H. Breen, "Creative Adaptations: Peoples and Cultures," in *Colonial British America: Essays in the New History of the Early Modern Era*, ed. Jack P. Greene and J. R. Pole (Baltimore: The Johns Hopkins University Press, 1984), 195–232; and Daniel K. Richter, "Whose Indian History?" *WMQ*, 3d. ser., 50 (1993): 379–93.

[23] See also Colin G. Calloway, *The American Revolution in Indian Country: Crisis and Diversity in Native American Communities* (New York: Cambridge University Press, 1995), especially 292–301.

over the possession and "proper" use of land, ways different peoples viewed the connection between land and identities, and the means by which land served to mark the place of Indian people in New England. The colonial encounter involved a fundamental and enduring collision between two very different conceptions of the connection between land and identity that can be read through the emergence and transformation of the social order of English colonialism. In this study, I look at the connection between Indian land and identity in colonial Natick as a way of understanding the paradox of Indian persistence and change under an imposed social order through forms of adaptation that by the early nineteenth century rendered them invisible to Euro-Americans. New England Indians and English colonizers had different conceptions about the connection between land and identity, and these different ways of thinking about land help us understand how and why Natick Indians remained within their homelands, why they eventually became landless, and how New Englanders could come to regard landless Indians as marginal to the English cultural world and thus disappearing.

From the Indian perspective, the connection to homeland as the place where kin and community are sustained remained at the center of their identity despite the transformation of many of the traits that are usually interrogated as the building-blocks of identity, such as language, religion, political organization, and economic systems. Even the land itself was transformed, and so was the place of land in social transactions. By looking beneath the stories of diplomacy, fur trade, and wars, and by including not just massive tribal dispossession but also the minute transactions of Natick individuals, we can detect a story different from the usual one of wholesale tribal displacement, acculturation, assimilation, or extinction. It is a story with echoes into the late nineteenth and twentieth centuries, when the allotment policy of the United States government accomplished massive Indian dispossession on the individual level in remarkably similar ways.[24] Attention to the details of land allows the reconstruction of a narrative that is not easily told by focusing exclusively on the extent to which a list of cultural traits did or did not change. And it is for its records about changing connections of Indians to the land that Natick makes such a rich and informative case study.

[24] See Frederick E. Hoxie, *A Final Promise: The Campaign to Assimilate the Indians, 1880–1920* (Lincoln: University of Nebraska Press, 1984); and Melissa L. Meyer, *White Earth Tragedy: Ethnicity and Dispossession at a Minnesota Anishinaabe Reservation, 1889–1920* (Lincoln: University of Nebraska Press, 1994). On constructing alternatives to the assimilation/persistence dichotomy, see Richard White, *The Middle Ground: Indians, Empires, and Republics in the Great Lakes Region, 1650–1815* (New York: Cambridge University Press, 1991); and Clifford, "Identity in Mashpee," in *The Predicament of Culture*. For the closest parallels to Natick's history, see Jeanne Ronda and James P. Ronda, "'As They were Faithful': Chief Hendrick Aupaumut and the Struggle for Stockbridge Survival, 1757–1830," *American Indian Culture and Research Journal* 3 (1979): 43–55; Edward Byers, *The Nation of Nantucket: Society and Politics in an Early American Commercial Center, 1660–1820* (Boston: Northeastern University Press, 1987), especially 15–101, 160–4; Patrick Frazier, *The Mohicans of Stockbridge* (Lincoln: University of Nebraska Press, 1992); and Lion G. Miles, "The Red Man Dispossessed: The Williams Family and the Alienation of Indian Land in Stockbridge, Massachusetts, 1736–1818," *NEQ* 67 (1994): 46–76.

By examining the history of Natick as an Indian place, I also hope to shed light on larger issues surrounding New England Indian survival. Throughout New England, the extinction paradigm that has always applied to some extent in the popular perception of Native Americans became uniquely potent. As elsewhere, but at an even more intense pitch, the siren song of disappearance drowned out the voices of Indian resistance and persistence. The pattern of Indian survival amid the dominating paradigm of disappearance is no more dramatically displayed in North America (with the possible exception of California) than it is in New England. Within this larger context, the history of Natick allows us to examine in particularly bold relief the emergence and dynamics of the disappearance story that missed the reality of Indian persistence in New England. Through the long-term negotiation of the colonial relationship in Natick, we can see the ways in which the erasure of the Natick Indian story is a metaphor for the erasure of New England Indian history more generally.

Natick was not the only "Praying Town" or persisting Indian place in New England, and it was never a rigidly sealed community, as I will show. But in the richness and variety of its records it stands alone, in part because Natick was different, which is not to say its history is unique. Natick brought together individuals and families from several different Indian groups in southeastern New England, and thus its history is not a "tribal" one in the conventional sense.[25] Rather, it is a story about "refugees" torn loose from their villages in the wake of invasion and the disruptions it wrought: wars, epidemics, and "economic and ecological imperialism."[26] Though not unparalleled as a composite community, its origins as such are important to recognize in the larger context of its history. Natick Indians as a group came into existence in the colonial context as a refugee community, and it came apart in protracted and complicated fashion by the early nineteenth century. Ever since then, the problem of what happened to Natick Indians has been something of a puzzle.

C. *"My land": Indian resistance to colonial erasure*

The Praying Town of Natick became a place for Indians to rebuild kin connections and community within their homelands in the wake of English invasion. Indians rooted themselves in Natick in Indian ways, although their relationship to their land and the English colonial society changed over time. In this book, I explore these crucial transformations. In Chapter 1, I probe the ways in which New England Indians and English colonizers conceptualized the social order, particularly in connection with their different ideas about land and identity. In Chapter 2, I examine cultural negotiations involved in bounding Natick as a Praying Town, and the cultural accommodations that occurred as individuals

---

[25] Merrell, *The Indians' New World*; and William C. Sturtevant, "Creek into Seminole," in *North American Indians in Historical Perspective* ed. Eleanor Burke Leacock and Nancy Oestreich Lurie (Prospect Heights, IL: Reissued by Waveland Press, Inc., 1988), 92–128.
[26] White, *The Middle Ground;* and Cronon, *Changes in the Land*, 162.

and families came to Natick. In Chapter 3 I focus on the social construction of the category "Friend Indian" after the last New England Indian military resistance in 1675, which especially involved negotiations over cultural boundaries, Indian claims to English protections of their land rights, and Indian defense of lands in Natick. In Chapter 4 I consider transformations in cultural practices that Indians continued to reshape, and especially the reconfiguration in Indian landownership that occurred within the town in the first four decades of the eighteenth century. In Chapter 5 I break from the chronological narrative of the book to concentrate on the different ways individuals and families used their lands and negotiated cultural changes, and I trace the perpetuation of Natick Indian lineages. Finally, in Chapter 6 I examine the process of Indian dispossession in the late eighteenth century, consider Indian and English responses to Indian dispossession, and focus on the reformulation of the category "wandering Indian" in the context of Indian dispossession. By examining the changing connections of Indians in Natick to their land, I hope to illuminate their shifting place within the social order of colonial New England, demonstrate the persistence of Natick Indians, and examine how English colonists and Euro-Americans tried to erase Indians from the landscape by uprooting them.

In his 1830 history, William Biglow, who wrote about the rooting of Natick's remarkable trees, offered a commentary on the importance of naming and an implausible interpretation for the Algonquian word *Natick*, claiming it means "a place of hills."[27] He endorsed a proposal that "the present uncouth name be changed . . . to Eliot, or Eliotville," thus sanctioning a further colonial appropriation.[28] But according to eastern Algonquian linguistic material provided by John Eliot and others, "place" is signified by "ayeuonk," and "hill" by "wadchu" or "wachook," which sound nothing like "Natick."[29] Earlier, an English colonist who dabbled in linguistics and argued that Indians possessed rights to their land that required a legal process to extinguish offered a different interpretation for the word in the Narragansett language. Roger Williams wrote in 1643 that "Nittauke" means "my land."[30] Not "ground," or "earth," or "land," but "my land." Indians who came to Natick resisted such colonial erasures. They found remarkable ways to defend kin and community that offer vivid testimony about the centrality of their land to their persistent yet changing identity.

[27] Biglow, *History of Natick*, 4.
[28] Biglow, *History of Natick*, 10.
[29] Ives Goddard and Kathleen J. Bragdon, *Native Writings in Massachusett*, 2 vols. (Philadelphia: American Philosophical Society, 1988), 1:278, and 2:609, for example.
[30] Roger Williams, *A Key into the Language of America*, ed. John J. Teunissen and Evelyn J. Hinz (Detroit: Wayne State University Press, 1973), 167. This conforms with usages analyzed by Goddard and Bragdon: "nittokeim 'my land.'" Goddard and Bragdon, *Native Writings in Massachusett*, 2:499. In the related Angonquian language Ojibwe, "ni" signifies "my," and "aki" is "land." See John D. Nichols and Earl Nyholm, *A Concise Dictionary of Minnesota Ojibwe* (Minneapolis: University of Minnesota Press, 1995).

1

Peoples, land, and social order

Awaunaguss, suck. *English-man, men.*
This they call us, as much as to say, These strangers.[1]

A. *Strangers*

In the New England colonial encounter, Native peoples and the English who came to their lands confronted each other as strangers. To be sure, Native peoples had been engaging in sporadic relations of exchange with various Europeans throughout the sixteenth century, which provided Native peoples with a bedrock of selective information about Europeans. Likewise, the English consumed the burgeoning literature on the "New World" that served up fact and fancy about aboriginal peoples and their lands, some of which grew out of English efforts to gain a foothold in the European invasion of the Western Hemisphere. These accumulated bodies of partial and incomplete knowledge that resulted from actual or recorded experiences partly conditioned the shape and interpretation of interactions between Indians and the English. Still, "strangeness" remained, and in early encounters, peoples with little intensive experiences with one another struggled for comprehension. Not surprisingly, in their effort to understand the differences between themselves, they made frequent recourse to their own cultural categories to craft explanations about how the others saw, and lived, their lives.[2]

A crucial aspect of the colonial encounter involved a collision between peoples who held deeply ingrained and dramatically divergent notions about how a properly constituted social order should be composed. The culturally different notions about the social order ranged from what constituted "good manners" to the larger question of the divine source of social relations, and touched on just

[1] Roger Williams, *A Key into the Language of America*, ed. John J. Teunissen and Evelyn J. Hinz (Detroit: Wayne State University Press, 1973), 137.
[2] See, for example, Douglas R. McManis, *European Impression of the New England Coast, 1497–1620*, Research Paper 139 (Chicago: University of Chicago, Department of Geography, 1972); McManis, *Colonial New England: A Historical Geography* (New York: Oxford University Press, 1975); and Robert F. Berkhofer Jr., *The White Man's Indian: Images of the American Indian from Columbus to the Present* (New York: Vintage Books, 1978). On cultural misunderstandings, see James H. Merrell, " 'The Customes of Our Countrey': Indians and Colonists in Early America," in *Strangers within the Realm: Cultural Margins of the First British Empire*, ed. Bernard Bailyn and Philip D. Morgan (Chapel Hill: University of North Carolina Press, 1991), 117–56; and Richard White, *The Middle Ground: Indians, Empires, and Republics in the Great Lakes Region, 1650–1815* (New York: Cambridge University Press, 1991).

about everything else in between.[3] In this chapter, I examine the broad outlines of two versions of social order that collided in colonial New England, focusing particularly on the ways in which Indians and the English conceptualized the nexus of land, identity, and the shape of social relations, and how these categories relate to the problem of sorting out essential aspects of the strangeness of the colonial encounter.

B. *Native peoples of southeastern New England*

The strangers who came to the place they renamed New England encountered an abundant landscape with "many goodly groues of trees, dainty fine round rising hillucks, delicate faire large plaines, sweete cristall fountaines and cleare running streames that twine in fine meanders through the meads."[4] Springing from the rolling hills dotted with ponds and drained by river systems were large stretches of forest with many varieties of trees, including oak, hickory, chestnut, pine, ash, elm, beech, walnut, cedar, maple, and, particularly northward, different species of birch. Also found were plum and cherry trees, cranberries, strawberries, blueberries, whortleberries, and more.[5] Forests, ponds, and waterways constitued a rich habitat for wildlife, and supported "Fowles in abundance, [and] Fish in multitude."[6] The abundant "fowles" included swans, geese, ducks, cranes, turkeys, pheasants, partridges, crows, hawks, quails, and falcons. Forest habitats sustained deer, elk, beaver, otter, wild cat, raccoon, fox, wolf, bear, muskrat, hare, and squirrel populations. Ponds teeming with fish dotted the region, and richly stocked river systems carved their way from the interior into the sea, which contained fish, shellfish, and mammals. The ocean abounded with large and small fish, including cod, bass, sturgeon, salmon, herring, eel, smelt, flounder, and shad, as well as shellfish such as lobsters, oysters, and clams. Fresh-water ponds contained trout, carp, pike, perch, eels, and alewives.[7] In the words of Thomas Morton, "if this Land be not rich, then is the whole world poore."[8]

But however much it seemed to the English a wilderness, the landscape was shaped by the Native peoples to whom it was home. The hardwood forests appeared open and parklike at intervals to some English observers, the result of the Native practice of periodically burning the woods to clear large stretches of dense underbrush: "this custome of firing the Country is the meanes to make it passable; and by that meanes the trees growe here and there as in our parks: and makes the Country very beautifull and commodious."[9] Within the forests that

---

[3] Merrell, "'The Customes of Our Country'"; and White, *Middle Ground*.

[4] Thomas Morton, *The New English Canaan*, ed. Charles Francis Adams (Boston, The Prince Society, 1883. Reprinted, New York: Burt Franklin, 1967), 180. On the ecology of New England, see William Cronon, *Changes in the Land: Indians, Colonists, and the Ecology of New England* (New York: Hill and Wang, 1983).

[5] Cronon, *Changes in the Land*, 3, 28, 40, and 144.   [6] Morton, *New English Canaan*, 180.

[7] Cronon, *Changes in the Land*, 4 and 39.   [8] Morton, *New English Canaan*, 180.

[9] Morton, *New English Canaan*, 173; and Cronon, *Changes in the Land*, 25, 49–51.

had been shaped by Native burning practices were trail systems that linked together villages, the rich coastline, and interior resource sites in a dense network of places that helped bound Native homelands. Controlled burning of the forests also helped promote abundant game, encouraged the growth of bushes that produced berries of various sorts, and kept pests under control. Within the extensive stretches of forests, Indians planted maize, beans, pumpkins, and squash in multi-crop fields that had been further cleared by girdling trees.[10]

Whereas the English who encountered the New England landscape viewed it through cultural lenses that conditioned them to see economic resources, for Native peoples, natural resources and landmarks defined their place in a created world inseparable from an Indian spiritual realm: "They will generally confesse that God made all: but then in speciall, although they deny not that *English-mans* God made *English* Men, and the Heavens and Earth there! yet their Gods made them, and the Heaven and Earth where they dwell."[11] Agriculture, hunting, fishing, and gathering were accompanied by rituals and ceremonies performed by individuals and groups to maintain spiritual balance that marked economic activities as also essentially religious.[12] In a universe infused with manitou (power), reciprocal relations, including the proper performance of ritual and the maintenance of a ceremonial cycle, kept the world in balance, and ensured the well-being of the people: "If they receive any good in hunting, fishing, Harvest &c. they acknowledge God in it. Yea, if it be but an ordinary accident, a fall, &c. they will say God was angry and did it. *musquantum manit* God is angry."[13] Within this larger spiritual universe, Indian shamans, called "powwaws" in New England, acted as intermediaries. They demonstrated their relationship with the spirit world through dream interpretation, healing, and prophecy. Because the status of powwaws depended on their success in demonstrating their ability to manipulate spiritual forces through ritual means, their influence waxed and waned.[14]

[10] Cronon, *Changes in the Land*, 48–51.
[11] Williams, *Key into the Language*, 189; William S. Simmons, "Southern New England Shamanism: An Ethnographic Reconstruction," in *Papers of the Seventh Algonquian Conference*, ed. William Cowan (Ottawa: Carleton University, 1976), 217–56; William Simmons, *Spirit of the New England Tribes: Indian History and Folklore, 1620–1984* (Hanover: University Press of New England, 1986), especially Chapter 3; Henry W. Bowden and James P. Ronda, eds., *John Eliot's Indian Dialogues: A Study in Cultural Interaction* (Westport, CT: Greenwood Press, 1980), 19–21; Constance A. Crosby, "From Myth to History, or Why King Philip's Ghost Walks Abroad," in *The Recovery of Meaning: Historical Archaeology in the Eastern United States*, ed. Mark P. Leone and Parker B. Potter (Washington: Smithsonian Institution Press, 1988), 183–209; and Kathleen J. Bragdon, *Native People of Southern New England, 1500–1650* (Norman: University of Oklahoma Press, 1996), 53–4 and chapters 8–10.
[12] Simmons, *Spirit of the New England Tribes*, 45–6, 59.
[13] Williams, *Key into the Language*, 189; and Neal Salisbury, *Manitou and Providence: Indians, Europeans, and the Making of New England, 1500–1643* (New York: Oxford University Press, 1982), 35–6.
[14] Simmons, *Spirit of the New England Tribes*, 41–4, 48–58; Simmons, "Southern New England Shamanism"; and Bowden and Ronda, *Indian Dialogues*, 13–16.

While the Natives of southeastern New England from whom Natick drew its population shared many cultural practices, they also possessed adjoining but bounded homelands that were central to their identity as separate peoples. In the words of Roger Williams, "The *Natives* are very exact and puntuall in the bounds of their Lands, belonging to this or that Prince or People, (even to a River, Brooke, &c.)."[15] Together they numbered between 70,000 and 144,000 before the epidemic of 1616–19 reduced the Indian population dramatically.[16] The Indians of southeastern New England – from the Pawtucket in present-day southeastern New Hampshire and northeastern Massachusetts, south to the Massachusett, whose land contained the rivers that drained into the bay named after themselves, and further south to the contiguous Wampanoag along Martha's Vineyard to the eastern shore of Narragansett Bay, west to the Narragansett people on the western shore of the bay and their neighbors the Pequot and Mohegan of eastern Connecticut, and north to the Nipmuck of central Massachusetts – differed from groups to the north in their reliance on horticulture as a crucial element of their economies, and the higher density of their populations.[17] Important linguistic and cultural divides and hostilities of unknown antiquity distinguished them from Iroquoian speakers to the west. To the south, they were connected to Algonguian speakers of Long Island through longstanding relations of trade. Speakers of related eastern Algonquiañ languages, New England Native peoples nonetheless also differed from one another in "the varietie of their Dialects and proper speech within thirtie or fortie miles" of each other.[18]

Prior to the 1616–19 epidemic, each separate Native group of southeastern New England was composed of several villages of a few hundred people. The villages themselves included extended families from several lineages who were interconnected through kinship networks within and beyond the bounds of particular villages. Marriage outside of the village produced extensive webs of relatives tied together through kin loyalties in other places, and provided individuals with options for relocating their village affiliation as well as a network of places for visiting.[19] Kinship entailed reciprocal bundles of obligations and rights surrounding justice, caretaking, and other social arrangements: "If any

[15] Williams, *Key into the Language*, 167.

[16] See Cronon, *Changes in the Land*, 42 for the lower end, and Salisbury, *Manitou and Providence*, 26–7 for the upper end.

[17] Bert Salwen, "Indians of Southern New England and Long Island: Early Period," in *Handbook of North American Indians: Northeast*, ed. Bruce G. Trigger (Washington: Smithsonian Institution, 1978), 160–76. On the diversity of economic systems within southern New England, see Bragdon, *Native People*, especially Chapter 1.

[18] Williams, *Key into the Language*, 174.

[19] On villagers and kinship see Kathleen Joan Bragdon, "'Another Tongue Brought In': An Ethnohistorical Study of Native Writings in Massachusett" (Ph.D. diss., Brown University, 1981), 95–8; Bragdon, *Native People*, Chapter 6; Elise Melanie Brenner, "Strategies for Autonomy: An Analysis of Ethnic Mobilization in Seventeenth-Century Southern New England" (Ph.D. diss., University of Massachusetts, 1984), 40–5; Cronon, *Changes in the Land*, 37 and 58–60; and Salisbury, *Manitou and Providence*, 41–2.

murther, or other great wrong upon any of their relations or kindred, be committed, all of that stock and consanguinity look upon themselves concerned to revenge that wrong, or murder, unless the business be taken up by the payment of wompompeague, or other satisfaction, which their custom admits, to satisfy for all wrongs, yea for life itself."[20] Roger Williams detected the centrality of kinship even in Narragansett language usage: "Nickquenum. *I am going home:* Which is a solemne word amongst them; and no man will offer any hinderance to him, who after some absence is going to visit his Family."[21] In these ways and others, lineage and kinship networks formed a principal source of identity and a sense of place that included but also transcended natal village.

The Narragansett word "Nqussutam. *I remove house,*"[22] gave expression to a mobile way of life geared toward reaping the seasonally available resources that fundamentally shaped the relationship of Indians to the land as well as the size and location of Native villages: "they use not to winter and summer in one place . . . but . . . remoove for their pleasures; sometimes to their hunting places, where they remain keeping good hospitality for that season; and sometimes to their fishing places, where they abide for that season likewise: and at the spring, when fish comes in plentifully, they have meetinges from severall places, where they exercise themselves in gaminge and playing of juglinge trickes and all manner of Revelles."[23] In the spring, having used slash-and-burn techniques to clear the forest, they planted nutrient-preserving multi-crop fields of maize, beans, squash, and pumpkins in central village sites. Within eight or ten years, soil exhaustion required newly cleared land and shifting sites for central villages. During the summer, because the mixed fields inhibited weeds, the crops needed little attention until harvest. While the crops grew, Indians moved away from agricultural sites on expeditions to gather nuts, berries, and wild plants in the summer and into the fall. These foods, added to the crops that they raised, accounted for perhaps three-fourths of the Indian diet in southern New England.

Native agricultural practices thus both required a degree of fixity and fostered mobility to pursue other economic activities. Indians reaped fish and shellfish in abundance "in the spring, summer and fall of the leaf,"[24] and they dried and smoked some of their catch to preserve for future use. Fishing activities

[20] Daniel Gookin, *Historical Collections of the Indians in New England* (Reprinted: New York: Arno, 1970), 9.
[21] Williams, *Key into the Language*, 117.
[22] Ibid., 127–8.
[23] Morton, *New English Canaan*, 138. On the mobile southeastern New England Indian economies see Cronon, *Changes in the Land*, 37–53. For a discussion of Indian mobility in southern New England as "conditional sedentism," see Bragdon, *Native People*, 36–9, chapter 1.
[24] John Josselyn, "An Account of Two Voyages to New England, Made during the Years 1638, 1663," *Collections of the Massachusetts Historical Society* (hereafter cited as *MHSC*), 3rd ser., 3 (1834): 305.

included gathering the spring runs of spawning fish on the river drainages
within the homelands of each group, which drew large gatherings of Indians
from many villages, as well as smaller-scale excursions throughout the summer
to engage in hook-and-line angling, trapping fish with weirs constructed in
rivers, and coastal fishing and shellfish gathering. Summer was a time for some
hunting, which also entailed mobility. In the fall, activity focused on additional
gathering, but the larger village reassembled to reap the crops, and celebrations
surrounding the "ingathering of their ha[r]vests, [drew] all their neighbours,
kindred, and friends, [to] meet together."²⁵ Between October and December,
villages broke into smaller groups and moved away from the central village for
intensive hunting. By late December, the villagers congregated once again, and
in winter, they harvested "all manner of fowls of the water and of the land, and
beasts of the land and water, [and] pond-fish."²⁶ This mobile, mixed economy
procured an abundance of food, although between seasons, especially in late
winter, Indians might experience times of scarcity. Accumulation of material
goods made little sense in the context of Indian mobility, and even wood-frame
wigwams with grass or bark mats were portable: the women would "carry their
houses on their backs, sometimes to fishing places, other times to hunting places,
after that to a planting place where it abides the longest."²⁷

Within villages, Indians lived in extended households characterized by a
gendered division of labor, and these divisions thus gendered mobility. Women
assumed principal responsibility for agriculture: "[They] set or plant, weede,
and hill, and gather and barne all the corne, and Fruites of the field."²⁸ Women
gathered nuts, berries, and other wild foods, and collected shellfish on the coast.
Occasionally they caught fish, processing some of them through drying and
smoking techniques. Many observers noted that "in their removals from place
to place . . . for their fishing and hunting at the several seasons, the women carry
the greatest burthen: they also prepare all the diet."²⁹ In addition to all of these
tasks, women also made clothing, mats, and baskets, and assumed principal
responsibility for child rearing.³⁰

While female activities usually kept them near the central village site, male
pursuits often drew men away. The hunting activities of men included two

---

²⁵ Gookin, *Historical Collections*, 13.
²⁶ William Wood, *New Englands Prospect*, ed. Alden T. Vaughan (Amherst: University of
   Massachusetts Press, 1977), 86.
²⁷ Wood, *New Englands Prospect*, 113; Peter A. Thomas, "Contrastive Subsistence Strategies
   and Land Use Factors for Understanding Indian–White Relations in New England," *Ethnohistory* 23 (1976): 1–18; Salisbury, *Manitou and Providence*, 30–9; and Howard S. Russell,
   Indian New England Before the Mayflower (Hanover, NH: University Press of New England, 1980), 123–81.
²⁸ Williams, *Key into the Language*, 170.   ²⁹ Gookin, *Historical Collections*, 9.
³⁰ On the gender division of labor see Robert Steven Grumet, "Sunksquaws, Shamans, and
   Tradeswomen: Middle Atlantic Coastal Algonkian Women During the Seventeenth and
   Eighteenth Centuries," in *Women and Colonization: Anthropological Perspectives*, ed. Mona
   Etienne and Eleanor Leacock (New York: Praeger, 1980), 43–60; Cronon, *Changes in the*

basic approaches: "First, when they pursue their game (especially Deere . . .) they pursue in twentie, fortie, fiftie, yea two or three hundred in a company . . . Secondly, They hunt by Traps of several sorts . . . they goe ten or twentie together, and sometimes more, and withall (if it be not too farre) wives and children also."[31] In addition to hunting, men procured fish, were traders, and warriors, and they engaged in politics and diplomacy. They made hunting and fishing equipment, including dugout canoes, and out of wood they carved "dishes, pots, and spoons."[32]

But even given culturally specific expectations about male and female roles, some overlap occurred, as in hunting expeditions near village sites. Although women attended to agriculture, cultivation of tobacco (a ritual crop) was "commonly the only plant which men labour in."[33] Other times, in working with the crops "the man himselfe, (either out of love to his Wife, or care for his Children, or being an old man) will help the Woman which (by the custome of the Countrey) they are not bound to do."[34] Likewise, "When a field is to be broken up, they have a very loving sociable speedy way to dispatch it: All the neighbours men and Women forty, fifty, a hundred &c, joyne, and come in to help freely."[35] The building of wigwams also involved some male labor – they crafted the poles.[36] And women assisted men in the hunt by hauling game back to camp and processing the animals. In addition, women could become sachems, and thus engage in trade, diplomacy, and politics.[37]

As with kinship, village life, and the gendered shape of the economy, the intricate workings of Native leadership also were rooted in homelands – in their use, their defense, and how Indians belonged on the land, as well as how personal relationships were inscribed on the land. "Their Kings or Governours called *sachimauog* . . . and . . . Rulers, doe govern: Their Priests, performe and manage their Worship: Their wise men and old men (of which number the Priests are also,) . . . make solemne speeches and Orations, or Lectures to them, concerning Religion, Peace, or Warre and all things."[38] Sachems, to whom the English mistakenly ascribed monarchical authority, attained their positions through inheritance: "It is the custom for their kings to inherit, the son always taking the kingdom after his father's death. If there be no son, then the queen rules; if no queen, the next to the blood-royal."[39] The emphasis on hereditary leadership accounts for the presence of some female sachems. The evidence suggests that there may also have been hierarchical arrangements between sachems, who engaged in reciprocal gift giving to regulate relations with each other. In keeping with notions of reciprocity, part of the harvest went to the

Land, 44–8; Salisbury, *Manitou and Providence*, 39–41; and Bragdon, *Native People*, 49–53 and chapters 3 and 7.

[31] Williams, *Key into the Language*, 224.   [32] Gookin, *Historical Collections*, 11.
[33] Williams, *Key into the Language*, 103.   [34] Ibid., 170.
[35] Ibid., 170.   [36] Ibid., 128.
[37] Grumet, "Sunksquaws, Shamans, and Tradeswomen."
[38] Williams, *Key into the Language*, 192.   [39] Wood, *New Englands Prospect*, 97.

sachems in the form of "tribute," and in turn they distributed gifts in order to demonstrate their generosity and cement ties with villagers, and to provide hospitality to visitors.[40]

Though sachems were born into their positions as village leaders, their power and following depended on their charisma, power of persuasion, and demonstrated skill in securing the best interests of the group. Sachems with rich networks of relatives could display power through their ability to mobilize kin support; they married into other groups and sometimes practiced polygyny to enhance kin connections. Other villagers, "chief men, that [the sachem] consults with as his special consellors,"[41] influenced the shape of activities that involved the group as a whole, such as selecting the location of family garden plots within a village, planning for hunting, guiding trade outside the group, and engaging in intergroup diplomacy. Consultation with counselors, coupled with the ability of villagers to abandon leaders and join kin elsewhere, acted as a check on the power of sachems and marked group actions as largely consensual: "Their sachems have not their men in such subjection, but that very frequently their men will leave them upon distaste or harsh dealing, and go and live under other sachems that can protect them: so that their princes endeavour to carry it obligingly and lovingly unto their people, lest they should desert them, and thereby their strength, power, and tribute would be diminished."[42] But customs that valued broad consultation within the group were also shaped by the notion that age and experience brought wisdom: "the younger are allwayes obedient unto the elder people . . . in all councels, (as therein they are circumspect to do their acciones by advise and councell, and not rashly or inconsiderately,) the younger mens opinion shall be heard, but the old mens opinion and councell imbraced and followed."[43]

Indian ideas about property and land tenure, often misunderstood by Europeans, reconciled individual and collective ownership of goods and places and were shaped by Native patterns of mobility as well as the principles of sharing and reciprocity that undergirded Native ways of life: "they love not to bee cumbered with many utensilles, and although every proprietor knowes his owne, yet all things, (so long as they will last), are used in common amongst them."[44] Corporate ownership of a group territory was reckoned in the person of the

[40] On political organization see Simmons, *Spirit of the New England Tribes*, 12–3; Bragdon, "'Another Tongue Brought In,'"119–35; Brenner, "Strategies for Autonomy," 31–45; Henry W. Bowden and James P. Ronda, eds., *Eliot's Indian Dialogues: A Study in Cultural Interaction* (Westport, CT: Greenwood Press, 1980), 9; Salisbury, *Manitou and Providence*, 42–3; Cronon, *Changes in the Land*, 58–60; Salwen, "Indians of Southern New England," 166–8; Grumet, "Sunksquaws, Shamans, and Tradeswomen." Bragdon argues that Native political organization was becoming more centralized and hierarchical prior to English invasion. Bragdon, *Native People*, 40–49 and chapters 5 and 6.

[41] Gookin, *Historical Collections*, 14.

[42] Gookin, *Historical Colletions*, 14; and Salisbury, *Manitou and Providence*, 42–3.

[43] Morton, *New English Canaan*, 149.   [44] Ibid., 177.

hereditary sachems whose "ownership" of land was analagous to the "ownership" that European monarchs asserted over their nations. But decisions about
land depended on the approbation of individuals who could express their dis-
satisfaction with sachems by abandoning them, thus diffusing their power.
Within this system of property, Indians based their notions of landownership
on usufruct principles. Indian households "owned" the use of the land where
their wigwams stood and where the women planted the fields, and they owned
the crops raised by the women. Because Indians moved their fields every few
years to avoid soil exhaustion, landownership shifted with land use as well as
with the seasons. Ideas about property rights in hunting, fishing, and gathering
related to ecological use: Group members enjoyed the privilege of harvesting
many resources wherever they found them, which in effect conferred their possession to them, although individuals or kin groups might enjoy exclusive ownership of traps, nets, and sometimes the location where they were placed.
Indian concepts of ownership of other goods revolved around their manufac-
ture: They owned the things they crafted.[45]

Taken together, ideas about the social order held by Native peoples of southeastern New England involved elaborately intertwined customs and beliefs
about kinship, village life, and identity as separate peoples that were intimately
connected to their notions about "bounding" peoples and working out Indian
ways of belonging on the land. Separate peoples possessed bounded homelands, but marriage ties sometimes connected peoples across these boundaries.
Within each group, seasonally fragmenting villages were the principal residential location. Within and between the villages, kinship networks defined social
relations and delineated social rights and obligations such as justice and caretaking, which operated according to Native notions of reciprocity and the
imperative of rectifying imbalance. Even the hereditary but flexible political
structure of Native peoples in southeastern New England was importantly
shaped by kinship. Native leaders needed to mobilize their kin to pursue con-
certed group activities, and dissatisfied villagers might abandon leaders to join
kin elsewhere. The gendered mobile economy likewise reconciled fixity and
mobility implicit in the cross-village kinship system. Indian ways of belonging
on the land held mobility and fixity in tension: Indians moved between resource
sites, visited relatives in other villages, and sometimes entirely relocated their
village affiliation based on kin relations. But principles of mobility existed alongside notions of fixity, as in movements between central village sites and, for
example, the annually abundant fish spawning sites. In sum, lineage and kinship
constituted the central component of Indian identity, and its multi-village geography, in concert with Indian seasonally mobile economies, underscored the
ways in which a larger Indian sense of place connected many separate locations

[45] On "property," "sovereignty," and land see Cronon, *Changes in the Land*, 58–68; and Bragdon, *Native People*, 43, 137–9

together in an intricately webbed landscape. The creative tensions between mobility and fixity and between male and female roles were deeply etched in Indian societies and their histories, comprising and delineating crucial Native ways of belonging on the land. These central cultural blueprints, which English colonists worked hard to redraw, remained principal imperatives through which Indians negotiated their identities in the colonial encounter.

C. *English notions: fixity and social order*

The English understood landownership very differently, but they too connected ideas about land to identity and to understanding an individual's place within an orderly society.[46] English colonizers stressed fixity on the land; Indian mobility contradicted English requirements for social stability.[47] The geographically bounded and "settled" New England town symbolized both a way of ordering the landscape in an overwhelmingly agricultural society, and replicating what the English viewed as the divinely ordained social order in a bounded place. They employed various land distribution systems drawing upon local English customs, which conferred ownership of land on individuals, and provided a means of reproducing a hierarchial society in fixed and ordered places. Through colonization, the English imposed their notions about property rights upon the landscape, bounded land differently, turned it and its products into commodities, altered its ecological uses, and eventually linked it to a new Atlantic economy driven by the market. Arrangements about land were underpinned by a legal system that enforced exclusive ownership, and contained bureaucratic procedures for property transfers and inheritance of property.[48]

[46] For several important studies of how Europeans forged distinctive colonial identities partly by defining themselves against Native people, African slaves they imported, the lands they invaded, and in comparison to the metropolis they left behind, see Nicholas Canny and Anthony Pagden, eds., *Colonial Identity in the Atlantic World, 1500–1800* (Princeton: Princeton University Press, 1987). For considerations of the ways in which Indians and the "wilderness" informed English colonial and Euro-American identity, see Roy Harvey Pearce, *Savagism and Civilization: The Study of the Indian in the American Mind* (Baltimore: The Johns Hopkins University Press, 1953); and Richard Slotkin, *Regeneration through Violence: The Mythology of the American Frontier* (Middletown, CT: Wesleyan University Press, 1973).

[47] Cronon, *Changes in the Land*, 53.

[48] Cronon, *Changes in the Land*, especially chapters 4, 7, and 8; Kenneth A. Lockridge, *A New England Town: The First Hundred Years* (New York: Norton, 1970); Philip J. Greven Jr., *Four Generations: Population, Land, and Family in Colonial Andover, Massachusetts* (Ithaca: Cornell University Press, 1970); John R. Stilgoe, *Common Landscape of America, 1580 to 1845* (New Haven: Yale University Press, 1982), 43–58; David Grayson Allen, *In English Ways: The Movement of Societies and the Transferral of English Local Law and Custom to Massachusetts Bay in the Seventeenth Century* (Chapel Hill: University of North Carolina Press, 1981); Peter M. Briggs, "Timothy Dwight 'Composes' a Landscape for New England," *American Quarterly* 40 (1988): 359–77; McManis, *Colonial New England*; Roy Akagi, *The Town Proprietors of the New England Colonies* (Philadelphia: University of Pennsylvania

In Massachusetts Bay, the commonwealth at least in theory regulated the orderly replication of towns by granting land to particular groups of colonists who distributed land among themselves (thus transferring it to individual ownership according to English fee simple notions), and imposing requirements for "improving" the land and building town institutions. Towns generally distributed lands unequally, which reinforced ideas about social rank and proper place within the social order. In rather chaotic practice by the end of the seventeenth century and in law by the early eighteenth century, the original group attained separate legal status as sole proprietors of the town with exclusive rights to further divisions of town lands. The commonwealth directed recipients of town grants to "improve" the land by breaking ground for monocrop agriculture and fencing fields. Recently occupied places fell into the category "plantation" until the General Court granted town status upon petitioning settlers. Town status carried privileges and duties, including the obligation to support a minister and church, convene a town meeting for local affairs, elect a representative for the colonial assembly, provide relief for poor town residents, maintain roads, support a school, and regularly perambulate town boundaries.[49]

The English preoccupation with fixity and the social order also translated into legal provisions about family life and gender roles. The family reproduced patriarchal relations of power in which the obedience of wives, daughters, and children was thought to be religiously prescribed. Husbands and fathers stood at the apex of family government, ensuring training in and pursuit of economic routines, inculcation of religious values, and the maintenance of orderly social relations within the household. Women had few legal rights. As "feme coverts," their property and earnings belonged to their husbands. As "deputy husbands," they could manage household economic affairs, but only in the absence of their spouses. As widows, they legally were entitled to benefit from one-third of the real estate of their husbands during their widowhood, and to receive supplies from adult children with whom they often resided, but husbands controlled the ultimate dispensation of family property. Women could control only the distribution of property coming from previous marriages in order to protect the interests of the children from those marriages, which fit into patrilineal assumptions

Press, 1924); John Frederick Martin, *Profits in the Wilderness: Entrepreneurship and the Founding of New England Towns in the Seventeenth Century* (Chapel Hill: University of North Carolina Press, 1991); and Sumner Chilton Powell, *Puritan Village: The Formation of a New England Town* (Middletown, CT: Wesleyan University Press, 1963).

[49] Martin, *Profits in the Wilderness*, 282–3; Michael Zuckerman, *Peaceable Kingdoms: New England Towns in the Eighteenth Century* (New York: Norton, 1970), especially 10–45; James T. Lemon, "Spatial Order: Households in Local Communities and Regions," in *Colonial British America: Essays in the New History of the Early Modern Era*, ed. Jack P. Greene and J. R. Pole (Baltimore: The Johns Hopkins University Press), 86–122; Joseph S. Wood, "Village and Community in Early Colonial New England," *Journal of Historical Geography* 8 (1982): 333–46; Patricia J. Tracy, "Reconsidering Migration within Colonial New England," *Journal of Social History* (hereafter cited as *JSH*) 23 (1989): 93–114; and McManis, *Colonial New England*, 53–66.

as well. While women could obtain prenuptial agreements with regard to property, this right was seldom exercised. Legal provisions subsumed unrelated and unmarried male and female indentured servants within the family government of the household in which they lived and worked. Within the household, women cooked, cleaned, raised children, and cared for garden plots; they might engage in dairying, spinning, weaving, making clothing, and trading surplus with other local women. Outside the mercantile sector, men directed the activities of the household as the basic unit of agricultural production, pursued plow agriculture, raised livestock, or were artisans: masons, coopers, millers, blacksmiths and the like. Only men enjoyed a political voice, or an acknowledged public role outside the household.[50]

Expectations about fixity and order found bold expression in the system of poor relief, which was based on the idea of determining who properly belonged in particular towns. Drawing upon Elizabethan poor law, English colonists located responsibility for impoverished persons in the individual's town of origin. In many ways this system simply reflected the desire of localities to avoid the costs of relieving the impoverished, but "vagrancy" also sparked fears of crime and disorder. And although later laws created procedures for changing one's status as inhabitant of a town, the underlying assumptions about fixity remained, and the practice of "warning out" that sent non-residents back to their natal town continued even after the commonwealth eliminated the system in law.[51]

Property ownership, especially landownership, also conferred political privileges and obligations at the town level. In early modern England, to borrow E. P. Thompson's felicitous phrase, "the greatest offence against property was to have none."[52] Male heads of household participated in town governance because as

[50] Edmund S. Morgan, *The Puritan Family: Religion and Domestic Relations in Seventeenth-Century New England* (New York: Harper and Row, 1966); John Demos, *A Little Commonwealth: Family Life in Plymouth Colony* (New York: Oxford University Press, 1970); Laurel Thatcher Ulrich, *Good Wives: Image and Reality in the Lives of Women in Northern New England, 1650–1750* (New York: Vintage Books, 1980); Marylynn Salmon, *Women and the Law of Property in Early America* (Chapel Hill: University of North Carolina Press, 1986); Kathleen M. Brown, "The Anglo-Algonquian Gender Frontier," in *Negotiators of Change: Historical Perspectives on Native American Women*, ed. Nancy Shoemaker (New York: Routledge, 1995), 26–48; and Ann Marie Plane, "Colonizing the Family: Marriage, Household and Racial Boundaries in Southeastern New England to 1730" (Ph.D. diss., Brandeis University, 1994).

[51] David J. Rothman, *The Discovery of the Asylum: Social Order and Disorder in the New Republic* (Boston: Little, Brown and Co., 1971), 3–56; Walter I. Trattner, *From Poor Law to Welfare State: A History of Social Welfare in America*, 5th ed. (New York: Free Press, 1994), 16–28; Douglas Lamar Jones, "The Strolling Poor: Transiency in Eighteenth-Century Massachusetts," *JSH* 8 (1975): 28–54; and Jones, "Poverty and Vagabondage: The Process of Survival in Eighteenth-Century Massachusetts," *New England Historical and Genealogical Register* (hereafter cited as *NEHGR*), 133 (1979): 243–54.

[52] E.P. Thompson, *The Making of the English Working Class* (New York: Vintage, 1963), 61. I thank Russell Menard for reminding me about this.

property owners they were thought to have a legitimate stake in society and therefore be deserving of a political voice. Deliberation about issues occurred in regular town meetings governed by consensual politics. Status arrangements in part determined which men led. Political hierarchy proceeded from the crown, to commonwealth, to town government, and finally, to the male-headed household.[53]

New England towns thus, in theory, constituted both a geographically bounded place and a location in which one's place in a cohesive and divinely mandated hierarchical social order was enacted. Broad but unequal landowner-ship would attest to status arrangements and provide a competent living for industrious nuclear families in the market economy. Patriarchical households would fix individuals within "little commonwealths," reinforce gender ideals, and ensure the fulfillment of religious obligations. Local governance by proper-tied males in town meetings would contribute to the construction of "peaceable kingdom[s]."

These notions about the social order operated as ideals and values that the actual behavior of colonists frequently contradicted. Land speculation began early in the seventeenth century, undermining expectations about the orderly expansion of towns. By the second or third generation of a town, land short-ages propelled children outward in search of land. Mandates about the devel-opment of town institutions often were violated. Within towns, individuals hauled each other into court regularly. Conflicts over issues ranging from the condition of fences to the location of the meetinghouse set neighbors against one another. Especially in the eighteenth century, the expanding ranks of the "strolling poor" attested to economic struggles and mobility that flew in the face of expectations about fixity.[54] The actual mobility of English colonists, a continuation and reformulation of early modern European patterns, followed the continued success of the English demographic regime and the growth of the British Atlantic economy, and led to even more rapid geographical expan-sion and town proliferation in the eighteenth century.[55]

[53] Edward M. Cook Jr., *The Fathers of the Towns: Leadership and Community Structure in Eighteenth-Century New England* (Baltimore: The Johns Hopkins University Press, 1976); and Zuckerman, *Peaceable Kingdoms.*

[54] Greven, *Four Generations*; Lockridge, *A New England Town*; Kenneth Lockridge, "Land, Population, and the Evolution of New England Society, 1630–1790," *Past and Present* 39 (1966): 62–80; Stephen Innes, *Labor in a New Land: Economy and Society in Seventeenth-Century Springfield* (Princeton, NJ: Princeton University Press, 1983); Paul Boyer and Stephen Nissenbaum, *Salem Possessed: The Social Origins of Witchcraft* (Cambridge: Har-vard University Press, 1974); Robert A. Gross, *The Minutemen and their World* (New York: Hill and Wang, 1976); Carol Karlsen, *The Devil in the Shape of a Woman: Witchcraft in Colonial New England* (New York: Norton, 1987); Martin, *Profits in the Wilderness*; and Alan Taylor, *Liberty Men and Great Proprietors: The Revolutionary Settlement on the Maine Frontier, 1760–1820* (Chapel Hill: University of North Carolina Press, 1990).

[55] Bernard Bailyn, *The Peopling of British North America: An Introduction* (New York: Vintage Books, 1986), especially 20–43; John J. McCusker and Russell R. Menard, *The Economy of*

Despite these realities, English ideas about fixity on the land and its connection to the impulse to assign everyone a proper place in the social order informed their interpretations of Indian ways of life, and moreover, their notions of land provided them with justifications for dispossessing Indians. Most English observers who looked at Indian mobility saw aimless wandering, not seasonal migration that secured a livelihood. The expansive homelands required for the Indians' diversified economies, homelands that included forests as well as fields, looked to the English like unimproved lands. Building upon these ideas so they could replicate their own social order on the land, seventeenth-century English colonists used two devices to dispossess New England Indians: they declared lands "vacuum domicilium" (empty of habitation), and thus available to be put to "higher uses," and, especially at the prompting of Roger Williams, they purchased lands, which entailed an admission of Indian ownership legitimately transferred to themselves. The English rejected full Indian sovereignty over their lands by subsuming Indian transactions within English legal procedures and choosing to interpret transactions according to English principles. When Indians gave deeds to the English intending to extend usufruct privileges, for example, the English interpreted them as transfers of the land itself. Even when they did claim land through purchase, the English assumed that their land rights really emanated from crown grants secured through right of discovery, and the biblical directive for Christians to "subdue the earth and multiply." They also extracted formal submissions of sachems to colonial authority, which aimed to subsume Indians within English colonial regimes.[56]

D. *John Eliot and the bounding of Natick*

Using English ideas about fixity and the social order, John Eliot and other English Calvinist missionaries could imagine a place for Indians within the colonial regime. Eliot, educated at Cambridge, arrived in Massachusetts Bay in 1631,

British America: 1607–1789 (Chapel Hill: University of North Carolina Press, 1985); Allan Kulikoff, "Households and Markets: Toward a New Synthesis of American Agrarian History," *William and Mary Quarterly* (hereafter cited as *WMQ*), 3d ser., 50 (1993): 342–56; Winifred B. Rothenberg, "The Market and Massachusetts Farmers, 1750–1855," *Journal of Economic History* 41 (1981): 283–314; Winifred B. Rothenberg, *From Market-Places to a Market Economy: The Transformation of Rural Massachusetts, 1750–1850* (Chicago: University of Chicago Press, 1995); Thomas R. Cole, "Family, Settlement, and Migration in Southeastern Massachusetts, 1650–1805: The Case for Regional Analysis," *NEHGR* 132 (1978): 171–85; Tracy, "Reconsidering Migration"; Linda Auwers Bissell, "From One Generation to Another: Mobility in Seventeenth-Century Windsor, Connecticut," *WMQ*, 3d ser., 31 (1974): 136–49; Douglas Lamar Jones, *Village and Seaport: Migration and Society in Eighteenth-Century Massachusetts* (Hanover, NH: University Press of New England, 1981); John W. Adams and Alice Bee Kasakoff, "Migration and the Family in Colonial New England: The View from Genealogies," *Journal of Family History* 9 (1984): 24–43; and Gregory H. Nobles, *Divisions Throughout the Whole: Politics and Society in Hampshire County, Massachusetts, 1740–1775* (New York: Cambridge University Press, 1983).
56 Cronon, *Changes in the Land*, especially chapters 4, 7, and 8.

took a position as teacher in the Roxbury First Church in 1632, and remained there until his death in 1690. Eliot was one of the few in the seventeenth century who answered the call of working toward Indian conversion to English Calvinism, which was articulated as "the principall Ende of this Plantation" in the 1629 Massachusetts Bay charter.[57]

The ideology of conversion John Eliot developed involved fixing Indian candidates for conversion in geographically bounded places called "Praying Towns" where English ideas about land use and ownership would prevail, gender roles would be transformed, and English institutions would instruct Indians about their place in the social order before extending them full religious rights in formally gathered Indian congregations. He viewed religious conversion as embedded in total cultural transformation. In the 1640s he told Indians who had inquired about the rituals of English Calvinism that they were "incapable . . . to be trusted therewith, whilst they live so unfixed, confused, and ungoverned a life, uncivilized and unsubdued to labor and order."[58]

In keeping with the exclusiveness of English Calvinism, strict scrutiny of Indian converts was required. For Indians, as for the English, full membership in a congregational church (or full communion) required scriptural knowledge, blameless behavior, and a convincing conversion experience related in public and evaluated by others already judged to be part of the visible church. Full membership qualified individuals for communion and their children for baptism. For both Indians and the English, establishing a congregation would take assembling a core of individuals admitted to full communion who could then enter a church covenant, call a minister, and administer church ordinances.[59]

Having studied the Algonquian language, Eliot tentatively made excursions to groups of Indians near Roxbury in the 1640s. In 1646 at the Indian village of Neponset, Eliot got little attention from Massachusett leader Cutshamekin and his followers, and he retreated. Six weeks later, he received more encouragement from Waban and his followers at Nonantum. Thereafter, he made biweekly visits from Roxbury to Nonantum and other villages where he delivered his message in Algonquian and English, instructed Indians in prayer, catechized children and adults, and encouraged Indians to ask questions. He preached the harsh message of English Calvinism in the Native tongue to the best of his ability. He spoke about the fall of man, the uncertainty of salvation, the omnipotence of God who sent divine retribution for sinners in this life and punished them in the afterlife, the consequences of breaking commandments, the rewards of heaven,

[57] On John Eliot see, for example, Nehemiah Adams, *The Life of John Eliot with an Account of the Early Missionary Efforts Among the Indians of New England* (Boston: Massachusetts Sabbath School Society, 1847); Francis Convers, *Life of John Eliot, the Apostle to the Indians*, The Library of American Biography, Conducted by Jared Sparks (New York: Harper & Brothers, 1854); and Ola Elizabeth Winslow, *John Eliot, "Apostle to the Indians"* (Boston: Houghton Mifflin Company, 1968).

[58] Edward Winslow, "The Glorious Progress of the Gospel, amongst the Indians in New England," *MHSC*, 3d ser., 4 (1834): 90. See also Axtell, *Invasion Within*, especially 131–78.

[59] Axtell, *Invasion Within*, 221; and Jennings, *Invasion of America*, 228–53.

and especially the pains of hell. He then spoke of repentance, the promise of God's forgiveness, and eternal salvation for followers of the "true" word.[60]

In peddling his message, Eliot quickly grasped that pursuading Indians to listen would be most effectively achieved by working through the Indian social order: "I doe endeavour to engage the Sachems of greatest note to accept the Gospel, because that doth greatly animate and encourage such as are well-affected, and is a dampening to those that are scoffers and opposers: for many such there be, though they dare not appear before me."[61] Eliot succinctly encapsulated Native leadership through persuasion in this passage. On the other hand, he paid attention to Native religious ideas so that he could undermine them. He focused the brunt of this attack on Native powwaws, who were viewed by Eliot and other colonists as satanic, and whose shamanistic activities were banned by the General Court. As powwaws were healers as well as spiritual intermediaries in general, Indians resisted Eliot's campaign: "If [we] leave off Powwowwing, and pray to God, what shall [we] do when [we] are sick?"[62] In the meantime, the ineffectiveness of Indian curing for smallpox and other epidemic diseases dramatically undermined their faith in customary healing anyway. Eliot gleefully claimed in 1648 that Indians were rejecting powwaws, and that the powwaws themselves were turning to prayer.[63]

Having gained the ears of at least some Indians, Eliot proposed the establishment of an English-style town composed of Indian listeners in order to accelerate the conversion process:

> For the further progresse of the work amongst them, I doe perceive a great impediment; Sundry in the Country in divers places would gladly be taught the knowledge of God and Iesus Christ, and would pray unto God, if I could goe unto them, and teach them where they dwell: but to come to live here among or neer to the English they are not willing, because they have neither tooles, nor skill, nor heart to fence their grounds; and if it be not well fenced, their Corne is so spoyled by the English Cattell . . . that its a very great discouragement to them and me . . . So that I plainly see the way to do them good must be this. A place must be found . . . some what remote from the English, where they must have the word constantly taught, and government constantly exercised, means of good subsistence provided, incouragements for the industrious [and a] meanes of instructing them in Letters, Trades, and Labours.[64]

[60] Francis Jennings, "Goals and Functions of Puritan Missions to the Indians," *Ethnohistory* 18 (1971): 197–212; and James Naeher, "Dialogue in the Wilderness: John Eliot and the Indians' Exploration of Puritanism as a Source of Meaning, Comfort, and Ethnic Survival," *New England Quarterly* 62 (1989): 346–68.

[61] Winslow, "Glorious Progress," 83.

[62] Shepard, "The Clear Sun-shine of the Gospel Breaking Forth upon the Indians in New-England," *MHSC*, 3d ser., 4 (1834): 56.

[63] Ibid., 50.   [64] Winslow, "Glorious Progress," 81.

Figure 1. Southern New England in the early 1670s

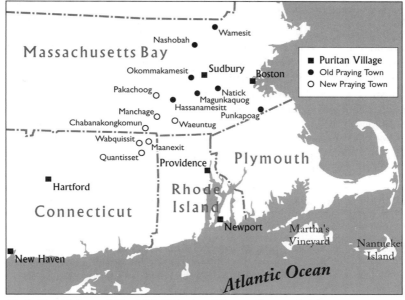

Map by Mark Lindberg and Allan Willis, University of Minnesota Cartographic Laboratory

Fencing fields would eliminate conflicts with English farmers, impose order on the landscape, and encourage intensive English-style agriculture that would replace mobility with fixity. Finding a location "remote from the English" would placate Indians unwilling to live too near them, and buy time for Indian cultural transformation. Gathering Indians into towns would confine them, and facilitate social control as well as cultural and religious instruction.

The establishment in 1649 of the Corporation for Promoting and Propagating the Gospel among the Indians in New England (known as the New England Company) provided financial support for Eliot's activities and a broad range of missionary overtures made in southeastern New England that would continue through the eighteenth century.[65] By the time of the American Revolution, the

---

[65] Beginning in 1643, a campaign was initiated to encourage Parliamentary support for missionary activities. The first "Eliot Indian Tracts" were part of this campaign. In 1649, largely through the efforts of Edward Winslow, "An Act for the promoting and propagating the Gospel of Jesus Christ in New England" was passed. The corporation, which should not be confused with the later Anglican Society for the Propagation of the Gospel, was empowered to appoint overseers in New England to "receive and disburse the money sent across the Atlantic by the Society" and was given the usual rights and powers of a corporation. Collections were to be made in England and Wales. William Kellaway, *The New England Company, 1649–1776: Missionary Society to the American Indians* (London: Longmans, 1961), 15–6.

initiatives of seventy-two English missionaries had attracted Indian attention in
at least ninety-one localities in New England, and twenty-two Indian churches
had been established. One hundred and thirty-three Indians had become preachers and teachers. But in the seventeenth century, John Eliot's work at Natick and
thirteen other Praying Towns designated between 1650 and 1671 received the
most attention and support from the Company.[66] (See Figure 1.)

Yet however much naming Natick a Praying Town argued an English position with regard to Indian acceptance of various English ideas – their religion,
notions about a fixed and bounded geographical place, and the essential aspects
of a different social order – for Indians who came to Natick, a different agenda
guided their actions. After the early years of their encounter with the aggressive "strangers," Indians who came to Natick envisaged an Indian future there
that they could substantially shape. By using the institutions of the imposed
English colonial order, they could rebuild kin connections and community
within their homelands. Thus Natick at its founding, and as always, was an
Indian place.

[66] Axtell, *The Invasion Within*, 273. For slightly different numbers, see Alden T. Vaughan and
Daniel K. Richter, "Crossing the Cultural Divide: Indians and New Englanders,
1605–1763," *Proceedings of the American Antiquarian Society*, Part I, 90 (1980): 23–99.

2

The sinews and the flesh

Natick comes together 1650–75

> Then he said unto me, Son of man, these bones are the whole house
> of Israel: behold . . . Our bones are dried up, our hope is lost . . .
> Therefore prophesy and say unto them . . .
>> Behold . . . I will open your graves, and cause you to come up
>> out of your graves . . . .
> And shall put my spirit in you, and ye shall live, and I shall place you
> in your own land.
>
>> Ezekiel 37.11–14[1]

A. *Metaphor and place*

Between 1650 and 1675, twenty years after the establishment of Massachusetts Bay, Natick came together as a Praying Town. One of John Eliot's favorite texts provided a metaphor for the coming together of Natick, and a point of convergence between the English religion and Native belief. Ezekiel 37 contained a message that gave play to Eliot's millennium-driven preoccupation with the conversion of Israel and his conviction that New England Indians were descended from the Ten Lost Tribes of Israel.[2] The text uses the analogy of bare, dry bones to refer to unconverted Israel; prophesied conversion is given visual content by describing "bone joining bone," "the sinews and the flesh come upon them," and the spirit being breathed into them "that they may come to life."[3] Whether by design or coincidence, Eliot's chosen passage reverberated among his Indian listeners:

> the first Text out of which Mr. Eliot preached to the Indians was
> about the dry bones, Ezek. 37. where it's said, Vers. 9, 10. that by
> prophesying to the wind, the wind came and the dry bones lived;

[1] King James version, *The New Layman's Parallel Bible* (Grand Rapids, MI: Zondervan Bible Publishers, 1981), 2210.
[2] J. F. MacClear, "New England and the Fifth Monarchy: The Quest for Millennium in Early American Puritanism," *William and Mary Quarterly* (hereafter cited as *WMQ*), 3d ser., 32 (1975): 223–60; and James Hollstun, *A Rational Millennium: Puritan Utopias of Seventeenth-Century England and America* (New York: Oxford University Press, 1987).
[3] Ezekiel 37.9–10:
> Then said he unto me, Prophesy unto the wind, prophesy, son of man, and say to the
> wind, Thus saith the Lord GOD; Come from the four winds. O breath, and breathe
> upon these slain, that they may live.
>
> So I prophesied as he commanded me, and the breath came into them, and they lived, and
> stood up upon their feet, an exceeding great army.

The New Layman's Parallel Bible, 2211.

> now the Indian word for Wind is Waubon, and the most active Indi-
> an for stirring up other Indians to seek after the knowledg of God in
> these parts, his name is Waubon, which signifies Wind, (the Indians
> giving names to their children usually according to appearances of
> providences) although they never dreamt of this, that this their
> Waubon should breathe such a spirit of life and incouragement into
> the rest of the Indians . . . some of the Indians themselves that were
> stir'd up by him took notice of this his name and that Scripture
> together . . . Mr. Eliot . . . professing that he chose that Text with-
> out the least thought of any such application in respect of Waubon.[4]

Perhaps struck by the coincidence himself, Eliot used the metaphor of "dry bones" repeatedly in his preaching, and he "applyed [it] to their condition."[5]

If Indian listeners found it remarkable that Eliot's favorite text incorporated the name of a local leader, they could not have missed the message of the next four verses of Ezekiel, which became principal themes in the missionary encounter. Those whose "hope is lost" would be redeemed; the dead would be resurrected; the infusion of spirit would preserve life; and they would be settled on their land.

The term "Praying Town" indicates a conjuncture between ideology (English Calvinism as a particular expression for "Englishness") and a particular location for fixing Indians in a geographically bounded place on which cultural negotiations would occur. In this sense, the Praying Town itself stood as a metaphor for an early form of cultural accommodation. Eliot's ideas about missionization envisioned the transformation of Indian land use, social institutions, and cultural forms as precursors to actual religious conversion. That vision included the idea of "reducing them to civility," or transforming Indian lifeways into conformity with English expectations about social order. Within this context, disputes over land became central to the ways in which cultural conflicts were resolved. The coming together of Natick after 1650 involved negotiating rules over what land would belong to whom and how it would be used as much as it had to do with religion.

B. *Siting the community: negotiating place*

Bounding the site that would become Natick occurred in the context of cultural negotiations over place. In theory, the idea of fixing Indians willing to entertain

---

4 Thomas Shepard, "The Clear Sun-shine of the Gospel Breaking Forth upon the Indians in New-England," *Collections of the Massachusetts Historical Society* (hereafter cited as *MHSC*), 3d ser., 4 (1834): 62–3.
5 Eliot periodically made reference to this scripture in his published works. See, for example, Thomas Shepard, "The Day-Breaking, if not the Sun-Rising of the Gospel with the Indians in New-England," *MHSC*, 3d ser., 4 (1834): 15 and 22; Shepard, "Clear Sun-shine," 62–3; Henry Whitfield, "The Light Appearing Towards the Perfect Day: Or, a Farther Discovery of the Present State of the Indians in New-England. Concerning the Progresse of the Gospel Amongst them," *MHSC*, 3d ser., 4 (1834): 122, 126, and 128.

the possibility of conversion in geographically circumscribed Praying Towns met with official approval when the General Court directed a committee to purchase land "for ye incuragmt of yr Indians to live in an orderly way amongst us."[6] But in practice, bounding Natick collided with the local interests of the townspeople of neighboring Dedham, who pressed a vigorous battle against the project. In creating Natick as a Praying Town, disputes about bounding the land involved John Eliot as a kind of cultural intermediary, the General Court as the political body of the commonwealth, respected elders from other towns, as well as townspeople in Dedham and Indians who would build Natick. Although the disputes were adjudicated within English legal and political institutions, even the English disputants understood that Indian rights importantly informed the terms of debate.

Conflict over boundaries began with the founding of Natick in 1650, erupted into an angry legal battle in 1661, and festered just beneath the surface for the duration of the seventeenth century. Even General Court intervention did not settle land matters. Contested oral agreements, ambiguous territorial descriptions, and the failure of authorities to provide an explicit town grant or act decisively in the dispute, despite their 1646 charge, contributed to an atmosphere of mutual distrust.[7] At the center of the battle lay the undecorous spectacle of Eliot and Dedham minister John Allen accusing one another of faulty memory if not willful misrepresentation, and engaged in intense bickering over the niceties of boundary making.

The process of selecting the town site, which John Eliot made appear somewhat mysterious in a published tract, set the stage for the persistent land dispute. According to Eliot, an expedition that included Indians predisposed toward establishing a Praying Town searched for a suitable location. Disappointed by one place "of some hopeful expectation," the group was forced to turn back because a member of the party became ill. As they were returning

> the Jndians in our company, upon inquiry describing a place to me, and guiding us over some part of it, the Lord did both by his providence then, and after more diligent search of the place, discover that there it was his pleasure we should begin this work . . . I purpose, God willing, to call them together this Autumne to break and prepare their own ground against the Spring, and for other necessary works.[8]

---

[6] Nathaniel B. Shurtleff, ed., *Records of the Governor and Company of the Massachusetts Bay in New England* (1628–86) (hereafter cited as *Mass. Records*), 5 vols. (Boston, 1853–54), 2:166, 4 Nov. 1646; and James Axtell, *The Invasion Within: The Contest of Cultures in Colonial North America* (New York: Oxford University Press, 1985), 139.

[7] For a discussion of disorder and irregularity in land recording in Essex County, see David Thomas Konig, "Community Custom and the Common Law: Social Change and the Development of Land Law in Seventeenth-Century Massachusetts," *American Journal of Legal History* 18 (1974): 137–77.

[8] Whitfield, "Light Appearing," 138.

Eliot's providential explanation about the town's origins, designed to impress those who offered financial support for Indian conversion, appears disingenious when his later testimony is taken into account:

> These lands lying wthin the lines of Dedhams grant by the Gen: Court, our first motion was, to request Dedhams love & consent, for our siting downe at Natick, to make a Towne, where some of the Praying Indians then planted, & had done of old, even beyond the memory of the oldest man alive, I requested mr Allin & [Lieut.] Fisher to move it to the Towne, & giue me a speedy answer. mr Allin returned to me an answer of appbation & consent wherupon we pceeded to begin our Towne, this was in the spring 1650.[9]

This version, which acknowledged that the chosen site fell partly within an already bounded English town, suggests that Indians forced Eliot to act as their advocates in securing the Native rights to a particular place. Selection of the site was guided less by the hand of God than by some determined Indians who wanted explicit English legal confirmation of the lands they already lived on and planted "even beyond the memory of the oldest man alive."

But that was not the claim that stuck in Dedham's craw. Their version of the Indian plantation differed in fundamental respects from the one offered by Eliot. Dedham proprietors insisted that the lands the Indians had settled on belonged to them, and that Eliot had failed to gain permission to begin there. Dedham residents rested their claim on its General Court town grant of 1635, their own interpretation of a 1651 agreement between Eliot and the town of Dedham to provide some of its land for Natick (endorsed by the General Court), and on the testimony of inhabitants designated to oversee the establishment of the Indian plantation.[10] Unfortunately the 1651 agreement, which became the lynchpin of the dispute, was worded vaguely enough to permit conflicting interpretations; oral negotiations between individuals exacerbated the potential for controversy.

Nobody disputed the fact that the site chosen by the Indians fell squarely within the bounds of land the General Court had already granted to Dedham, or that other grants in the area limited the possibilities for carving out the Natick plantation. In 1651 Eliot and the inhabitants of Dedham struck a compromise: Dedham "tendered" 2,000 acres to the Indians, "provided they lay downe all clajmes in that toune elsewhere, and sett no trapps in vninclosed ground."[11]

---

[9] Don Gleason Hill, ed., *The Early Records of the Town of Dedham, Massachusetts, 1659–1673* (hereafter cited as *DTR*) 4 vols. (Dedham: The Dedham Transcript, 1894), 4:255. Records relating to the Dedham-Natick dispute are reprinted in the Appendix of Volume 4. This quotation comes from Eliot's 1662 plea for the Natick Indians.

[10] Cf. John Frederick Martin, *Profits in the Wilderness: Entrepreneurship and the Founding of New England Towns in the Seventeenth Century* (Chapel Hill: University of North Carolina Press, 1991), 300–2.

[11] *DTR*, 4:242, and 4:263–5.

Figure 2. Natick in 1750

Map by Mark Lindberg and Allan Willis, University of Minnesota Cartographic
Laboratory, based on Samuel Livermore's Plan of Natick dated August 1, 1749,
Massachusetts Archives, Massachusetts State Archives at Columbia Point, Boston,
Map Collection 3d ser., 33:17:633

Subsequent disagreements centered around the issue of which 2,000 acres each
party had in mind; the agreement itself contained no clear instructions.

For their part, Dedham residents insisted that they had stipulated that their
grant to Natick be laid out on Dedham's western bounds and be confined to the
north side of the Charles River. (See Figures 2 and 3.) Eliot claimed that in the
spring of 1650 he had obtained consent from Dedham, communicated orally to
him by Rev. John Allen, for the Indians to continue where they were, on both
sides of the Charles River. Allen remembered the events differently. He acknowledged that he had viewed the location with Eliot in the spring of 1650, but asserted that when he referred the issue to the townspeople they refused to give up
lands on the south side of the river, and that Eliot had been informed of this decision. In July 1650 Dedham appointed a committee to supervise the establishment
of Natick, since it was "a matter of great Concernemt in many respects."[12] One
month later, Eliot composed his letter depicting the providential origins of

[12] Ibid., 4:241.

Figure 3. Lands disputed between Natick and Dedham 1650–62

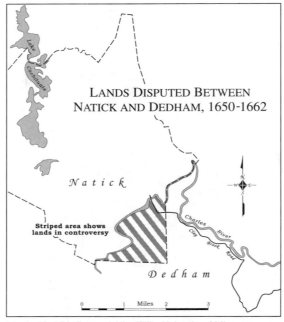

Map by Mark Lindberg and Allan Willis, University of Minnesota
Cartographic Laboratory, based on Frank Smith, "Controversy over
Dedham's Grant to the Natick Indians," *Dedham Historical Register* 9
(1898): 37–41

Natick; he neglected to mention the complicated dispute in which the plantation
was already embroiled.[13]

For the next decade, each party periodically initiated efforts to settle their differences.[14] The General Court appointed a committee to mediate the dispute in
1651. Two years later, representatives for Dedham petitioned the colony for relief
"in respect of some affronts offred them by the Indians, as also . . . some difference
in relation to land betweene them." Although directed to bring suit to gain satisfaction, they decided to wait and try to settle the problem informally. In 1658 Eliot
asked the General Court to finish laying out Natick's boundaries, yet the committee did nothing about the festering dispute. In 1660 surveyors found Natick to be

[13] The letter published in the pamphlet was dated 21 August 1650. Dedham appointed their
committee to oversee the settlement of Natick on 21 July 1650. Eliot, "Light Appearing,"
135–45.

[14] Kenneth Lockridge, *A New England Town: The First Hundred Years* (New York: Norton,
1970), 83. Lockridge described this battle as Dedham's "most notable failure" in maintaining
a peaceful community. He argued for the legality of Dedham's claim against Natick, but also
that "no amount of legal right could have justified the deceptions, retaliations, and lasting
bitterness which characterized Dedham's role in the case." (The quotation is from p. 84.)

far smaller than was intended and badly compromised by previous English grants and a scarcity of meadow "wch tendeth much to the discouragement of the poore natives, wch are willing to shroud themselves vnder our protection from the malice of such as theire & our ennemyes." A meeting in the same year between elders from Dedham and Roxbury contained the essence of the eventual resolution. They asked Eliot to acknowledge that his behavior in encouraging the Indians in the struggle for lands that Dedham claimed appeared "very irregular" to the townspeople of Dedham. They confirmed Dedham's rights in the dispute, and asked Dedham to concede the lands to the Indians "considering how grievous it will bee to those poore natives to bee put from the Lands which they have so long possessed." Dedham should be compensated with lands elsewhere, and the Indians should desist from further "encroachment," acknowledge Dedham's gift of lands, and eschew any claim of Native-based title, the elders said.[15]

The September 1660 meeting of elders was designed to forestall a more aggressive course of action already begun by Dedham. Planning a division of land to proprietors, they decided in July 1659 to include the Indian lands in the distribution. Debating the conditions of the 2,000-acre tender, they concluded that the agreement

> is heerby made voyde; and did forwith pceed to this vote . . . .
> That the 2000 Acres formerly granted to the Indians at Natick shall be layd out at the westerly end of our Towne Bounds. and that the other lands of our Towne neere Naticke wheresoeuer. shall be searched out and viewed and what Land shall . . . be founde fitt to be laid out in deuident . . .shall be layd out to the Inhabitants of the Towne [of Dedham].[16]

That November, they clarified what was meant by lands "neere Natick whatsoeuer":

> they intend all the land that is fitt for corne Land. first on the southe east side of Charles Riuer and neere or adjoyneing thereto, and allso a playne that lye neerer our Towne conteyning about 100 acres. more or lesse and allso the remainder of that playne where vpon Naticke meeting house stand. and allso the land betwixt Naticke brooke and the drye heard house. and about that house and all about Mayns his wigwam and downe towards the Riuer there. that is so much thereof as is fitt for impuemt for corne.[17]

Nine years after Natick had been bounded, Dedham residents proposed to seize the lands as properly belonging to them. At this point they did not confine their

---

[15] *DTR*, "affronts": 4:243, "discouragement": 4:246, and "how grievous": 4:247–9.
[16] Ibid., 4:9–10.
[17] Ibid., 4:12–13. "Mayns" probably refers to Indian John Magus. The Dedham Town Records are transcribed and published; I suspect the name was misread.

claims to the south side of the Charles River, but demonstrated their determination to dismantle Natick by lumping into the division lands on the north side of the river on which the Indians had built their meetinghouse.[18] Perhaps because it might prove useful for them, they voted to allow the sawmill the Indians were building even though it also fell on lands Dedham claimed.[19]

In September 1661, rejecting the recommendation of the elders, Dedham voted to prosecute their claims against the Indians in county court and to sue for all the lands the Indians had improved.[20] The town issued writs of attachments against the persons and property of several prominent Natick residents, collected depositions from its own inhabitants, and worked to build its case.[21] John Eliot did not exaggerate when he declared that "If these lands sued for be taken from us Natik is overthrowen fro being a Towne . . . our meeting house & other publik buildings are lost & uselesse to us," since the inhabitants would be forced to move at least two miles away from where the buildings had been erected.[22]

The decisions about Natick disclosed a deeply seated ambivalence on the part of authorities about the place of Indians in the colony, and left the townspeople of Dedham dumbfounded. While the jury in county court found in Dedham's favor in the cases (split into three separate actions), the magistrates refused the verdicts and referred them to the Court of Assistants for action. The General Court dictated a settlement in May of 1662 that confirmed Dedham's legal rights, but found for the Indians anyway:

> although the legall right of Dedham thereto cannot in justice be denyed, yet such haue binn the incouragement of the Indians in their improovements thereof, the which, added to their native right, wch cannot, in strict justice, be vtterly extinct, do therefore order, that the Indians be not dispossessed of such lands as they at present are possessed of there.[23]

The court weighed two versions of justice in its decision: Dedham's "legall right" (invented by the ideology of English conquest) could not justly be refuted, but neither could "native right . . . in *strict* justice" be wholly dismissed. Significantly, Indian improvements to the land, evaluated according to English criteria, tipped the scales. In adjudicating Natick's boundaries, Native right, in combination with Indian possession of lands in ways that resembled English patterns, discouraged colonial officials from dispossessing them. The court designated a committee to set the boundaries of the settlement, which encompassed

---

[18] Lands on the north side of the river had been a point of contention as well, though Dedham seemed more willing to compromise about that part of Natick. Dedham selectmen recommended that proprietors who drew lots placing them on Natick plain "shall haue optunitie to treat or accept of a Treay wth the Indians or any in their behalfe & conclude therein as they se cause." Ibid., 4:29.

[19] Ibid., 4:12–13.   [20] Ibid., 4:36.

[21] Ibid., 4:250–5, and 4:261–9.   [22] Ibid., 4:259.

[23] Ibid., 4:270.

6,000 acres.[24] Compensation for Dedham came in the form of 8,000 acres to be laid out as a new town.[25]

Not satisfied that justice had been served, residents of Dedham continued to harass their Indian neighbors. In 1668 Dedham complained about Indian encroachments.[26] The next year, Eliot objected that Dedham violated the boundaries, prevented Indians from working the grounds they had planted, ripped up the fence rails that enclosed them, and sold Indian lands much to the "trouble and wonderment of the Indians."[27] At this point, relations between the reverends deteriorated to the level of scripturally based personal insult. Allen cited Leviticus 19.15: "Thou shalt not respect ye pson of ye poore in judgmt." Not less exasperated, Eliot in turn accused Allen of at least the appearance of persecuting the Indians: "my plea . . . yt we should not so injure the pore you answer by two texts of scriptures, yt we must not unjustly favor the pore. I accept your intimation, & desire to watch against the eror on yt hand, as I desire you to watch against opprssing ym, or of seeming so to doe."[28] The committee was asked once again to reset the bounds. This time, Dedham's version prevailed.[29]

The General Court had agreed in principle to extending land grants for Praying Towns in 1646 when they appointed a committee to purchase land for Indians willing to "live in an orderly way amongst us."[30] There was nothing orderly about the way Natick was established. In selecting the site, Eliot acted as a cultural intermediary for Indians who, by going along with the idea of Praying Towns, gained security for ancestral lands by having them bounded within the English legal system. He failed to carefully identify lands not bounded as English towns. Instead, probably because he needed to secure his relationship with the Indians in order to proceed with his cultural agenda, he responded to what they wanted and then tried to gain post facto legal concessions.[31] No English authority conceded that he had acted properly. Security for the town was gained not because the magistrates agreed he had proved their unassailable rights; Eliot's logic in presenting the Indian case was in fact rather murky and relied on hearsay.[32]

---

[24] William Biglow, *History of the Town of Natick, Massachusetts from the Days of the Apostolic Eliot, 1650, to the Present Time, 1830* (Boston: Marsh, Capen, and Lyon, 1830), 21.

[25] The grant resulted in the settlement of the Connecticut River Valley town Deerfield. Martin, *Profits in the Wilderness*, 239–40; and Richard I. Melvoin, *New England Outpost: War and Society in Colonial Deerfield* (New York: Norton, 1989).

[26] *DTR*, 4:152–3.   [27] Ibid., 4:279.

[28] Ibid., 4:282.

[29] Ibid., 4:279–83. The Allen quote is from p. 280, and the Eliot quote from p. 282.

[30] Shurtleff, *Mass. Records*, 2:166, 4 Nov. 1646.

[31] Shepard, "Day-Breaking," 17 and 20; Whitfield, "Light Appearing," 124.

[32] The main thrust of his argument was that Allen had conveyed an "inclination" to accede to Eliot's request, and that because Dedham had not prevented the Indians from beginning their plantation, this "inclination" was tantamount to consent. Dedham then, according to Eliot, granted Natick 2,000 acres without restricting the location. Natick thus had

The General Court found for Natick because the moral claims upon which Eliot based his arguments in the dispute caught the attention of the magistrates. English guilt over dispossessing the Natives surfaced in the 1662 settlement. Arguing that the Native right "cannot, in strict justice, be vtterly extinct" could have opened the door for insecurity of colonial claims, a dangerous concession that no English settler would want to entertain seriously.[33] What is so surprising is that the possibility received written expression at all.

The whole notion of the English granting land to Indians who remained in their ancestral homelands seems astounding. This irony was not lost on those involved in building Praying Towns. Daniel Gookin offered a defense of the practice:

> If any should object, that it is not necessary, that the English should grant them land, forasmuch as it was all their native country and propriety, before the English came into America; the answer is ready: First, that the English claim right to their land, by patent from our king. Secondly, yet the English had the grant of most of the land within this jurisdiction, either by purchase or donation from the Indian sachems and sagamores, which were actually in possession, when the English came first over. Therefore the propriety is in the English; and it is necessary for the Indians, as the case stands, for their present and future security and tranquillity, to receive the lands by grant from the English, who are a growing and potent people, comparatively to the Indians.[34]

Gookin theoretically conceded the legality of Native title, which he regarded as extinguished through a combination of abandonment and purchase.[35] But he cited the crown grant first and implied that the English, backed by a growing

the right to the 2,000 acres based on first possession, tacit consent, and Indian right. Eliot also falsely implied that Dedham townspeople waited ten years before pursuing action. *DTR*, 4:255–61.

33 Ibid., 4:270.

34 Daniel Gookin, *Historical Collections of the Indians in New England* (Reprinted: New York: Arno, 1970), 39. Gookin was an avid speculator and participant in English town founding, gaining several large grants from the colony for his services. In acting as Indian superintendent, Gookin extracted land cessions in central Massachusetts. See Martin, *Profits in the Wilderness*, 15, 23–4, 32. "Sagamore" was the equivalent term for Native leaders in northern New England. Neal Salisbury, *Manitou and Providence: Indians, Europeans, and the Making of New England, 1500–1643* (New York: Oxford University Press, 1982), 42.

35 The best discussion of conflicting notions of landownership and sovereignty is William Cronon, *Changes in the Land: Indians, Colonists, and the Ecology of New England* (New York: Will and Wang, 1983), 54–81. For treatments of English justifications for their land tenure see Chester E. Eisinger, "The Puritans' Justification for Taking the Land," *Essex Institute Historical Collections* 84 (1948): 131–43; Wilcomb E. Washburn, "The Moral and Legal Justification for Dispossessing the Indians," in *Seventeenth-Century America: Essays in Colonial History* , ed. James M. Smith (Chapel Hill: University of North Carolina Press, 1959), 16–25; and Francis Jennings, "Virgin Land and Savage People," *American Quarterly* 23 (1971): 519–41. Jennings explores English techniques for gaining Indian deeds in *The Invasion of America: Indians, Colonialism, and the Cant of Conquest* (New York: Norton, 1975), 128–45.

population and the ability to wield power, should prevail even lacking transfer of Native title. Granting Indians' own lands back to them underscored the relations of power and authority that had come to govern the Massachusetts Bay region.

Despite Gookin's pat explanation, English colonists were not so sure. The Natick-Dedham dispute included messy debates over Native title, and it was Eliot who brought the issue to the fore. In arguing Natick's case in 1662, he used the rhetoric of English justification for colonization, but he pushed it in directions that made the magistrates uneasy:

> Touching the Indians right. our right we hold (said the Court) by or [letters] of Patent fro the Kings Maty. & by our right coming into vacuum domicilum where we so find it, but where the Indians have a rigt, we doe religiously take care that it be lawfully alienated, wch we doe not see evident touching these lands in question.[36]

Dedham argued that the lands had been ceded to the English by the Massachusett sachem Chickataubut at a meeting in Dorchester. Eliot claimed he had been present at the meeting and insisted that the lands were not Chickataubut's to give, but rather belonged to his son Josias Wampatuck through his maternal grandfather. Futhermore, "Josias, alias Wompituk, did in the yeare 50 . . . solemly in God's prsence, give up his right in these lands, unto God, to make a towne, gather a church, & live in civil order in this place."[37] By 1651, Native rights in other lands that made up the Natick town site had also been given to the town in a public ceremony: "John Speen and his bretheren and kindred . . . gave away all their right and interest . . . unto the public interest of the town" for a gratuity and reserved interest in their fish weirs on the Charles River.[38] Eliot paid attention to Indian systems of landownership and used them to defend their site.

Others had betrayed nervousness over just this issue. When Roxbury and Dedham elders intervened in the dispute in 1660, one of the stipulations of the proposed settlement zeroed in on the problem of proper land title. Indians were directed to acknowledge that their lands in Natick had been granted to them, and aside from property "they were in actual & imediate possession & improvement of before Dedham was planted," the rest had come from Dedham's "Love & Christian condescendency . . . & not from ye right of Any Indian Title out bidding theirs."[39] This provision disclosed a sensitivity about legal title that did

---

[36] *DTR*, 4:258–9.

[37] Ibid., 4:259. Josias did not remain with the group. Gookin wrote in 1674 that "for several years last past, [he] was separated from the praying Indians, and was but a back friend to religion." Gookin, *Historical Collections*, 26. The sachem generally was referred to as Josias Chickataubut.

[38] Oliver N. Bacon, *A History of Natick from its First Settlement in 1651 to the Present Time* (Boston: Damrell & Moore, Printers, 1856), 10.

[39] *DTR*, 4:249.

not disappear. In hammering out the 1662 settlement, the General Court could not ignore the seeds of doubt Eliot had planted.[40]

C. *Ordering the site: cultural negotiations*

Natick also became a site of struggle for Indians with conflicting agendas. Most surrounding Indian peoples fervently opposed any missionary initiatives.[41] Eliot wanted to establish Natick quickly because he worried that delaying the town would "embolden their adversaries to despise the work (for all the country of Indians are in expectation of it)."[42] He complained that the sachem Cutshamekin, who eventually and ambivalently came to Natick, "openly contested with me against our proceeding to make a Town; and plainly told me that all the Sachems in the Countrey were against it."[43] Even after bounding the town, difficulties surfaced because "a considerable pt of the Indians . . . did earnestly desire to have pitched or first stake in another place."[44] Natick and other Praying Towns subsequently established suffered from raids by the Mohawk in the 1660s.[45] Concern over opposition may have contributed to the decision to construct a palisade in Natick for its defense. Eliot asserted that if the Indians could not obtain "Guns, Powder, Shot, [and] Swords," they would use "Slings, Bowes, and other Engines" to ensure their security.[46]

Amid the bitter struggle over boundaries and the opposition of Indians who made other choices, Indians came together on the Natick town site. They came from local groups within at least three of the major sociopolitical divisions in the

[40] Dedham, and most other existing Massachusetts towns, scrambled to gain quitclaims for land during the 1680s charter crisis. See Chapter 3. Interestingly, one land sale of the 1680s was made by John and Sarah Magus, who, it was acknowledged, owned that land "according to Indian law & custom." This 1685 deed was confirmed by Massachusett sachem Charles Josias, successor to Josias Wampatuck Chickataubut. Dedham, Masssachusetts, Deeds from the Indians of the Town of Dedham, Ayer Collection Mimeo, The Newberry Library, Chicago, IL.

[41] See, for example, James P. Ronda, "'We are Well as We are': An Indian Critique of Seventeenth-Century Christian Missions," *WMQ*, 3d ser., 34 (1970): 66–82; Henry W. Bowden and James P. Ronda, eds., *John Eliot's Indian Dialogues: A Study in Cultural Interaction*, (Westport, CT: Greenwood Press, 1980); Axtell, *Invasion Within*; Alden T. Vaughan and Daniel K. Richter, "Crossing the Cultural Divide: Indians and New Englanders, 1605–1763," *Proceedings of the American Antiquarian Society*, Part I, 90 (April 1980): 23–99; and Neal Salisbury, "Toward the Covenant Chain: Iroquois and Southern New England Algonquians, 1637–1684," in *Beyond the Covenant Chain: The Iroquois and Their Neighbors in Indian North America*, ed. Daniel K. Richter and James H. Merrell (Syracuse: Syracuse University Press, 1987), 61–74.

[42] Whitfield, "Light Appearing," 134.

[43] Ibid., 140. Sachems feared loss of their power and, according to Eliot, loss of tribute especially.

[44] Eliot to Mr. Steele, 8 Oct. 1652, *New England Historical and Genealogical Register* (hereafter cited as *NEHGR*) 36 (1882): 295.

[45] Salisbury, "Toward the Covenant Chain."   [46] Whitfield, "Light Appearing," 143.

region: the Massachusett, the Pawtucket, and the Nipmuck.[47] In Eliot's words, "Some of Sudbury Indians, some of Concord Indians, some of Maestick Indians, and some of Dedham Indians, are ingenious and pray unto God, and sometimes come to the place where I teach and hear the word."[48] Some of these Indians had powerful connections in several Indian groups. The reluctant Cutshamekin, brother of the deceased Massachusett sachem Chickataubut, held influence as regent to Chickataubut's minor son, Josias Wampatuck. Waban had married Tasunsquaw, daughter of the Pawtucket sachem Tahattawan, and gained additional authority in part through his early association with Eliot. The Speen families were acknowledged owners of much of the land that made up the Praying Town site. Awassamug was the nephew of the Nipmuck sachem Wuttawushan, and had married Yawata, the daughter of the Pawtucket sachem Nanapeshamet and his wife, Squa Sachem. Natick settlers included followers of local leaders at Neponset (Cutshamekin) and Nonantum (Waban), the two principal sites where Eliot preached, as well as people from other villages surrounding Natick.

The bounded place of Natick became a site where different cultures collided and new ways were negotiated.[49] The English stressed orderliness and industriousness as central to properly constituted societies; these ideals were to be symbolized in the physical layout of a town and the structuring of lifeways within that space. The English assumed that religious conversion would be preceded by Indian "civility," demonstrated by Indians' learning English work skills, fencing fields, forming nuclear families, and accepting gender roles that met with English approval. Men should work the fields; women belonged in the household, rearing children and, ideally, engaging in household production

---

[47] Political groupings in the Massachusetts Bay region are difficult to sort out with precision given the disruption of early epidemics. This description draws from Bert Salwen, "Indians of Southern New England and Long Island: Early Period," in *Handbook of North American Indians: Northeast*, ed. Bruce G. Trigger (Washington: Smithsonian Institution, 1978):160–76; Cutshamekin: Salisbury, *Manitou and Providence*, 120–1, 214; as regent: Ebenezer Clapp Jr., *History of the Town of Dorchester, Massachusetts* (Boston: David Clapp, Printer, 1859), 11; Josias Wampatuck: *DTR*, 4:258–9; Waban: Elise M. Brenner, "Strategies for Autonomy: An Analysis of Ethnic Mobilization in Seventeenth-Century Southern New England" (Ph.D. diss., University of Massachusetts, 1984), 103; and Kathleen J. Bragdon, "'Another Tongue Brought In': An Ethnohistorical Study of Native Writings in Massachusett" (Ph.D. diss., Brown University, 1981), 153; Speens: Bacon, *History of Natick*, 10; Awassamug: Richard Frothingham Jr., *The History of Charlestown, Massachusetts* (Boston: Charles C. Little & James Brown, 1845), 34–5; and Josiah H. Temple, *History of Framingham, Massachusetts, Early Known as Danforth's Farms, 1640–1880* (Framingham, MA: Published by the Town, 1887), 8 and 40.

[48] Temple, quoting Eliot in 1649, in *History of Framingham*, 8.

[49] Holstun explores the "reorganization of Algonquian social life according to a new utopian scheme of social space, time, and proceedure" in his analysis of John Eliot's utopian millennialist thought. *A Rational Millennium*, 123–7. This analysis also draws from Axtell, who interprets missionization in terms of English perceptions that Indians were deficient in order, industry, and manners, and analyzes the significance of English obsession with "reducing [them] to a state of greater civilization." Axtell, *Invasion Within*, 131–78. Quotation is from 135.

such as carding and spinning wool.[50] Even the building of heavy frame houses and adoption of English material culture might counteract Indian mobility and fix them in Praying Towns.[51]

Very quickly, Natick began to take on the aspect of an English-style permanent village, yet it was unmistakably an Indian place. Indians laid out streets, carved out house lots, planted orchards, and built English houses "while living in *Wigwams*, whereof there is a good store neer the hill side."[52] In the first year, they worked on a footbridge across the Charles River and broke fields for spring planting.[53] The next year they completed a round fort of whole trees, and within it they erected a 50-by-25-by-12-foot meetinghouse "after the English manner . . . with chimneys in it, with one or two days assistance from an English carpenter."[54] This structure served several functions; it became the gathering place for religious activities, a location for the Indian schoolmaster to instruct the children, a storage area, and a place for Eliot to stay when he visited every other week.[55] They also finished their stone-and-timber footbridge, which stood undamaged while an English-constructed bridge in Medfield was destroyed by ice and flood waters.[56] New notions of spatial organization found expression in street building; measuring and dividing of individual house-lots with planted orchards lent the impression of English ideas about property, land use, and ownership. Yet the presence of large numbers of wigwams and a weir for catching alewives at the bridge provided evidence that Native practices would coexist in the town.[57]

Indians had altered their subsistence ways even before Natick was bounded, which reflected a century of trade with Europeans that preceded the permanent arrival of the English. At Nonantum in the 1640s, some Indians had fenced their cornfields, produced new crafts, and marketed their surplus in a market economy:

> they begin to grow industrious, and find something to sell at Market
> all the year long: all winter they sell Brooms, Staves, Elepots, Bas-

[50] Shepard, "Clear Sun-shine," 59; and Letter from the Commissioners of the United Colonies to Hon. Robert Boyle, 10 Sept. 1668, which asks for cards for women, in J. W. Ford, ed., *Some Correspondence Between the Governors and Treasurers of the New England Company in London and the Commissioners of the United Colonies in America, the Missionaries of the Company, and Others Between the Years of 1675 and 1712* (London: Spottiswoode and Company, 1896), 20.

[51] Axtell, *Invasion Within*, 137–41.

[52] Henry Whitfield, "Strength out of Weaknesse: Or a Glorious Manifestation of the Further Progresse of the Gospel Among the Indians in New-England," *MHSC*, 3d ser., 4 (1834): 177.

[53] Whitfield, "Light Appearing," 138–9.

[54] Whitfield, "Strength out of Weaknesse," 177; and John Eliot, "Tears of Repentance: Or, a further Narrative of the Progress of the Gospel amongst the Indians in New-England," *MHSC*, 3d ser., 4 (1834): 227.

[55] Ibid.; and Whitfield, "Strength out of Weaknesse," 174.

[56] Whitfield, "Strength out of Weaknesse," 177–8.   [57] Ibid., 177.

kets, Turkies. In the Spring, Craneberries, Fish, Strawberries; in the Summer Hurtleberries, Grapes, Fish: in the Autumn they sell Craneberries, Fish, Venison, &c. and they find a good benefit by the Market, and grow more and more to make use thereof; besides sundry of them work with the English in Hay time, and Harvest.[58]

Indians participated in a cash economy by selling fruits and fish, which they had always gathered, venison yielded from hunting, craft items such as baskets and brooms, and new goods such as staves. They also earned wages by laboring for English farmers.[59] Subsistence strategies continued to follow the rhythm of a seasonal round; new products and practices complemented older hunting and gathering routines.[60] In Natick, agriculture continued. By 1662, they had "fenced & broaken vp two great Feilds, & seuerall lesser Feilds."[61] Some Indians procured livestock, an adaptation that was not limited to those Indians living in Praying Towns, and used English tools on their farms.[62]

Material culture reflected the retention of Native as well as the borrowing of English products. In their houses, most of which were still made "after their old mode" in 1671 because Indians found wigwams warmer and more comfortable, they used Indian-crafted goods and English-manufactured items. English-made tin cups and pails complemented pottery, and wooden dishes, spoons, and ladles carved by men. Women weaved mats for covering wigwams and for interior uses, and made birch-bark containers and woven baskets. These were supplemented by English-manufactured metal kettles, "knives, combs, scissors, hatchets, hoes, guns, needles, awls, [and] looking glasses."[63] Widespread replacement of skins by cloth, and alteration of hair and clothing styles toward the English mode served as markers of Praying Indians.[64] Women continued to value "bracelets, necklaces, and head bands, of several sorts of beads, especially black and white wampum" for personal ornamentation.[65]

[58] Shepard, "Clear Sun-shine," 59.
[59] Wage labor continued after the establishment of Natick. Gookin, *Historical Collections*, 26.
[60] Brenner, "Strategies for Autonomy," 246–9.
[61] Committee report, November 1662, *DTR*, 4:273. The committee estimated that there were about sixty families there.
[62] Daniel Gookin, "An Historical Account of the Doings and Sufferings of the Christian Indians in New England, in the Years 1675, 1676, 1677," in *Transactions and Collections of the American Antiquarian Society*, 2 vols. (New York: Johnson Reprint Corporation, 1971), 2:451 and 512. Even some Indians who opposed missionaries began keeping livestock, especially hogs, as a cultural adaptation in the context of their disrupted subsistence economies. Swine keeping, in contrast to raising cattle, entailed fewer disruptions in cultural patterns, and they served as a partial replacement for hunted animals. Domesticated animals were an early and enduring source of friction between Indians and the English. See Virginia DeJohn Anderson, "King Philip's Herds: Indians, Colonists, and the Problem of Livestock in Early New England," *WMQ*, 3d ser., 51 (1994): 601–24; and Cronon, *Changes in the Land*, 130–7.
[63] Gookin, *Historical Collections*, 12.   [64] Axtell, *Invasion Within*, 171–7.
[65] Gookin, *Historical Collections*, 12.

Discounting Indian ways of working as producing little more than idleness and leisure, the English emphasized that shifts in the culture of work would go along with modifications in economic organization and material culture.[66] Civil codes drawn up before the bounding of Natick sought to inculcate English ideals "that they may fall upon some better course to improve their time," and refrain from being "idle."[67] English observers were obsessed with what they saw as Indian idleness; industriousness (English work habits and organization of time) became a principal indicator of cultural conversion. Countering charges that Praying Indians lacked sincerity, Richard Mather declared: "if there be any work of Grace amongst them, it would surely bring forth, and be accompanied with the Reformation of their disordered lives, as in other things, so in their neglect of labor, and their living in idleness and pleasure."[68] In Natick, he wrote:

> they have more applied themselves unto Labor then formerly: . . .
> The Grounds . . . they have fenced in, and clawed and broken up . . .
> It is true, that considering the manner of their bringing up, being
> little accustomed to labor, but the contrary, it is not much to be mar-
> veled if they be not comparable therein to some English, who from
> their Child-hood have been trained up thereto; yet we see they are
> coming to it.[69]

In this formulation, fenced fields stood for cultural conversion secured through English work habits.

Eliot also stressed the centrality of labor to Indian transformation, and he tried to inculcate English values about individually owned property and accumulation. He welcomed "strangers" to Natick as long as they did not openly oppose the religious ends of the community, and "if they be willing to labour," they received wages.[70] Even his apparently contradictory decision to retain most tools as community property fit into the larger scheme of transformation through work: "I give small gifts & these but seldo. [What] shall come to my hand of these tooles I intend to keepe in a comon stock to lend to one as well as anothr, that no man may sit idle, or loose a days wrk for want of a toole."[71] There was more to this concern than seeing to it that labor would counteract "idleness." He also wanted to prevent Indians from giving away what they received, since "many of them . . . will easily [part with what] they have not prsent use of."[72] This attests to the fact that Native ideas about property and

---

[66] For an analysis of the centrality of labor to English missionary ideology, see Axtell, *Invasion Within*, 148–67.

[67] Shepard, "Day-Breaking," 20; and Shepard, "Clear Sun-shine," 39.

[68] Eliot, "Tears of Repentance," 223.   [69] Ibid., 224.

[70] Eliot to Mr. Steele, 8 Oct. 1652, *NEHGR* 36 (July 1882): 296.

[71] Eliot to Winslow, 20 Aug. 1651, Ibid., 294.

[72] "First Accompt sent over from New-England to ye Corporation, January 1653," Ibid., 297.

sharing persisted. Communal principles existed in uneasy tension with notions of private property and individual accumulation.

Gender roles were heavily implicated in English critiques of Indian work habits, and they singled out Indian men in particular for rebuke. Commentaries on the Indian division of labor stressed male "laziness" and the massive burden of female labor: "Their way of living is infinitely barbarous: the men are most abominably slothful; making their poor squaws, or wives, to plant and dress, and barn and beat their corn, and build wigwams for them."[73] Indian hunting, an activity marked as leisure and reserved to the aristocracy in England, challenged English hierarchical assumptions and suggested to them that Indian men were idle.[74]

Focusing most of their energies on changing men's work habits, the English said little about how Indian women's lives should change beyond implying they should be banished from the fields. According to Eliot, some women embraced the opportunity to learn English skills: "The women are desirous to learn to spin, and I have procured wheels for sundry of them, and they can spin pretty well. They begin to grow industrious, and find something to sell at Market all the yeer long[.]"[75] In a description of one exemplary female convert, Eliot made the connection between work, order within the household, and religious devotion: "She was industrious, and did not goe about to English houses a begging, as sundry doe, (though it is well reformed now with many of them) but kept house, kept her children to labour, making baskets to sell, &c. She quickly learned to spin well. Her life was blameless after she submitted to the Gospel."[76] Like this exemplar, Indian women should work hard and produce for the market, but do so while staying put in the household, preferably engaging in English female household manufacturing such as spinning. They should keep households orderly by attending to them and by seeing to it that their children also worked – although, interestingly, he approvingly noted that these children made baskets, a Native activity. As principal rearers of children, women occupied a position of importance in inculating values and skills.

For the English, nuclear families headed by men who worked the fields were the essence of well-ordered societies. Civil codes Indians adopted in the late 1640s dictated that "Every young man if not anothers servant, and if unmarried, . . . shall be compelled to set up a *wigwam* and plant for himself, and not

---

[73] Cotton Mather, *Christi Magnalia Americana: The Ecclesiastical History of New England* (Hartford: Silas Andrus and Son, 1855), 559. He speculated that all this hard work might account for "their extraordinary ease in childbirth."

[74] Axtell, *Invasion Within*, 152–9; and Kathleen Brown, "The Anglo-American Gender Frontier," in *Negotiators of Change: Historical Perspectives on Native American Women*, ed. Nancy Shoemaker (New York: Routledge, 1995), 26–48.

[75] Shepard, "Clear Sun-shine," 59.

[76] Edward Winslow, "The Glorious Progress of the Gospel, amongst the Indians in New England," *MHSC*, 3d ser., 4 (1834): 79–80.

live shifting up and downe to other *wigwams*."[77] The directive discouraged
extended household structure, looked toward the formation of nuclear families,
and insisted that agriculture constituted a male sphere. By placing Indian children in apprenticeships with English families, these notions might be inculcat-
ed at an early age.[78]

Eliot devised a scheme for civil order in Natick based on Mosaic law in
order to bolster the religious ends of the community. The Indians elected a
ruler of one hundred, two rulers of fifty, and ten rulers of ten, all to be organized hierarchically. Each ruler was expected to be accountable for the behavior of his followers to those placed over him. Male leaders led "numerous small
paternal states," with women, children, and servants "virtually comprehended
in their father's covenant."[79] The system called for them to select their own
rulers: "every man chose who should be his ruler of ten, the rulers standing in
order, and every man going to the man he chose, and it seemed unto me as if I
had seen scattered bones goe, bone unto his bone, and so lived a civil political
life."[80] Once again, Eliot used the imagery of Ezekiel 37 to describe Natick
coming together.

The hybrid government of Natick incorporated elements from three kinds
of polities: English, Indian, and scriptural.[81] Elective government introduced
an English innovation, as did the administration of justice through a bureaucratic structure. Selecting rulers to exercise power in a fragmented system permitted a degree of choice in leaders that had been central to Indian political
organization and provided an important continuity. The foundation and
espoused purpose was religious. Government in Natick struck a compromise
among colonial magistrates who demanded Indian order and submission; millennialist Eliot, who sought to demonstrate the power of a pristine religious
polity; and Indians who actively searched for an alternative social order that
would sustain them, even while they selectively retained and reshaped Indian
cultural practices.

---

[77] Shepard, "Day Breaking," 20. On the ramifications of missionization for ideas about
Native marriage and justice systems, see Ann Marie Plane, " 'The Examination of Sarah
Ahaton': The Politics of 'Adultery' in an Indian Town of Seventeenth-Century Massa-
chusetts," in *Algonkians of New England: Past and Present*, ed. Peter Benes, The Dublin
Seminar for New England Folklife Annual Proceedings, 1991 (Boston: Boston University,
1993), 14–25.

[78] This practice began as early as 1643 as an element of missionary approaches. [John Eliot],
"New England's First Fruits; In Respect, First of the Conversion of Some, Conviction of
Divers, Preparation of Sundry of the Indians," in *The Founding of Harvard College*, ed.
Samuel Eliot Morison (Cambridge: Harvard University Press, 1935), 3; Shepard, "Day-
Breaking," 18; Shepard, "Clear Sun-shine," 58; and Axtell, *Invasion Within*, 159–61.

[79] Holstun, *A Rational Millennium*, 153. The second phrase is from Eliot, "Christian Commonwealth," 145–6, as quoted in Holstun.

[80] Whitfield, "Strength out of Weaknesse," 171–2.

[81] Susan L. MacCulloch, "A Tri-Partite Political System among Christian Indians of Early
Massachusetts," *Kroeber Anthropological Society Papers* 34 (1966): 63; and Brenner,
"Strategies for Autonomy," 240–1.

In practice, when Indians elected their leaders, they chose individuals from families who had been in positions of community leadership.[82] Cutshamekin, despite the fact that Eliot remained "doubtfull in respect of the thoroughness of his heart," was chosen the chief ruler.[83] With elegant simplicity Eliot explained, "Cutshamekin, the chiefe Sachem, and therefore [he was] chosen the chiefe."[84] Waban was voted a ruler of fifty; rulers of ten included Tother-swamp, Nataous, Peter, and Piambouhou.[85] The potential for molding the political order remained in the hands of experienced Native leaders, who may have lost some existing institutions to wield power (tribute, which leaders probably adapted to fit tithing schemes), but gained others (legitimized access to colonial officials).[86] Even seemingly innocuous actions might be shaped to fit older notions of leadership. For example, by placing some of the tools "unto the hands of or rulers of tennes . . . to be distributed," Eliot provided rulers with a means to enhance their prestige, demonstrate their generosity, and influence the behavior of others.[87]

The polity charged rulers with overseeing compliance with codes of behavior Indians had agreed to at Concord and Nonantum in the 1640s, which aimed to transform the Indian social order within the Praying Town. Codes stressed monogamy and nuclear, male-headed households, imposed fines for fornication, sodomy, and adultery, and aimed to eliminate the Native custom of female separation from the household during menstruation. English notions of secure personal property and a well-regulated market found expression in rules that circumscribed idleness, and in prohibitions against Native games of chance,

[82] MacCulloch, "A Tri-Partite System."

[83] Whitfield, "Strength out of Weaknesse," 173. Cf. MacCulloch, "A Tri-Partite Political System," 67. She concluded that Waban was made ruler of 100. Eliot explicitly stated that Waban was a ruler of fifty in the beginning; he may have become ruler of one hundred after Cutshamekin's death. John Eliot, "Tears of Repentance," 232.

[84] Whitfield, "Strength out of Weaknesse," 173.

[85] Eliot, "Tears of Repentance," 232; and John Eliot, "A Late and Further Manifestation of the Progress of the Gospel amongst the Indians in New-England," *MHSC*, 3d ser., 4 (1834): 273. One of the Speens was also chosen a ruler, but he died by 1652. I have been unable to identify which one. In John Speen's confession, he laments that "God hath afflicted me, in taking away my brother, a Ruler." (Eliot, "Tears of Repentance," 247.) Rulers were to be approved by "a superior authority." (Gookin, *Historical Collections*, 37.)

[86] MacCulloch, "Tripartite Political System," 66–7; and Axtell, *Invasion Within*, 142–3. See also Harold W. Van Lonkhuyzen, "A Reappraisal of the Praying Indians: Acculturation, Conversion, and Identity at Natick, Massachusetts, 1646–1730," *NEQ* 63 (1990): 401–2 and 406. He sees Eliot as a "Cultural Patron" and Indian preachers as "Big Men" who also became brokers.

[87] "First Accompt sent over from New-England to ye Corporation, January, 1653," *NEHGR* 36 (July 1882): 298. Elise Brenner has found that Indians in southern New England used English material culture in burials to symbolize their power, status, and authority in a period when such relations were no longer so clear. Elise M. Brenner, "Sociopolitical Implications of Mortuary Ritual Remains in Seventeenth-Century Native Southern New England," in *The Recovery of Meaning: Historical Archaeology in the Eastern United States*, ed. Mark P. Leone and Parker B. Potter Jr. (Washington: Smithsonian Institution Press, 1988), 147–81.

which contradicted English ideas about frugality and accumulation of property. Indians were instructed to "pay their debts to the English." Codes banned the curing rituals of Native powwaws, mandated regular prayer in families, and penalized profaning of the Sabbath with a twenty-shilling fine. They sought to eradicate cultural traits that symbolized "disorder" and "barbarity" to English observers, such as Native mourning rituals, hair styles, and the use of bear grease to protect the skin. Other regulations stressed peaceful interaction, and acquiescence in punishment for social and legal transgressions. Indians should accept their proper place in a deferential society, suppressing pride for humility.[88] English notions of privacy gained endorsement through insistence that Indians knock before entering an English house (and vice versa), to counter more flexible ideas about private spaces. The impact of these proscriptive and prescriptive mandates on actual behavior is difficult to assess because the system left enforcement to Native rulers. Many of the regulations surely had as much to do with English obsessions about Indian cultures as they did with mores that Indians wanted to alter.[89]

Responsibility for monitoring the behavior of Praying Indians fell to rulers, who also settled disputes that arose among them. Indian rulers were to ensure that Indians obeyed English laws as well, because those Indians who had not formally submitted themselves to the English government did so by implication when coming to Praying Towns. Participation in political and legal matters gave the Indians considerable latitude for shaping local governance.

But the formal submission to the commonwealth of several sachems, which may have been a prerequisite for missionary beginnings, technically lodged legal authority over Indians within colonial legal structures.[90] The commonwealth elaborated a special judicial mechanism for Indians when Daniel Gookin was appointed as superintendent of Indians in 1656.[91] The system Gookin implemented followed the precedents of the submission agreements and Praying Town codes, while creating a structure of Indian magistrates operating under the ultimate supervision of the English. There was to be no mistaking who gained ultimate power. Gookin as superintendent received the authority to appoint Indian commissioners "to hear and determine all such matters that do arise among themselves, as one magistrate may be amongst the English; with officers to execute all commands and warrants, as marshal and constables."[92] In conjunction

---

[88] Axtell, *Invasion Within*, 138.

[89] Codes are in Shepard, "Day-Breaking," 20–1; and Shepard, "Clear Sun-shine," 39–40. For more on the codes, see Axtell, *Invasion Within*, 169–78.

[90] Shurtleff, *Mass. Records*, 2:55–6, 1644; and Axtell, *Invasion Within*, 220.

[91] Gookin, *Historical Collections*, 37. Gookin continued as superintendent until 1687. There is no record that the position continued after 1709. Yasuhide Kawashima, *Puritan Justice and the Indian: White Man's Law in Massachusetts, 1630–1763* (Middletown, CT: Wesleyan University Press, 1986), 29–31.

[92] Gookin, *Historical Collections*, 38. Indian magistrates were designated beginning in 1647. Shepard, "Clear Sun-shine," 59.

with the superintendent, the Indian magistrates received the power of a county court, with the English magistrate responsible for determining the time and place for hearings. This body heard cases involving appeals, life or limb, banishment, divorce, and other cases of a severe nature; lesser matters could be managed by Indian magistrates without assistance. The General Court further empowered the English superintendent to influence Indian life in Praying Towns by

> the making of orders, and giving instructions and directions, backed with penalties, for promoting and practising morality, civility, industry, and diligence in their particular callings: for idleness and improvidence are the Indians great sin, and is a kind of second nature to them, which by good example and wholesome laws, gradually applied, with God's blessing may be rooted out.[93]

Gookin made provisions to collect tithes "at the ingathering and threshing of their grain . . . for support of those that attend public service."[94]

Natick Indians performed new rituals in their transformed civil and legal institutions and in their practice of religion.[95] Acceptance of a covenant drawn up by Eliot accompanied codification of the governmental system. The Indians commemorated these events by conducting their first formal day of fasting and prayer.[96]

D. Narrating the site: religion and Indian voices

Even though Indians rapidly implemented their government and subscribed to a religious covenant (based on English practice), formal establishment of a church was long delayed. Elders from several English towns made three separate public examinations of Indians between 1652 and 1659. Hesitation related to the logistics of translating the confessions from Massachusett to English, and especially, to English reluctance to trust the Indians "with that Treasure of Christ, lest they should scandalize the same."[97] As an intermediate step, elders placed some Indians in tutelage in English churches, which made them unavailable for keeping Sabbaths in Natick.[98] In 1660 elders finally sanctioned full communion for eight Indian confessors in a formally gathered Natick congregation.

---

[93] Gookin, *Historical Collections,* 38.   [94] Ibid.
[95] See Neal Salisbury, "Red Puritans: The 'Praying Indians' of Massachusetts Bay and John Eliot," *WMQ,* 3d ser., 31 (1974): 51; Kathleen J. Bragdon, "Native Christianity in Eighteenth-Century Massachusetts: Ritual as Cultural Reaffirmation," in *New Dimensions in Ethnohistory: Papers of the Second Laurier Conference on Ethnohistory and Ethnology,* ed. Barry Gough and Laird Christie, Canadian Ethnology Service, Mercury Series Paper 120 (Hull, Quebec: Canadian Museum of Civilization, 1991), 120; and Van Lunkhuyzen, "A Reappraisal."
[96] Whitfield, "Strength out of Weaknesse," 172–3.   [97] Eliot, "Tears of Repentance," 227.
[98] John Eliot, *A Further Account of the Progress of the Gospel Amongst the Indians in New England* (1659) (New York: Reprinted for Joseph Sabin, 1865), 1–2; and F. J. Powicke, ed.,

Taken together, the public confessions expressed Indian perceptions that the crucial nexus of personal relationships, kinship, community, and land could be preserved through English Calvinism. Coming to Natick would entail cultural compromises, but also offered attractive options in the context of aggressive English expansion. The bounding of the town within the English legal structure offered more secure Native tenure on a site they selected, albeit in a drastically circumscribed place. Subsistence patterns had to be modified somewhat. In particular, the English expected Indians to reject seasonal removal, though it is quite clear that this expectation was among many that were not entirely realized.[99] Essential elements of Indian culture remained, with Indians incorporating some aspects of English material culture, such as metal tools and livestock keeping. The political system bore some resemblance to pre-Natick forms, and Indians continued to select acknowledged leaders. The new system did offer the opportunity to eliminate or at least modify objectionable demands for tribute by some sachems; this reform appealed to some.[100] The acceptance of a new religious system offered a whole set of new community relationships, complete with collective rituals to reinforce the social unit.[101]

The eighteen Indians who were examined, all men, reveal Indian interpretations of the coming together of Natick that often challenge English claims about the missionary project.[102] Although the English often conveyed the impression that many Praying Indians were instantaneously receptive to Christianity, their own confessions tell a different story. For example, Eliot consistently portrayed Waban as a model convert who quickly became convinced to accept the Gospel. According to Waban, however, his reasons for listening to the English had little to do with a sudden high regard for their religion. At first, he despised "the knowledge of God" and continued to practice his own religion. One of his confessions related the fear that "if we did not pray, the English might kill us."[103] In a third confession, he revealed that one of his primary reasons for continuing to listen was that "they would give me good victuals."[104] Waban was not alone in acting on his own interests. Monotunkquanit testified that his "heart laughed at praying" and that he "went to Cohannit, not for praying, but to gather clams."[105]

But Indian confessors moved beyond passive disinterest, the lure of small gifts, or fear of the implicitly threatening English presence to consider larger rewards that might be secured through tolerating Eliot's preaching. John Speen said he prayed "because I saw the English took much ground, and I thought if I

"Some Unpublished Correspondence of the Rev. Richard Baxter and the Rev. John Eliot, 'Apostle to the American Indians,' 1656–1682," *Bulletin of the John Rylands Library* 15 (1931): 159.
[99] Brenner, "Strategies for Autonomy."   [100] Whitfield, "Light Appearing," 140–1.
[101] Salisbury, "Red Puritans," 51.
[102] Examinations of Indian conversion experiences include Axtell, *Invasion Within*, 218–41; and Naeher, "Dialogue in the Wilderness," 346–68.
[103] Eliot, *Further Account*, 31.   [104] Ibid., 72.
[105] Ibid., 65.

prayed, the English would not take away my ground."[106] Even though he felt ambivalent and considered leaving his people, Magus reasoned that "if I do go away, I shall lose my ground."[107] For the Indians, their homelands held symbolic meaning, defining characteristics of their proper place in the created world, and were regarded with deeply felt affection. Land was not viewed in English terms as a commodity.[108] When Nishohkou began to pray, "it was because I loved our place and dwelling."[109]

Personal relationships and family figured prominently in shaping Indian responses. John Speen testified: "when I first prayed to God, I did not pray for my soul, but only I did as my friends did, because I loved them."[110] Staunchly unconvinced, Anthony decided: "I will abide with my brothers, because I love them, but not because I would pray."[111] More substantial belief came for him, as for many others, only later.

Community ties and Indian leadership patterns also shaped Indian responses. The confessors included one former powwaw (Robin Speen) and one who aspired to that status (Waban).[112] Seven of the eighteen confessing Indians attributed their eventual conversion either to leaders Waban or Cutshamekin. Nataous credited his praying directly to Cutshamekin's influence.[113] Though it was especially his brothers who convinced him, Anthony also cited the example of Wampooas, Totherswamp, and Waban.[114] At Sudbury, Wuttasukoopauin "heard Waban prayed to God." Although Wattasukoopauin was at first "not glad of it," Waban eventually convinced him to "pray to God, and carry our children to Roxbury, that they might learn to pray."[115] Awassamug related how first Waban, and then many others began to pray. He reported that fleeing only removed him from his personal support system and exposed him to other threats: "When some of my neighbors began to pray, I went always into the Country, but I could find no place where I was beloved . . . last year, I sought to go away afar off, but I could think of no place, but I should be in danger of being killed."[116] He decided to remain both because of his connections to the group and because he perceived danger everywhere he turned. Indians who came to Natick lived in a world that seemed to offer them few viable options.

---

[106] Ibid., 58.   [107] Eliot, "Tears of Repentance," 252.

[108] Cronon, *Changes in the Land*; and Bowden and Ronda, *Indian Dialogues*. Constance Crosby has argued that Indians in colonial southern New England extended the meaning of the concept of "manit" (some thing or person with spiritual power) to Europeans, their material culture, and the by-products of European conquest such as epidemics in order to give meaning to, and try to control, the European presence. She also argues that land became a symbol or metaphor for Indian group and personal identities, filled with meaning and power even when Indians lost land, positing a transition in Indian ideology from myth to landscape and historical time. Constance A. Crosby, "From Myth to History, or Why King Philip's Ghost Walks Abroad," in *The Recovery of Meaning*, 183–209.

[109] Eliot, *Further Account*, 39.   [110] Eliot, "Tears of Repentance," 246.

[111] Eliot, *Further Account*, 12.   [112] Eliot, "Tears of Repentance," 248 and 231.

[113] Ibid., 233.   [114] Eliot, *Further Account*, 10.

[115] Ibid., 27.   [116] Eliot, "Tears of Repentance," 258.

The retention of personal relationships and loyalties figured prominently in the decisions of Indians who came to Natick.

Some Indians expressed their desire to gain access to English skills.[117] At an early Indian lecture, Monequassin, who became schoolmaster in Natick, asked, "How should I get wisdom?" The answer he received made him consider praying. At the next lecture he was taught that "if any man lack wisdom, let him ask it of God, who giveth liberally to all that ask, and upbraideth noone."[118] Nishohkou, Poquanum, and Nookau all referred to an early desire to learn.[119] Anthony's brother convinced him to become a servant in Roxbury, where he might learn smithery.[120] During the early lectures, several young Indian men arranged to place themselves into servitude with Englishmen, and several children were sent to live with English families.[121]

Indian ideas about the connection between religion and healing provided a fertile ground for casting the theological seeds of English Calvinism. In emphasizing the anger and vengeance of an angry English God and the healing powers that would convey salvation and eternal life, Eliot struck a responsive chord among Indians still reeling from the rippling effects of imported diseases.[122] Many responded to rhetoric that dwelled upon Indian afflictions as supernatural retribution, and even attached literal meaning to the notion of Christ as the Physician. John Speen revealed in 1659 that he "heard that Christ healed all manner of diseases, therefore I believed that Christ is the son of God, able to heal and pardon all."[123] Waban explained his thought process on the matter,

---

[117] Although references to material gain are largely absent in Indian confessions, accounts of pre-Natick Indian lectures contain hints about the effect of gifts on Indian willingness to listen to Eliot. For instance, Shepard writes of an old man who consistently attended the lectures. On one occasion, Eliot told the Indian he would get some clothes for him. The Indian responded, "God I see is merciful." Shepard, "Clear Sun-shine," 46.

[118] Eliot, "Tears of Repentance," 237–8.   [119] Ibid., 249, 253, 255.

[120] Anthony's master refused to train him in smithery, because then "Indians might learn to make [Flintl]ocks and Guns." Eliot, *Further Account*, 11. It was presumably in his one-year stay in Roxbury that Anthony learned his carpentry skills.

[121] Desire for material possessions was probably the least important incentive for Indians who decided to consider Christianity. Cf. Alden Vaughan, *New England Frontier: Puritans and Indians, 1620–1675* (Boston: Little, Brown, and Co, 1965), 61. For different interpretations of Indian views of European material culture, see Jennings, *Invasion of America*; Axtell, *Invasion Within*; and Nancy Oestreich Lurie, "Indian Cultural Adjustment to European Civilization," in *Seventeenth-Century America: Essays in Colonial History*, ed. James Morton Smith (Chapel Hill: University of North Carolina Press, 1959), 39.

[122] According to Simmons, seventeenth-century shamans divided curing into two sorts, one "caused by the creator's anger, which they could not prevent," and the other "caused by the sorcery of another shaman, over which they had some control." He found some evidence that epidemics were regarded as attributable to the creator's anger. William S. Simmons, *Spirit of the New England Tribes: Indian History and Folklore, 1620–1984* (Hanover, NH: University Press of New England, 1986), 55–6. For other discussions of epidemic disease and the theme of crisis as background to Indian conversion, see Axtell, *Invasion Within*; and Naeher, "Dialogue in the Wilderness."

[123] Eliot, *Further Account*, 19.

and disclosed a recurrent theme of Indian conversion experiences: "a little while ago after the great sickness, I considered what the English do, and I had some desire to do as they do, and after that I began to work as they work; and then I thought I shall quickly die, and I feared lest I should die before I prayed to God."[124] Epidemics produced penetrating doubts in survivors; Indian listeners considered English lifeways and religion as alternatives to Indian ways that failed to control European diseases. In all, nine out of the eighteen confessing Indians singled out the death of friends and family as a factor in persuading them to pray.[125] Whether Eliot considered its instrumental aspects or not, the message of Ezekiel 37, dwelling as it does upon hope recaptured, resurrection, spiritual revitalization, and the preservation of life and homeland, conveniently encapsulated the overriding concerns of Indian listeners.

In the missionary encounter, correspondences between Indian and English notions of otherworldly intervention in worldly affairs provided a flash point for religious debates.[126] Eliot fastened onto the mutually agreed upon connection between the natural and supernatural worlds, and added English points of doctrine and ritual observances in his preaching. Indians interpreted the message from their own perspectives, and some considered the healing potential implicit in the English religion. For Indians, curing practices were embedded in religious belief and practice. And for Indians as well as the English, a society in crisis constituted concrete evidence of spiritual relationships out of order. Piambouhou refused to pray to first. He thought "if they were any of them sick, the Pawwaws could make them well . . . Then my wife and children died," which undermined his faith in Native medicine.[127] Indian fear of sickness and death was convenient for Calvinists, since the religion offered two interpretations of the connection between Indian maladies and the will of God. If sick Indians prayed and were cured, a clear and positive causal relationship could be established. If Indians died, however, the calamity could be attributed to a lack of sincerity or some other deficiency in Indian devotion and practice. Indians

[124] Eliot, "Tears of Repentance," 231.
[125] In addition to sickness and fear, Monequassin cited the death of his wife and child. (Eliot, "Tears of Repentance," 239.) John Speen lost a brother, who was a ruler at Natick, and many of his children. (Eliot, *Further Account*, 18; and Eliot, "Tears of Repentance," 247.) Robin Speen, a former powwaw, witnessed the death of his three children. (Eliot, "Tears of Repentance," 248.) Anthony lost his brothers "and kindred." (Eliot, *Further Account*, 12.) Ponampam's mother and two children died. (Ibid., 22.) Wuttasukoopauin outlived his children and two wives. (Ibid., 63.) Nishohkou lost a wife and a child, (Ibid., 40) and Piambouhou his wife and his children. (Ibid., 68.) Totherswamp had decided "that if my friends should die, and I live, I then would pray to God." His was the first confession presented at the first examination. (Eliot, "Tears of Repentance," p. 229.)
[126] Naeher described a dialogue between Indians and Eliot in which Indians led him to address their greatest concerns. Naeher, "Dialogue in the Wilderness," 348.
[127] Eliot, *Further Account*, 68–9. Powwaws gained their followings through demonstrated ability and held them only as long as they were successful in curing. Bowden and Ronda, *Indian Dialogues*, 13.

were not alone in making the connection between disease and divine providence. The English believed that gaining a foothold in New England came
about because God "in sweeping away great multitudes of the Natives by the
small Pox, a little before we went whither . . . [made] room for us there."[128]

Many Indian confessors underscored their concerns about the perpetuation of
Indian people that epidemics made even more critical by placing particular
emphasis upon children. Doubting himself, John Speen expressed an anxiety that
had to do with his own posterity: He "remembered that many of my children are
dead; This is Gods punishment on me, because of my sins."[129] Ponampum cited
scripture in giving voice to his concern over his progeny: "I heard Gods promise
to Abraham, To increase his Children as the Stars for *number*, but I beleeved not,
because he had but one Son: and thus I cast off the word."[130] Magus captured the
despair of many parents who suffered through the deaths of their children in his
literal interpretation of the Genesis story: "I believe that word which God told
Eve, That in sorrow she should bring forth Children, and I see it dayly to be true.
I beleeve that word of God, that sin brings misery, and all shall die."[131]

Some individuals testified to the direct and positive effects that the new religion had produced for them. Deeply conflicted about the religion, Anthony
experimented with praying when "my Brothers were sick, and others also . . .
But they dyed; then I thought . . . that God heareth not our prayers, and that
God is not." He decided to reject the religion and run away.[132] Later, he
resigned himself to the fact that "whether I go or stay I shall die."[133] Thoroughly ambivalent, Anthony wavered for a long time. But after he sustained a head
injury while working on the Natick meetinghouse, he finally struck a bargain:
"When I was near death, I prayed unto God, Oh Lord give me life, and I will
pray to God so long as I live . . . after this, God gave me health, and then I
thought, truly, God in Heaven is merciful."[134] For others, the process was much
more complex and far less convincing.

Nishohkou's deep ambivalence about praying turned on the priorities of
place, family, and illness:

> I desired to pray to God, and would not go away, but it was because I
> loved our place and dwelling, I prayed, but I believed not, I consid-
> ered not Eternal Life, but only this worldly life: And this went on,
> till they chose rulers at NATICK, they chose me, and I refused,
> because I believed not: After that my Wife and Child died, and I was
> sick to death, but lived again, and being well, I thought I could not
> pray, I was a child, and therefore could not, I put off praying to God,
> my Relations died, and why should I pray? but then again I consid-

---

[128] Eliot, "First Fruits," 20. The disease probably was not smallpox. John Duffy, *Epidemics in Colonial America* (Baton Rouge: Louisiana State University Press, 1953), 43.
[129] Eliot, *Further Account*, 18.   [130] Eliot, "Tears of Repentance," 241.
[131] Ibid., 252.   [132] Eliot, *Further Account*, 48–9.
[133] Ibid., 49.   [134] Ibid.

ered, why does God punish me; yea the Minister spake to me about
it, and said, It may be it was because I refused to do God's work.[135]

Nishohkou remained with the group because of his passion for place. He prayed
without believing, and was chosen a ruler despite his deep skepticism about the
religion. In the end, the message of curing captured his imagination because he
witnessed the deaths of so many people close to him. If Nishohkou entertained
any doubts about the connection between physical well-being and the new religion, Eliot did his best to dissuade him. His technique was deliberate. Describing the conversion process, he wrote, "It pleaseth God to try them with great
sicknesse and mortality . . . by the Lords assitanc, they doe the more judg themselves for their sinnes, and cry for mercy, pardon, and grace in Christ."[136]

Some individuals who came to Natick simply followed acknowledged leaders
or accompanied their families; even many confessors described an extended
period of skepticism about the English religion. Eliot acknowledged at the time
of the second public examination that some that "are among them that Pray
unto God, . . . are hemmed in by Relations, and other means, to doe that which
their hearts love not, and whose vices satan improveth to scandalize and
reproach the better sort withall; while many, and some good people, are too
ready to say they are all alike."[137] It is likely that many Natick inhabitants never
embraced the religion fully, if they ever believed at all.[138]

Indian preachers merged new concepts with established systems of meaning
in their public exhortations and emphasized religious healing as a central
theme. A 1658 day of fasting and prayer, conducted in "preparation for gathering a church, and because of much rain, and sickness and other tryalls," provided an occasion for several Indians to address their townspeople.[139] Waban
preached from Matthew 9.12–13, which reads:

> But when Jesus heard *that*, he said unto them, They that be whole
> need not a physician, but they that are sick.
> But go ye and learn what *that* meaneth, I will have mercy, and not
> sacrifice: for I am not come to call the righteous, but sinners to
> repentance.[140]

[135] Ibid., 39–40.
[136] Eliot letter, 5 May 1657, in Wilberforce Eames, ed., *John Eliot and the Indians,
1652–1657: Being Letters Addressed to Rev. Jonathan Hanmer of Barnstaple, England* (New
York: The Adams and Grace Press, 1915), 26.
[137] Eliot, "Late and Further Manifestation," 273.
[138] Gookin states, "I have no doubt, but am fully satisfied, according to the judgment of charity, that divers of them do fear God and are true believers; but yet I will not deny but that
there may be some of them hypocrites, that profess religion, and yet are not sound heart-
ed." Gookin, "Historical Collections," 183.
[139] John Eliot, *A Further Accompt of the Progress of the Gospel Amongst the Indians in New-
England, and of the Means Used Effectually to Advance the Same* (1659) Sabin's Reprints,
Quarto-Series, No. 4 (New York: Reprinted for Joseph Sabin, 1865), 8–9.
[140] *The New Layman's Parallel Bible*, 2470.

In applying this scripture to the gathering, Waban emphasized cultural change and healing:

> we have many at this time sick in body . . . but more are sick in their souls: we have a great many diseases and sicknesses in our souls (he instanced, as Idlenesse, neglect of the Sabbath, Passion, &c.) There-fore what should we doe this day? goe to Christ the Phisitian; for christ is a Physitian of souls. He healed mens bodies, but he can heale souls also.[141]

Indians and English Calvinists viewed bodily illness as an outward manifesta-tion of spiritual malfeasance, though they held quite different notions of causa-tion and the larger religious context. Elementary agreement on some principles isolated concepts and practices to be debated. As largely invisible, concepts were especially subject to personal interpretation; malleable cultural practices could be read by observers in myriad ways.

Other Indian preachers focused on the acknowledged themes of the day of fasting and prayer: preparation for church establishment, excess rain, and sick-ness. Nishohkou spoke of Noah's offerings, and the ending of the Lord's pun-ishment (Genesis 8.20–21): "God hath chastised us of late with such raines, as if he would drown us." Wuttasukoopauin chose the curing of the leper (Matthew 8.2–3): "So let us this day cry to Christ, and worship him, and if we do it in faith then he will heal us." John Speen endorsed fasting and repentance to appease God's anger, drawing from Matthew 9.14–15. Anthony's reading of Matthew 6.16 betrayed a literal interpretation of scripture based on Native practices of mourning: "we must not be like hypocrites in our fasting, for they disfigure their faces." ("Moreover when ye fast, be not, as the hypocrites, of a sad countenance: for they disfigure their faces, that they may appear unto men to fast.")[142] Piambouhou found resonance and solace in the beatitudes (Matthew 5.1–10).[143]

E. *Indian resistance to English fixity and order*

Despite the eventual cooperation the narratives outlined, resistance permeates Natick conversion experiences. "Converts" described hesitations that ranged from passive disinterest to occasional flight from the community to avoid English

---

[141] Eliot, *Further Accompt*, 9–10. Van Lunkhuyzen reads Native preaching on this biblical passage as evidence for "a new concept of human nature, or responsibility, and ultimately, of community" which had to do with individual healing and internal culpability. Van Lonkhuyzen, "A Reappraisal," 417.

[142] His whole text was Matthew 6:16–18.

[143] Nishohkou: Eliot, *Further Accompt*, 11–2; Wuttasukoopauin: Ibid., 20; John Speen: Ibid., 15–17; Anthony: Ibid., 12–14; and Piambouhou: Ibid., 18–19. The only printed texts available in Massachusett at this time were Genesis, Matthew, and "a few psalms." Ibid., 21. Eliot used this pamphlet to make an impassioned plea for publishing the Bible in Massachusett.

messengers.[144] Others found active means to undermine the community.[145] The three Indians who pursuaded the eleven-year-old son of the ruler Totherswamp to join them in a drinking episode in 1654 must have realized how mortifying the incident would be for Eliot. Timing their actions just before the second public examination of Natick Indians for church establishment maximized the detrimental effect of their behavior and sent a strong message about the differential level of commitment to the religious enterprise. Flouting English-influenced rules, such as proscriptions against abuse of alcohol, disrupted the community.[146] Less visible resistance remained possible by continuing Native practices but hiding them from the view of observers. Even those who adopted certain English behaviors could resist holistic change by infusing them with Native meanings, as many may have done in thinking about English religion as healing, for example.[147]

By going along with the selection of the site for Natick, Eliot provided the means for additional internal strife. He hoped that by incorporating all Indian listeners in a single Praying Town, regardless of group affiliation, they would offer each other mutual support and would be isolated from the influence of Native opponents and malicious English neighbors. According to Eliot, when the site was selected, "this choyce of mine did move in the Cohannet Indians a jealousie that I had more affection unto those other Indians, then unto them."[148] After Cutshamekin died and Josias Wampatuck succeeded to the sachemship, many Cohannet Indians broke off and formed their own Praying Town in Punkapoag.[149] Indians succeeded in using conversion as a strategy to maintain particular lands of overriding cultural importance.

Indian opponents of Christianity also intervened to disrupt the formation of mission communities. Indian confessors feared the reaction of sachems should they respond to Eliot.[150] He noted how neighboring Indian groups actively worked to undermine conversion.[151] In one case, he used the differential impact of disease to counteract their resistance campaign:

> There is a company of profane Indians that lately are come to a place
> near Wamouth, not farre from our Indians, who do not onely refuse

---

[144] See analysis of confessions, above, and Powicke, *Some Correspondence*, 4.

[145] Examples include threats from within the group: Shepard, "Day Breaking," 17; lack of interest: Shepard, "Clear Sun-shine," 47; and asking disruptive questions: Gookin, "Historical Collections," 183.

[146] Van Lunkhuyzen sees this episode as evidence that Indians had rejected Native resolution dispute for English mechanisms, because Totherswamp decided to whip his son for punishment along with the other offenders. "A Reappraisal," 417.

[147] Bowden and Ronda, *Indian Dialogues*, 33.

[148] Eliot, "Late and Further Manifestation," 270.

[149] Ibid.

[150] Ponampum and Monotunkquanit, *Further Account*, 54 and 65.

[151] These included both sachems and powwaws (Shepard, "Clear Sun-shine," 38 and 50–1; Whitfield, "Light Appearing," 139–41; and Mather, *Magnalia Christi Americana*, 533–6), and other non-listeners from outside proselytized groups (Eliot, "First Fruits," 2).

to pray unto God, but oppose and apprehend that they were sent thither, if not by the policie of some Pawwaws, yet by the instigation of Sathan, on purpose to seduce that younger sort from their profession, and discourage others . . . .Now it pleased God that this company of wicked Indians, were smitten with the Pox, and sundry cut off, and those which were cut off, were of the worst and mischievious of them all; which Providences, all the good Indians do take a great notice of and doth say that the Lord hath wrought a wonder for them.[152]

The favorable comparison recurred the following winter, when Natick lost only three inhabitants to smallpox. Eliot used such incidents to drive home the point that real benefits devolved to true believers.

Despite the fact that listeners demarcated themselves by joining Praying Towns, contact between them and strict opponents of missionization continued. External groups made their presence felt through persistent scoffing of Praying Indians.[153] Relatives became particular targets of apostasy campaigns. Eliot reported that one devout woman on her death bed called her two grown daughters to plead that they ignore their unbelieving relatives:

when I am dead, your Grand-Father and Grand-mother, and Vncles, &c. will send for you to come live amongst them, and promise you great matters, and tell you what pleasant living it is among them; But doe not beleeve them, and I charge you never hearken unto them, nor live amongst them; for they pray not to God . . . I charge you live here.[154]

A painful splintering of family is described here. The missionary presence complicated relations within families and among groups of Indians. Religion became a factor in the creation of group alliances, and it provided an arena of conflict both inside and outside of the physical bounds of community.[155]

F. *Defending the site: Natick and King Philip's War*

The Indian resistance movement known as King Philip's War, which erupted in 1675, laid bare the precarious position of Natick and other Praying Towns, tested Indian commitment to the community, and seemed for a time to threaten the future of the English colony. By the time the English gained the upper hand in

[152] Whitfield, "Light Appearing," 133–4.
[153] Shepard, "Day-Breaking," 22–3; Shepard, "Clear Sun-shine," 50–1, 57, 63; Winslow, "Glorious Progress," 81; and Whitfield, "Light Appearing," 133–4, 139, 142–3.
[154] Winslow, "Glorious Progress," 80.
[155] See, for example, Daniel Richter, "Iroquois versus Iroquois: Jesuit Missions and Christianity in Village Politics, 1642–1686," *WMQ*, 3d ser., 40 (1983): 528–59; and Bruce G. Trigger, *The Children of Aatentsic: A History of the Huron People to 1660* (Montreal: McGill-Queen's University Press, 1976).

1677, the Wampanoag, with those Nipmuck, Pocumtuck, and Narragansett who allied themselves with the sachem Metacom (King Philip), had destroyed more than a dozen English towns. Indian defeat terminated their political autonomy and provoked fierce English revenge.[156] Through the duration of the conflict, Praying Indians faced pressures from all sides. Indians who rejected missionary initiatives "did very industriously endeavour to bring the Christian Indians into disaffection with the English, and to this end raised several false reports concerning them."[157] The English, on the other hand, viewed Praying Indians with suspicion and hatred, refusing to distinguish between enemy, neutral, and ally.

Natick Indians offered early warnings of the imminent crisis in order to clarify their position in the impending conflict. First in April, and again in May of 1675, "Waban . . . came to one of the magistrates on purpose, and informed him that he had ground to fear that Sachem Philip and other Indians, his confederates; intended some mischief shortly to the English and Christian Indians."[158] Throughout the war, Indians from Natick and other Praying Towns served as guides, informants, and soldiers for the English.[159] They joined other erstwhile allies, the Mohegan, Pequot, Nauset as well as the Mohawk, who especially helped turn the events of the war. Despite the Praying Indians' services, most English colonists seized on them as convenient scapegoats to blame for scattered acts of violence and English military disasters early in the conflict. Critics of Praying Indians found evidence for perfidy in the dispersal of Nipmuck Indians from the seven newest of Eliot's fourteen Praying Towns, many of whom joined the confederacy.[160]

Public outcry against Indians culminated in a General Court order calling for the internment of Natick Indians on Deer Island in October of 1675.[161] English officials hoped to prevent Praying Indians from becoming complicit in the Indian resistance, to protect Praying Indians from the actions of vindictive English people, and to temper English fears about the Indian presence. Indians faced dreadful conditions on Deer Island in Boston harbor from October 1675 until the General Court permitted Gookin and Eliot to transport them back to the mainland in May of 1676, at their own expense.[162] During the period of confinement, Praying Indians from Nashobah and Punkapoag joined the Naticks on Deer Island.[163]

---

[156] On King Philip's War see, for example, Douglas Leach, *Flintlock and Tomahawk: New England in King Philip's War* (New York: The Macmillan Company, 1958); Jennings, *Invasion of America*; Philip Ranlet, "Another Look at the Causes of King Philip's War," *NEQ* 61 (1988): 79–100; Russell Bourne, *The Red King's Rebellion: Racial Politics in New England, 1675–1678* (New York: Atheneum, 1990); Jill Lepore, "Dead Men Tell No Tales: John Sassamon and the Fatal Consequences of Literacy," *American Quarterly* 46 (1994): 479–512; and Lepore, "The Name of War: Waging, Writing, and Remembering King Philip's War" (Ph.D. diss., Yale University, 1995).

[157] Gookin, "Historical Account," 2:462.   [158] Ibid., 2:440–1.

[159] Leach, *Flintlock and Tomahawk*; George M. Bodge, "Soldiers in King Philip's War," *NEHGR* 44 (1890): 270–9; and Ibid., 44 (1890): 373–81.

[160] Gookin, "Historical Account," 2:436.   [161] Shurtleff, *Mass. Records*, 5:57, 13 Oct. 1675.

[162] Shurtleff, *Mass. Records*, 5:86, 5 May 1676.   [163] Gookin, "Historical Account," 2:485–92.

While on Deer Island, approximately five-hundred Indians suffered severe deprivation. Their sudden removal had prevented them from preparing for their confinement. Deprived of their material possessions,

> The poor Indians were discouraged, and in want of all things almost, except clams, which food (as some conceived) did occasion fluxes and other diseases among them; besides, they were very mean for clothing, and the islands were bleak and cold with the sea winds in spring time, and the place afforded little fuel, and their wigwams were mean.[164]

The General Court arranged to have corn left at Natick delivered to Indians a little at a time. The Corporation also provided some food and clothing.[165] The interned Indians' sufferings, claimed Hassanamisco Indian minister Tuckapaw-illin, made other Indians "mock and scoff at me, saying, 'Now what is become of your praying to God?'" Some of the English accused him of religious hypocrisy; others had stolen his corn, cattle, and tools. His wife and eldest son had fled, and he had "no where to look, but up to God in heaven to help me."[166] The court finally acknowledged the miserable conditions Praying Indians endured and permitted them to leave Deer Island, mainly because of the military service of the Praying Indians.

Natick Indians paid a heavy price for defending their position as allies to the English, but Daniel Gookin's sympathetic account of the experience of Praying Indians during King Philip's War concluded that confinement on Deer Island at least preserved them from the blind anger of the English. He also observed that "they carried themselves patiently, humbly, and piously, without murmuring or complaining against the English for their sufferings . . . there appeared among them much practical Christianity in this time of their trials."[167] Indians who came to Natick in 1650 had decided, for a plethora of individual and corporate reasons, to make cultural accommodations to find a place in a world where the sheer exercise of English power threatened their survival. Twenty-six years later an overwhelming majority of these Indians stood by their decisions by enduring confinement on a bleak island, or acting as crucial allies of the English in the military campaign.

G. *Convergence*

In the Praying Town of Natick, a convergence occurred between English colonial ideology, which could envision a place for Indian people as religious and cultural converts fixed in bounded geographical places, and Indian resistance to

---

[164] Ibid., 2:516–17.   [165] Ibid., 2:485, 518.

[166] Ibid., 2:503. I have standardized the spelling of this Praying Town in conformity with eighteenth-century usage. In the seventeenth century, it was usually referred to as "Hassanamesit."

[167] Gookin, "Historical Account," 2:485–86.

crushing English colonial expansion that envisioned the preservation of Indian kin and community on Indian lands secured through institutions of the imposed colonial order. Bounding Natick involved negotiations about what land belonged to whom, and in what ways it would be owned. Although the terms of debate emanated from the English colonial order, Indian desires shaped the dialogue. Because they made cultural compromises, some Indians could still claim Natick as "my land."

The Praying Town of Natick came together because an English missionary message included incentives for Indian individuals and families; they sought a course of peaceful coexistence holding the promise that an Indian future could be negotiated within the context of English expansion. Eliot, bolstered by official support for Indian conversion, developed a blueprint for a missionary regime that Indians could shape to fit their own objectives. Eliot compromised repeatedly to advance his own cause, and even argued a claim of Native rights to land that penetrated the collective conscience of colonial magistrates. Coming to Natick appealed to some Indians because they saw much to gain, and they viewed the changes expected of them as modifications, not cultural suicide.

The new religious beliefs were the most drastically different principles the English expected Indians to adopt in reordering their lives. Interpreting individual crises within the context of spiritual intervention in their lives, some Indians became convinced that the English religion might offer instrumental benefits. Elsewhere, Indians made different decisions. On Martha's Vineyard, Thomas Mayhew noted that many Indians "laid the cause of all their wants, sicknesses, and death upon their departing from their old heathenish ways."[168] Some Indians appear to have been pursuaded that Native forms of spiritual interaction no longer functioned effectively. The unfavorable comparison of Indians in crisis with the English thriving all around them formed one aspect of Indian self-doubt. The readily apparent ineffectiveness of Indian powwaws in curing epidemic illness constituted another.

Indians may have reconciled the political system even more easily. The fragmented nature of the new form of government contained continuities in basic ideas about voluntary allegiance to leaders who had proved their ability. Indians chose their own rulers, and were given wide berth in self-government. Influential Indians for the most part retained positions of leadership. English magistrates reinforced the colonial legal system in Praying Towns, but most Indians had already acknowledged formal strictures, and in practice much of the administration of local affairs remained in Indian hands.

Indians accepted individual initiative and voluntary participation to some extent on every societal level. Individuals and families from several local groups made a commitment to Natick, and not all members of these groups followed. Within Praying Towns, individuals determined the nature of their political and

[168] Whitfield, "Light Appearing," 110.

religious participation. The desire to remain part of a functioning community with familiar support systems convinced some Indians that they might secure an Indian future in their ancestral territory through Natick. Those who made that choice encountered the hostility of Indian opponents and aggressive English neighbors. Pursuing neutrality during King Philip's War subjected them to an intensified version of these threats. Yet in the end, Indians who came to Natick remained committed to the community and to the Native strategies it represented. Once it had come together, Natick did not easily come apart.

3

"Friend Indians"

Negotiating colonial rules 1676–1700

[B]e more carefull for future that no spoyle or wrong be . . . don to any of
our freind Indians, let none of yours come nere to Naticke, Puncapauge,
Hassanamesit, or Waymesit, nor among any of our tounes where our freind
Indians are . . . there are other Indians for you to fall vpon, whose pursuing
& destroying wee shall take kindly from your hand.[1]

A. *Friends and enemies: bounding peoples*

In issuing this directive to Mohawk leaders in 1677, colonial magistrates used a
special language for thinking about the position of Praying Indians in the aftermath of King Philip's War. Having recruited Mohawks to bring an end to the
Native resistance that continued in northern New England, English officials
unwittingly exposed Praying Indians to Mohawk raids.[2] The most devastating loss
resulted in the capture of twenty-two Indians from a cornfield at Magunkaquog
near Natick in 1678. Mohawk leaders attempted to disassociate themselves from
the incident, but also argued: "ye Indians of Magoncog are not ye lesse to blame,
they not dwelling as frind Indians in ye Woods, haveing a Castell so well fortifyed
wth stockadoes, which frind Indians need not have, Therefore did Imagine them
to be Enemyes."[3] The Mohawk explanation was almost certainly disingenuous,
given that their raids against Praying Indians had begun at least as early as the
1660s.[4] But the English and Mohawk agreed in principle that a distinction should
be made between "frind Indians" and "Enemyes." Their negotiations centered on
the problem of how to tell the difference between the two.

The Mohawk response pointed to a military criterion that lay at the center
of the problem. Why would "frind Indians" require "stockadoes" for protection? "Frind Indians" resided "in ye woods," not barricaded within a fortress in
the shadow of English settlements.

---

[1] Nathaniel B. Shurtleff, *Records of the Governor and Company of the Massachusetts Bay in
New England* (1628–86) (hereafter cited as *Mass. Records*), 5 vols. (Boston, 1853–4), 5:165,
12 Oct. 1677.

[2] This Massachusetts communication stemmed from the murder of a Natick Indian and the
capture of two Natick women near Hassanamisco.

[3] E. B. O'Callaghan, ed., *Documents Relative to the Colonial History of the State of New York*,
15 vols. (Albany, NY: Weed, Parsons and Co., Public Printers, 1853–87), 13:528.

[4] Neal Salisbury, "Toward the Covenant Chain: Iroquois and Southern New England Algonquians, 1637–1684," in *Beyond the Covenant Chain: The Iroquois and their Neighbors in
Indian North America*, ed. Daniel K. Richter and James H. Merrell (Syracuse, NY: Syracuse University Press, 1987), 61–73.

The English distinction between Indians also centered on the issue of alliance: "we haue reason to take care of them, who were true to us in all the time of our warre, and ventured their liues for us; and now we shall not lett them loose theire lives by our freinds that haue engaged to carry it freindly to us and them, as you haue done."[5] Their military contribution entitled Praying Indians to English protection. They categorized the Mohawk as friends, too, because of their alliance with them, and viewed their raids on "freind" Indians as depredations. But their notion of where "freind Indians" within Massachusetts resided differed from that of the Mohawk. The English cited four towns: Natick, Punkapoag, Hassanamisco, and Wamesit. These Indian settlements carried English implications about boundaries, and the sedentary organization of town activities.

Praying Indians did not hesitate to remind English authorities of their role in the military conflict, and the obligations to them the English had incurred. They believed their actions entitled them to more than just protection from Mohawk raids:

> Haveing approved our selves faithfull to ye English interest, In ye
> Late Warr, and joined them most of us As Souldiers, wherein Some
> of or Relation lost there Lives, we Doe hereby Declare to the hond
> Court yt wee or pdeceser had & have a Naturall Right to Most of
> the Lands Lying in the Nipmuck Country . . . for which we Desire
> the Country & Genll Court will give us a Compensation . . . that so
> Before God and Man, things May be Clear [i]n after time Between
> us and our Posterrity, & the English and yr posterrity.[6]

In this 1681 petition to the Massachusetts General Court, inhabitants of three of the four Praying Towns that survived King Philip's War made a potent declaration of their ownership of lands the English aimed to carve into English towns. They sought acknowledgment of their "Natural Right," compensation for English seizure of their lands, and clarification of a colonial relationship that threatened to overwhelm them.

After King Philip's War, the issues of "friendship" and "boundaries" became linked in struggles that played out very concretely in land transactions, but also were implicated in the questions "Who is a friend Indian?" and "What can friend Indians expect from the English?" As "friends," Praying Indians translated their alliance into assertions of their rightful ownership of land they expected the English to defend. When calculating English land speculators swarmed among them, they argued for Native customary rights, used the English political and legal systems, and agreements among themselves to stave off their complete dispossession. Magistrates acknowledged in their official actions

5 Shurtleff, *Mass. Records*, 5:165, 12 Oct. 1677.
6 Massachusetts Archives (hereafter cited as MA), Massachusetts State Archives at Columbia Point, Boston, 30:257, 1681.

that Native systems of ownership continued to operate and that Indian lands required special protection. But they framed a system to defend Native ownership so narrowly, and enforced it so sparingly, that it could not help but fail miserably. The magistrates themselves accomplished far more Indian dispossession than a few wily individuals could manage.

Despite their rhetoric of protection and their rebuke to the Mohawk, the English had in mind an unmistakably subservient role for Indians within Massachusetts. They attempted to regulate Indian residence patterns and lifeways in conformity with settled town life through periodic legislation, a secular version of missionary prescriptions of earlier years. Together with legitimizing their land tenure by offering minimal compensation for the vast hereditary territories of Indians who remained in Massachusetts, English magistrates sought to clarify what they regarded as a legitimate place for "friend Indians" in the colonial society. They used several mechanisms to unambiguously stabilize the category "friend" by regulating Indian residency in towns, confining them there during military conflicts, monitoring Indian indentured servitude, controlling their use of firearms, and supervising Indian trade at the Boston market. Though they recognized the "Naturall right" of Indians to lands in the Nipmuck Country and elsewhere, they did so principally for the purposes of rationalizing their own colonial regime. Indian claims to the obligation of "friendship" proved a slender reed for Indians in the clarification of relations between two peoples.

B. *Social and cultural boundaries: the ambiguity of Indian identity*

When permitted to return to the mainland from confinement on Deer Island in May of 1676, Natick Indians settled in four separate locations with English supervisors nearby. A group of twenty-five, consisting of James Rumneymarsh and his relatives, went to Medfield. Fifty others settled near Natick, and seventy-five returned to Nonantum Hill. Waban led a contingent of sixty to the falls of the Charles River.[7] These locations all fell within or near Natick's bounds. English neighbors employed some of these 210 Natick Indians in various tasks, such as cutting wood, making stone walls, and spinning.[8] But Indians continued to rely primarily upon a mobile diversified economy: "There is but here and there a spot of good land, fit for planting corn, with accommodation of fishing; these spots of good land lie att a great distance from each other; some four or five miles, some eight or nine miles; some ten or twelve miles." John Eliot

---

[7] Daniel Gookin, "An Historical Account of the Doings and Sufferings of the Christian Indians in New England, in the Years 1675, 1676, and 1677," *Transactions and Collections of the American Antiquarian Society*, 2 vols. (New York: Johnson Reprint Corp., 1971), 2:532.

[8] Indians from the Praying Towns of Punkapoag, Hassanamisco, Magunkaquog, Okommakamesit, and Wamesit, as well as some from Pakachoog, were settled in small groups under similar arrangements. Daniel Gookin wrote that 597 Praying Indians survived the ordeal on Deer Island. Gookin, *Historical Account*, 2:517–19.

explained that the mobile Indian economy meant that dispersed locations were required for religious observations: "It is impossible for them, especially with women and children, to meet at one place; therefore all, that live together at one place, meet to worship God on the sabbath day."[9] Occasional meetings were also held "at places of fishing, hunting, gathering chestnuts in their seasons," and at the several forts that had been erected for defense against Mohawk raids.[10]

Colonial legislation reduced the number of Praying Towns, sought to regulate Indian activities permitted in and around these towns, and addressed ambiguities about the position of Indians who remained in Massachusetts.[11] Indian allies would be set apart from still-autonomous groups, and their presence would be tolerated within the colony provided they accept the notion of drastically reduced territories and residence within the English-imposed town system. In 1677 the General Court directed that all Indians within the English government of Massachusetts Bay reside in one of four Praying Towns granted to Indians: Natick, Punkapoag, Hassanamisco, and Wamesit. They appointed English overseers to inspect the towns regularly and to provide an annual census of all Indian residents. They prohibited friend Indians from entertaining any "stranger or forrein" Indians without permission of the authorities appointed to inspect them. They repealed laws that legalized English murder of any Indians found outside of their bounded places, and they permitted hunting provided Indians obtain a certificate from an English official, since it was "not easily discoverd whither [they were] freinds or not."[12] The law directed hunting Indians to lay down their arms and present certificates upon demand in the woods. If they failed to do so, they could be regarded as enemies and have their weapons seized.

Ambiguities over Indian identity resurfaced during times of military conflict. Confinement orders were reiterated at those times. As with the internment on Deer Island during King Philip's War, English magistrates passed these

[9] John Eliot to Robert Boyle, April 22, 1884, *Collections of the Massachusetts Historical Society* (hereafter cited as *MHSC*), lst ser., 3 (1794): 185–6.

[10] Ibid., 185.

[11] Yasuhide Kawashima interpreted regulation of Indians beginning in this period as the basis for a reservation system in colonial New England, and the period after King Philip's War as the time when the English extended full "legal imperialism" over Massachusetts Indians. Kawashima, "Legal Origins of the Indian Reservation in Colonial Massachusetts," *American Journal of Legal History* 13 (1969): 42–56; Kawashima "Jurisdiction of the Colonial Courts Over the Indians in Massachusetts, 1689–1763," *New England Quarterly* 42 (1969): 532–50; and Kawashima, *Puritan Justice and the Indian: White Man's Law in Massachusetts, 1630–1763* (Middletown, CT: Wesleyan University Press, 1986). Ronda argued that the war marked a turning away from the equitable treatment for Indians in the English legal system, but Koehler argued that the English were only fair to Indians when their safety was at stake. James Ronda, "Red and White at the Bench: Indians and the Law in Plymouth Colony," *Essex Institute Historical Quarterly* 110 (1974): 200–15; and Lyle Koehler, "Red-White Power Relations and Justice in the Courts of Seventeenth-Century New England," *American Indian Culture and Research Journal* 3 (1979): 1–31.

[12] Shurtleff, *Mass. Records*, 5:136–7, 24 May 1677.

measures ostensibly to protect friend Indians from Indians involved in the conflicts as well as from vindictive English neighbors. In July 1689 the General Court directed Indians to remain in their assigned towns during the conflict for their own security and to prevent them from aiding the enemies of the English. The law cited "a more than ordinary Recourse of Indians to the Towns of Boston and Charlestown to the disquieting of the People and danger of Exposing such Indians as are friendly unto us to mischiefes and Violence besides other inconveniences that may attend the same."[13] Indian visitors to Boston included Mohawks, who acted as messengers between the colony and their own leaders. All entrances to the towns were to be secured by guards, who would search their baskets or bundles for contraband. The law empowered magistrates or military officers to interrogate individuals they regarded as suspicious. Within all towns, inspectors were to keep watch during Sabbath days for "Idle walkers."[14]

Even though the broad objectives of colonial policy toward Indians in the aftermath of King Philip's War centered on residential confinement, other legislation demonstrated that Indians resisted the imposition of fixed locations and interacted extensively with the English outside of Praying Towns. A 1677 order addressed the "experience of ye Indians Coming Dayly to Boston upon the occasions of Market & otherwise," and the problem of drunk and disorderly behavior of some of these visitors. The law designated Tuesdays and Fridays as market days, erected a system where they brought their wares to the town wall, and identified individuals among themselves to conduct their trade. At other times, appointed Indians were to obtain necessary supplies. Transgressors were to be "whipt out of town with ten stripes."[15] Two years later an act passed to prevent the abuse of liquor on military training day and during other public events. It concerned the "many people; both English and indians that come to such meetings" and engaged in disruptive behavior and "neglect of duty."[16]

Magistrates built in exceptions to strict confinement even in residency legislation. The most visible of these involved the continued recruitment of "friend Indians" for military duty. In 1689 the General Court ordered that ninety Indians be mustered from Natick, Punkpoag, and from among "other friend Indians" for service in King William's War.[17] A year later, it recruited two-hundred Indians for an expedition against the Eastern Indians.[18] Officials also sanctioned economic activities outside Praying Towns. The initial regulation allowed Indians to hunt outside of towns, albeit only through a licensing system. Legislation in 1690 specifically exempted women and children who gathered clams, and Indians who fished at the lower falls of the Charles River or at Neponset mill.[19]

[13] MA 30:313, 1689.   [14] Ibid.
[15] MA 30:243, 1677.   [16] MA 47:43, 1679.
[17] Massachusetts Historical Society Photostat (hereafter cited as MHS Photostat), Massachusetts Historical Society, Boston, MA, 1689 Aug. 21.
[18] MA 30:317, 1690.   [19] MA 30:315, 1689/90.

Engaging in wage labor and indentured servitude also constituted legitimate cause for living outside of designated towns. The 1690 confinement measure ordered wage laborers, but not indentured servants, to return to their Indian towns:

> It being difficult to Discern between Friends & Foes . . . This Court doth order and appoint that . . . such as are not [abroad] are forthwith to return to their respective stations, as also such as are Sojourning within any of our Towns excepting only those who are constant dwellers in English houses.[20]

This provision fit with English notions about household structure, which envisioned indentured servants as part of family government.

Failure to regulate Indian servitude resulted in English manipulation of the institution. Indians complained loudly enough about abuses of the labor system that they prompted colonial officials to regulate English behavior. The statute addressed the complaints of

> some of the Principal and best disposed Indians within this Province [who] have Represented and complained of the Exactions . . . which some of the English exercise toward the Indians by drawing them to consent to covenant or bind themselves or children Apprentices or Servants for an unreasonable Term, in pretence of, or to make Satisfaction for some small debt contracted or damage done by them.[21]

The bill directed that indentures would henceforth be binding only with the approval of five or more justices of the peace as assurance for equitable and reasonable contracts. It also empowered justices of the General Sessions of Peace to evaluate and act upon any indenture not yet expired.

Residency requirements set the broad parameters of interaction between "friend" Indians and their English neighbors. But even the legislation itself testifies to the extensive permeability of boundaries, especially for economic purposes. Defining the category "friend Indian" did not require rigid separation except when military conflicts that involved any Indians heightened the ambiguity of their identity. The experience of King Philip's War persuaded magistrates of the need to restrain the English from persecuting their allies. The principal motivation in creating a review process for servitude arrangements was to constrain English abuse of Indians, which took the form of lengthy servitude stints extracted on specious grounds.

C. Legal boundaries and land

Problems stemming from English manipulations designed to obtain Indian land

---

[20] Ibid. For a discussion of Indian servitude in Rhode Island, see John Sainsbury, "Indian Labor in Early Rhode Island," *New England Quarterly* 48 (1975): 378–93.

[21] MA 30:458, 1700.

proved even more problematic for English officials. Magistrates had begun to regulate land transactions in the early years of colonization. In 1634 the General Court passed its first law regarding the purchase of Indian lands: "And it is Ordered, that no Person whatsoever, Shall henceforth buy land of any Indian without License first had and obtained of the General Court, and if any offend herein, such Land so bought shall be forfeited to the Country."[22] In 1665 the General Court broadened regulations explicitly to cover the lease of Indian lands.[23] Grants of Praying Towns included specific restatements of the alienation clause.[24] Despite these restrictions, regular violations of the law occurred. In an attempt to prevent fraud and confusion over land titles, the General Court periodically restated proscriptions. Laws prohibited English individuals from purchasing, receiving as a gift, or leasing land from Indians without prior approval (often referred to as license) from the General Court. The law directed Indians to seek relief from fraudulent dispossession through the English court system.[25]

These regulations operated on four levels. First, they implicitly codified English assumptions about the colonial land relationship: Land rights proceeded in hierarchical fashion from the crown grant, to the General Court as the governing body of the colony, to the town, and finally to individuals. Second, magistrates acknowledged that some basis for Indian rights to the land existed either by explicitly extinguishing title through English legal means (sometimes through questionable means), or by declaring lands vacant and thus available for English taking (vacuum domicilium). Colonial officials intended to provide the basis for the orderly transfer of title from Indians to the English governing body, to prevent conflicts over land title, and to pay some attention to Indian rights while attempting to prevent an array of fraudulent devices to dispossess Indians. Third, General Court oversight of Indian land transactions implicitly enacted a trust relationship whereby Indian interests might be protected by the English legal system.[26] In creating a system of oversight, magistrates reinforced the colonial relationship and acknowledged a moral obligation to Indians. Magistrates further elaborated supervision in 1694 by appointing commissioners to oversee Indians within the colony.[27] Fourth, land regulations included penalties for violators, though the exact meaning of these penalties remained ambiguous. The wording of the original law, declaring that lands transferred "without license first had and obtained of the General Court . . . shall be forfeited to the Country,"[28] implies

---

[22] *General Laws and Liberties of the Massachusetts Bay Colony, Revised and Reprinted, May 15, 1672* (Cambridge, MA: Printed by Samuel Green, for John Usher, 1672), 74–5. Restated in "An Act Prohibiting the Purchasing of Lands of the Indians," MA 30:348, 1694.

[23] Shurtleff, *Mass. Records*, Part I, 4:282, 11 Oct. 1665.

[24] Shurtleff, *Mass. Records*, Part I, 4:192, 14 May 1654, and Part I, 4:408, 12 Nov. 1659.

[25] *Laws and Liberties*, 74–5; and Kawashima, *Puritan Justice*.

[26] See Ronda, "Red and White at the Bench," for a discussion of similar developments in Plymouth.

[27] Kawashima, *Puritan Justice*, 32–3, 97.   [28] *Laws and Liberties*, 74–5.

that the land would devolve to the colony to the exclusion of the fraudulent purchaser, not to the Indians. But at least in grants to Praying Towns, such transactions were pronounced "illegal & vojd in lawe."[29] In one land dispute involving a
Praying Town, a restatement of Indian land policy recited both stipulations.[30]

In spite of periodic legislation, fraudulent land transactions continued to
plague magistrates who entertained a vision of orderly English land title. An act
that became law in 1701 revisited the problems that undermined Indian land
policy, and added teeth to the enforcement mechanism. It proclaimed:

> Sundry persons for private Lucre have presumed to make purchas-
> es of Land from the Indians not having any Licence or Approbation
> . . . to the injury of the Natives & great disquiet and disturbance of
> many of ye Inhabitts of this Province in the peaceable possession of
> their Lands and Inheritances.[31]

The act restated the principle of prior license from the General Court and the
authority of the English court system in resolving disputes, but it moved
beyond nullifying transactions or transferring jurisdiction over these lands to
"the Country." Violators would be punished by fines (not to exceed double the
value of the land) or six months' imprisonment. Illegal purchases concluded
after 1667 were subject to the provisions. This act, like those that came before,
exempted transactions between Indians from the licensing process.[32]

This emphasis on regulation reflected an important reality, since Indians
connected to Natick were involved in a large number of land transactions and
disputes between 1675 and about 1700. Land transactions of this period fall
into several types: town boundary disputes and adjustments, Indian quitclaims
to already settled English towns, large-scale corporate sales of land outside of
the town, and individual land transactions in and around Natick.

D. *Boundaries with neighbors*

Between 1675 and 1690, the geographical boundaries of Natick were the object
of both negotiation and conflict with neighboring English towns. Natick negotiated an exchange of land with Sherborn designed to benefit both towns. In the
case of Dedham, continuing animosity between the communities had its roots
in the initial struggles over bounding Natick.

In March of 1677 a committee appointed by the General Court to investigate
a proposed exchange of land between Natick and Sherborn filed its report. The
committee hoped to meet with Daniel Gookin Sr. and John Eliot and other concerned parties. Gookin and Eliot failed to appear, sending a letter with two Indians which asked that nothing be done at that time. The committee investigated

---

[29] Shurtleff, *Mass. Records*, Part I, 4:408–9, 12 Nov. 1689.
[30] Shurtleff, *Mass. Records*, 5:487, 4 June 1685.   [31] MA 30:474, 1701.
[32] Ibid.

anyway and found that Sherborn had almost no land near the place the towns-people wanted to erect their meetinghouse. The committee reported that it was doubtful "whither they be like to be a toune, if some considerable tract of land be not procured from the Indians, either by exchange or purchase, or both."[33] The committee made some specific recommendations about how an exchange of land should be arranged.

In April 1679 representatives from Sherborn and Natick endorsed articles of agreement for a 4,000-acre exchange between the two towns. The parties agreed to an equal exchange of acreage, with Sherborn contributing 200 bushels of Indian grain to Natick as well. Out of the land Sherborn received from Natick, forty acres were to be set aside for a free school for Indian and English children, the site to be chosen by Gookin, Eliot, the commissioners of the United Colonies, and the Indian rulers.[34]

Natick's other boundary problems were rooted in the continued aggression of Dedham townspeople. Animosity between the towns was not limited to land struggles; Dedham townspeople found much to criticize in their Indian neigh-bors.[35] In 1681 Dedham inhabitants complained bitterly about Indians in their vicinity. They argued that Indians engaged in objectionable behavior toward the English, drunkenness, wasteful hunting practices, pilfering of corn and provisions from their fields, and refusal to work, "except upon unreasonable terms," or to engage in settled agriculture. They added that the "soberest Indi-ans at Natick complain yt their young men are ruined by these Indians."[36] They also directed their constable to warn "several Indians [who] were residing in the town" to return to Punkapoag, Natick, or Wamesit.[37]

But continuing struggles over boundaries remained the most intractable issue. In 1685 the General Court directed a surveyor to reset the original bounds of the exchange made in 1662 in order to end bickering between the towns.[38] In 1700 Natick inhabitants protested that Dedham's usurpations came from two directions: In addition to encroaching on Natick land on the south side of the Charles River, the Indians said, Dedham residents had in the previ-ous two years "run A new circular Line from the west part their Township . . . And by their soe doeing have jnclosed fourteen hundred Acres or more, where-in lyeth fourty orchards & fivety corn fields old & new & upon where Indians doe dwell."[39] Dedham had sold the lands they enclosed to Samuel Morse of

[33] Shurtleff, *Mass. Records*, 5:229–30, 28 May 1679.   [34] MA 30:247–8, 16 April 1679.

[35] See Kathleen J. Bragdon, "Crime and Punishment among the Indians of Massachusetts," *Ethnohistory* 28 (1981): 23–32, for a good discussion of English attitudes toward Indians, which locates English indignation about Indian behavior within their notions of hierarchi-cal society.

[36] MA 30:261a, 1681.

[37] Herman Mann, *Historical Annals of Dedham, from Its Settlement in 1635 to 1847* (Dedham, MA: Herman Mann, 1847), 20.

[38] Shurtleff, *Mass. Records.* 5:485, 4 June 1685.

[39] MA 30:457, 1700.

Sherborn.[40] After a series of hearings, the General Court ordered a new committee to redraw the original bounds of Natick and Dedham once again.[41] In these actions, the court persisted in defending Indian land rights.

E. *Negotiating Native land claims*

The English desire to obtain more secure title to land that had already been granted by the General Court and settled as towns lay behind another kind of transaction that involved Indians with connections to Natick. Indians were engaged in numerous land sales and quitclaims to English towns, mostly in the 1680s, in response to the vacating of the Massachusetts Bay charter in 1684 and the actions of Dominion of New England governor Sir Edmund Andros, who challenged the legality of the New England land system.[42] Towns rushed to form committees or designate individuals to extract Indian deeds for substantial tracts encompassed by the towns' bounds to gain protection for English land titles.[43] Even Dedham, which had so confidently asserted its title in the 1660s, got into the act. The town secured a confirmation of its Indian deeds from Chickataubut's grandson Charles Josias in 1685.[44]

More than forty Indian men and women who were from Natick, or who had kin connections there, sanctioned quitclaims to English towns in four Massachusetts Bay counties in the late seventeenth century: Middlesex, Essex, Norfolk, and Worcester. Some Indians were grantors to three or four towns, sometimes located in more than one county. The number of Indian grantors to a particular town ranged from one individual to more than a dozen, because some English agents worked to encompass as many Indian claimants as possible in their quitclaims.[45] These land transactions illustrate the connection of Indians associated with Natick to a network of locations throughout present-day

---

[40] MA 30:457, 1700.

[41] Massachusetts General Court, Council, *The Acts and Resolves, Public and Private of the Province of the Massachusetts Bay* (hereafter cited as AR) 21 vols. (Boston: Wirth & Potter Printing Co., State Printers, 1895–1922), 7:245, Appen. 2, Chap. 17, 15 June 1700/01; AR 7:267, Appen. 2, Chap. 33, 18 Feb. 1700/01; AR 7:287, Appen. 2, Chap. 3, 6 June 1701; and AR 7:297, Appen. 2, Chap. 25, 27 June 1700/01.

[42] See Theodore Lewis, "Land Speculation and the Dudley Council of 1686," *William and Mary Quarterly*, 3d ser., 31 (1974): 255–72; Kawashima, *Puritan Justice*, 50; and Martin, *Profits in the Wilderness*, 260–7.

[43] See, for example, Samuel A. Green, *The Early Records of Groton, Massachusetts, 1662–1707* (Cambridge, MA: University Press, John Wilson & Son, 1880), 194–96; and Charles Hudson, *History of the Town of Marlborough* (Boston: Press of T.R. Marrin & Son, 1862), 89–91.

[44] Dedham, Massachusetts, Ancient Deeds from the Indians of the Town of Dedham, Ayer mimeo, The Newberry Library, Chicago, IL, 18 April 1685.

[45] See O'Brien, "Community Dynamics in the Indian-English Town of Natick, Massachusetts, 1650–1790" (Ph.D. diss., University of Chicago, 1990), 116–17. On the mechanisms behind English extraction of Indian deeds see Francis Jennings, *The Invasion of America: Indians, Colonialism, and the Cant of Conquest* (New York: Norton, 1976), 128–45.

central and eastern Massachusetts. The grantors were described as rightful heirs to the lands in question; the distribution of locations suggests the wide geographical scope from which Natick drew its population.

The largest tracts acquired by the English lay in the Nipmuck Country in central Massachusetts. These transactions occurred in the 1680s and involved huge tracts, measured in approximate square miles instead of acres. From the English perspective, extinguishing Native title to the Nipmuck Country prior to English occupation of the region would pave the way for regularized English town expansion into the region and avert questions about land titles that surfaced during the Massachusetts charter crisis. The Nipmuck transactions brought to the fore a debate in which Indians solicited English officials to defend their land rights based on Native practices.

Between May 1681 and February 1682, inhabitants of Natick, Punkapoag, and Wamesit repeatedly asserted their ownership of the Nipmuck Country. The Indians called on the General Court to defend their right to these lands, citing their faithfulness and loyalty to the English, but especially their "Naturall Right" to the land. During protracted negotiations, Indians challenged English pretensions to concluding Indian land transactions without reference to Native custom.

Indians continued to think about land in terms of customary ownership. As Kathleen Bragdon has argued, the inclusion of a large number of Indians in endorsing deeds demonstrated the broad participation of Indians in decision making about land, not just sachems. This practice fit into Native ideas in which a sachemship was dependent on the support of community members, who could transfer allegiance to another sachem if they became dissatisfied with the leadership. The central issue of most land disputes within an Indian community, then, was the legitimacy of the sachem, not the right of the sachem to alienate land.[46]

But while customary notions did continue to govern Indian land tenure, Praying Indians also recognized that by drawing upon the English legal system to solidify their ownership of hereditary lands, they could resist outright dispossession. Before 1677, Indians had entrusted Indian John Wampus "(because he spake English well & was aged wh the English) to inquire after & in our names & for our use to declare & Enduce(d?) to get settled & recorded, the Indians title & Right to these those lands."[47] Wampus's language skills qualified him to negotiate the strategic use of the English legal system to gain security for Indi-

[46] Kathleen J. Bragdon, "'Another Tongue Brought In': An Ethnohistorical Study of Native Writings in Massachusett" (Ph.D. diss., Brown University, 1981), 107–8. Bragdon uses the example of John Wampus in making this point. She also suggests that corporate control of this sort continued into the eighteenth century, but the group underwent a transformation to correlate with the Chrisitanized community instead of the sachemship. (See p. 113.) This seems to be the case with some transactions made by Indians associated with Natick.

[47] MA 30:259a, 1681; and MA 30:260a, 1681.

an lands. Indians tried to draw upon both customary practices and English legal forms to defend their ancestral lands.

Unfortunately, Wampus proved a poor choice to act as their attorney. Instead of fulfilling his duty to the community, John Wampus usurped Nipmuck lands as his own and sold them to English purchasers. According to "several Aged & principal Indians," including Waban, Piambouhou, and John Wampus's uncles Anthony and Tom Tray, Wampus "was no sachem, and had no more Right or title to Any lands in Nipmuck Country . . . then other comon Indians." Daniel Gookin attested that he had been present at a meeting in September 1677 when Indians gathered to challenge Wampus about his bold claims to Nipmuck lands and his audacity in proposing to sell them as his own. Indian elders denied Wampus's claims and charged that "hee was an Evel instrumt to disquiet them, & all hee aymed at was to gett mony to be drunke & spend upon his lusts." They ordered him to desist, and withdrew their request that he act as an attorney on their behalf.[48]

In this forum, the Indian elders advanced arguments based on Native notions of land rights and ownership, arguing that Wampus was not a sachem, nor was he acting in the collective interest of the Indians. Wampus had no more right to corporate lands "then other comon Indians." Only a sachem could sell these lands. Selected as an agent for the communal owners because of his familiarity with English, Indians charged him to gain English legal recognition of their title to the Nipmuck Country. Instead of protecting their interests, Wampus had betrayed the community.

The General Court appointed William Stoughton and Joseph Dudley to act as agents for the colony in extinguishing Indian ownership at the same General Court session in which they first heard the Indian complaints about John Wampus.[49] They empowered Stoughton and Dudley "to take particcular care & inspection into the matter of the land in Nipmug country, what titles are pretended to by Indeans or others, and the validity of them" and to report back to the court.[50]

An initial meeting that consisted of all Indian claimants, John Eliot, other interpreters, plus Stoughton and Dudley "found them willing enough to make clajme to the whole country, but litigious & doubtfull amongst themselves."[51] They adjourned the meeting after the Indians agreed to decide their claims among themselves and compromise "on the countrys behalfe."[52] In September, the parties met again. Stoughton and Dudley, along with the principal claimants, spent a week evaluating the land. It fell into three territories. Groups of Indians

[48] MA 30:259a, 1681.
[49] Stoughton and Dudley were only two well-connected individuals who were engaged in large-scale land speculation throughout New England during the mid-1680s. Lewis, "Land Speculation," 259; and Martin, *Profits in the Wilderness*.
[50] Shurtleff, *Mass. Records* 5:315, 11 May 1682; and Lewis, "Land Speculation," 259.
[51] Shurtleff, *Mass. Records*, 5:328–9, 17 Oct. 1681.   [52] Ibid.

under the leadership of Black James owned the southern lands, which Stoughton and Dudley judged good land for English expansion. They described the far nothern area around Nashaway as the best in the territory, but the Natick Indians were willing to part with only a small parcel near Hassanamisco. Stoughton and Dudley were particularly interested in obtaining this tract. Though the Indians were unwilling to sell, the English thought that they might "vpon reasonable termes, be, so farr as respect the Indian clajme, taken into the countrys hands, which wee offer our advise as best to be donne, least the matter grow more difficult by delays."[53] Hassanamisco Indians currently residing in Natick claimed the central section, north of Sherborn and Marlborough. This was the territory the activities of John Wampus had brought into question. Stoughton and Dudley summoned the executors of Wampus's will to Boston and investigated. They found "their clajme very vncertajn, but, if allowed, will be to to [sic] the ruine of the midle part of the country, of which the Indians made complaint to this Court."[54] In accepting this return, the General Court advised that clear title be obtained to these lands on the easiest possible terms in order to avoid further "troubles and pretentions."[55]

By March of 1682, Stoughton and Dudley had purchased the southern part of Nipmuck Country, reserving the right for the Indians to a tract five miles square, to be laid out in one or two pieces, and the bulk of the Hassanamisco-Natick claim. These two tracts, measuring an estimated twenty miles by fifty miles, were purchased from the Indians for a total of fifty pounds and a coat, plus "small quantitjes, about fiue pounds, wee haue distributed amongst them."[56] The northernmost territory near Wachusetts remained unacquired, while the negotiators searched for the owners. In the agreement, these Indians had added to their plantations all the land lying between Natick and Hassanamisco near Medfield, Sherborn, Mendon, Marlborough, and Sudbury. This land was described as being "of very inconsiderable value."[57] As part of the bargains, English magistrates promised the Indians that their individual claims against towns and farmers who had taken up land without obtaining titles would be heard and settled justly.[58]

Dozens of Indians endorsed the deed for lands in the southern part of Nipmuck Country that had been forfeited by the group of Indians under Black James. Several of them were Indians with strong Natick connections, including James Wiser, John Maquah, and James Printer.[59] The five miles square reserved for them was located in two places, Quantisset and Maanexit, two of the seven "New Praying Towns" designated by John Eliot in the 1670s. They were surveyed and granted by deed from Stoughton and Dudley in May of 1685, and

[53] Ibid. [54] Ibid.
[55] Ibid. [56] Shurtleff, *Mass. Records*, 5:341–2, 17 Mar. 1681/2.
[57] Ibid. [58] Ibid.
[59] MA 30:265, 1681. I have standardized the spelling of "Moqua" in the document to "Maquah."

were confirmed by the General Court in June of 1685.[60] Waban's group of Indians gave deeds for Nipmuck Country land in February 1682. Virtually all of the endorsers of this deed had strong connections to Natick. The tract was described as comprehending all the land lying between the Nipmuck River to the southern border of Massachusetts, and over to Springfield.[61]

But the transactions made by John Wampus continued to affect land titles for years, and the actions of the magistrates demonstrate that they accepted Indian arguments that he lacked legitimacy. Only three years after the Nipmuck Country titles were supposedly settled, several English petitioners asked that land deeded to them by Wampus be confirmed to them. Magistrates asserted that "the Court knowes not of any land that Wampas, Indean, had any true or legal right vnto, he being no sachem, but a comon person."[62] They offered to reconsider their complaint if they could find any land to which they could prove Wampus's ownership.[63]

Obtaining deeds for the Nipmuck Country opened the way for rapid English occupation of the region. Within a year of the Nipmuck deeds, the General Court began making grants.[64] They gave Stoughton and Dudley an 8,000-acre town in partnership with another Englishman in May 1683, and two years later awarded them 1,000-acre farms.[65] Nipmuck land cessions provided the means for a group to emigrate from England in 1685.[66] Acquisition of title expanded available territory to colonists who relied upon high-status agents to prepare the way for English town expansion.[67]

F. *Transforming corporate Indian landownership*

In the wake of the Nipmuck transactions, and because individual English speculators had begun incursions into the town of Natick itself (detailed later in this Chapter), Praying Indians took steps to place their remaining landholdings on firmer ground. In 1682, "by a Generall Agreement of all the praying indian[s] they made this order that no indian or indians should sell any land belonging to yr townes without the unanimous consent of every proprietor."[68] This agreement aimed to transform Indian land tenure into a corporate issue that differed somewhat from existing customary practices by investing every Indian "proprietor" with a voice in transactions involving any town lands. The pact sought to prevent even sachems from alienating Praying Town lands. Indians with customary rights to Natick, the Speens and Josias Wampatuck, had already

---

[60] Shurtleff, *Mass. Records*, 5:488, 4 June 1685.
[61] Shurtleff, *Mass. Records*, 5:361–5, 27 May 1682.
[62] Shurtleff, *Mass. Records*, 5:442, 17 May 1684.   [63] Ibid.
[64] Shurtleff, *Mass. Records*, 5:409, 16 May 1683.
[65] Lewis, "Land Speculation," 260; and Shurtleff, *Mass. Records*, 5:488, 4 June 1685.
[66] Shurtleff, *Mass. Records*, 5:467, 28 Jan. 1684/5.
[67] Martin, *Profits in the Wilderness*.   [68] MA 30:285–6, 1684.

forfeited their control over the town site in public ceremonies during the establishment of the community. The agreement also aimed to preclude the English
from extracting deeds from individuals against the wishes and prerogatives of
the group, a long-standing device of dispossession.[69]

This corporate policy received a stiff test when English residents of the town
of Marlborough attempted a large-scale land acquisition of their own in 1684.
They submitted a request to the General Court for license to purchase the 5,800
acres remaining in the Praying Town of Okommakamesit (Whip Suffrage),
accompanied by a petition of Natick Indians.[70] In that petition, the Indians
explained that their "Need and Nessesity" prompted them to sell the land. The
Marlborough inhabitants reminded the General Court that they had been
promised first-purchase rights to contiguous Okommakamesit should the Indians
ever decide to sell their plantation.[71] The court refused the petitions for license.[72]

Failure to win approval did not deter Marlborough inhabitants, who produced a deed for General Court approval just two months later.[73] John Eliot,
Daniel Gookin, and Natick inhabitants themselves made passionate protests
and challenged the validity of the Marlborough deed and the methods
employed in acquiring it. Eliot and Gookin recited the technicalities of Indian
land policy, evoked the inherent trust relationship, and offered an analysis of
the methods by which Marlborough acquired its deed. In having "taken deeds
of sale; wch are acknowledged & recorded[,] made by Some Drunken &
debauched indians . . . to the great disatisfaction of other more sober indians, as
much [entitled] as any others," Marlborough residents engaged in "notorious
injustice & unrighteousness." The General Court could not allow the transaction to stand because it would dishonor the English colonial government, the
king, and the missionary company to ignore laws passed to protect Indians from
land fraud. They argued that confirmation would encourage "bold prsumtious
& covetous men" to follow their example, and that Indians would quickly be
dispossessed of what lands remained theirs. And "indians when they are thus
cheated & outed of their lands and Inheritances" would be forced "to mix
among the Barborous nations yt are enimes to the English; & to joyn wth them
in a new warr." Eliot and Gookin reminded the magistrates that English land
encroachment was "a principall cause of the late [King Philip's] warr."[74]

The Indians made a somewhat different argument, although they also
appealed to a sense of justice, the colony's trust responsibilities, and the letter
of the law:

> we doe understand that no man is to buy Indean land without leave
> from your Honr[s. W]e see dayly that Thomas Waban and great

---

[69] Jennings, *Invasion of America*, 128–45.
[70] MHS Photostat, 1684 May 8; and MHS Photostat, 1684 May 7.
[71] MHS Photostat, 1684 May 8.   [72] MA 30:285–6, 1684.
[73] MA 30:280, 1684.   [74] MA 30:285–6, 1684.

> James Doe Appropriate to themselves the Indian land at Malbury
> and sell it & yt Without order and keep all the pay themselves.[75]

Thomas Waban and Great James violated the Native principles of corporate ownership of Indian lands as well as the colony's Indian land policy. Community members lamented that the Marlborough deed broke the general agreement made by Praying Indians just two years earlier. Thomas Waban persisted in flouting the corporate pact; he endorsed a third Marlborough confirmation attempt just one month after Natick Indians protested his actions.[76]

In ruling in favor of the Indians in June of 1685, the General Court drew upon the colony's Indian land policy without mentioning the Indians' internal agreement. The 5,800-acre conveyance had been conducted illegally which rendered it null and void. Their order reiterated the restrictions on Indian land sales, and specifically emphasized that Indian land sales to the English required prior license from the court. It declared that all such sales, except those already confirmed and allowed, would be nullified.[77] Though the magistrates defended Indian landownership in this case, their actions failed to legitimate Indian land arrangements and instead adjudicated the dispute within English law.

Despite Indian actions to bolster colony restrictions on Indian land sales by requiring the unanimous consent of Indian proprietors, further erosion of Indian lands continued. Several English residents from Chelmsford and Concord asked for confirmation of deeds to the Indian lands at Nashobah in 1702. The petitioners argued that most of the Indians who had received the land grant and lived there "afterward Removed themselves and familys to Natick . . . . They and their Descendts that Remain . . . are reduced to very few."[78] They received confirmation of the deeds under the condition that they provide "a Convenient Settlement" for the Indians who remained at Nashobah.[79]

In another instance, notions of Native land rights overrode the corporate ban on land sales by Indian individuals. In May 1684 John Awassamug Sr. asked for permission to sell the remainder of his "hereditary lands now within the bounds of Medfield, Mendham, and Sherbourn."[80] Seven months later, he granted power of attorney to his son Thomas Awassamug "to looke after the Indian title that yet do remaine vnpaid for by English proprietors."[81] The younger Awassamug sold his inheritance to discharge debts he had incurred in maintaining his father in his illness and death. Edward Rawson, long-standing secretary to the General Court, moved for permission to purchase the Awassamug lands in May

---

[75] MA 30:301, 1684.   [76] MA 30:288, 1684.

[77] Shurtleff, *Mass. Records*, 5:486–7, 4 June 1685. Two hundred acres at Okommakamesit had been granted and confirmed earlier to Daniel Gookin Sr. in recognition of his services to them over the preceding twenty years. Shurtleff, *Mass. Records*, 5:216–7, 28 May 1679; MA 30:237, 1679; and MHS Photostat, 1677 May 2.

[78] MA 30:486, 1702.   [79] Ibid.

[80] MA 30:297a, 1684.   [81] Shurtleff, *Mass. Records*, 5:531, 1 Dec. 1684.

1685.[82] He had already procured a deed from Thomas Awassamug and his wife, Abigail.[83] The court granted his request.[84]

Before Rawson acquired the 2,000 acres from Thomas Awassamug, his right to sell the land was settled according to Native principles of ownership, but using the English land system. In January 1685 John and Samuel Awassamug, John Maquah, Peter Ephraim, and Eleazer Peegun granted their "whole native title" to the lands to Thomas Awassamug. They reckoned ownership through their "naturall right, descending to us from the cheife sachem Wuttawushan, vnlce to the sajd John Awassamoage, Sen, who was the cheife sachem of sajd land, and nearly related to us al."[85] John Awassamug controlled the land "according [to] the sagamore title."[86]

The Awassamug transactions merged Native and English practices in a way different from the earlier Nipmuck and Okommakamesit negotiations. In all probability, it was Edward Rawson who worked to establish an unassailable title to lands he wanted by guiding these Indians through the bureaucratic transactions. Nevertheless, it is instructive that his actions expressly acknowledged the legitimacy of Native land practices. Rawson, as the experienced secretary to the General Court, was in a position to know how English and Indian assumptions about "good title" worked, and what elements were involved in getting an Indian transaction approved. That the Indians did not contest the Awassamug transactions is also telling. They acknowledged Awassamug as the rightful heir through Native custom, and because the lands fell outside of Praying Town bounds, the transaction did not violate their corporate agreement.

G. *Defending land in Natick*

English colonists also engrossed Indian lands in and around Natick. Some of them capitalized on Indian decisions to exchange land for needed public works; others bought land from Indian individuals over the protests of the town. Natick Indians challenged the fraudulent activities of engrossers with some positive effect. Their corporate agreement, which addressed local land sales in addition to the large-scale land loss outside of the town, seems to have halted the threat of wholesale dispossession. But in the 1680s, four English intruders managed to gain a foothold in and around the town despite Indian protests, sometimes portraying themselves as defenders of Indian interests: John Grout, Matthew Rice, Samuel Gookin Jr., and Samuel How. Indians collectively agreed to make grants to three other Englishmen: Thomas Sawin, John Collar, and Thomas Eames.

[82] MA 30:297, 1685.   [83] Shurtleff, *Mass. Records*, 5:533, 21 Apr. 1685.
[84] Shurtleff, *Mass. Records*, 5:484, 4 June 1685.
[85] Shurtleff, *Mass. Records*, 5:531–2, Deed, 21 Jan. 1685.
[86] Shurtleff, *Mass. Records*, 5:531, power of attorney to Thomas Awassamug, 21 Apr. 1685. The document used "sagamore," the equivalent term for "sachem" among northern New England groups. Neal Salisbury, *Manitou and Providence: Indians, Europeans, and the Making of New England, 1500–1643* (New York: Oxford University Press, 1982), 42.

John Grout and Matthew Rice, both residents of nearby Sudbury, appeared as would-be purchasers of Natick land in the early 1680s. Natick rulers and inhabitants described the tangle of events involving Grout and Rice in two separate petitions to the General Court in 1683 and 1684. The problem began when Grout

> did privately Bargaine wth two or thre persons of our towne; for a parcill of land belonging to or towne without the townes . . . consent & did obtaine leave of ye General Court . . . to purchase of thos Indians about fifty Acres of land; but he so ordered the matter yt instead of 50 Acres hee Got a deed from the said Indians, for about 500 Acres.[87]

The Indians understood that Grout's initial purchase should fall outside of the town boundaries; they later determined that he had marked out 500 acres to himself within the town. When the Indians discovered his encroachment, they used "all faire measures . . . to shew him the wrong hee did the towne."[88] Then, using the legal mechanism for relief provided for in the Indian land policy, Natick Indians successfully sued in county court at Charlestown. In a magnanimous gesture, they allowed Grout to keep the fifty acres he originally bargained for and "for peace . . . also added to him near forty Acres more." They now asked that the General Court confirm 400 acres they regained and had since sold to Matthew Rice, and that Grout be refrained from harassing Rice in possessing the lands.[89] The parcel lay "in a remote Angle" of the town and was "almost surrounded by English mens lands." Rice, they argued, "is redy to pay us & wee want the pay being much of it in corne for to Suply or families."[90] Selling the land to Rice became a pressing concern for the Indians because "we are many of them in a sickly state, & at least forty persons yong & old have died within these twelve months."[91]

The General Court ordered a committee simultaneously to investigate the intertwined Grout-Rice claims.[92] Their report, composed by Daniel Gookin, recommended that Grout be allowed to lay out eighty acres, and that Rice be granted the 400 acres he requested. This resolution meshed with the stated wishes of Natick rulers and inhabitants. But John Eliot, designated to advise in the matter, entertained serious reservations about the arrangement: "For charity Sake I can suffer and Lett it be = but act in it I can not."[93]

[87] MA 30:277a, 1683.   [88] Ibid.
[89] MA 30:279a, 1684.   [90] MA 30:277a, 1683.
[91] MA 30:279a, 1684.
[92] Shurtleff, *Mass. Records*, 5:464, 24 Oct. 1684; and 5:486, 4 June 1685. As long as they were at it, the committee was asked to describe the boundary between Natick and Dedham once again.
[93] Middlesex County Court, Grantee and Grantor Records (hereafter cited as MCG), Cambridge, MA, 10:448, 1685/1685. The first date refers to the year the deed was consummated, and the second, to the year the deed was registered with the county court.

The John Grout–Matthew Rice land controversy offers a revealing demonstration of the Massachusetts land policy in operation. Grout obtained prior license to purchase land, acquired a deed, and then engrossed ten times as much land as the Indians bargained for. Natick Indians pursued the available legal channels to negate the transaction and won their case in court. They expressed dismay that Grout had contracted with individuals instead of the town as a whole, but they honored the bargain in the breach and sought to appease Grout by doubling the size of the tract. Matthew Rice made no pretense of gaining prior license, but instead ingratiated himself to the Indians and pursuaded them to argue for legal confirmation of the balance of land that had reverted to Indian possession from the lawsuit.[94] This was not the first time Rice ignored the licensing provision; in 1683 he entered a deed for 208 acres from Waban, John Magus, and Thomas Waban that he had obtained in April 1681.[95]

English officials enforced the Indian land policy selectively in these intertwined negotiations. Grout obtained prior consent from the General Court; Rice did not. The General Court compromised the prior consent provisions, but apparently did so at the request of the Indians. Even though John Eliot registered his dismay about the arrangement, colonial officials sanctioned the resolution.

Grout and Rice employed different strategies in gaining access to Natick lands. Grout approached individuals; his technique must have been one factor in the development of a corporate protection policy by Indians. His fraudulent engrossment provided a wedge for Rice to enter the scene. Pleading dire need arising out of epidemic illness, the Indians decided to sell to Rice instead of retaining the lands Grout had laid out to himself. Rice, who was prepared to pay, must have seemed preferable to Grout, who had already tried to swindle them. But if the Indians entertained any illusions about the fairness of Rice, they had been shattered by May of 1700. Rice was just one of several English settlers charged with engrossing Natick land in that year. He was singled out as particularly blatant in his trespass and bold in his flouting of Indian rights: "Some of us have discursed with him about it he sayd wee are poore creatures and have noe money & if you goe to law & I cast you you must goe to prison & there Lye & rott."[96] Rice did not hesitate to use intimidation and threats to forestall Indians from using the English protections available to them. Other aggressive English neighbors no doubt shared his mentality.

Not all English efforts to obtain Indian land succeeded. In 1702 Isaac Rice and Hopestill Bent of Sudbury tried to acquire 1,000 acres of Natick land plus nine acres of meadow bordering on some small parcels of land they already owned. Thomas Waban, town clerk of Natick, endorsed the petition, which described a struggling community: "several of the Indians of the Sd Plantation

---

[94] The deed he registered actually was for only 300 acres. MCG 10:647, 1685/1686.
[95] MCG 11:178, 1681/1693.
[96] Though a committee was appointed to investigate the charges of the Indians, no record of its conclusions is extant. MA 30:457, 1700.

of Natick are lately gone to Sea, having left their wives and many Small children in a very poor and needy condition, who cannot Subsist without some relief."[97] The land bordered on English-owned land and was not under improvement by the Indians. The committee appointed to investigate the proposed land sale recommended that it be prevented, "not findeing that the Indians are Under a prsent Necessitie to make sale of their land." The General Court barred the transaction.[98]

The most dramatic land grab within Natick involved Samuel Gookin Jr. of Cambridge and Samuel How of Sudbury. Gookin and How appeared in Natick through one of several arrangements that involved exchanging Natick lands for the erection of public works designed to benefit the community as a whole. In 1682 five Natick Indians, described as proprietors of Whip Suffrage (Okommakamesit), granted to Samuel Gookin of Cambridge the right to construct a sawmill on any suitable run of water. In exchange for "a valuable sum of mony," Gookin gained the right to use up to three acres of land and as much pine timber as he needed in building the mill. The bargain took the form of a thirty-year lease, and directed Gookin to protect the Indian interest in timber and land from trespass for the duration of the agreement. The General Court allowed the transaction because it tended to promote the public good; the order directed that the sawmill be operated as a public utility for both Indians and the English.[99]

At exactly the same time, Gookin and How gained a deed, apparently without prior license but endorsed by "the principall men of Natick," that conveyed to them 200 acres "of Remote and waste land . . . lying at the utmost westerly bounds of Naticke." Stoughton and Dudley recommended that the deed be confirmed, since "having Inquired into the matter wee conceive it will be no prejudice or Inconvenience to the Indians or their plantation."[100] This tract, described as being mostly encompassed by English lands, was confirmed to them by the General Court.[101]

In May of 1694 Thomas Sawin of Sherborn, son-in-law of Matthew Rice, complained that Gookin and How had "by fraudulent carriage" engrossed eight-and-a-half times as much land as was actually allowed in the 1682 transactions. A surveyor's plat showed that they had extended the 200-acre tract to encompass nearly 1,700 acres. Gookin and How had proceeded to sell about 1,200 acres of this land to "sundry persons" in the intervening twelve years, including 300 acres to Samuel How's son. Sawin explained that the Indians

> have been for these [diverse] yeares past much disquieted there-
> about & continually complaining of ye wrong done them thereby by

[97] MA 30:487b, 1702.
[98] MA 30:487c, 1702; AR 7:348, Appen. 2, Chap. 31, 17 Oct. 1702; and AR 7:352, Appen. 2, Chap. 44, 3 Nov. 1702.
[99] MA 30:267, 1682. Acceptance of the agreement was based on the recommendation of Stoughton and Dudley. Shurtleff, *Mass. Records*, 5:355, 27 May 1682.
[100] MA 30:271, 1682.   [101] Shurtleff, *Mass. Records*, 5:355, 27 May 1682.

ye abovesd partners and to ye great griefe of many English in ye adjoyning Townes who look upon such dealings as highly injurious and most Abhorrent, Especially at such a time when God is contesting with us by ye heathen.[102]

Acting under power of attorney from the Indians, Sawin argued that the Indians should be protected as "wards of the Honrd Court." In making the case against the encroachments of Gookin and How, Sawin recited the essence of the Indian land policy: "ye Indians . . . [are] no wise enabled to make sale of any lands untill qualified thereunto by your Honors in the first place . . . that such colourable pretences may not avalye to ye irregular deprivin Natives of yr just rights &c."[103] According to Sawin, the Indians were unwilling to have settlers on the engrossed land removed from their improvements, but wanted to be compensated for the land that was fraudulently obtained. He proposed that a committee of "discreet persons of Sudbury & Sherborn" be selected to determine the value of the land before it had been improved, and that the unsold portion revert back to Natick.[104]

The General Court summoned Gookin and How to respond to the complaint and ordered a committee to survey the land in question.[105] In 1697 the court extended legal confirmation of the 1,700 acres to Gookin and How and their "tenants," one of whom was Matthew Rice.[106] In turn, the court allowed the Indians 1,000 acres adjoining Sherborn.[107] Even though the land may have been different in value, and in spite of the court's favorable ruling, the Indians lost approximately 500 acres in this contested transaction.

Thomas Sawin had arrived in Natick three years after the Gookin and How transactions, also as a contractor for a public work. In 1685 Natick inhabitants petitioned for license to grant Sawin a tract of land not to exceed fifty acres in exchange for Sawin erecting a corn mill: "haveing noe Corn mil near us . . . [we] are forced to goe with much difficulty to have our Corn Ground, Some time to Watertown, and Sometime to Medfield or Sudbury, or Sometime by Reason of floods or great snows we cannot go to either of the mills round us."[108] The Indians added that Sherborn had no mill, and had no "stream Convenient to Set a mil on."[109] The General Court allowed the arrangement without further investigation.[110]

---

[102] MA 30:361, 1694.   [103] Ibid.
[104] Ibid.   [105] Ibid.
[106] These included John Bent (MCG 12:327, 1683/1699, 60 acres); John Adams (MCG 17:437, 1683/1715, 200 acres); David Rice (MCG 13:701, 1683/1705, 60 acres); Thomas Pratt (MCG 10:275, 1685/1693/4, 30 acres); Thomas Walker (MCG 5:91, 1688/1691/2, 60 acres); Thomas Drury (MCG 13:704, 1688/1705, 50 acres); John How (MCG 17:437, 1688/1689, 200 acres); Thomas Rice (MCG 15:24, 1688/1709, 300 acres); John Pratt (MCG 12:58, 1694/1697, 50 acres); David Stone (MCG 8:411, 1683/1683, 200 acres); and Matthew Rice (MCG 10:338, 1694/1694/5, acreage unknown).
[107] MA 30:361, 1694.   [108] MA 30:307a, 1685.
[109] Ibid.   [110] Ibid.; and Shurtleff, *Mass. Records*, 5:510–1, 16 Feb. 1685–6.

The only land transactions the Indian community as a whole willingly participated in during the last quarter of the seventeenth century involved reciprocal arrangements. Sawin received land in exchange for a corn mill; Gookin and How, laying aside their fraudulent behavior (which should have called into question the magistrates' wisdom in designating Gookin to protect the Indians' timber and land from trespass), erected a sawmill. The town also acquired a new meetinghouse through a reciprocal arrangement. In 1699 nineteen Indian men endorsed a petition asking for permission to grant "a small nook of our plantation containing about 200 acres" to John Collar Jr., a carpenter. They described a fragmented community still committed to religion:

> [Because of] the death of many and removall of [others], who during the time of the late wars have been Sojourning among the English for their support, and are not yet returned to their plantation, we are now greatly deminished & impovereshed. [Our] meeting-house where wee were wont constantly to meet Sabath days and lecture days to worship God is fallen down and we are not able to build us another.[111]

The General Court extended approval for this transaction in 1705.[112]

These corporate transactions served community needs. Another English family received a corporate land grant for very different reasons, though the transaction was also governed by notions of reciprocity. In 1695 a committee of Indians petitioned for the confirmation of a tract of land conveyed to Thomas Eames at an Indian court held at Nonantum in 1676.[113] Eames's family had been attacked during King Philip's War after several Magunkaquog Indians discovered that corn they had stored there had been pilfered. In retaliation, the Indians burned Eames's farm while he was away, killing or capturing his family.[114] After the war, Eames settled on Natick land near Sherborn along with three of his children who had escaped captivity. Eames had died by 1695 and had never obtained a legal conveyance of this land. The Indian committee asked that they be confirmed to his son, John Eames, in exchange for twenty-two pounds. In explaining their reasons for selling this tract, the Indian petition cited

> the great suffering of ye sd Thomas Eames by those Indians that burnt his house barn and Cattle and killed his wife and three children and Captivated five more, thereof only three returned who are now dwelling on ye said Lands whom now to ruin a second Time by turning them off these Lands we are not willing to be any occasion thereof.[115]

[111] MA 30:503, 1699, punctuation added.
[112] MA 30:502, 1702; and AR 8:117, Appen. 3, Chap. 1, 6 June 1705.
[113] MA 30:366, 1695.   [114] MA 30:211, 1676.
[115] MA 30:366, 1695.

The petition also mentioned relief given by Eames to John Awassamug, a "Chiefe proprietor" of the land in question. Confirmation of the land to Eames finally passed both houses of the General Court in 1702.[116]

The transaction to the Eames family was embedded in relations between them and the Indians. Even though Natick Indians disavowed responsibility for the attack on Eames's family, they were willing to indemnify them for their losses.[117] Granted, the settlement occurred under the duress of a lawsuit. But the petitions also indicate that the parties engaged in a reciprocal relationship. The Indians allowed the Eames family to remain on lands that belonged to the community for more than twenty years without legal conveyance. During this time, Eames supported an impoverished Indian who was an heir to land in that vicinity according to Native custom. These informal arrangements persisted for an extended period of time, and represented a kind of reconciliation that reflected new realities. Natick Indians and the Eames families had come to an understanding that moved beyond the events of the war.

H. *"Friend Indians" defined*

English hostility toward Indians in the aftermath of King Philip's War undermined commitment to the missionary enterprise. The conflict shattered John Eliot's vision of expansive conversion, "haveing greatly vitiated the spirits of our youth both English & Indians."[118] Eliot continued regular visits to Natick, assisted by a servant in his old age, with virtually no support or attention except from the missionary society.[119] Arranging for a reprinting of the Indian Bible consumed most of his energy.[120] Only Daniel Gookin Jr., minister at Sherborn, expressed any interest in Praying Indians by lecturing at Natick once a month to English and Indian listeners. In 1684 sixteen Natick men wrote to John Eliot asking that Gookin be encouraged and supported financially, since their "great poverty especially since the wars" rendered them unable to do so themselves. They noted that they learned some English through the monthly lectures, and that attending services with Sherborn residents tended "to promote not only

---

[116] This complicated transaction was enmeshed in a large-scale land exchange between the towns of Sherborn and Natick, which is discussed elsewhere in this chapter. MA 30:484, 1701; and AR 7:25, Appen. 2, Chap. 86, 25 Feb. 1702.

[117] Three Indians were executed for this attack. William Barry, *A History of Framingham, Massachusetts* (Boston: James Munroe & Co., 1847), 29.

[118] Thomas Danforth et al. to Hon. Robert Boyle, 26 Dec. 1679, in *Some Correspondence Between the Governors and Treasurers of the New England Company in London and the Commissioners of the United Colonies in America, The Missionaries of the Company, and Others Between the Years 1657 and 1712*, ed. J. W. Ford (London: Spottiswoode & Co., 1896), 59.

[119] William Stoughton et. al. to Hon. Robert Boyle, 29 May 1682, Ibid., 59.

[120] A second edition was published in 1685. William Stoughton, et. al., to Hon. Robert Boyle, 1 Mar. 1683/4, Ibid., 72; Eliot to Boyle, 15 Mar. 1682/3, *MHSC*, lst ser., 3 (1794): 181; 21 June 1683, Ibid., 182; and 27 Nov. 1683, Ibid., 182.

Religion but Civility amongst us."[121] Natick Indians looked to ministerial guidance from within their own ranks as well. Daniel Takawampbait served as the Natick pastor from at least 1683, and he continued in that role until his death in 1716.[122]

Eliot's death in 1690 set back the missionary effort further. Increase Mather reported in 1697 that since then "there has bin a signal blast of heaven on ye Indian work, very many of the most pious Indians (both professors & preachers) being dead also, & others of equal worth not appearing to succeed them."[123] Grindall Rawson and Samuel Danforth visited the plantation in 1698 and reported only ten church members, seven men and three women, out of 110 adults and 70 children under the age of sixteen who were living there.[124]

The position of Indians in the aftermath of King Philip's War had less to do with missionary imperatives than it did with a series of negotiations that defined a limited place for "friend Indians" in the colonial society. The English, operating from a position of insurmountable power, dominated the process of definition. But "friend Indians" compelled English authorities to acknowledge their rights to different treatment from Indians outside the parameters of colonial society.

For the English, the category friend Indians was occupied by those Indians who had acted as military allies during King Philip's War. But there was more to the category than that. Friend Indians were those Indians who at least espoused English Calvinism and English lifeways, and who recognized the primacy of English governance. Friend Indians were those who could be thought of as bounded, settled, and controlled.

Defining a position for friend Indians in the last quarter of the seventeenth century had much to do with the English rationalizing their colonial regime, especially with bounding the land according to their own expectations about the legal status of landownership.[125] But in entrenching the colonial society, English authorities felt compelled to acknowledge the existence of Native peoples whose wartime behaviors entitled them to different treatment from other Indians. Setting friend Indians apart involved residency restrictions, which defined physical spaces for friend Indians. Magistrates acted to control Indian movements during times of military conflict, which heightened the ambiguous position of Indian allies. But the wording of legislation attests to the extensive permeability of physical and social boundaries that normally elicited little

---

[121] Sixteen Natick Indians to John Eliot, 19 Mar. 1683, in Ford, *Some Correspondence*, 74–6.

[122] MA 30:276, 1683; and Thomas W. Baldwin, comp., *Vital Records of Natick, Massachusetts to the Year 1850* (Boston: Stanhope Press, 1910). A day book reprinted in *NEHGR* 8 (1854): 19, cites 29 July 1683 as Takawampbait's ordination date.

[123] Increase Mather to William Ashhurst, 20 Jan. 1697, in Ford, *Some Correspondence*, 81.

[124] Grindall Rawson and Samuel Danforth, "Account of an Indian Visitation A. D. 1698," *MHSC*, 1st ser., 10 (1809): 129–34.

[125] William Cronon, *Changes in the Land: Indians, Colonists, and the Ecology of New England* (New York: Hill and Wang, 1983), 54–81.

comment, including the extensive participation of Indians in hunting, wage and indentured labor, and public events such as market days and military training days. Intensive supervision of friend Indians was impractical in any event, particularly in a society that lacked institutional mechanisms for such control.[126]

In exchange for their participation as allies in King Philip's War and their ostensible acceptance of English institutions and certain behavioral proscriptions, the English recognized obligations to friend Indians. English magistrates moved to regulate the indenturing of Indian servants after hearing vociferous complaints from Indians who were victimized by English settlers in search of laborers. Concerns about "good title" to land preoccupied English authorities even more. By regulating transactions between Indians and the English, magistrates erected a slender structure to forestall rampant fraudulent dispossession of friend Indians, and acknowledged a moral obligation to protect rightful Indian ownership of land. But the legal system they developed served mostly to rationalize massive dispossession and bar English individuals from land encroachments to the exclusion of the colony. Large-scale land acquisition, sanctioned by the General Court and managed by high-status individuals such as Dudley and Stoughton, further reduced the territory Natick Indians could claim as their own. The English may not have allowed them to "loose their lives," but their lands were another matter.[127]

For Indians, their position as friends entitled them to make claims to special treatment within the colonial relationship. Having acted as allies, Indians demanded acknowledgment of their rightful ownership of vast territories within the colony and compensation for their dispossession. They merged Native notions of landownership with English political and legal protections sparingly extended to them to defend their rights. In compacting with English authorities to cede their ownership of the Nipmuck Country, Indians acknowledged the overwhelming power of the colonial regime. They recognized that only modest compensation remained feasible in making things "Clear [i]n after time Between us and our Posterity, & the English and yr posterrity."[128] But on the local level, they used the English political and legal system, as well as corporate agreement among themselves, to protect Natick lands. Nonetheless, some English individuals from towns bordering Natick used an array of devices to enrich themselves on Indian lands. Though still only minimally breached in 1700, to Indians, Natick must have seemed surrounded.

---

[126] Brenner makes the point that Indians in Praying Towns used the towns as "an open, geographically unbounded system, allowing the towns to resist total political domination." Elise M. Brenner, "Strategies for Autonomy: An Analysis of Ethnic Mobilization in Seventeenth-Century Southern New England" (Ph.D. diss., University of Massachusetts, 1984), 252–4. The quotation is from page 253.

[127] Shurtleff, *Mass. Records*, 5:165, 12 Oct. 1677.

[128] MA 30:257, 1681.

Magistrates heard, investigated, and settled Indian complaints about land improprieties. Some attempts at enforcing restrictions against purchasing land without prior approval resulted in the nullification of transactions, but in most cases officials dictated a settlement. Magistrates did not grant petitions for land sales as a foregone conclusion. Nevertheless, land complaints were reviewed on a case-by-case basis, and, in practice, judgments were rendered according to invisible criteria that makes land regulation seem irregular. In most cases Indians suffered a net loss in acreage in the disputes.

Friend Indians faced severe challenges in the postwar period. Officially sanctioned dispossession surpassed the impact of small-scale land engrossment by aggressive English neighbors. Tempted or manipulated, Indians such as Thomas Waban and John Wampus sometimes served as agents for English encroachment. Partial reliance on wage and indentured labor outside of the town, seafaring, and military service fragmented the community and left women and children alone. Mohawk raids besieged them into the 1680s. But despite the challenges, friend Indians, and Natick itself, endured.

4

Divided in their desires, 1700–40

> It is very sure, the best thing we can do for our Indians is to Anglicise them
> in all agreeable Instances; and in that of Language, as well as others. They
> can scarce retain their Language, without a Tincture of other Salvage Incli-
> nations, which do but ill suit, either with the Honor, or with the design of
> Christianity. The Indians themselves are Divided in the Desires upon this
> matter. Though some of their aged men are tenacious enough of Indianisme
> (which is not at all to be wondered at) Others of them as earnestly wish that
> their people may be made English as fast as they can.[1]

A. *Cultures in dialogue*

In his 1710 characterization of Praying Indians as "Divided in the[ir] Desires"
over culture change, New England Company official Samuel Sewall captured an
important dynamic of community life in early eighteenth-century Natick. Indians drew upon both Indian and English cultural practices in shaping their community, as they had from the beginning. Though Sewall emphasized language
as a central point of contention, which it surely was, cultural debates involved a
full range of social institutions in the community. But it was the outcome of
cultural negotiations about land, in particular, which stemmed from the Indians' divided desires, that both magnified crucial divisions within the Indian
community, and created the fault lines that eventually eroded Indian autonomy
by facilitating English landownership in Natick.

Between 1715 and 1720, Indians altered a land system that at the beginning
of the century involved the community acting as a whole to assign land rights
broadly to its members using a relatively flexible method that drew upon Indian usufruct principles, and also some English ideas about land measurement
and usage. An English proprietary system was implemented in the community
that individualized land distribution and ownership according to English
notions, and restricted landownership as well as future rights to land to an
exclusive core of Indians. This transformation institutionalized a mechanism
for reifying the divided desires Indians held about cultural practices around
land into social and economic divisions, and jeopardized exclusive Indian
landownership in the community by rendering it more easily transferred
through the workings of the market economy. The new proprietary system
entirely excluded some Indians from landownership, rendered a fluid system
rigid, and created places for English surveyors, clerks, and overseers to become

---

[1] Samuel Sewell, "Letter Book of Samuel Sewell," *Collections of the Massachusetts Historical
Society* (hereafter cited as *MHSC*), 6th ser., 1 (1886): 401.

involved in the community's internal affairs. It laid the groundwork for the development of a market in Natick land during a time of overcrowding and land scarcity in eastern Massachusetts English towns.[2] The abandonment of corporate protections for Indian landownership, along with the arrival of an English minister in 1721 and Indian willingness to allow English participation in local governance, attracted English residents to the community and jeopardized Indian control over Natick.

After 1720, a complicated system of land transfer that built upon proprietary bureaucratization emerged in the community. Those Indians who were accorded exclusive rights to future land divisions as proprietors drew upon their land privileges to different degrees, more evidence of their divided desires, and transferred real estate to Indian and English purchasers using the proprietary system. Indians also used the English deed registration system to transfer land to other Indians, and they sold land to English purchasers under the supervision of the commonwealth. A land market involving English buyers and sellers also began to emerge, reflecting Indian land loss from the seventeenth century as well as the ongoing transfer in property from Indian owner to English purchaser and the presence of land-short Englishmen with ready cash. In the 1730s debt began to plague some Indians, who turned to the land market for capital in a dramatic shift from Indian to English ways of using and valuing land. But even though some Indians had begun to treat land as a market commodity, land transfers within the Indian community still outstripped other kinds of transactions through the 1730s. Because of the dramatic transformation of the land distribution system, even though Natick remained an unmistakably Indian place in 1740, the social and institutional groundwork had been laid for Indian dispossession that would play out in excruciatingly gradual fashion from the middle through the latter decades of the eighteenth century.

Other institutions and practices also evidenced cultural tensions. Into the early decades of the eighteenth century, Natick Indians continued to use the Massachusett language; acquisition of literacy (for some) resulted in the recording of community actions in both Massachusett and English. Despite widespread adoption of English names, many Indians continued to observe Native naming practices; still others refused either to abandon Native custom or to use English ways exclusively, instead using both Indian and English names. And the governance system, while it came to resemble more closely political institutions

---

[2] See, for example, Kenneth Lockridge, *A New England Town: The First Hundred Years* (New York: Norton, 1970); Philip J. Greven Jr., *Four Generations: Population, Land, and Family in Colonial Andover, Massachusetts* (Ithaca: Cornell University Press, 1970); Douglas Lamar Jones, *Village and Seaport: Migration and Society in Eighteenth-Century Massachusetts* (Hanover, NH: University Press of New England, 1981); and Douglas R. McManis, *Colonial New England: A Historical Geography* (New York: Oxford University Press, 1975).

found in English communities, still bore its own unique character which preserved Indian autonomy to a degree. While acceding to be governed within the
broad but somewhat distant parameters of commonwealth law, Indians nonetheless chose their own local officials. In sum, Indians were "divided in their
desires," but not as sharply as Sewall put it when he described a split between
some who were "tenacious enough of Indianisme" and others who "earnestly
wish that their people may be made English." Indians held these two cultures in
tension, participating in the transformation of Native practices without categorically embracing English ways. The identity of Natick as an Indian place was
negotiated and asserted as Indian through these practices.

The tension between "Indianisme" and Anglicization glimpsed by Samuel
Sewall in the first decade of the eighteenth century found expression in material
culture and economic strategies as well as language and other "agreeable
instances." Thus, differing Indian attitudes about Indian and English cultural
practices as well as the institutionalization of different kinds of privileges with
regard to land also created divisions within the Indian community. Sewall
implied that different perspectives on culture change did not break down along
generational lines, as they often did in Indian communities. Some individuals
used their land to raise capital for building English-style farms, incorporating
animal husbandry and erecting frame houses and barns. Still others avoided
involvement in the land market and eschewed their right to draw upon their
proprietary privileges to expand their own landownership. The replacement of
wigwams in favor of English-style houses and barns, beginning in the 1720s or
earlier, was motivated for some by "a great desire to Live more like my Christian English neighbours," and probably for others by the difficulty in "getting
materials any where near us, wherewith to build Wigwams."[3]

The cultural transformations in the first four decades of the eighteenth century provide a graphic illustration of how a minority community in a colonial
relationship must be culturally "bilingual," whereas the group that has
achieved a position of dominance no longer needs to struggle for cultural
understanding.[4] In the cultural dialogue of early eighteenth-century Natick,
Indian voices communicated diverse choices with regard to the tension between
"Indianisme" and Anglicization. But given the colonial relations of power and
their ideas about race that can be read in struggles over land and social institutions that were increasingly differentiated within the community, the English
who became involved in Natick could be culturally monolingual, and refuse to
accord full validity to Indian cultural differences.

---

[3] Massachusetts Archives (hereafter cited as MA), Massachusetts State Archives at Columbia Point, Boston, 31:135, 1726.
[4] See also James H. Merrell, "'The Customes of Our Countrey': Indians and Colonists in
Early America," in *Strangers within the Realm: Cultural Margins of the First British Empire*,
ed. Bernard Bailyn and Philip D. Morgan (Chapel Hill: University of North Carolina
Press, 1991), 117–56.

B. *Language and literacy*

Tensions surrounding language and literacy illustrate the reconfiguration of Indian identity in early eighteenth-century Natick and the diverse choices made by Indian individuals with regard to cultural practices. According to Samuel Sewall, "such . . . [Indians] as can speak English, find themselves vastly accomodated for the entertaining and communicating of knowledge, beyond what they were before." Sewall's concerns revolved around what little remained of the English proseltizing impulse, especially the problem of how effectively the Eliot Bible disclosed the religious content of Christianity.[5] Sewall had been informed that Indians grieved over the Eliot Bible's shortcomings, which apparently involved problems of dialect and imprecision. He cited an observation that "there seems to be [as] much difficulty to bring them unto a competent knowledge of the Scriptures, as it would be to get a sensible acquaintance with the English Tongue."[6] Yet the Massachusett religious texts, though intended to Anglicize Indians in the matter of religion, also reinforced the use of the Massachusett language. These texts helped preserve the use of the language at least into the late eighteenth century, especially in Mashpee, on the island of Nantucket, and at Gay Head on Martha's Vineyard, although by 1729, no Natick Indians could read in Massachusett.[7]

Mixed use of Massachusett and English is also evident in Natick naming practices. Since the beginning of English colonization, Indians throughout New England had blended English and Indian naming conventions. Into the early eighteenth century, some Natick Indians continued to use two names: one Massachusett and one English. Capt. Thomas Waban, the most prominent writer of Massachusett and English in Natick, also used his Indian

5 Sewell, "Letter Book," 401. The New England Company, sponsor of missionary activities, continued to provide oversight and financial support to Natick and other Indian communities until 1786. Expenditures to English neighbors for services, provisions, implements, books, as well as salaries for Indian "rulers," "justices," and schoolmasters, were regularly made. The company, which envisioned Christianity and "Civility" as inextricably linked, also sanctioned placing Indian children in English homes to learn trades. Ledger of Commissioners of the New England Company, 1708–19, Samuel Sewall Collection, Massachusetts Historical Society, Boston, MA (hereafter cited as New England Company Ledger); Frederick Weis, "The New England Company of 1649 and its Missionary Enterprises," *Publications of the Colonial Society of Massachusetts* 38 (1947–51): 134–218; and Kellaway, *New England Company.*
6 Sewall, "Letter Book," 401.
7 Ives Goddard and Kathleen J. Bragdon, *Native Writings in Massachusett*, 2 vols. (Philadelphia: American Philosophical Society, 1988), 1:11. This indispensable source translates all known surviving Massachusett writings by Indians. Included are a grammatical treatment and an overview of the uses of Native literacy in Massachusett. A 1729 survey found that none of fifty Natick families could read in Massachusett, and only thirteen, former servants to English families, could read and write in English. Kathleen Bragdon, "'Another Tongue Brought In': An Ethnohistorical Study of Native Writings in Massachusett" (Ph.D. diss., Brown University, 1981), 56. Rates of bilingualism remain unknown. Ibid., 77–8.

name, Weegramomenit. Dual name usage included women and men, such as Susannah Ephraim (Muttassonshq), and John Thomas Sr. (Naamishcow).[8]

Changing naming practices did not represent a rejection of Indian identity, but a blending of English and Massachusett signifiers. Indians used several methods when altering names to reflect more typically English usage. Some families inscribed a distinctly Indian signifier upon themselves and their progeny instead of borrowing English names wholesale, by using an aboriginal name as a surname, such as the Wabans, the Awassamugs, and the Wamsquans. Then they passed surnames down, patrilineally, in English fashion.[9] This had been the case for some families since the founding of Natick. Others used shortened versions of a Native name, including the Peeguns (Unqunpeegun), Comechos (Sokomecho), and Paugenits (Kenepaugenit).[10] Still others adopted an English surname, often choosing names usually thought of as Christian names, such as Ephraim, Abraham, and Thomas. Territorial associations may account for some surnames, such as the Rumneymarsh family, which had ties to the Pawtucket region and English town of that name. Some Massachusett surnames may have indicated clan associations, as is likely in the case of Kenepaugenit (codfish). Indians had begun to change their names in the seventeenth century, and this practice continued into the early eighteenth century. For example, sometime before 1719 John Takichape became known as John George.[11]

Some shifts in naming practices among Natick residents marked a radical departure from Native usage. Native customs included taboos against uttering the name of a deceased person out of fear that the individual would be summoned from the otherworld.[12] But at least by the eighteenth century, some Natick Indians gave their exact names to children and distinguished themselves with the suffixes junior and senior. For example, there were at least four Thomas Wabans. Marriages led to the replication of other Natick names.

[8] Bragdon, "'Another Tongue Brought In,'" 73. Bragdon, citing Experience Mayhew's observation that the use of different names depended mainly on whether the context was Indian or English. Weegramomenit: Bragdon, "'Another Tongue Brought In,'" 73; Muttassonshq: Goddard and Bragdon, *Native Writings*, 1:273, (1720); and Naasmischow: Ibid., 2:768.

[9] Bragdon offers a good discussion of changes in naming practices, as well as an analysis of linguistic change as a reflection of cultural change. Much of this paragraph is based on that work. Bragdon, "'Another Tongue Brought In,'" 72–4.

[10] Unqunpeegun: Goddard and Bragdon, *Native Writings*, 2:764; and Kenepaugenit: Middlesex County Court, Probate Records (hereafter cited as MCP), Cambridge, MA, #13133, Eleazar Paugenit, Admin., 1741.

[11] Land Grants to Proprietors, Freeholders, and Inhabitants of the Town of Natick, 1719 (hereafter cited as NPB1), Morse Institute Public Library, Natick, MA.

[12] See, for example, Edward Winslow, "The Glorious Progress of the Gospel amongst the Indians in New England," *MHSC*, 3d ser., 4 (1834): 80; Roger Williams, *A Key into the Language of America*, ed. John J. Teunissen and Evelyn J. Hinz (Detroit: Wayne State University Press, 1973); and William Scranton Simmons, *Cautantowwit's House: An Indian Burial Ground on the Island of Conanicut in Narragansett Bay* (Providence: Brown University Press, 1970), 58–60.

According to customary practice, these names should have been changed when one of them died; it seems that rarely occurred. In sum, the broad range of choices made by Natick Indians with regard to naming displayed both dramatic transformation and cultural bilingualism.

At the beginning of the eighteenth century, at least some Natick Indians could speak and write in both languages. The Indian scribe who kept records for the town, Capt. Thomas Waban, was bilingual.[13] The extent to which Massachusett remained in use is evident in his writings in English. His phonetic spelling in some instances indicates Algonquian pronunciation: "Tark" is used instead of "dark," "Bromised" instead of "promised," and "pushill" instead of "bushel."[14]

Part of the value of literacy lay in providing a better understanding of the English colonial society, and bilingualism in particular could help protect Indian interests. But also, as Kathleen Bragdon has argued, persistence of the Native language with the addition of literacy can be seen as "a source of community strength which helped to preserve their distinctiveness as Indians." She argued that these skills were adjusted to meet Native needs and concepts, coexisted with but did not replace conventional forms of communication, and became a source of cohesion. She identified the home, and interaction with other Native communities as arenas for retention of Massachusett until about 1750.[15]

Bilingualism offers an important commentary on colonial relationships. The use of Massachusett in addressing community affairs may have been simply a natural way of communicating about transactions within the town, but at the same time, it made a statement about whose place Natick was. In choosing Massachusett, Indians defined their personal and physical boundaries and engaged in a process of self-affirmation. And in writing about land, in particular, in Massachusett, Indians may have sought to protect their interests from

[13] There is some confusion over his identity. There were at least three Thomas Wabans in Natick at this time. Goddard and Bragdon concluded that Capt. Thomas Waban was the eldest son of Waban, Eliot's first convert, and that he died in 1727, but his death is recorded as occurring in 1722. Thomas W. Baldwin, comp., *Vital Records of Natick, Massachusetts to the Year 1850* (hereafter cited as *NVR*) (Boston: Stanhope Press, 1910). On Thomas Waban, see also Daniel Mandell, "'Standing by His Father': Thomas Waban of Natick, circa 1650–1722," in *Northeastern Indian Lives 1632–1816*, ed. Robert S. Grumet (Amherst: University of Massachusetts Press, 1996), 166–92. Bragdon discussed the connection between bilingualism and the occupation of positions of importance in her dissertation, citing the example of Indian Minister John Neesnumin. Bragdon, "'Another Tongue Brought In,'" 60. Capt. Thomas Waban seems to be an even more forceful example.

[14] Original Indian Record Book (hereafter cited as OIRB), Morse Institute Public Library, Natick, MA, 22 June 1704.

[15] Bragdon, "'Another Tongue Brought In,'" 64 and 78. The quote is from p. 64. Bragdon estimated that 30 percent of Natick Indians were literate in 1720, and 20 percent in 1750 and 1770, based on "descriptions of contemporaries, signatures, and surviving writings." Bragdon, Ibid., 55. See also Bragdon, "'Emphaticall Speech and Great Action': An Analysis of Seventeenth-Century Native Speech Events Described in Early Sources," *Man in the Northeast* 33 (1987): 101–11.

English outsiders by casting Native actions into an English (written) form. They may have hoped that by using their Native language in conjunction with the English practice of writing, they could both reaffirm their Indianness and defend their lands against English encroachment. This constituted an important signal about power: English colonists no longer needed to learn Indian languages to communicate with Indians in Natick, and they certainly did not need literacy in Massachusett to safeguard their possessions.

Indians used literacy in strategic ways that demonstrate their cultural bilingualism and resistance. Documents recorded exclusively in Massachusett pertained to affairs internal to the town, where Indian autonomy could flourish: land arrangements prior to 1719, fines for nonattendance at the town meeting, settlement of an internal dispute, and some of the town elections.[16] Those recorded exclusively in English, on the other hand, related to affairs that in some way concerned English neighbors: settlement of boundaries, keeping track of livestock captured in Natick belonging to English neighbors, and the corporate sale of the former Praying Town Magunkaquog. By using English to make records of these social transactions, Indians could defend themselves against the possibility the English would creatively interpret these interactions. Town elections were recorded in either English or Massachusett, and sometimes in both. Though they regulated internal affairs, officials also dealt with problems involving English towns. For example, a 1715 ordinance against selling wood to the English, recorded in both languages, also involved English outsiders and the community's concern about English usurpation of their resources. The town asserted collective ownership of trees, and declared that timber did not constitute an appropriate good for market transactions with English neighbors.[17]

C. Land between cultures

By 1700, the manner in which Indians managed their lands also held Indian and English elements in tension, particularly in terms of the concepts of land use, property description, and entitlement. Community members participated in decision making about landownership, and recognized corporate actions as authoritative. They recorded land actions in the Massachusett language, occasionally using English loan words for untranslatable concepts that stemmed from different notions of time and space.[18] Here, the land itself became a

[16] Town records in Massachusett are translated in Goddard and Bragdon, *Native Writings*. Town records in English are in OIRB. Only fifty-two pages of the Original Indian Record Book survive, "a fraction of the original book." Ten leaves were recorded in Massachusett; the others are in English. These records are arranged in fairly chaotic form, and provide scattered information on town officers, proprietary divisions, and other official matters. Goddard and Bragdon, *Native Writings*, 1:272. The book begins with the heading "72 bages." Ibid., 1:271 (1720).

[17] Goddard and Bragdon, *Native Writings*, 1:277 (18 Apr. 1715); and OIRB, 18 Apr. 1715.

[18] Goddard and Bragdon, *Native Writings*, 1:17.

common language where cultures might otherwise have been untranslatable to each other.

Indians used Massachusett words to describe most features of the landscape: swamps, rivers, and brooks. Lands that came to be used in English ways, such as meadows and orchards, prompted the use of English loan words.[19] They differentiated at least seven separate meadows by attaching Massachusett names to the English word "meadow": "The same Wunneeteoommak meadow. At the property of Samuell Apraim, from the north over (?) to the end to the northwest, that is the property of the one named David Ummoonehmun."[20] Indians expressed directions, "property," and "boundary" in Massachusett. Dates and English units of measurement (acres and rods) appeared in English, reflecting different notions of time and space.

Grants inscribed exclusive ownership on parcels of land using natural and altered markers of boundaries rather than carving land into squares and rectangles:

> to the north from that little path that goes to the orchard of
> Thomas Waban, Senior, from that brook, near that path and maybe
> up to the swamp, maybe up to the spring out of which flows the
> brook, and as far as that same spring . . . this is the property of
> Solomon Thomas.[21]

Other landmarks by which to demarcate location included the old stone fort and the meetinghouse.[22] Grants do not appear to have been surveyed; their terse descriptions suggest they may have been used as mnemonic devices that evoked more complete memories.[23]

Property transactions attest to the fluidity of land arrangements sanctioned by the community. They suggest a conjunction between Native usufruct rights (land belongs to an individual, through group confirmation, only as long as it is being used) and English legal rights (land is an exclusive possession transferred through the operation of the market, sanctioned by bureaucracy). To Natick Indians, exclusive ownership did not necessarily mean perpetual ownership. Pre-1715 land grants by the town distinguished among at least three different terms of land tenure: perpetual, lifetime, and conditional.[24] The town granted Thomas Peegun two acres as his "property fo(r)ever."[25] Wunnuhkonnosk, on

---

[19] Ibid., 1:11.   [20] Ibid., 1:311 (n.d.).

[21] Ibid., 1:327 (n.d.).   [22] Ibid., 1:293 (1700); and 1:333 (n.d.).

[23] Bragdon, " 'Emphaticall Speech and Great Action,' " 107; and Goddard and Bragdon, *Native Writings*, 1:19, where Natick town records are characterized as "almost telegraphic in style with much relevant information clearly intended to be understood by the clerk and townspeople and hence not written down."

[24] Cf. Goddard and Bragdon, *Native Writings*, 1:14–15.

[25] Ibid., 1:313 (n.d.). Bragdon argued that land grants from sachems could be made for an individual's lifetime or could confer permanent possession that might be passed on to heirs. " 'Another Tongue Brought In,' " 106.

the other hand, received the use of two acres in 1702, "only as long as she (?) lives. When she (?) dies, then the land and the appletrees shall instead return to Peter Ehprai[m]."[26] One Natick Indian received a grant of two acres, "only as long as [he is] magistrate. That also goes away from him."[27]

These notions coexisted in Natick before 1719. For example, the town acted as a whole to confirm the legitimacy of needs expressed in requests for land. In 1700 Thomas Waban and John Wamsquan each asked for and received land grants for their sons; Isaac Wuttasukoopauin solicited and was given two acres of meadow for himself. The town also took actions to transfer use rights from one individual to another: "What John Thomas Sr. once had a little of, and now Eleazer Kanuppakinit has it: it has been given to him from this town." John Tauinmau lost the use of his meadow through town action; Peter Uppakata[__] had two acres reconfirmed to him in 1700: "he once had it before, but now it is properly his, at this time."[28] One agreement sanctioned a use arrangement between an Indian and an Englishman, and directed the future disposition of land:

> And now John Thomas, Senior, remaines where he is regarding that meadow, except only that he has lent a little of it to [Englishman] Jonathan Rice. But whenever that comes open, then it shall be the property of Isaac Wuttasukkooppauin. Then after that John Thomas, senior, shall have . . . from Wunnetomag [meadow] two acres.[29]

The fact that Indians regulated this land arrangement and recorded it in their own language attests to Indian power and control in Natick.

Land transactions, according to Natick practice, required public confirmation to be considered valid. The recorded transactions thus both attest to the communal nature of land oversight and offer evidence about Indian rules of land transfer that in many respects stand in contrast to English rules and practices. One entry acknowledged Eleazer Peegun's land sales to his brothers Thomas and Solomon, and confirmed their ownership of the properties. Another included the terms of a transaction. John Thomas Jr. owned a two-acre tract that he "sold . . . to the one named Eleacer Kanpaginit. And he now has that property for three pounds. Know this." Another sale transferred property from Englishman Thomas Mansfield to Indian Eleazer Peegun. Mansfield was the only English grantee of Natick land in the first two decades of the eighteenth century, receiving two acres in a gesture of reciprocity "because he always repairs the bridge."[30]

[26] Question marks are in the translation, indicating uncertainty. Goddard and Bragdon, *Native Writings*, 1:307 (before 1702).

[27] Ibid., 1:321 (n.d.).

[28] Waban, Wamsquan, and Wuttasukoopauin: Ibid., 1:321 (1700); Thomas and Kanuppakinit: Ibid., 1:323 (n.d.); Tauinmau: Ibid., 1:287 (1700); and Uppakata[__]: Ibid., 1:287 (1700).

[29] Ibid., 1:311 (1702).

[30] Peeguns: Ibid., 1:283 (n.d.); Thomas and Kanpaginit: Ibid., 1:321 (n.d.); Mansfield and Peegun: Ibid., 1:277 (1703); and Mansfield: Ibid., 1:277 (n.d.).

The act of recording brought together family history, descent of property, and community recognition in an identifiably Indian voice. Particular parcels of land became locations that evoked family relationships. The community sanctioned inheritance arrangements by committing them to public record, often recapitulating the histories of land transfers:

> Babokoothessik meadow. The one north and following along the river: that is the property of . . . Benjamen Wawobequnnont, about 4 acres. Before, it was once the property of Thoma[s] Tray. Then, when he died, afterwards Benjamen Wawobequnnont. Because he was his father's brother is why he has the estate. This was done. Know this about that 4 acres of mead[ow].[31]

Wawobequnnont's inheritance from his father's brother may have followed Native notions of family obligation, rewarded a favored nephew, or confirmed land from an uncle who left no surviving children. The complexity of some recorded land histories, which often detail several property transfers, suggests that oral agreements coexisted with written records and remained legitimate even when Indians started using writing.[32] The earlier system whereby a sachem, supported by the followers, controlled land distribution had been transformed to correlate with the townspeople acting jointly as a community.[33] This practice may have been established in the 1680s, when Indians adopted their corporate agreement against alienating land without community consent.[34] Unlike other Indian communities along Martha's Vineyard, Nantucket, and elsewhere, they ceased to use the term "sachem."[35]

Unlike the English, who denied married women a separate legal identity and subsumed women's property under the control of their husbands, Indian women in Natick could own land in their own right:

> Whatever John Swomp had first, . . . when he died then it was the property of the one named Hannah Speen, and then when she also died then on[ly?] after that that meadow was the property of the one named Abraham Speen, because she had been his wife . . . Then th[at] Abraham Speen afterwards, he turned it all over to his own son, the one named Isaac Speen, e[ver]y thing that he had. With witnesses.[36]

---

[31] Ibid., 1:287 (n.d.).

[32] Land histories may have been recorded prior to transferring property. Ibid., 1:14–15. Goddard and Bragdon argued that the practice of bequeathing property emerged in the late seventeenth and early eighteenth century, and that specific families "gradually became associated with specific plots." Ibid., 1:18.

[33] Bragdon, "'Another Tongue Brought In,'" 113.   [34] See Chapter 3.

[35] See, for example, Goddard and Bragdon, *Native Writings*, 1:6, 1:10, 1:131 (1700), 1:135 (1701), 1:213 (1719), 1:153 (1735), and 1:223 (1756).

[36] Ibid., 1:281 (1718 or after).

John Swomp may have been Hannah Speen's father, brother, or a previous husband. But however she gained this parcel, the community affirmed her exclusive ownership despite her marital status. The land became her husband's property only after she died, and he passed it down to his son although the reasons for this dispensation are not clear.

Two other women received land from the division of a single estate:

> This is the judgment on August 18, 1703, concerning what was bequeathed by Jonas Muttahanit here in Natick. And now Esther, who is a widow there, only has two acres of meadow and also that one orchard that lies on the south side of the river next to John Bacon, only that . . . That is her property. But the other one, that afterwards is the property of the relatives of Jonas.[37]

Later, the town declared that "the one that has this property is one named Sarah, the wife of one named Mahthias Ahatun."[38] Esther may have been Jonas's widow, sister, or daughter, or even an unrelated woman whose needs the community sought to accommodate. Sarah, who inherited land as a married woman, most likely received her property as a relative, perhaps a daughter, sister, or niece, of Jonas Muttahanit.

Women also received land grants in their own right. Even after the land system had become a formalized proprietorship, one married woman received a twenty-acre grant in perpetuity: "Then the proprietors jointly and willingly released one piece of land . . . to the one named Muttassonshq, or Susannoh, the wife of Joseph Ephraim . . . And this has been lovingly given to Muttassonshq. She has that property forever."[39] Although grants to women constituted the minority of land actions in early eighteenth-century Natick, separate female ownership of land indicates that Indians did not adopt the English legal proscriptions of coverture (which subsumed female property under the control of their husbands), and suggests that at least some women continued to farm.[40]

D. Toward English rules

Beginning in 1715, Indians participated in a dramatic reconfiguration of their land management and distribution practices that carried crucial consequences for the future of the community. Possibly under pressure from English magistrates, who had passed legislation to codify town land systems in 1713, Indians implemented a more rigid English proprietary system that individualized landholdings according to English legal procedures.[41] These actions may also have

---

[37] Ibid., 1:301 (1703).   [38] Ibid., 1:301 (n.d.).
[39] Ibid., 1:273 (1720).
[40] Marylynn Salmon, *Women and the Law of Property in Early America* (Chapel Hill: University of North Carolina Press, 1986).
[41] More legislation was passed in 1723. See Roy Akagi, *The Town Proprietors of the New England*

been made with the encouragement of those families in whose hands the system concentrated landownership. Whatever prompted the transformation, the new system introduced hierarchical notions about land into the community by restricting rights to future land divisions to a small group of "proprietors," and it left some Indians completely out, including most women. In individualizing land according to English principles, Indians abandoned the corporate protections they had adopted in the 1680s to prevent their dispossession as well as the notion that the community as a whole should sanction land arrangements. These changes paved the way for the development of a land market that readily included English neighbors.

Transformation in the land system involved negotiations spanning several years. The first formal action that incorporated the language of the new Anglicized system occurred in 1715 and involved the town's last large-scale land transaction outside of its boundaries, the site of the former Praying Town Magunkaquog. The transaction derived from a seventeenth-century bequest made by Edward Hopkins to the New England Company. The trustees of Hopkins's estate approached Natick with a proposal that it sell a large tract of land, which would become part of Hopkinton, the proceeds of which would be invested and profits paid annually to Natick Indians. In September 1715 "At a Meeting of Proprietors of Natick orderly warned," the proposal was approved, and a committee of Indian inhabitants was "fully Impowered to Act in behalf of the said Proprietors" to complete the transaction.[42] English agents obtained General Court approval of the arrangement in advance; the Indian committee gave a deed for the lands the next month.[43] The invested proceeds came to be

---

Colonies (Philadelphia: University of Pennsylvania Press, 1924) for the evolution of the proprietary system, and particularly, p. 46 ff, for developments in the early eighteenth century. Akagi argued that the system emerged over time. Originally, proprietors and inhabitants were coterminous; in the second or third generation of a town, in response to land scarcity, the earliest settlers gained exclusive control over the distribution of land in a town. Frederick Martin has challenged this interpretation, arguing that New England towns were founded with the profit motive at the forefront and were dominated by elites who closed their ranks early on by conferring exclusive land privileges upon themselves. John Frederick Martin, *Profits in the Wilderness: Entrepreneurship and the Founding of New England Towns in the Seventeenth Century* (Chapel Hill: University of North Carolina Press, 1991).

[42] OIRB, 24 Sept. 1715.

[43] Massachusetts General Court, House of Representatives, *Journals of the House of Representatives of Massachusetts, 1715–1790* (hereafter cited as JH), 55 vols. (Boston: Massachusetts Historical Society, 1919–), 1:35, 14 June 1715; Massachusetts General Court, Council, *Acts and Resolves, Public and Private, of the Province of the Massachusetts Bay* (hereafter cited as AR), 21 vols. (Boston: Wirth & Potter Printing Co., State Printers, 1895–1922), 9:410, Appen. 4, Chap. 68, 20 July 1715; and Middlesex County Court, Grantee and Grantor Records (hereafter cited as MCG), Cambridge, MA, 17:627, 1715/1715/6. The deed gave 8,000 acres for 600 pounds. New England Company funds were used to pay surveyor's and other charges to complete the transaction. New England Company Ledger, 56 (1715), and 64–6 (1717).

called the Magunkaquog rents; Natick Indians selected English trustees to manage the income.[44]

The fact that fully implementing the English proprietary system took four years indicates that the process was contested. Indians negotiated about who would be designated as proprietors, what privileges this status would carry, and how inhabitants at large would be accommodated. In 1716 they declared that six Indian men would receive 100 acres each; the rest would be granted sixty or thirty acres apiece. Three years later they voted "that all ye Speens is ye Proprietors of ye sid natick."[45] Finally in May 1719, the town committed its negotiations to public record. The meeting addressed three principal concerns. First, the categories of proprietor and freeholder were created as distinct from each other and "from ye Other Inhabitants of Natick."[46] Second, they addressed the problem of how to prevent "Unnecesary Selling of Timber wood or Trees from Lands Comons." Third, they agreed to hire an English surveyor to lay out individual allotments. They also agreed that Englishman Francis Fullam, during the "Continuanc of His Care of & Govrmt Over ye Indians," would collect and distribute the Magunkaquog rents, record the land allotments, and pay the English surveyor Samuel Jones, who had begun preliminary work as early as 1717.[47]

By unanimous vote the town declared that nineteen men and one woman "shall be Hence forward Allowed, Held, Reputed & distinguished to be ye Only & true proprietors of Natick." Each proprietor received a sixty-acre grant, sole rights to remaining undivided lands, and the annual Magunkaquog rents. Indian minister John Neesnumin also received a conditional proprietary right, "if he Live & Dye in ye Worke of ye Gospel Ministry." They designated an additional twenty-five men and two women as freeholders "Having No Right to Any of ye Rent money . . . Or to Any After Divisions of Land" unless they obtained proprietary rights through grant or purchase. Freeholders received one-time-only land grants ranging from thirty to sixty acres each.[48]

In designating land rights in 1719, Indians actually restricted landownership to a smaller number of families than had previously enjoyed land rights. On the surface, the two land systems seem to have accommodated Indian landowners

[44] AR 9:432, Appen. 4, Chap. 118, 2 Dec. 1715/6. English efforts to purchase the Magunkaquog lands had commenced by at least 1711, when a group of Englishmen petitioned the General Court for approval. MA 31:84, 5 June 1711. This group included at least three men who purchased Gookin and How lands obtained from Natick in the 1680s. Thomas Drury: MCG 13:704, 1688/1705, 50 acres; David Rice: MCG 13:701, 1682/1705, 60 acres; and Thomas Walker: MCG 11:91, 1688/1689, 60 and 32 acres.
[45] OIRB, 17 May 1719.   [46] NPB1.
[47] Ibid. Fullam presided over the meeting, and continued to act as overseer. In 1735, the proprietors voted for him to continue "under Such pay as as [sic] he has when he serves the English by the Day." Natick Proprietors Book of Record, 1723–1787 (hereafter cited as NPB2), Morse Institute Public Library, Natick, MA, 2 Jan. 1734/5. In 1717, Samuel Jones was paid five pounds by the New England Company for surveying in Natick for 12 1/2 days. Samuel Sewall, New England Company Ledger, 1708–1721, 66.
[48] NPB1.

in roughly the same proportion. The new system granted land to forty-seven individuals, two more than the number of landowners who appear in the surviving records from 1700 to 1715. But these relatively similar numbers mask a process of land concentration apart from the creation of differential access to future land divisions. Grants dating from 1700 to 1715 went to individuals with thirty-five different surnames (including two women whose grants were recorded using their Massachusett names); on the other hand, the total number of surnames for all freeholders and proprietors in 1719 was twenty-four, and this figure includes five that do not appear in the pre-1715 land records. Even if the names of four individuals who had died before 1719 are included, there were still seven fewer surnames represented in the new system. The number of surnames thus declined by between one-third (32 percent) and one-fifth (20 percent). Sixteen surnames never again appeared in connection with Natick.[49]

The proprietary system also concentrated land resources within particular families. Ten individuals became the only landowners with their surname. Thirteen other surnames accounted for two or more land grants, including seven Speens, four Thomases, and three Wamsquans, Ephraims, Pittimees, and Comechos.

More importantly, the English proprietary system created different classes of individuals with greater and lesser community rights. Proprietorship carried the privilege of future rights to the remaining undivided land in the town. Only fourteen surnames were represented in the proprietary ranks, 60 percent fewer than had received land in the pre-1715 land system. The town accommodated freeholders with one-time land grants. Others received nothing from the outset, including most Indian women.[50]

Moreover, the Anglicized land system removed control over land transactions from the Indian community as a whole and placed it within English legal and bureaucratic procedures that treated land as an individually owned commodity whose possession was regulated by the market. It also imposed a new rigidity in providing access to land to community members, compromising the town's latitude for responding to individual needs, on the one hand. And on the other, it released the constraints on individual transactions to the English that the 1680s corporate agreement against such sales had implemented. Subsequently, non-proprietors could be accommodated only through informal mechanisms, inheritance, or market transfers of property. Indian landowners could permit others to use their land, but such arrangements involved negotiations between individuals, not the community as a whole responding to individual requests.

Even though the system entailed unequivocably English ideas about landownership, in conferring proprietary status on nineteen individual Indians under-

---

[49] Based on a comparison of NPB1, NPB2, OIRB, and documents compiled in Goddard and Bragdon, *Native Writings*. Early records undoubtedly understate landownership, since only a fraction of the record book has survived.

[50] Ibid.

scored the tension between "Indianisme" and Anglicization that shaped the community. Nearly all of the proprietors derived status from at least one of three claims: descent from customary owners of land in or near Natick, descent from Indians acknowledged as leaders before Natick was bounded, or descent from prominent original converts. Six Speens, descendants of seventeenth-century founding converts, dominated the list, constituting a third of the proprietary group.[51] Other proprietors linked to founding converts include Capt. Thomas Waban, Simon Ephraim, Isaac Monequassin, and John Awassamug's heirs.[52] Half of the proprietors (ten of twenty) could claim connections to early converts; only about one-fifth (five of twenty-seven) of freeholders seem to have had similar direct links, and all but one of these (Isaac Nehemiah) had surnames that were represented among the proprietors. The families of freeholders Joseph and Andrew Ephraim, Thomas Waban Jr., and Bethiah Speen, wife of James Speen, were among the proprietors. Extending proprietary status to other members of these families reinforced the standing that came with town founding.[53]

Several proprietors traced their lineage through Native leadership structures that existed prior to town establishment.[54] Solomon Thomas was a grandson of the Concord sachem Tahattawan. His father, John Thomas (designated a freeholder) was between ninety and a hundred in 1719, beyond his productive years by the time land-right status was ascribed; his son was a more logical candidate for managing and passing on a proprietary right. Capt. Thomas Waban was a descendant, perhaps a son, of the convert and leader Waban. Old Waban had been married to a daughter of Tahattawan. The heirs of John Awassamug were given a proprietary right, perhaps because of the family's descent from the Nipmuck sachem Wuttawushan. Besides John Thomas and his sons, only one freeholder seems to have claimed similiar connections: John Wamsquan, who may have been a son of the sachem Great James.

At least two of the families represented among the proprietors were recognized through Native custom as owners of the land in and around Natick. During the founding of the town, the Speen family forfeited its Native ownership

---

[51] The Speens were remarkable for their dominance of positions of leadership in the seventeenth century. See Elise M. Brenner, "To Pray or To Be Prey: That is the Question[:] Strategies for Cultural Autonomy of Massachusetts Praying Towns," *Ethnohistory* 27 (1980): 144. The family's ties to traditional leadership structures remain obscure, however, and territorial associations may account for their prominence.

[52] Indians with these names had their doctrinal confessions recorded by John Eliot in the 1650s. John Eliot, "Tears of Repentance: Of a Further Narrative of the Progress of the Gospel Amongst the Indians in New England," *MHSC*, 3d ser., 6 (1834): 198–260; and John Eliot, *A Further Account of the Progress of the Gospel Amongst the Indians in New England* (1659) (New York: Reprinted for Joseph Sabin, 1865).

[53] The possibility exists that other Indians who were directly connected to early missionary efforts were counted among freeholders, but this rough measure does suggest that a tie to original converts was a vital factor in determining proprietary rights.

[54] Bragdon made the general point that prominent families were represented in town leadership structures as well. Bragdon, "'Another Tongue Brought In,'" 132.

rights to the town.[55] The community remembered the Speens's hereditary rights in admitting all male Speens to the proprietorship. Townspeople also conferred a proprietary right on the Awassamug family, whose customary ownership of lands around Natick Indians continued to acknowledge.[56]

Whereas the principles underlying this distribution evidenced cultural blending, the system of recording them was exclusively English, and that aspect of the transformation in reckoning landownership resulted in an insidious English encroachment on the Indian community in the very process of managing their lands. Land actions recorded by Indian scribe Capt. Thomas Waban were quickly supplanted by land records in English kept by English clerks using English terms of measurement. The English technical language of surveyors replaced the descriptive boundary making previously recorded in Massachusett. In stark contrast to earlier Indian ways of marking boundaries, many of the allotments took on rectangular or square shapes, rather that following natural markers such as rivers and brooks: "Laid out to Simon Ephraim Sixty Acres of Land in Natick In full of his first Division Granted to Him & His Heires for Ever Adjoyning to Sherburn Line ye Length of this Lott is 60 Rodds And the Width is 62 Rodds this Lott Hath Near Right Angles."[57] Even when lots bounded on the Charles River, the surveyor imposed right angles on property.[58]

Though the 1719 allotment was described as the "first division" of land, at least some of the plots codified existing arrangements. For instance, the surveyor "Laid Out to James Wiser 40 Acres Takeing in His Wigwam." Two other situations suggest that some communual notions prevailed as well. James Speen (proprietor), his wife, Bethiah (freeholder), and their son John Speen (proprietor) had their 180 acres laid out together in a large family plot. Part of the allotments of Samuel Bowman (proprietor) and Daniel Will (freeholder) were adjoined, with a line run through the middle. These arrangements suggest cooperative land use, and as such a blending of Indian and English forms. Allotments also revealed the impact of the corporate transactions of the 1680s. Moses Speen's sixty-acre parcel was next to the land of an Englishman named Pratt. Joshua Wamsquan had "mr Rice" as a neighbor. Two Pratts and three Rices had purchased land acquired by Samuel Gookin and Samuel How; Matthew Rice added that parcel to land he had already acquired on his own.[59]

55 See Chapter 2. Recognition of this family's right to the territory in and around Natick speaks to Native conceptions of land and property. As noted earlier, Bragdon has argued that sachems conferred to individuals the right to use land or its products either as a permanent inheritance or on terms of lifetime tenure. There is no evidence that the Speens were sachems, but perhaps they had gained permanent control over this land through such a grant. Bragdon, "'Another Tongue Brought In,'" 106.
56 Indians had not challenged his right to sell land in the late seventeenth century. See Chapter 3.
57 NPB1.   58 Isaac Speen's grant, for example. NPB1.
59 MCG 10:275, to Thomas Pratt, 1685/1694, 30 acres; MCG 12:58, to John Pratt, 1694/1697, 50 acres; MCG 10:385, to Matthew Rice, 1694/1694/5, acreage unknown; MCG 13:701, to David Rice, 1682/1705, 60 acres; MCG 15:24, to Thomas Rice, 1688/1709, 30 acres;

Minor adjustments and clarifications in landholdings accompanied implementation of the new land system. The Massachusett land history involving Hannah Speen explained Isaac Speen's land inheritance; awarding him a proprietary right underscored the long-term commitment of this family to the community. The twenty-acre grant to Susannah Ephraim [Muttassonshq] made in 1720, the last surviving Natick town record in Massachusett, apparently rectified an oversight in the extending freeholder lands. The month before proprietary establishment, Simon Ephraim received an additional two acres to allow for a highway through his lot.[60] Thomas Waban Jr. deeded "Waban's orchard," which had been passed down from his grandfather through his father to himself, to Samuel Ompetowin in March 1716; it was in the place Ompetowin had selected for his lot.[61]

Many of the allotments clustered on the south side of the Charles River or on Dedham's line, in the area that had been disputed between the two towns almost continuously since the founding of the community. Several plots were laid out contiguously, though common and undivided land remained in between some of the parcels. Some Indians located just across the river, near the meetinghouse and burying ground. Other allotments were set near Cochituate pond (at least four), the Needham line (at least three, possibly near the meetinghouse), and in "northerly" Natick (one). Most Indians seem to have been concentrated at the original locus of the town, near the meetinghouse on both sides of the Charles River.[62]

E. *Land distribution and transfer under the proprietary system*

The new land system in Natick performed a variety of functions for community residents. Proprietors evaluated land claims and requests regarding land at meetings conducted according to English legal forms.[63] Acting as a restricted group instead of the community as a whole, they not only allotted land among themselves but also recorded exchanges of land between individuals, purchases of undivided land from proprietors, confirmations of ownership, and forfeitures of land already laid out. As in earlier years, the proprietors continued to use Natick land to acquire public works and bolster community institutions. In 1736 they sold a thirty-acre lot to establish an educational fund to be managed by the treasurer of the missionary society as trustee.[64] In 1730 they granted the

---

MCG 10:448, to Matthew Rice from Natick Indians, 1685/1696; MCG 10:647, to Matthew Rice, 1685/1686, 300 acres; and MCG 11:178, to Matthew Rice, 1681/1693, 200 acres.

[60] OIRB, 13 Apr. 1719.   [61] MCG 20:595, 1716/1721.

[62] NPB1.

[63] The records of eighteen meetings held between 1723 and 1740 are preserved in the proprietors' book. The fact that allotments were also made independently of the formal meetings suggests that some kind of standing committee tended to proprietary matters as well.

[64] NPB2, 42, and 45; JH 14:130–1, 3 Dec. 1736; and AR 12:336, Appen. 7, Chap. 169, 24 Jan. 1736/7.

use of land to John Gleason and Henry Lealand in exchange for their erecting a grist mill and the privilege of free grinding for Indians for thirty years.[65]

Proprietors allotted land irregularly between 1720 and 1740, parceling out mostly small plots, probably at the request of individuals. Although they voted at a 1737 meeting to equalize the holdings of each proprietor, as of 1740 the nineteen Indians had received between sixty and just over 146 acres each.[66] Three proprietors received no land between 1720 and 1740: Isaac Monequassin, Israel Rumneymarsh, and Moses Speen. Other proprietors or their heirs received land divisions as many as twelve times up to 1740 in parcels ranging from less than an acre to sixty-five acres. Of the parcels 93 percent were twenty acres or less, however, and 59 percent were less than five acres.[67]

Management of Natick lands after 1719 occurred along a racially based division of labor that in effect compromised Indian autonomy. Indian proprietors exercised authority over granting access to land resources, acted as moderators at proprietary meetings, and formed committees to allot lands, but Englishmen from nearby towns performed bureaucratic and technical services such as land surveying and recording proprietary actions. Francis Fullam supervised proprietary affairs until at least 1750, William Rider served repeatedly as clerk, committee member, and surveyor of land allotments; Ebenezer Felch replaced him as surveyor in 1739.[68]

The development of a market in Natick land, monitored by commonwealth regulations about Indian land sales, emerged out of the individualization of landholdings. Restrictions on English acquisition of Indian land had been implemented in the seventeenth century and were still in effect through the eighteenth century. Commonwealth supervision of Indian land transactions to English purchasers proceeded from assumptions about Indian incapacity in negotiating the English legal system, and the problem of fraudulent English seizure of Indian land. At the same time, English magistrates regarded selling land to raise capital for physical improvements as part of the process of encouraging "civility." Thus they viewed Indian land sales as entirely valid, despite the ramifications for a dwindling land base. By allowing them to sell land to discharge debt, they underscored the fact that Indians would be held accountable for their participation in the market economy, like the English.

After they had individualized landownership, thus releasing land from the control of the Indian community as a whole, some Indians began selling mostly small parcels to English purchasers in order to raise capital for specific purposes.

[65] JH 9:20–21, 2 July 1729; AR 11:425, Appen. 6, Chap. 46, 1 Sept. 1729. Three years later, Gleason and Lealand sold the mill to Benjamin Kendall of Framingham for 10 pounds, reiterating the provisions of the original transaction. MA 31:178, 1730. Ironically, just ten years earlier, Indians had complained to the General Court that "Henry Lealand has for some years Encroached upon" their lands. JH 2:251, 20 July 1720.
[66] NPB2, 1–65. The vote is recorded at p. 47.   [67] NPB2, 1–65.
[68] Fullam: Ibid., 121; and Felch, Ibid., 66.

Figure 4. Indian land sale petitions, 1720–40

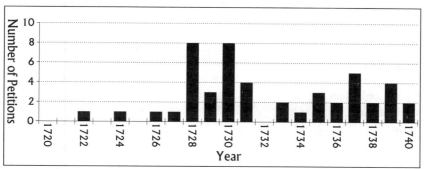

Sources: Massachusetts Archives, Massachusetts State Archives at Columbia Point, Boston, vol. 31; Massachusetts General Court, House of Representatives, *Journal of the House of Representatives of Massachusetts, 1715–1790*, 55 vols. (Boston: Massachusetts Historical Society, 1919–), vols. 2–18; and Massachusetts General Court, Council, *Acts and Resolves, Public and Private, of the Province of the Massachusetts Bay*, 21 vols. (Boston: Wirth & Potter Printing Co., State Printers, 1895–1922), vol. 10, Appen. 5–vol. 12–Appen. 7.

Between 1720 and 1740, Natick Indians petitioned the General Court forty-eight times for license to engage in these transactions.[69] Petitions were filed only four times prior to 1728; they peaked at eight in 1728 and 1731. Forty-two percent of were filed between 1728 to 1730, three years of higher than average Indian mortality.[70] (See Figure 4.) In the cases where the amount of land to be sold can be determined, the parcels ranged between five and ninety acres. Rounding the figures to the nearest five acres, 52 percent of the requests proposed to sell twenty acres of land or less. Only five petitioners sought to sell more than forty acres in a single petition.[71] In restricting the size of parcels transferred, most Indian sellers indicated their willingness to part only with small parcels of land to achieve specific ends rather than engaging in large-scale land liquidation.

[69] Province law required that Indians who wished to sell land present their case to the General Court in the form of a petition. Petitions included specific information on the amount of land to be sold, the proposed application of the proceeds, and often, the most detailed descriptions of Indian experiences, expectations, goals, and lifeways available for the eighteenth century. Indians were not required to obtain permission for sales or exchanges among themselves. Most petitions appear to have been recorded by English clerks, who received fees for their services, although some Indians penned their own. Once submitted, the petition was deliberated on by both houses of the General Court, and if the petition was approved, the court's actions constituted a license of sale. Petitions were not preserved uniformly; only nine survive through 1740. I have supplemented information on Indian requests with the legislative actions of the house and council to gain a fuller sense of the emerging market.

[70] 1728 (thirteen deaths); 1729 (fifteen deaths); and 1730 (twelve deaths). Peabody and Badger Records, Church of Natick, 1725–1795 (hereafter cited as NCR), Typescript copy, Massachusett Historical Society, Boston, MA. A total of 141 deaths were recorded in the Natick church records for fifteen years between 1722 and 1740, which would average 9.4 deaths per year.

[71] See O'Brien, "Community Dynamics in the Indian-English Town of Natick, Massachusetts, 1650–1790" (Ph.D. diss., University of Chicago, 1990), 240.

Table 1. *Factors motivating Indian land sales, 1720–40*[a]

Kind	1720–29		1730–40	
	Number	Percent	Number	Percent
Improvements	8	53%	6	19%
Debt	3	20%	10	32%
Estate settlement	2	13%	1	3%
Combination[b]	2	13%	14	45%
Totals	15	99%	31	99%

[a] In 46 of 48 cases where reasons can be determined.

[b] The category "combination" encompasses petitions that present an array of reasons, none of which was given particular emphasis by the petitioner.

Sources: Massachusetts Archives, Massachusetts State Archives at Columbia Point, Boston, vol. 31; Massachusetts General Court, House of Representatives, *Journals of the House of Representatives of Massachusetts, 1715–1790,* 55 vols. (Boston: Massachusetts Historical Society, 1919–), vols. 2–18; and Massachusetts General Court, Council, *Acts and Resolves, Public and Private, of the Province of the Massachusetts Bay,* 21 vols. (Boston: Wirth & Potter Printing Co., State Printers, 1895–1922), vol. 10, Appen. 5–vol. 12–Appen. 7.

These Indian land sales to the English represented a different kind of involvement in the market economy than the corporate transactions of the seventeenth century, which really arose out of diplomatic negotiations as much as anything, and reflected both the different economic and cultural priorities of some Indians as well as the consequences of debt relations for Indian individuals who possessed land in their own right. During the 1720s Indians requested permission to sell land seven times to raise capital for building houses, and once for purchasing cattle.[72] (See Table 1.) Three more had incurred debts that landed them in the courts.[73] In sharp contrast, during the 1730s Indians filed six requests for improvements, which included not just houses and livestock, but also land, husbandry implements, barns, and household goods.[74] The ten petitions that cited debt incurred through illness, injury, financial overextension, and support as the sole factor prompting them to sell land represented more than a threefold increase over the previous decade.[75] In addition, while Indians

[72] AR 10:225, Appen. 5, Chap. 190, 16 Nov. 1722 (cattle); MA 31:135–7, Feb. 1726 (house); HR 8:87, 3 Jan. 1727 (house); AR 11:317–8, Appen. 6, Chap. 51, 12 June 1728 (house); JH 8:355, 17 Oct. 1728 (house); JH 8:415, 11 Apr. 1728 (house for son); JH 9:132–3, 26 Nov. 1729 (house); and JH 9:147, 5 Dec. 1729 (house).

[73] JH 6:56, 13 June 1724 (debts: sued); JH 8:192–3, 5 June 1728 (debts: son sued for theft); and JH 8:355 and 360, 17 and 24 Oct. 1728 (debts: fined for "being in a riot.")

[74] JH 10:286, 5 Oct. 1731 (house, cart); AR 12:66, Appen. 7, Chap. 133, 10 Dec. 1734 (cattle, husbandry implements); JH 15:55, 16 June 1737 (barn and land); JH 15:189, 7 Dec. 1737 (land, cattle, sheep, husbandry implements); JH 15:220–1, 20 Dec. 1737 (finish barn, sheep, household utensils); and JH 16:72, 23 June 1738 (enlarge house, husbandry tools).

[75] AR 11:501, Appen. 6, Chap. 86, 25 Sept. 1730 (debts: sickness, support); AR 11:602, Appen. 6, Chap. 52, 20 July 1731 (debts: sickness); JH 9:279, 23 Sept. 1730 ("relief"); JH

cited a combination of factors in two requests in the 1720s, they did so fifteen times in the 1730s, and all but one of these fifteen included debt or relief in their explanations.[76] Overall, debt was a factor in only 33 percent of land-sale requests prior to 1730 (five of fifteen cases), but rose to 74 percent (twenty-three of thirty-one cases) between 1730 and 1740. In cases where a final action can be determined prior to 1730, 85 percent of requests were allowed; after 1730, 97 percent were granted. None of the three petitions that were disallowed cited debt as a motivating factor. In effect, individual ownership of land made alienation far easier, despite commonwealth supervision of Indian land sales, and created the conditions whereby some Indians began using land as a means of exchange for debt rather than some kind of payment or future tangible return.

In the two decades after the switch to the proprietary system, 1,739 acres of Natick land, or nearly one-third of the entire land base of Natick, changed hands through 151 transactions in an enormously complicated land market.[77] Land transactions proceeded on two levels. In practice, transactions from proprietors

10:321, 16 Dec. 1731 (debts); JH 10:286, 5 Oct. 1731 (debts); JH 11:284, 4 Oct. 1731 (debts: mortgage retirement); JH 13:176, 20 Dec. 1735 (debts: sickness, support); JH 16:48, 16 June 1738 (debts: sickness, support); MA 31:258, 13 Dec. 1739 (debts: sickness, sued); and MA 31:286, 9 June 1740 (debts: injury, support).

[76] 1720s: AR 11:365, Appen. 6, Chap. 191, 31 Aug. 1728 (debts: sickness, deaths in family; land); and AR 11:457, Appen. 6, Chap. 130, 17 Dec. 1729 (house, subsistence). 1730s: AR 11:479, Appen. 6, Chap. 28, 3 July 1730 (leaving Natick, building house elsewhere); MA 31:175, 18 Feb. 1730 (debts: sickness, barn, husbandry tools, land); JH 9:231, 2 July 1730 (see previous entry); AR 11:566, Appen. 6, Chap. 64, 19 Mar. 1730/1 (debts, cattle); JH 10:284, 1 Oct. 1731 (house, "comfort"); JH 11:268–9, 23 Aug. 1733 (debts, husbandry tools); AR 12:150, Appen. 7, Chap. 54, 23 June 1735 (house, comfort in old age); AR 12:198, Appen. 7, Chap. 169, 24 Dec. 1735 (debts: sickness, house, livestock); JH 13:258, 16 Jan. 1735 (debts, husbandry tools, barn, land); JH 14:212, 11 Jan. 1736/7 (debts, house, husbandry implements, livestock); JH 15:80, 24 June 1737 (debts, land); MA 31:247, 12 June 1739 (son's debts, land); MA 31:254, 19 Sept. 1739 (debts, support, house or wigwam); and MA 31:263–4, 10 Dec. 1739 (debt: mortgage, land, barn).

[77] The data on the Natick land market comes from two sources: the second Natick proprietors' book (NPB2), which records scattered conveyances, and the Middlesex County Court Registry of Deeds (MCG), which contains hundreds of deeds involving Indians. I meshed the records: When deeds recapitulated direct land transfers recorded in the proprietary records, I used only the deed. I collected deed information by searching for any transaction made by an Indian in Natick land using a list of Indian names compiled from the Natick proprietors' records and published vital records for the town. Then I compiled a list of English names from these transactions and searched the records for any deed in Natick land these individuals engaged in with other English individuals. The data on the English-to-English market in the town thus is an incomplete sample that captures some unknown portion of the total land market. I converted acreages to the nearest quarter-acre, disregarding small amounts of land recorded in rods.

I excluded four kinds of transactions from my analysis: exchanges, land transfers resulting from legal judgments, land sales by administrators of estates, and gifts of property that represented parental estate settlements. My objective was to analyze voluntary land transfers occurring in a market setting without distorting the data with nonmonetary transactions (exchanges), involuntary transfers (judgments and sales by administrators), or

Figure 5. Number of land transactions by type, 1720–40

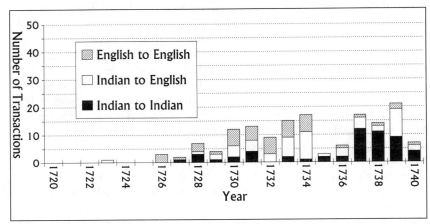

Sources: Natick Proprietors Book of Record, 1723–1787, Morse Institute Public Library, Natick, MA; and Middlesex County Court, Grantee and Grantor Records, Cambridge, MA.

Figure 6. Acreage sold by type, 1720–40

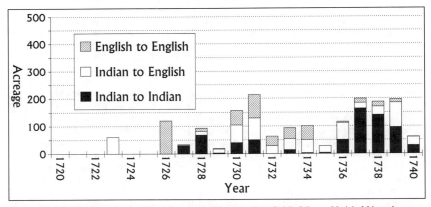

Sources: Natick Proprietors Book of Record, 1723–87, Morse Institute Public Library, Natick, MA; and Middlesex County Court, Grantee and Grantor Records, Cambridge, MA.

to both Indian and English purchasers were logged in their own record books, although General Court permission was required for transfers to the English. In addition, many of both sorts of land transfers were confirmed through county deed registration procedures.

Although individual ownership of land gave would-be English purchasers

familial transactions. Some transactions between relatives are included, but only when monetary payment accompanied the arrangement.

Figure 7. Size of parcels transferred by type, 1720–40

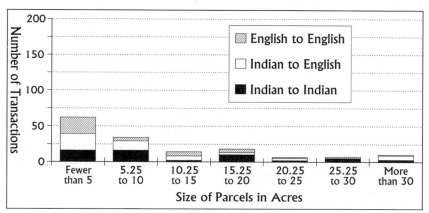

Size of Parcels in Acres

Sources: Natick Proprietors Book of Record, 1723–1787, Morse Institute Public Library, Natick, MA; and Middlesex County Court, Grantee and Grantor Records, Cambridge, MA.

easier access to Indian lands, large-scale catastrophic Indian land loss did not follow as a matter of course. The Natick land market included transactions between Indians, from Indians to English purchasers, and between English buyers and sellers. Significantly, only once did an Indian buy land from an English seller.[78] In fact, between 1723 and 1740 transactions between Indians composed the largest segment of the land market in terms of acreage; fifty-four of these involved 691 acres of land. An additional fifty-four Indian sales to English purchasers turned over possession of just over 600 acres. Forty-three land transfers between English parties turned over 447 ¼ acres more. (See Figures 5 and 6.) The overwhelming majority of transactions involved tracts of land ten acres or smaller; fewer than 10 percent of deeds transferred parcels larger than 30 acres, the size of a tract the proprietors and freeholders had apparently decided constituted the minimum for a viable farm.[79] (See Figure 7.)

Even the new emphasis on individualism evidenced by the land market existed in tension with persistent communal ideals that spanned beyond Natick's bounds. Individualization of Natick lands, which suggested a closed and fixed Indian community, did not mean that Indians had abandoned entirely notions of their larger territorial propriety or their connections to Indians in other localities. On three separate occasions between 1723 and 1734, Natick Indians filed petitions with the General Court asserting their rights to land outside of Natick. The first of these was a corporate petition in which Indians asked for a share in the proceeds of a sale of land in Hassanamisco.[80] A committee designated to

[78] This transaction is not included in the figures on the Natick land market. MCG 49:71, Moses Fisk to Joseph Ephraim, Jr., 1739/1740, 6 1/2 acres.
[79] This was the smallest grant given freeholders in the 1719 codification of the land system.
[80] JH 4:134, 5 Dec. 1722; and AR 10:231, Appen. 5, Chap. 206, 7 Dec. 1722.

investigate reported that they had met the Natick Indians at Hassanamisco, and that

> We Could Not Learn by all they had to say to us that ever they had
> any Right there[.] The Weightiest argument, which they Used with
> us was that when Land was Sold at Natick Hassanamisco Indians
> had Part of the Money, Therefore they ought to have Part of the
> Money that Hassanamisco Land is or may be Sold for.[81]

Ten years later Joseph Ephraim filed a petition on his own behalf claiming a right in Hassanamisco lands, based on the fact that his father, Peter Ephraim had been a "real and true Proprietor" of lands there.[82] Natick Indians made a claim to lands in Nashobah as descendants of proprietors there, too.[83] The court also dismissed these petitions.[84]

The response to these requests represented a startling reversal of policy. English magistrates had been willing to accept the claims of Indians from these same families when they were extinguishing Native title to the "Nipmuck Country" in the 1680s, and they endorsed the corporate Magunkaquog transaction outside of town boundaries in 1715. Even though Indians continued to argue for their hereditary rights in other places, by the 1720s English magistrates no longer validated broader notions of corporate Indian ownership. English rejection of the larger territorial vision Natick Indians continued to hold coincided with institutionalization of individual landownership operating in conformity with the English proprietary system.

F. *The bureaucratization of inheritance*

The extension of English probate procedures followed and reinforced individualization of landownership according to English legal forms and reflected the

---

[81] AR 10:441–2, Appen. 5, Chap. 27, 4 and 5 June 1724. A different proprietary system operated in the Indian community at Hassanamisco. English-style proprietary rights were ascribed much more narrowly and the entire system evolved differently. Seven proprietors were designated in 1728 and received land. In addition, these Indians and their descendants were entitled to interest earned on the 2,500 pounds that forty English families had paid to extinguish Indian title and settle the town of Grafton. They received periodic dispersals from the Hassanamisco Trustees, Hassanamisco Trustees Accounts, 1718–1857, John Milton Earle Papers, American Antiquarian Society, Worcester, MA, octavo vol. 1, 4 (1729), and throughout.

[82] JH 12:48, 20 June 1734; AR 12:25, Appen. 7, Chap. 47, 21 June 1734; and AR, 12:66, Appen. 7, Chap. 133, 10 Dec. 1734. The petition was later dismissed. JH 12:80, 20 June 1735.

[83] JH 5:176, 11 Sept. 1723. This was probably the son of Capt. Thomas Waban.

[84] JH 5:237–8, 16 Nov. 1723. Elise Brenner's conclusions about Natick in the seventeenth century also held true in the eighteenth: "Praying Indians used the praying town as an open, geographically unbounded system." She saw their geographic mobility as vital in their resistance to political domination. I would argue that Natick Indians were already politically dominated in the eighteenth century, but they exercised considerable control over their internal affairs. Brenner, "Strategies for Autonomy: An Analysis of Ethnic Mobilization in Seventeenth-Century Southern New England" (Ph.D. diss., University of Massachusetts, 1984).

enmeshment of Indians and English neighbors in one another's lives. Technically, commonwealth law subsumed Indians under English probate jurisdiction in 1692, but it was not until 1725 that the first Natick Indian estate entered probate court.[85] Seven others were settled according to English probate procedures up to 1740. Englishmen and Indians became involved in settling Indian estates. Indian relatives of the deceased acted as administrators in five of the eight estates that went through probate court up to 1740. Only once did an Indian serve as an appraiser, however, and he was designated such along with three Englishmen.[86]

Three Indians left wills, which permitted them to express their desires about dispensation of their property quite different from what English intestate laws would have dictated. Hannah Tabumsug left a large plot of land to a daughter who had cared for her, and selected her as executrix despite that fact that she had living sons. Her other daughter received an insignificant bequest of ten shillings. Capt. Thomas Waban willed estates to benefit his children, but he also remembered a granddaughter and a distant relative for reasons of his own. However, a lengthy list of debts incurred during his family's illness, which took the lives of his widow and three children, consumed the bulk of his estate. Possibly as a result of a patron–client relationship, James Coochuck willed his substantial real estate to an English family.

G. *Governance transformed*

The land market, which drew English residents into Natick and provoked the extension of probate procedures over Indian estates, also led to the reconfiguration of local governance. After the English presence in Natick mushroomed, English neighbors began to participate in town institutions and played a role in reshaping them to conform more fully with English expectations. The transactions of the seventeenth century had introduced some English landowners into the town, even if (as it appears) not all of them relocated there or regarded themselves as Natick residents. Between 1723 and 1740, thirty-two Englishmen purchased Indian land in Natick, fifteen of whom (45 percent) bought only one parcel. Twelve more acquired land from English individuals, three of them

[85] Yasuhide Kawashima, *Puritan Justice and the Indian: White Man's Law in Massachusetts, 1630–1763* (Middletown, CT: Wesleyan University Press, 1986), 36; and MCP #23401, Thomas Waban, Will, 1725.

[86] Estates administered by Indians: MCP #7004, Hannah Ephraim, Admin., 1733 (James Coochuck, brother, admin.); MCP #7005, John Ephraim, Admin., 1730 (Joseph Ephraim, exact relationship unknown, and Benjamin Tray, admins.); MCP #22642, Hannah Tabumsug, Will, 1731 (Mary Tabumsug Coochuck, daughter, admin.); MCP #22412, Solomon Thomas, Admin., 1736 (Jacob Chalcom, son-in-law, admin.); and MCP #23401, Thomas Waban, Will, 1725 (Nathaniel Coochuck, son-in-law, admin.). Three other Indian estates were administered by the same Englishman, David Morse: MCP #4957, James Coochuck, Will, 1740; MCP #15319, Isaac Monequassin, Admin., 1733; and MCP #22413, Solomon Thomas Jr. Admin., 1737. Indian Benjamin Tray acted as an appraiser on the estate of Hannah Tabumsug.

through parental deeds. Nine individuals (20 percent) indicated Natick as their
residence in deeds. All but one of the rest came from towns bordering on Natick or located nearby.[87]

Even before the English presence in Natick expanded, Indians had transformed local political institutions of the founding years into a system that
resembled English town meetings. When they came to the community in the
seventeenth century, Indians embraced the scripturally influenced polity John
Eliot designed, and shaped local governance by selecting leaders with claims to
prominence that predated Natick. The system allowed for continuity in Natick
expectations that a proven ability, personal relationships, and voluntary alliance
underlay governance. As late as 1685, Natick still designated "rulers"; by 1707
the town elected selectmen and from time to time filled a range of other English
offices, such as highway supervisors, fence viewers, and tithingmen.[88] Natick
Indians annually filled the positions of selectman and constable, which were
most likely the two major offices with remuneration attached.[89] As in English
towns, selectmen served as principal local leaders.

At least prior to 1720, Indians appear to have relied upon community needs
and objectives in structuring officeholding instead of simply mimicking English
patterns. Offices other than selectman or constable were filled most likely when a
specific need arose. An intensification in disputes over livestock entering fields
may have spurred the town to elect a fence viewer in 1707; conflicts over roaming swine may have become acute around 1716, prompting them to designate a
hog reeve in that year.[90] While superficially they drew upon political institutions

[87] From Natick: Jonathan Carver, John Collar, Thomas Ellis, Moses Fisk, Joseph Mills Jr.,
    Lydia and Solomon Mills, David Morse, Jonathan Richardson, and John Winn. From
    Needham (12/27%): Henry Bacon, Stephen Bacon, Timothy Bacon, James Beals,
    Hezekiah Broad, Nathaniel Bullard, John Drury, Jeremiah Gay, John Goodenow, Joseph
    Mills, Jonathan Mills, and Edward Ward. From Sherborn (11/25%): Benoni Adams,
    Nehemiah Allen, Isaac Coolidge, Eleazar Fairbanks Jr., Benjamin Kendall, Henry Lealand,
    Jonathan Lealand, Joseph Perry Jr., Samuel Perry, Samuel Perry Jr., and Joseph Travis.
    From Dedham (2/5%): Hezekiah Allen and Nathaniel Battle. From Framingham (2/5%):
    Daniel Biglow and John Gleason. From Sudbury (2/5%): Joseph Beal and Thomas Dun-
    ton. From Weston (2/5%): Ebenezer Felch and John Felch. From Andover (1/2%):
    Samuel Ames. From Medfield (1/2%): Samuel Sady. Unknown (2/5%): Jonathan Dew-
    ing and Daniel Pratt. Extracted from deeds, MCG.
[88] MCG 10:647, 1685/1686 (deed from "Rulers"); and OIRB, 1707. New England Company
    officials continued to use the terminology "rulers" in ledger books. But Capt. Thomas
    Waban, the town clerk, used the English term "Selectman" in recording the results of
    town elections even when he wrote in Massachusett. A town might elect as many as a
    dozen or so town officers. See Edward M. Cook Jr., *The Fathers of the Towns: Leadership
    and Community Structure in Eighteenth-Century New England* (Baltimore: The Johns Hop-
    kins University Press, 1976), 23–62.
[89] The New England Company paid at least some town officers for their services. In ledger
    books, entries include payments for Indian "Rulers." New England Company Ledger, 6
    (1708), 9 (1709), 62 (1716), and 69 (1717), for example.
[90] O'Brien, "Community Dynamics," 180

of English towns, Indians seem to have molded them to address their own concerns and reflect their own priorities.

Through the first four decades of the eighteenth century, Natick relied on acknowledged Indian leaders whose status had been reinforced through the proprietary system. Nine of nineteen proprietors (47 percent) served at least one term as selectman, in contrast to the three freeholders of twenty-seven (11 percent) who were elected to this office.[91] Fifteen of nineteen proprietors (79 percent) held at least one town office, compared with twelve of twenty-seven freeholders (44 percent). Sixteen of thirty-two men (50 percent) who held lesser town offices had either inherited land in their own right or through their wives, or had purchased land.

Further changes in political arrangements followed institutionalization of the Anglicized land system. Francis Fullam, the justice of the peace from nearby Weston who acted as overseer for proprietary meetings, also attended Natick town meetings beginning in the 1720s.[92] He may have imposed alterations in town governance on Natick to make political gatherings more fully conform to the shape of "Generall Town Meeting[s] . . . [for] the Choyce of Town officers as the Law Directs."[93] These changes resulted in further reconceptualization of how authority would be institutionalized by dictating specialized political offices rather than retaining flexible Native notions about political action as responsive to particular problems.

Beginning in the 1720s, English landowners in Natick began to win elective office alongside Indians.[94] At least eight of the thirteen Englishmen who served as town officers registered deeds from Indians before 1740.[95] Indians held 98 percent of all offices in the 1720s (forty-five of forty-six terms), but in the 1730s, after English landownership in the town began to increase, Indian officeholding declined to 60 percent of all offices filled (forty-one of sixty-eight terms).[96]

Town government remained slightly unorthodox, with the community filling different offices erratically. The offices of selectman and constable were

---

[91] Three of the selectmen either inherited proprietary rights directly or obtained them through marriage (Deacon Joseph Ephraim, Thomas Waban Sr., and Nathaniel Coochuck), raising the percentage of proprietors represented in the highest rank of town leadership to 63 percent (twelve of nineteen).

[92] OIRB, 14 Mar. 1719/20; 11 Mar. 1722/3; and 16 Mar. 1723/4.

[93] OIRB, 11 Mar. 1722/3.

[94] Town officer lists are available for nine years between 1720 and 1740. The gap between 1728 and 1735 complicates any analysis of officeholding because only one Englishman held any office before 1735. Thomas Dunton served as hog reeve in 1724. In 1735, Englishmen occupied exactly half of Natick town offices, their largest proportion in the period.

[95] James Beals (2 deeds, 23 acres); Hezekiah Broad (3 deeds, 39 1/2 acres); Jonathan Carver (2 deeds, 14 acres); Thomas Dunton (1 deed, 2 acres); Ebenezer Felch (1 deed, 7 1/2 acres); Joseph Mills (3 deeds, 5 acres); David Morse (7 deeds, 67 acres); and John Winn (2 deeds, 22 acres). MCG.

[96] OIRB, 14 Mar. 1719/20, 11 Mar. 1722/3, 16 Mar. 1723/4, 27 Mar. 1724/5, 11 Mar. 1727/8, 10 Mar. 1734/5, 8 Mar. 1735/6, 28 Mar. 1737, and 19 Mar. 1738/9.

the only ones filled on an annual basis. But whether because of the incorpora-
tion of English residents in Natick or the mandates of Justice of the Peace
Francis Fullam, a more elaborate roster of town offices was filled in the 1730s.
Ten offices were filled in 1736 and 1737, nine in 1737, and seven in 1739, whereas only four offices had been filled in any given year before 1720.[97]

Indians continued to hold the most important local office in terms of authority (selectman), which constituted official recognition that Natick was still an
Indian place, but the machinery of relations in the town was infiltrated and
operated by the new English residents. Indians held formal authority, whereas
the English began to capture the power that regulated the daily lives of town
residents in serving with Indians as surveyors of highways, assessors, field dri-
vers, fence viewers, haywards, and hog reeves. Sometimes residents elected
both Indian and English individuals to serve in a position in the same year, suggesting either shared authority or stark separation in administering local affairs.
Paralleling changes in the operation of the land system, English officers came to
dominate bureaucratic positions, serving as town clerks, treasurers, and moderators more frequently than Indians in the 1730s.[98]

Before English involvement in town meetings, Indians had incorporated
some English notions into local governance. They mandated broad Indian participation in public forums to discuss and act upon community issues, apparently in Massachusett, and imposed fines for nonattendence.[99] In 1707 the town
resolved a dispute between Mohshontanum and Waohquonchum, a woman:
"Waohquonchum gives six shillings to Mohshontanum because of the accusation against her that was made, and then she also gives 3 shillings to this meeting."[100] In issuing fines, they clearly used an English mechanism, but it was also
in keeping with Native notions about restoring balance in personal relationships in the community.[101]

Indian officers consulted with community members and appointed representatives when issues arose that involved other towns. In 1702, for example,
the town appointed John Thomas Sr. and Peter Pakatook Jr. to negotiate with
selectmen from Watertown to renew the lines between the towns. The town also

[97] O'Brien, "Community Dynamics," 180, 225, and 226.
[98] Ibid., 225–6.
[99] I infer the use of Massachusett from the fact that surviving records from town meetings
were recorded in Massachusett. "This is the law at this time, on the 31 of May in this year
. . . whatever the time of the meeting is, whenever it is appointed, then whoever does not
come to the meeting . . . these shall pay [a fine]." Seven men were fined for failing to
attend. Goddard and Bragdon, *Native Writing*, 1:277 (n.d.).
[100] Ibid., 1:301 (1707).
[101] Bragdon saw Indian town meetings as forums for joint decision making and the resolution
of grievances, with powers of self-government increasingly restricted in the eighteenth
and nineteenth centuries. She argued that persistence of the town meeting constituted a
factor in the maintenance of Native distinctiveness in New England. Such was not the
case in Natick after the mid-1740s, as I will argue in Chapter 6. Bragdon, "'Another
Tongue Brought In,'" 134–5.

empowered the committee to examine the lines between Natick and Framingham, consulting with Englishmen Joseph Sherman of Watertown and Thomas Sawin of Sherborn.[102]

In their joint meetings, in all probability conducted in English, Indian and English officers arranged for schoolmasters, attended to community needs such as repairing the meetinghouse and building town pounds for roaming livestock, and debated laying out highways.[103] They paid for services out of assessments made upon all community members. On one occasion they voted that "all in the Town be rated alike and that all out of the Town that have land in the Town pay the same."[104] This suggests that not all landowners chose to participate fully in community life, and absentee ownership was a problem. This stipulation could be construed to apply equally to Indians not currently residing in the town as well as absentee English landowners.

H. *The abandonment of a Native ministry*

The tensions between "Indianisme" and Anglicization and between Indian and English residents of Natick are even more clearly visible in transformations in religious arrangements than in governance in early eighteenth-century Natick, and in the withering in Indian commitment to Christianity. The religion itself, ostensibly the most important factor in bounding Natick, symbolized Indian cultural transformation from the beginning and constituted a battleground for Indian listeners and opponents in the seventeenth century. For the English, on the other hand, the single most important local institution was a fully established congregational church. In fact, the location of the meetinghouse itself (in addition to the abilities and religious inclinations of the minister himself) became a bitterly contested issue in town after town throughout New England, as it would indeed later in Natick. Ironically, the placement of English minister Oliver Peabody in Natick in the 1720s, supported by the New England Company as the missionary sponsor for Indians, made Natick a viable residence for English landowners and became an opportunity for them to displace Indians from positions of authority in the institution that justified bounding Natick in the first place. Peabody's ministry also shows that although at least some Indians valued the English minister, he felt ambivalent about his partly Indian congregation. But his very presence drew English listeners to Natick.

Up to the 1720s, the New England Company envisioned a Native ministry in Natick and elsewhere. A succession of Indian preachers served in Natick through

---

[102] OIRB, 27 July 1702. This entry seems to have been made by one of the Englishmen in attendance.

[103] Proceedings from only three town meetings held in 1734 and 1735 survive, but they suggest meetings were held regularly. These records are all in English. OIRB, 2 Sept. 1734, 29 Nov. 1734, and 18 Sept. 1735.

[104] OIRB (n.d.), immediately following record from 29 Nov. 1734.

1720. After Indian minister Daniel Takawampbait's death in 1716, the New England Company selected John Neesnumin to replace him.[105] Neesnumin, who had
received a conditional proprietary right to remain as Natick minister, died in
1719. During the first two decades of the eighteenth century Indians John
Thomas and Josiah Shonks also preached in Natick.[106] English ministers Daniel
Gookin Jr. and Daniel Baker, both of neighboring Sherborn, received stipends
from the New England Company for occasional preaching until at least 1719.[107]

But after that, the New England Company abandoned its vision of an Indian
ministry in Natick. In 1721 the selection of Peabody to preside over religious
matters, whether intentional or not, removed the lack of an appealing religious
establishment as an obstacle for English commitment to Natick as a primary
residence.[108] Eight years later, they authorized the formal gathering of a mixed
Indian and English congregation and deaconage, and decided to ordain
Peabody as minister, finding "that the natives 'especially younger persons' were
all satisfied in Mr. Peabody's preaching."[109] The commissioners recorded their
observations on services at Natick:

> As to publick singing Mr. Peabody at present sets the Psalm &
> sometimes an Indian and sometimes an English man reads it and
> [there] having been some difficulty upon this head we told them that
> it is the Minister's part to appoint who shall read and set the Psalm . . . .
> The English & Indians agree well together in their attendance on
> publick Worship and the Indians were willing the English should
> attend with them.[110]

Adam Winthrop reported that eight English families from Natick and thirteen
families from other towns attended services there.[111]

[105] Takawampbait: *NVR*; Neesnumin: William Kellaway, *The New England Company,
    1649–1776: Missionary Society to the American Indians* (London: Longmans, 1961),
    152–3, 237; and New England Company Ledger, 71 ff. Neesnumin had assisted mission-
    ary Experience Mayhew in translating religious texts into Massachusett for publication.
    Goddard and Bragdon, *Native Writings*, 2:763.
[106] Thomas: New England Company Ledger, 77 (1718); and Shonks: OIRB, 19 Dec. 1720.
    Thomas had preached at Nashobah between 1669 and 1714, and Shonks at Mashpee in
    the 1680s. Weis, "The New England Company," 171, 174.
[107] Kellaway, "New England Company," 120 and 236–7; Gookin: New England Company
    Ledger, 30, 33, 35; and Baker: New England Company Ledger, 48, 55, 73, 79.
[108] A 1721 graduate of Harvard, Peabody did not relocate to Natick until 1723. "Oliver
    Peabody," *Biographical Sketches of Graduates of Harvard University, in Cambridge, Massa-
    chusetts*, ed. John Langdon Sibley (Cambridge, MA: C. W. Sever, 1873–1975), 6:529.
[109] Ibid., 530.
[110] Ibid. Quoted from Harvard College Records. See also Kathleen J. Bragdon, "Native
    Christianity in Eighteenth-Century Massachusetts: Ritual as Cultural Reaffirmation," in
    *New Dimensions in Ethnohistory: Papers of the Second Laurier Conference on Ethnohistory
    and Ethnology*, ed. Barry Gough and Laird Christie, Canadian Ethnology Service, Mer-
    cury Series Paper 120 (Hull, Quebec: Canadian Museum of Civilization, 1991), 117–26.
[111] "Oliver Peabody," *Biographical Sketches*, 530.

In November, Joseph Ephraim Sr., Joseph Ephraim Jr., and John Brooks were admitted to full communion in the church, which was formally gathered the next month on a day of fasting and prayer. These three Indians entered into the church covenant with five Englishmen "belonging to & living in Natick." In January of 1730 church members elected Joseph Ephraim Sr. the first deacon. Although the English accepted Indian deacons, there may have been tensions in the congregation. Peabody noted: "He being an Indian I think every English man in the Church voted for him & ye Indians voted for English men not unanimously."[112] In the next four years they added Englishmen Ebenezer Felch and Nathaniel Chickering.[113] But unlike the continued dominance of Indians as selectmen in town governance, English church members outnumbered Indians from the first year of Peabody's ministry. Nineteen Indians joined the church between 1729 and 1740, compared with fifty-three English communicants.[114] The English commitment to Christianity clearly outstripped that of the Indians, who were the reason the congregation existed in the first place, and on whose behalf it was supported by the New England Company.

Despite the Anglicization of their church, some Indians did retain interest, and even provided supplemental financial support for Peabody. Instead of levying regular ministerial rates, Indians gathered voluntary contributions for Peabody once a month and "Uncapable of Giving any Other Encouragemt," they also generously supported him by extending him a proprietary right.[115] He used this right twelve times between 1723 and 1740 to add just over fifty acres to the eighty acres granted him when he settled in the town. He received more allotments than any other proprietor, and compiled the fourth largest estate.[116] Peabody pleaded for more money from the missionary society, arguing that there weren't "above two or three men of any Estate Considerable to help and they were taxed to support the ministry in neighboring towns,"[117] meaning Englishmen, and suggesting that he regarded Indians as paupers without economic potential. He was voted a salary of twenty pounds a year.[118]

Peabody apparently felt discomfort as minister to Indians in Natick; most likely he accepted the call as an obligation to repay the scholarship to Harvard

---

[112] NCR, 2.   [113] Timothy Bacon declined to serve. Ibid., 2, 5.

[114] Ibid. Prior to reestablishment, Indians were baptized in neighboring towns. Between 1726 and 1729, ministers from Sherborn, Needham, Medway, and Boston recorded the baptisms of eleven Indian children and sixteen Indian adults. With the gathering of the church in 1729, Peabody began to keep church records.

[115] AR 10:249, Appen. 5, Chap. 264, 2 Jan. 1722/3; JH 4:177, 2 Jan. 1722/3; and AR 10:296–7, Appen. 5, Chap. 22, 2 Jan. 1723/4.

[116] Peabody received a sixty-acre allotment in 1723, and a deed for the twenty-acre house lot previously given to Indian minister John Neesnumin. As was the case with Indian proprietors, most of Peabody's allotments were smaller than five acres. NPB2; and MCG 25:516, from Natick Proprietary Committee, 1722/1723, 20 acres.

[117] Sibley, *Harvard Graduates*, 6:529.   [118] Ibid.

he had received.[119] His uneasiness about his place within the Indian community prompted him to endorse a request for a land sale by Indian Samuel Abraham to an English purchaser, arguing:

> In as much as it is very lonesome, uncomfortable & disadvantageous to live at Such a distance from Neighbours as I am from any English (ye nearest English family being about a mile distant & no more within near two miles) & if I might have two or three near me it would (I believe) render my Life much more pleasant & Easy . . . with one Neighbour about as near again as my nearest is at Present.[120]

Peabody's endorsement laid bare his racial ideas about his Indian flock. Apparently he regarded them neither as fit nor pleasant neighbors, and viewed his residence among them as a "disadvantage." And in urging the court to act, he in effect sponsored the inclusion of an additional English resident in Natick, housewright Samuel Ames of Andover, who purchased the land and later entered into the church covenant in Natick.[121] A great many more would follow.

The existence of a fully established church with an English minister, supported mostly by or because of Indians, benefited English landowners in Natick and made residence in the town more appealing for them. Peabody's presence lured English neighbors to services he conducted in English. In response to their complaints about the inconvenience of traveling great distances to attend church, the court freed groups of farmers to attend services in the meetinghouses of other towns, including "Eleazer Ellis and the 13 [from Dedham] who usually go to Natick [meetinghouse, who] are to pay the same rate as they would to Dedham to Natick."[122] Even English farmers who lived on the borders used the proximity of the Natick meetinghouse to wage battles in their own towns about the location of their own meetinghouses.[123] In 1723 farmers from the south end of Sudbury gained a General Court order to relocate their meetinghouse more centrally by presenting their annexation to Natick as an alternative.[124] In 1724 seven Englishmen from Needham, which had been part of Dedham until being set off in 1711, unsuccessfully attempted the same strategy.[125] English inhabitants

[119] Ibid. Peabody received a scholarship from the missionary society requiring that he enter the Indian service or repay the gift. Kellaway, *The New England Company*, 237.

[120] MA 31:137, 1726.

[121] The transaction was not formalized until several years later, perhaps because Ames then sold the land to an English purchaser. MCG 35:104, Samuel Abraham to Samuel Ames, 1732/1733, 22 acres; and MCG 39:543, Samuel Ames to Jonathan Carver, 1732/1738, 22 acres.

[122] JH 9:198, [1729]. The group became Springfield precinct in the same year. Lockridge, *A New England Town*, 97–102.

[123] See, for example, Lockridge, *A New England Town*.

[124] JH 5: 54–5, 22 June 1723; JH, 5:129, 17 Aug. 1723; and JH 5:237, 16 Nov. 1723.

[125] JH 6:95, 14 Nov. 1724; and JH 9:265, 18 Sept. 1730. The location of the Natick meetinghouse would continue to be an issue for Needham residents, as I will discuss in Chapter 6.

of the westerly part of Dedham, which eventually became Dover (1836), petitioned for precinct status in 1729.

I. *Community tensions*

If Indians were "divided in the[ir] desires" about cultural change, so, too, were the English divided in their visions about the Indian presence in Massachusetts Bay. In the first decade of the eighteenth century, Samuel Sewall wrote to John Higginson regarding "agitation . . . [about] whether it be not for the Honor of the G[overnor] and of N[ew] E[ngland] to reserve entire, and untouch'd the Indian Plantation of Natick, and Other Land under the same Circumstances[.]"[126] Sewall addressed the question from a religious perspective, arguing "that the lying of those Lands unoccupied and undesired by the English, may be a valid and lasting Evidence, that we desire the Conversion and Welfare of the Natives, and would by no means extirpate them as the Spaniards did[.]"[127] But for many English neighbors of Indians, theoretical issues about honor and the English historical legacy took a distant second place to their own desires for land. English settlers who surrounded Natick were not nearly so concerned as Sewall to leave the land unbreeched as a monument to the purity of English intensions.

Contrary to Sewall, Natick's lands were not "unoccupied." But the way in which Natick Indians used the land, including the probable continued use of some Indian agricultural techniques, may have blinded Sewall to the existence of the Indian community. In this way, he was much like Peabody, who, living among his Indian flock, looked around and saw no neighbors. Neither were these lands "undesired by the English," as Sewall asserts.

By portraying the central dynamic in the Indian community as a debate over whether "to Anglicise . . . in all agreeable Instances" versus the stubborn retention of "Indianisme," Sewall created a false dichotomy. In naming practices, language use, and working out the details of governance, Indians in Natick held English and Indian cultural practices in tension, at least for a time. Questions about land tenure before 1715 were resolved by using both Indian and English notions. Perhaps it was these blended practices in conjunction with their separatist ideas about race that convinced some English observers, who held rigid expectations about cultural forms, that Natick's lands were unoccupied, and convinced Peabody that he lacked neighbors.

But developments after 1715 did lay the groundwork for other kinds of divisions within the town, which carried implications not readily apparent at the time. The institutionalized proprietary system created divisions within the Indian community by conferring relatively greater rights to land upon a select group of Indian proprietors, lesser rights to a second group of freeholders, and

---

[126] "Letter Book of Samuel Sewall," 326.   [127] Ibid.

denied all rights to still other Indians by mandating individual landownership that would be regulated by the market. Implementation of the proprietorship reified what had been a fluid land system, and concentrated land rights into the hands of fewer Indian families. The system reinforced existing status arrangements and reduced the ability of Indians as a community to accommodate individual needs.

Despite the blizzard of documents produced in connection with reconfiguring the Natick land system, just what prompted the transition remains unclear. It is tempting to conclude that English magistrates insisted upon bringing the Indian town into conformity with the English model as part of their impulse to "Anglicise" Indians "in all agreeable instances," although only the Indian community of Stockbridge witnessed full implementation of the proprietary system elsewhere in Massachusetts Bay.[128] English neighbors such as Francis Fullam, Samuel Jones, and Ebenezer Felch certainly stood to benefit financially from providing supervisory and surveying services, as did English neighbors in land-scarce towns. Still, no evidence exists to support so stark a claim about English domination of the transformation process. To the contrary, the evidence shows that at least some Indians actively participated in working out the technicalities of the proprietorship, and those admitted to the privileged group had claims to longstanding preeminence in the community. Furthermore, those who sold land to build houses and farms, in particular, may have endorsed individualization. Other Indians may have contested the transition, especially those excluded, such as most of the women as well as freeholders barred from future land divisions, although no evidence survives to suggest that they did.

Whether some Indians resisted the transformation or envisioned the future erosion of Indian landownership, individualization compromised the autonomy and future of the Indian community. In 1700 Indians held full corporate control over the town's lands, except the relatively small amount lost in the seventeenth century or exchanged for community services such as mills, and they determined the ways in which the lands were possessed. They shaped their own system of local governance and chose their own leaders even while the colonial relationship with the commonwealth impinged upon full sovereignty. Native ministers played an active though not exclusive role in religious matters for those committed to Christianity.

By 1740, Natick Indians still retained their dominance in the town, but their control was precarious. Indian landownership had already declined. More than 1,000 acres, or about one-sixth of the land base, had passed into English hands between 1723 and 1740. And although Indian proprietors maintained power over remaining common lands, English supervisors and surveyors controlled the technical aspects of the land system, and English clerks replaced Indian scribes casting

[128] Patrick Frazier, *The Mohicans of Stockbridge* (Lincoln: University of Nebraska Press, 1992); and Lion G. Miles, "The Red Man Dispossessed: The Williams Family and the Alienation of Indian Land in Stockbridge, Massachusetts, 1736–1818," *NEQ* 67 (1994): 46–76.

records in Massachusett. In the 1730s, Indians shared power in town governance with Englishmen, but they retained exclusive control over the most important position in local leadership, the office of selectman. After 1729, Indians became deacons in the reestablished church, but Natick never saw another Indian minister. But because the New England Company retained control over the church as part of its missionary initiatives, even the presence of an English minister and a majority of English communicants did not erase Indian influence in religious affairs.

During the 1720s and 1730s, Indians incorporated the newly arrived English landholders into the town meeting and the religious establishment seemingly without severe tensions. Indians recognized at least some English landowners as participants in the community by allowing them to participate in the church, and in permitting their election to town offices beginning in the 1730s. The town meeting served as an arena for addressing issues affecting the community as a whole. These developments constituted recognition that some English settlers had become functional members of the racially mixed community. But in the ensuing decades, community relations deteriorated and cooperation gave way to divisiveness, as Indians became steadily divided *from* their *land*.

5

Interlude

The proprietary families

A. *"Vanishing Indians": family, lineage, and the myth of extinction*

Scrutinizing the different life experiences of the relatively elite group of proprietary families yields a closer look at the divided desires of Indians in eighteenth-century Natick. These families' stories afford insight into the ways Indians took up English lifeways as a means of defending Natick as an Indian place. Indicators such as the abandonment of an Indian ministry, increasing numbers of English officeholders, and the commodification of land and emergence of a land market might suggest that Indians, and Indianness, were slowly disappearing. The records of the everyday lives of Natick Indians offered a more nuanced picture of Indian life histories. Indian individuals and families responded variously to the contest of cultures in Natick. Many of them used their land resources in English ways, selling off parcels of land, building English-style farms, furnishing frame houses with English goods. However, in doing so, they managed to perpetuate their families and retain claim to their place even though they no longer enjoyed exclusive occupancy of the land. Portraits of the nineteen proprietary lineages flesh out the complexity of cultural change and social relations in the shifting terrain of eighteenth-century Natick.

Telling stories about Native peoples whose lives have long been obscured, marginalized, and erased from histories of colonial New England involves a fair amount of detective work, and at least as much frustration when terse documentary evidence fails to answer pressing questions. I have constructed the narratives that constitute this chapter by following leads suggested in incomplete sources and by finding personal narratives in unexpected places such as records of land transactions. Knit together, these bits of scattered evidence speak of how Indian lifeways shaped and were shaped by the history of colonial New England. The evidence speaks haltingly, however, and often ambiguously, and at times it remains mute. Even when relatively abundant, it never answers all the questions that need explication.

I came to this study trained in the methodology of social history, expecting to reconstruct the story of Natick in records of marriage patterns, birthrates and death rates, and other demographic information, as well as to examine land distribution patterns, officeholding, and the shape of religious institutions within the community. But I found these records were too fragmentary, which suggested that Natick's history required a different approach. In turn, earlier social histories had defined New England towns as closed, bounded communities. More recently, social historians have abandoned this romantic notion of community to recognize a more permeable and fluid social order.

To take just one example of how conventional methods might miss a larger truth, the vital records include a great many Indian marriages, but clearly underrecord Indian births and deaths: Comparing the probate records to the death register shows that 36 percent of Indians for whom probate dockets were filed between 1741 and 1762 are entirely omitted from the death register (twenty-three of sixty-four); between 1764 and 1790, the figure rose to seventy-seven percent (ten of thirteen). This means that whereas legal documentation of Indian property was maintained throughout Natick's history, by the end of the eighteenth century neither the English minister nor the English town clerk took care to record the beginnings and ends of Indian lives. These records, which can be taken to document the "vanishing" of Natick's Indian population, instead narrate the gradual erasure of Indians from their own place. If I were to use conventional demographic methods, I could only reproduce the extinction narrative that has dominated the traditional account of Natick, "vanishing" Indians from its history. Similarly, if I were to apply uncritically the categories of analysis and questions tailored to plot changes in western European societies, I would run the risk of erasing the Indianness of social and cultural transformations in Natick.[1]

I focused on Natick individuals and families, compiled any evidence I could uncover about their lives, and worked to reconstruct Indian lineages. I identified a pool of individuals to trace that included any person who appeared in the Natick vital records, and I supplemented that roster by adding any Indian identified as being from Natick in pamphlets produced during the seventeenth-century missionary encounter, the Massachusetts Archives, and probate records in addition to Natick town meeting and proprietary records. I then traced the surnames through the Middlesex County land records to investigate all the land transactions involving Natick Indians, checked the Worcester County probate records, searched the vital records of more than 120 other New England towns, examined militia roles, looked at dozens of nineteenth-century local histories, and combed the records of the nineteenth-century Massachusetts state Indian Commissioner John Milton Earle in order to capture as much detail as possible about Indian life stories. Moving back and forth between these sources and scattered others, I worked to link information, sort out genealogies, and listen for Indian voices in documents that had been produced for other purposes.

[1] For attempts to do otherwise, see Kathleen Bragdon, "'Another Tongue Brought In': An Ethnohistorical Study of Native Writings in Massachusett" (Ph.D. diss., Brown University, 1981), which also includes a section reconstructing Indian lineages, including several Natick families, and Daniel Mandell, "'To Live More Like My Christian English Neighbors': Natick Indians in the Eighteenth Century," *William and Mary Quarterly* 3d ser., 48 (1991): 552–79.

I focused on lineages and family stories for two reasons. First, because it is possible to trace the lineages through the eighteenth century even if all the lines are not fully present. The persistence of these lineages contradicts the extinction myth. And second, looking at the everyday transactions of Natick families over time allows us to see Indians making strategic adaptations to colonialism. This genealogical approach makes it possible to shift the historical narrative about the erasure of Indianness to a more dynamic understanding of how the meaning of Indianness was transformed.

Not surprisingly, some proprietary families appear more frequently in the documentary record than others. In general, those Indians who can be extensively traced constitute a biased sample. Indians who entered the land market, joined the church, and acquired English material possessions were more likely to surface in the written record. If successful, their existence and evidence of their lifeways received confirmation through probate dockets created in the disposition of their estates. Members of the Ephraim family, for example, emulated English cultural and economic strategies, and much evidence about them has survived.[2]

Though perilous, interpreting silences in the record can also provide hints about the shape of Indian lives. The absence of personal estate inventories, even for many landowners, for example, suggests that some proprietary families may have rejected any substantial cultural alterations through adopting aspects of English material culture. While they benefited from their common rights and owned land that was passed on to heirs, it is difficult to determine exactly how these lands were used. Some Indians probably continued to farm them according to Native usage, or with selective adoption of some English techniques. Others confined their land dealings to other Indians, rejected the large-scale acquisition of English goods, or engaged in activities that reflected Indian cultural values, such as military service and seafaring, and stood aloof from English influences. Unlike Indians who used land resources to purchase tools, household goods, build houses and barns, other families seem to have remained further outside of the market economy. Or perhaps these families resisted the effect of English institutions on their lives by giving away their possessions before English probate proceedings intruded to override their wishes. Still, even when Indian landowners resisted change, they could not completely escape the increasingly institutionalized presence of the English legal system, which their English neighbors used to make claims against their property. Many Indian holdings were dissipated through probate proceedings.

A brief portrait of four proprietary lineages offers two distinct reinterpretations of the extinction myth as it applies to Natick. First, of the nineteen proprietors designated in 1719 only one family line entirely vanished from the documentary record in the eighteenth century, and a different lineage took its

---

[2] Unless otherwise indicated, all individuals mentioned in this chapter were Indians.

place in the proprietary ranks. Second, although three surnames disappeared, those family lines continued. More extensive stories about the other lineages argue that all the rest persisted.

In 1762, as they prepared to make a final division of the commons, the proprietors formally acknowledged the lapsing of the Will family. Noting that "Samuel & Daniel Will, Decd without heirs,"[3] the proprietors asked to have lands granted out of Samuel's right revert to them, and their request was granted. This is the story of the Will family land: A proprietary share had been awarded to the heirs of Samuel Will during codification of the Natick land system in 1719.[4] Between 1719 and 1740, a total of 180 acres were granted out of the commons in Samuel Will's right, mostly to daughter Hannah Speen, but none thereafter. This is the only request the proprietors made to reclaim a proprietary share based on death without heirs. The fact that the proprietors formalized their action in this manner stands as evidence that the Will family was the only one to meet with complete demographic failure. If other families failed to produce heirs, other lands would have been reacquired for distribution in this way.

Whereas the Will family left no heirs, other Indian couples left only daughters. Still others who left no children passed on their property and common rights to other relations. Just following direct patrilineal lines might suggest that these families, too, had lapsed; however, by taking into account female offspring and relatives, the demographic evidence affords insight into the persistence of these families. This is illustrated by the narratives of three other proprietary lineages: the Nehemiahs, Monequassins, and Ompetowins.

Thomas Nehemiah's name was entered as a proprietor in 1740 on behalf of his daughters, Hannah Nehemiah Abraham (wife of Samuel Abraham Jr.) and Patience Nehemiah Peegun (wife of Thomas Peegun Jr.).[5] Thomas Nehemiah, who appeared in a 1702 Natick petition, may have been a son of original Eliot convert Nehemiah, who was murdered by a hunting companion sometime before 1685.[6] Nehemiah was the son of Captain Tom (Wuttasukoopauin) and

---

3 Massachusetts General Court, House of Representatives, *Journals of the House of Representatives of Massachusetts, 1715–90* (hereafter cited as JH), 55 vols. (Boston: Massachusetts Historical Society, 1919–), Part 2, 37:356, 17 Apr. 1761; and Natick Proprietors Book of Record, 1723–87 (hereafter cited as NPB2), Morse Institute Public Library, Natick, MA, 138. Hannah Speen and her husband, proprietor John Speen, are discussed later in this chapter. While they left no direct heirs, there were many collateral descendants among Speen families. The only evidence I have located about Daniel Will is that he served in the military in 1723. Massachusetts Archives (hereafter cited as MA), Massachusetts State Archives at Columbia Point, Boston, 91:74–6, 1723, Muster Roll, Edmund Ward, Captain.

4 Samuel Will may have been the Samuel Williams who married Mary Speen, daughter of the original convert Robin Speen, sometime before 1684. Josiah H. Temple, *History of Framingham, Massachusetts, Early Known as Danforth's Farms, 1640–1880* (Framingham, MA: Published by the Town, 1887), 93.

5 NPB2, 68. Nearly 205 acres were granted in Nehemiah's right between 1740 and 1763.

6 John Eliot, *The Dying Speeches of Several Indians* (Cambridge, MA, 1685).

his wife, Mary (Neepanum).[7] He was probably the brother of Isaac Nehemiah, also known as Isaac Wuttasukoopauin, who appeared in the Original Indian Records for Natick after 1700. Thomas Nehemiah bore daughters to carry forth the family line, but no sons. The Natick surname Nehemiah, borrowed from English in the first place, thus disappeared, even though the Nehemiah descendants did not.

The same was true of the Monequassin family. Extensive use of the proprietary right of Isaac Monequassin was made beginning in 1742, first by "his heirs" (forty-two acres),[8] and thereafter by the wife of Nathaniel Hill. Isaac Monequassin had died in 1730, having received only his initial grant of sixty acres in 1719. The surname Monequassin never appeared again in connection with Natick.

Patience Quassont had married Nathaniel Hill in Newton in 1731, most likely using a shortened version of her surname, Monequassin.[9] At least three of their children were baptized in Brookline in 1741 (Abigail, Amos, and Elizabeth), though the Hill family was in Natick by 1749 when an Indian-generated census counted seven children in the household.[10] Sometime following his wife's death, Nathaniel returned to Brookline, where he died in 1772.[11] Two years later, Elizabeth Hill of Brookline "and others" (including Hannah Hill of Cambridge) petitioned the General Court to sell lands they were entitled to in Natick following the "demise of their father."[12]

Proprietor Samuel Ompetowin and his wife, Hannah, daughter of original convert Robin Speen, both died in 1722, leaving no children who have been identified.[13] In the course of a long and complicated settlement, Samuel's sister Mary Toss was made beneficiary of estate proceeds that were to earn interest for her support, and she became sole heir to his proprietary right.[14] Mary and Jeffrey Henry married in 1739, and they attempted to establish an English-style farm in Natick. Jeffrey moved to sell land in 1742 so he could procure oxen and some husbandry tools, needed because he had "cleared, fenced, and Brought to

---

[7] Temple, *History of Framingham*, 58.   [8] NPB2, 71 and throughout.

[9] *Vital Records of Newton, Massachusetts to the Year 1850* (Boston: New England Historical and Genealogical Society, 1905).

[10] *Vital Records of Brookline, Massachusetts to the Year 1850* (Boston: New England Genealogical and Historical Society, 1929); NPB2, 114; and Thaddeus Mason, "A List of the Names of the Indians Old and Young Viz. Parents with the Number of their Children Both Male and Female, which Live in or Belong to Natick; Taken July 16, 1749," *Collections of the Massachusetts Historical Society*, 1st ser., 10 (1792): 134–6.

[11] Thomas W. Baldwin, comp., *Vital Records of Natick, Massachusetts to the Year 1850* (hereafter cited as *NVR*) (Boston: Stanhope Press, 1910); MA 33:59–60, 1758; and *Brookline Vital Records*.

[12] Massachusetts General Court, Council, *Acts and Resolves, Public and Private, of the Province of the Massachusetts Bay* (hereafter cited as AR), 21 vols. (Boston: Wirth & Potter Printing Co., State Printers, 1895–1922), 18:774–5, Appen. 13, Chap. 129, 25 Feb. 1774.

[13] *NVR*; and Temple, *History of Framingham*, 93.

[14] AR 11:753–4, Appen. 6, Chap. 113, 31 Oct. 1733.

English grass a Good peice of Ground," and desired a "convenient Dwelling house." He also had care of his father, who was old and had been blind for twenty-five years.[15] Jeffrey claimed to be a proprietor, but it was his wife who held the common right.

Mary and Jeffrey Henry gave up their residence in Natick permanently sometime between 1742 and 1753. In 1755 they moved to sell "Divers Lotts of Land" in Natick "descended to the said Marcy from her brother Samll Umpinton Late of said Providence" as residents of Providence themselves.[16] Needing a means of support because they were "So far advanced in years that they are at present past hard Labour," the couple asked that the proceeds be managed by Englishmen Jonathan Olney and John Andrews of Providence, whom they had chosen as their English guardians, and John Jones and Jonathan Richardson, English guardians of the Natick Indians.[17] When Mary Henry's estate went to probate in Middlesex County in 1770, the small proceeds of her remaining assets went toward paying costs of administration, as well as for Mary's boarding and nursing charges brought by her daughter. The tiny inheritance left after discharging the debts was split between Mary's daughters, Hannah Toss and Mary Caesar, the nieces of proprietor Samuel and Hannah Speen Ompetowin.[18] The Ompetowin family did not die out, but tracing the line meant following the Ompetowin surname through its transfigurations into Toss, Henry, and Caesar.

Just as looking at Natick families through the lens of lineage broadly defined captures larger dynamics affecting the Native population, so too, does examining particular aspects of Indian life histories help bring Natick's history into clearer focus. Although family members pursued diverse courses of action in shaping their lives, different lineages illustrate important themes in the transformation of Indian lives particularly well.

The life stories in the rest of this chapter are arranged to illustrate crucial threads in a larger narrative of Indian social history in eighteenth-century Natick. I begin with the six Speen lineages and the Waban families, whose life experiences offer stark testimony about the ramifications of involvement in the market economy, and especially the ways in which debt relations, guardianship, and indentured servitude impinged on Indian lives. Next, in stories about the Awassamug, Abraham, and Thomas families, I explore the ways in which Indian marriages and gender relations were affected by structural rearrangements linked to the transformation of property relations. Then, I turn to the Ephraim, Peegun, Rumneymarsh, and Tray families to examine different ways Indians participated in the Natick land market. Finally, I tell stories about the Tabumsug and Bowman families in order to flesh out the regional dimensions of Indian

[15] MA 31:389, 1741.   [16] MA 32:618–9, 1755.
[17] MA 32:618–8, 1755.
[18] Middlesex County Court, Probate Records (hereafter cited as MCP) Cambridge, MA, #11173, Mary Henry, Admin., 1770.

networks that narrate Indian notions of place, which persistently resisted the fixity embedded in English colonial ideals.

By presenting stories about all nineteen proprietary lineages, all of them accented to one degree or another according to the larger themes of social and cultural change, I hope to make the case that the narrative of extinction does not explain the demise of Natick as an Indian place and explore some of the history that may have pursuaded observers otherwise. Although one lineage vanished (the Wills), and three surnames disappeared (Nehemiah, Mon-equassin, and Ompetowin), descendants of all but one proprietary family produced progeny that ensured the survival of Natick Indians in New England.

B. *Commodification of Indian lifeways: debt, guardianship, and indentured servitude*

Like other Natick Indians, at least some individuals from Speen and Waban families altered their lifeways to incorporate some English practices, economic pursuits, and material culture, which is visible in the surviving estate inventories. Some acquired English-style dwelling houses; furniture and other English household goods appeared in inventories as well. But land sales seem to have been the primary method of financing these alterations in lifeways, and there is no evidence that any of the Speens or Wabans became successful English-style farmers. Over the course of generations the land remaining in family hands continued to dwindle, reduced to smaller parcels that made only small-scale gardening possible. Small and scattered plots of land were of little use in gaining a secure livelihood. They came to be regarded more as an emergency resource to be drawn on in case of some financial predicament. Still, ownership of even small parcels could hold symbolic meaning in that it represented the continued Indian possession of some of their lands.

Judging from the fact that during their lifetimes many proprietors and their families made no use of common rights to accumulate land beyond the initial division in 1719, some Indians resisted values associated with the transformation to a market economy. Complicated estate settlements suggest that notions of communal usage and ownership may have continued to prevail among some Speen families. Husbandry tools formed a tiny portion of enumerated estates. These families may have relied upon Native cultivation tools and techniques that estate enumerators might have ignored or overlooked. Yet this absence does call into question whether the Natick lands possessed by many of the Speens and Wabans were being cultivated at all.

Whether or not the Speen and Waban families resisted cultural changes in Natick, once land became a commodity, they could not avoid the effect of structural changes that followed. After the division of Natick's lands into individually owned possessions, English institutions that undergirded the market economy in the colony impinged on the everyday lives of Indians to a far greater degree than they had previously. For the Speens, Wabans, and other Natick families, entering into relations of debt allowed the English to pry loose parcels of land by compelling Indians to liquidate their property and settle their financial obligations. A whole host of other English institutions also related to the commodification of Indian lifeways accompanied the emergence of the land market, including indentured servitude (always present, but now transformed into a debtor-creditor relationship), wage labor (made more urgent as Indians became landless), and guardianship arrangements for Indian children (which enabled English caretakers to claim expenses that would prompt the sale of Indian lands).[19] In turn, as the commodification of Indian lifeways accomplished a gradual transition from Indian to English landownership in Natick, the mushrooming presence of the English accelerated the infiltration of English institutions into the day-to-day lives of Natick Indians.

Indian servitude and guardianship scattered a great number of Indian children among English families in and around Natick. Indian fathers, too, bound themselves out to make financial restitution for their debts and the debts of their children. These practices helped account for the splintering of Indian families and must have reduced their own chances for economic independence. There is no question that the surrounding English community benefited from Indian labor through these arrangements, which often seem to have been made without recourse to formal legal procedures. Besides splintering Indian families, indentured servitude also became a principal location in which English ideas about households and family ideology created and maintained racial hierarchies in New England. These relations, in turn, helped shape the colonial English family.[20]

The nursing and guardianship arrangements detailed in Speen probate dockets illustrate recurrent themes in mid-eighteenth-century Natick. Both Indian and English claimants for these services secured payments in estate settlements. Indians recouped expenses, even from family members, which testifies to changes in the social welfare practices of Natick Indians. By Indian custom, caretaking constituted a kinship obligation. With Indian entanglement in a market economy, these services became a commodifiable expense for which the provider could gain financial compensation. It is quite possible that caretaking obligations could not have been met without extreme hardship because so many Indian lifeways had been affected by English domination. Whereas it may be that commodification of such services represents capitulation to English norms, it is also possible that these charges provided a means for relatives to assert indisputable claims to at least part of the estate, since debts were paid before any property could be divided among the heirs. By establishing them-

---

[19] See also John Sainsbury, "Indian Labor in Early Rhode Island," *New England Quarterly* 48 (1975): 378–93.

[20] Ann Marie Plane, "Colonizing the Family: Marriage, Household, and Racial Boundaries in Southeastern New England to 1730" (Ph.D. diss., Brandeis University, 1994), especially 254, 279, 405–11.

selves as creditors, family members could prevent themselves from being wholly deprived of their inheritances.

Shifts in landowning accounted for a steady influx of English farmers and artisans into Natick and gave shape to a diverse place where the lives of Indians and English settlers became intertwined in a complex patchwork. Several English people figured prominently in the lives of the Speens and other Indian families, acting as guardians, masters, administrators, and attorneys for them. Many of the English who became enmeshed in Speen lives were neighbors, who came to possess contiguous land. Englishman Isaac Coolidge acted as administrator of the estates of Hannah and John Speen and as a guardian for their children. He was also a neighbor of Samuel Speen.[21] Englishman Joseph Perry undertook the settlement of Robert and Benjamin Speen's estates. He was a neighbor of John and Josiah Speen.[22] As was the case for other Indians, participation of English settlers in the everyday lives of the Speen families had intensified by the mid-eighteenth century.

Speen family prominence dated back to the founding of Natick. The six Speen men designated proprietors in 1719 were descendants of John Eliot's first converts, several of whom held leadership positions in the early years of Natick. Their hereditary land rights to Natick had been acknowledged when John Speen and his kin surrendered exclusive privileges to land at the founding of the community; this recognition was underscored at a 1719 meeting when it was voted "that all ye Speens is ye Proprietors of ye said Natick."[23]

James Speen (d. 1736) was the eldest son of "Old Speen," a first-generation resident of the community. His eldest son, John (d. by 1741), also received proprietary privileges. Other Speens granted rights to the common lands appear to be third-generation residents of Natick and cousins or brothers to John Speen and one another: Isaac (d. 1738), Abraham (d. by 1754), Josiah (d. 1749), and Moses (d. 1749). All but Isaac had married at least once.[24]

Proprietor Isaac Speen received a sixty-acre lot in the land division of 1719, then made no use of his proprietary privileges until he sold them to another Indian, John Ephraim, sometime before 1737.[25] Ephraim's twenty-eight-pound bond plus five pounds interest constituted virtually all of Isaac's enumerated estate when he died in the care of an Indian who apparently was not a blood relation.[26] Yet while Isaac Speen's land activities and estate evidenced little in the way of

[21] MCP #21032, John Speen, Admin., 1742; MCP #21027, Hannah Speen, Will, 1742; MCP #21033, Hannah Speen, Gdn., 1742; and MCP #21039, Samuel Speen, Admin., 1755.

[22] MCP #21032, John Speen, Admin., 1742; and MCP #21034, Josiah Speen, Admin., 1749. Division Orders.

[23] Original Indian Record Book (hereafter cited as OIRB), Morse Institute Public Library, Natick, MA, 17 May 1719.

[24] NVR.

[25] Land Grants to Proprietors, Freeholders, and Inhabitants of the Town of Natick, 1719 (hereafter cited as NPB1), Morse Institute Public Library, Natick, MA; and NPB2, 50.

[26] MCP #21028, Isaac Speen, Admin., 1742.

involvement in the market economy, structural alterations in the community indicated that commodification of social welfare affected him nonetheless. Indian Eleazer Paugenit's estate inventory showed that he had boarded and nursed Speen, paid for a physician's services, and for Isaac's coffin when he died.[27]

Proprietor Abraham Speen did use his common rights after 1719. He had sold eighty-one acres from his right in eleven separate pieces ranging from one to twenty-four acres, only one parcel to an English purchaser.[28] When he died, he still owned nearly fifty-four acres in four parcels (less than his original sixty-acre grant and no longer a contiguous lot), the largest piece of which was located "near Speens Elewares." Debts required the sale of some of this remaining land. His fourteen-year-old daughter, Mary, was made a ward of Englishman Michael Bacon at that time.[29]

John Speen and his wife, Hannah, both brought proprietary rights to their marriage, John as a designated proprietor and Hannah as sole heir to proprietor Samuel Will.[30] As a result of their status, this family owned substantial lands in Natick: John owned more than 156 acres at his death, and Hannah brought at least 145 acres to the family. They resided in an English-style dwelling house complete with glass windows and furnished with chairs, chests, bedding, earthenware, ironware, pewter, brass, and books.[31]

These possessions suggest that John and Hannah Speen lived prosperously and in English fashion. Certainly the family aspired to many of the amenities of English material culture. Yet the evidence is mixed. No inventory of John Speen's personal estate has been preserved to examine for ownership of husbandry tools. Hannah's personal estate included not just English household goods but also "wompon and suckenhock," and "baskets and brombes[,] brombes and brombsticks," indicating both English and Indian cultural orientations and suggesting how Hannah may have earned income for the household. Indian women made a living selling baskets and brooms throughout New England well into the nineteenth century.[32]

---

[27] MCP #13111, Eleazer Kenepaugenit, Admin., 1741.   [28] NPB2.

[29] MCP #21024, Abraham Speen, Admin., 1754; and MCP #21035, Mary Speen, Gdn., 1752. A letter in the probate docket of Samuel Speen, who died before 1747, suggests Abraham was in financial straits by that time. Rev. Oliver Peabody asked permission of the probate judge for Samuel's administrator, Michael Bacon, to advance Speen some money to stave off a lawsuit. Though Peabody stated that "considerable" money was due to Samuel Speen's estate, the docket contains no documentation on the estate itself. MCP #21038, Samuel Speen, Admin., 1747.

[30] NPB1 and NPB2. I have determined that Hannah Speen was sole heir to Samuel Will through comparison of the index of grants in his right to the prose descriptions of actual land grants in NPB2.

[31] MCP #21032, John Speen, Admin., 1742; and MCP #21027, Hannah Speen, Will, 1742. This probate docket actually contains two separate estate settlements for two different Hannah Speens – one from 1742, and the other from 1767. Hannah Speen (1742) left a will; Hannah Speen (1767) died intestate, per administration order in docket.

[32] On New England Indian baskets, see *A Key into the Language of Woodsplint Baskets*, ed.

Separate probate proceedings on the sizable estates of John and Hannah Speen acknowledged that each held special proprietary positions. Hannah's estate settlement reveals that this was at least her second marriage and that she had elected to equip her children with English skills. Hannah remembered sons Samuel and Zachary, both from her previous marriage, with the lands that had come to her as sole heir to her father's proprietary right.[33] Reasoning that her daughter, Hannah, and son Joseph would benefit from their father's estate, she bequeathed to them only her share in the corporate rents and interest on the Magunkaquog lands.[34]

In the end, only one of the desires Hannah expressed in her will was fulfilled: Englishman Isaac Coolidge of Sherborn acted as her executor. Guardianship charges for son Zachary, who had resided with the executor since the age of two, nearly exceeded the value of Hannah's estate. Coolidge's account detailed charges for clothing, schooling, and "Taking Care of said Zachary in his Last Sickness when in the fifteenth year of his age." Sparing no detail, Coolidge listed nursing and doctors' charges, as well as 'Sugar, Raisons & other necessaries" and "funeral Charges as Gloves for ye minester[,] gloves for the bearers[,] Cofen[,] diging the grave and linen to lay him out in &."[35]

The same day Coolidge presented his final accounting on the estate, he filed guardianship documents for the deceased's daughter, Hannah, age fifteen, who lived only three more years.[36] Charges submitted by two English and one Indian physician (Peter Brand) were recouped in the final settlement of John Speen's estate. By this time John and Hannah Speen apparently had no surviving direct heirs. Instead, John Speen's siblings and their children received legacies in land of twenty to thirty acres each. Elizabeth Speen, daughter of Benjamin, was awarded the English-style dwelling house, valued at 100 pounds in the division order. Her English guardian arranged to lease out Elizabeth's holdings.[37]

Proprietor Josiah Speen also possessed a good-sized estate when he died in 1749, including more than eighty-seven acres of land and a dwelling house val-

Ann McMullen and Russell G. Handsman (Washington, CT: American Indian Archaeological Institute, 1987).
[33] The children's names are listed as "Samuel Speen and Zachary Speen alias Maynard" in Hannah's will. It is possible that her previous marriage may have been to another Speen or that more than one marriage had preceded this one. Aside from a mention in a 1741 land-sale petition of her "two small children," her will provides the only evidence that Hannah Speen had children.
[34] Hannah's bequest for her son Joseph was phrased as follows: "if sd Joseph be Alive & Live to return."
[35] MCP #21027, Hannah Speen, Will, 1742.
[36] MCP #21033, Hannah Speen, Gdn., 1742.
[37] MCP #21032, John Speen, Admin., 1742; and MCP #21026, Elizabeth Speen, Gdn., 1743. Joseph Perry's 1753 guardianship account includes proceeds for renting Elizabeth's land and house over the previous three years and nine months. She was probably residing with her guardian at this time.

ued at 250 pounds that was furnished with a table and chairs, a chest, a pewter pot, and pewter spoons. Nine acres were sold to reimburse the administrator of the estate, Englishman Benjamin Kendall, for provisions he provided for the Speen family during Josiah's last illness plus his funeral charges. Josiah owned "Tinker Tools and one pair of spoon Moulds" but no husbandry tools at the time of his death. He may have been beyond the age of field labor by this time: In 1744 he had sold land to discharge debts incurred through an illness "and [for] his more comfortable living in his old age." Still, the lands left to be divided among Josiah's heirs were described as "unimproved."[38]

At least three of Josiah and Judith Speen's children survived to adulthood: Daniel, Lydia, and Sarah. During his lifetime, Josiah Speen had arranged for his minor son Daniel to serve an apprenticeship with Jonathan Rice, an Englishman from Sudbury. Much to his father's chagrin, Daniel was accused of theft while serving with Rice. Rice agreed to settle the matter privately instead of bringing suit if Josiah would make restitution. Josiah agreed, and "moved . . . by the Advice of English friends As well as his own Parental Affection, became Bound unto the said Deacon Rice to make good the loss & damage by him Sustained." In order to extricate himself from this indenture, Josiah wanted to sell six acres granted him for services to the proprietors.[39]

Daniel and his sister Lydia took responsibility for caring for their aged mother when their father died, but alterations in the community had commodified such kinship obligations. Daniel gave Lydia a deed for "between Twenty & Thirty acrs of Valluable land," directing that Lydia in turn provide a predetermined sum of money for Judith's support. Lydia requested permission to sell land in 1752 to raise the money, particularly as her seventy-year-old mother was ill and already indebted to physicians.[40] But she retained her rights to her mother's thirds; her sister Sarah Ahauton gave her a quitclaim to them in 1769 as a resident of Bridgewater.[41]

Like his kinsman Josiah, proprietor Moses Speen died in 1749 owning land, a dwelling house, clothing, household goods, and furniture, but no husbandry tools. About the same time Josiah had sold land to support himself in his old age, Moses also pleaded for permission to sell land for income.[42] Moses had

---

[38] MCP #21034, Josiah Speen, Admin., 1749; JH 20:355, 22 Feb. 1743/4; and AR 13:481, Appen. 8, Chap. 45, 29 June 1745. The dwelling house was acquired sometime after 1729. JH 9:132, 26 Nov. 1726; and AR, 11:449, Appen. 6, Chap. 10, 2 Dec. 1729.

[39] MA 31:312, 1742. Josiah received this grant for serving on proprietary committees that supervised the laying out of land. NPB2, throughout. It may have been during this indenture that Daniel learned to write: his signature appears on the estate division order along with the marks of his two sisters.

[40] MA 32:296, 1752. Daniel had died prior to this time.

[41] Middlesex County Court, Grantee and Grantor Records (hereafter cited as MCG), Cambridge, MA, 98:517, Sarah Ahauton to Lydia Speen, 1769/1788, quitclaim to right in ten acres and a dwelling house in Natick.

[42] MCP #21036, Moses Speen, Admin., 1749; and MA 31:469, 1743. Also inventoried was "wampumpeague."

suffered a stroke "many years ago" that left him partially paralyzed. Though he had managed to keep his estate relatively solvent, his advancing age and disability led to indebtedness and the sale of twenty-two acres of his land. This parcel was sold out of a sixty-acre lot "lying remote" that he was physically unable to improve. Speen explained that he had only two daughters, one who was too young to assist him, and "the Eldest of whom is Married and Removed to Some Scores of Miles distance."[43] His use of his common right seems to have been his principal means of support during his lifetime: he sold just over eighty-eight acres to nine English purchasers, and thirty-six acres to three different Indians.[44] Despite his financial predicaments, eleven years later Moses Speen left an estate totaling more than 425 pounds and encumbered by only fifty-four pounds in debts. Twenty-five acres of land with a dwelling house was all that remained in his possession of the 180 acres he had been granted out of the commons.

The Natick vital records indicate that Moses Speen had outlived two wives and that his only child died in 1730. His petition, however, cites the two daughters. His probate documents add further detail. The account for administration includes a disbursement to his daughter Mary Peegun for 115 days nursing "in his Last Sickness."[45] Mary had chosen Englishman Jonathan Foster to administer the estate, who "has care of Sd Speen['s] Grand Sons now Liveing with him."[46] Though nothing further is known about this family, the linked documentation extends the lineage two generations further than the town's vital records taken in isolation.

Proprietor James Speen made virtually no use of his common right during his lifetime. His original grant out of the commons consisted of a sixty-acre home lot. This land had been laid out in 1719 contiguously with land given to his first wife, Bethiah (a sixty-acre freehold grant that did not entitle her to future land divisions) and the sixty acres his son John received as an initial proprietary right.[47] No other grants were made in his right until his estate was settled, when eighty-five acres more were granted directly to the heirs. An additional fourteen acres were sold in separate transactions to five different

[43] MA 31:469, 1743.

[44] To English: NPB2, 101, 1746, 5 acres to Josiah Whiting; NPB2, 101, 1746, 4 3/4 acres to Joseph Perry; NPB2, 101, 1746, 2 1/4 acres to Joseph Travis; NPB2, 104, 1746, 15 1/2 acres to Joseph Graves; NPB2, 109, 1748, 16 1/4 acres to Ebenezer Gleason; MCG 43:693, to Jonathan Lealand, 1744/1744, 6 3/4 acres; MCG 44:448, to Daniel Biglow, 1744/1744, 10 acres; MCG 44:449, to Daniel Biglow, 1744/1744, 12 3/4 acres; MCG 54:602, to Ezekiel Lealand, 1744/1757, 2 3/4 acres; and MCG 60:91, to Samuel Gleason, 1744/1762, 12 3/4 acres. To Indians: NPB2, 87, 1743, 10 acres to William Thomas; MCG 45:97, to William Thomas, 1731/1745, 10 acres; MCG 46:23, to Nathaniel Coochuck, 1746/1746, 12 acres; and MCG 46:41, to Jonathan Babesuck, 1742/1746, 4 acres.

[45] Mary Speen had married Jonathan Peegun of New Roxbury in 1730. OIRB. Another Indian woman, Sarah Francis, was also reimbursed for nursing. MCP #21036, Moses Speen, Admin., 1749.

[46] MCP #21036, Moses Speen, Admin., 1749.   [47] NPB1.

Englishmen; presumably, these lots were sold to raise capital for adminstration costs.[48]

James Speen had had at least five sons and two daughters by two wives, Bethiah Maquah, who died in 1730, and Abigail, who lived until 1759. Three of his children preceded him in death, sons John (the eldest) and Benjamin, and daughter Elizabeth. All three of these children left heirs to their grandfather's estate. The estate was divided among eight individuals: the widow, Abigail; sons Samuel, Robert, and Joseph; daughter Abigail Moheag; and three grandchildren whose parents were deceased: Elizabeth Speen, daughter of Benjamin; Bethiah Cole, daughter of Elizabeth Speen Cole; and Hannah, daughter of John Speen. All told, 130 acres were divided among the eight heirs. The division order provided each individual with a separately defined lot of land ranging from ten acres to twenty-two acres (the widow's thirds). Administrators noted that there were four heirs "here," implying that these were the only heirs resident in the community, and almost as an afterthought, added two sons who "are gone & we are ready to think Will never return, being Suspected of Murder."[49]

James Speen's widow Abigail outlived him by more than twenty years. In 1747 she asked the General Court to allow her to sell all of her remaining land in Natick (estimated at thirty acres). She complained that age and physical difficulties had rendered her unable to support herself. In dire circumstances, Abigail "cast herself" on Englishman Joseph Graves, who had supported her at his house for the past two years. Now, with "nothing to recompence Sd Graves with[,] nor to procure for her the Necessaries of life for the time present & to come," she wanted to pay her debts, and provide support and a "decent Christian Burial."[50]

Abigail Speen Moheag became a widow in 1745; her husband, John, was fatally injured when their wigwam burned.[51] Like her mother, Abigail faced the problem of shelter and sustenance. Until 1762, Abigail managed to support herself "by her Industery in the business of making Brooms Baskets and horse Collars." Infirmities had indebted her to physicians and others, and her situation was made worse by the lack of children and relatives who could take care of her. Abigail found herself homeless in 1764, "for her Cousens house

---

[48] NPB2, 82, 1743, 1 1/2 acres to William Rider; NPB2, 82, 1743, 2 acres to Daniel Dewing; NPB2, 82, 1743, 4 acres to John Coolidge; NBP2, 83, 1743, 1 1/2 acres to Thomas Russell; and MCG 43:440, to Joseph Perry, 1743/1743, 5 acres. All of these transactions were handled by Speen's administrator, Jonathan Lealand.

[49] *NVR*; NPB2; MCP #21031, James Speen, Admin., 1742; and Vault Materials, Morse Institute Public Library, Natick, MA, James Speen Estate Division Order. In fact, the division order for the estates provides the only direct evidence, with one exception, of the survival of this Speen family past the middle of the eighteenth century. The exception was James's son Benjamin, who died in 1740 and left an estate for his heir.

[50] MA 31:529, 1747. Abigail lived another ten years.

[51] AR, 13:500–1, Appen. 8, Chap. 96, 27 Sept. 1745.

where She used to live is taken Down and Carried off."[52] When she died in 1771 at about age seventy, no probate documents were filed.

Abigail Moheag had leased land to Joseph Graves.[53] Graves was intensively involved in the affairs of this Speen lineage. He provided caretaking and other services from which he benefited financially, and he also directly gained from the real estate holdings of the family. He had acted as a caretaker for James Speen's widow, Abigail, and was administrator of the estates of James's son Samuel, and James's granddaughter, Bethiah Cole. Her debts to him included room and board for her and her child, as well as nursing and funeral charges for her child.[54] Guardians of the Natick Indians had recommended Graves for joint administration of the Samuel Speen and Bethiah Cole estates, as he appeared to be the "greatest Creditor" to them.[55]

If alive, Samuel would have had cause to dispute the selection. Earlier, Samuel had requested that a deed be barred from registration in the county land records. Samuel argued "that by the Insinuations of Joseph Graves of Natick (a man that I have Confided in) I have ben indused to Sign Some Writings of Conveyance Which I aprehend to be to my damage." The writings in question were a forfeiture to his rights in his mother's thirds.[56] Graves administered the estate nonetheless, providing just over six acres for Samuel's widow, Esther. He levied a variety of charges against the estate, including a trip to the county court in Cambridge to block sale of the land Samuel disputed, services in the settling of John Speen's estate, attending a proprietors' meeting on his behalf, and "cash lent you."[57] The Natick guardians themselves harbored doubts about Graves's motives, despite the fact that they had recommended him as administrator. The surviving guardianship records for the Natick Indians included this undated notation: "Watch Graves as to Sam: Speens Land to be Sold – else will wrong be done – Graves wants to buy it &c."[58]

Samuel Speen had other entanglements with the English legal system. Some time before 1742, he obligated himself to make satisfaction on debts incurred by his brother Robert, who had become ill, recovered, and subsequently absconded.[59] He moved for license to sell ten acres of his anticipated inheritance "To be applied To Realeave your Petitioner out of the Difficulty he is in by becoming Bound for his Brother."[60] This land sale allowed Samuel to escape indentured servitude on his brother's behalf.

Samuel Speen later expressed his intention to engage in agriculture. In 1745 he and his sister Abigail Moheag filed a petition to sell land inherited from their

---

[52] MA 33:300–1, 1764.

[53] MCP #12363, Natick Guardians, Gdn., 1835. Graves leased four acres from Abigail Moheag and agreed to construct a fence on her land as part of the arrangement.

[54] MCP #21039, Samuel Speen, Admin., 1755; and MCP #4801, Bethia Cole, Admin., 1755.

[55] MCP #21039, Samuel Speen, Admin., 1755.

[56] Ibid. Samuel apparently signed and gave to his mother some sort of waiver of these rights.

[57] Ibid.   [58] MCP #12363, Natick Indians, Gdn., 1835.

[59] MCP #21037, Robert Speen, Admin., 1749.   [60] MA 31:419, 1742.

uncle John Speen. Samuel wanted the proceeds "laid out for the better cultivation and improvement of the estate he lives upon."[61] Thirty-one acres were enumerated in his estate inventory. Still, labor of some sort continued to form at least part of Samuel's economic livelihood. Among other expenses listed when his estate was settled was a trip to Boston "to git Samuel Speen's wages."[62]

Elizabeth Speen, another granddaughter of James Speen, was made a ward of Englishman Joseph Perry. He apparently provided Elizabeth with some education, charging her father's estate for expenses that included a "Primmer."[63] Elizabeth survived to adulthood and was married at least twice: first to Samuel Paugenit of Natick in 1754, then to "transient" Job Ahorton in 1770. Elizabeth's daughter Zibia Paugenit survived to marry sometime in the 1770s, preserving a genealogical line that ran back to the original Speen convert family of the mid-seventeenth century. This line of the Speen family constitutes one link between seventeenth-century converts and nineteenth-century survivors.[64]

The historically prominent Waban families also faced monumental struggles engendered by enmeshment in the market economy. Old Waban, a local headman, had been one of John Eliot's most important early converts. Capt. Thomas Waban, who was probably the son of Old Waban, achieved prominence in early eighteenth-century Natick that was in keeping with his family's pre-Natick status, though defined in very different terms. An officeholder and town clerk, the bilingual scribe Capt. Thomas Waban was a principal agent in negotiating between English and Indian ways in early eighteenth-century Natick.

Unlike the children of James Speen, some of whom inherited property and produced families of their own, financial distress and catastrophic illness affected the Waban family immediately following the proprietor's death in 1722. Whereas Speen left enough land to be divided among his eight heirs, Thomas Waban's estate was consumed by debts accrued between 1725 and 1727, when what may have been an epidemic claimed the lives of at least four family members.[65]

From then on, English colonial institutions impinged on the lives of the remaining Wabans. Isaac Waban, Capt. Thomas Waban's son, had encountered serious financial troubles as early as the 1730s. In 1739 he was imprisoned in Cambridge gaol because of two legal executions against him. Englishman Isaac

---

[61] AR, 13:500–1, Appen. 8, Chap. 96, 27 Sept. 1745. This land was described as a common lot even though the division order had detailed legal descriptions and precise boundaries to the lots.

[62] MCP #21039, Samuel Speen, Admin., 1755.

[63] MCP #21026, Elizabeth Speen, Gdn., 1743. Her cousin Bethiah Cole had also been made a ward of Joseph Perry at this time. MCP #4800, Bethia Cole, Gdn., 1743.

[64] *NVR*.

[65] MCP #22401, Thomas Waban, Will, 1725. See also Daniel Mandell, "'Standing by His Father': Thomas Waban of Natick, circa 1630–1722," in *Northeastern Indian Lives, 1632–1816*, ed. Robert S. Grumet (Amherst: University of Massachusetts Press, 1996), 166–92.

Coolidge of Natick satisfied Waban's obligations in exchange for an indenture. Waban remained bound to Coolidge for a couple of years but then deserted. Coolidge obtained a judgment against Waban at the Inferior Court of Common Pleas at Concord for twenty-four pounds, and had Waban's lands attached for satisfaction in 1741.[66]

Isaac was identified as a laborer when his estate was probated in 1746, even though he still owned real estate worth 190 pounds. The sum total of his personal estate was "an old Bible, Pot and Pothook, [and] other utensils."[67] The only heir to this very modest estate was his daughter, Mary, born about 1734 to Isaac and his wife, Hannah, daughter of Lt. John Wamsquan; Hannah had died in 1743.[68] Rev. Oliver Peabody suggested that the small piece of land Isaac had left could "be profitable to his Child were there an administr to take Care of it."[69] In 1749 orphaned Mary Waban of Newton chose Englishman Enoch Parker as her guardian. Her signature on the document is evidence that Mary had received at least some schooling.[70]

Thomas Waban, grandson of Capt. Thomas Waban, married Sarah Sety in 1738. Their only child, Sarah, was born twelve years later. Englishman Samuel Morse was made the child's legal guardian in 1753, the year after her mother died.[71] In 1755 Morse petitioned the General Court to sell land the child had inherited from her mother to pay for her support. He explained that the mother had died when Sarah was an infant, and the "Father of ye said minor Absconded and left it to Suffer."[72] Morse, who had hired an Indian woman to nurse the infant, had already sold part of Sarah's estate. He wanted funds for her future support.[73] Though described as sickly by Morse, Sarah survived as heir to the final division of lands in Natick in 1763.

Another grandson of Capt. Thomas Waban, Hezekiah Waban, attained no more success in life than did his brother. He had engaged in military service, and in 1744 was "feared lost" in Cuba when his three sons were still very young.[74] Hezekiah's estate was not probated until 1752 when his father's holdings were finally divided: Hezekiah received a thirty-five-acre bequest but left no personal estate at all.[75]

According to the probate docket, two of Hezekiah's sons had been placed with Englishmen, probably in their father's absence. One (unidentified) was lodged with William Eames, and the other, Jabez, with Benjamin Muzzy of Sherborn. When he turned seventeen in 1749, Jabez resisted this arrangement, fleeing from

[66] MA 31:336–8, 1741.   [67] MCP #23397, Isaac Waban, Admin., 1746.
[68] NVR; and MCP #23688, John Wamsquan, Will, 1746.
[69] MCP #23397, Isaac Waban, Admin., 1746.   [70] MCP #23398, Mary Waban, Gdn., 1746.
[71] NVR; and MCP #23403, Sarah Waban, Gdn., 1753.
[72] MA 32:694–5, 1755. According to the Natick church records, Thomas Waban died in military service. Peabody and Badger Records, Church of Natick, 1725–95 (hereafter cited as NCR), Typescript copy, Massachusetts Historical Society, Boston, MA.
[73] MA 32:694–5, 1755.   [74] NCR.
[75] MCP #23396, Hezekiah Waban, Admin., 1752.

his English guardian and enlisting on a "warship." At the request of Jabez's grandfather, Muzzy journeyed to Boston to retrieve the youth. Evidently, Jabez preferred not to be retrieved: Muzzy later complained that he ran away "Sundrea Times and often Stealing my Horses and Riding them to great Excese." During his final escape in 1750 Jabez contracted a fatal illness. Muzzy later petitioned Hezekiah's estate to recoup the expenses for Jabez's lingering sickness and death as well as for other costs of guardianship.[76]

Virtually every member of the Waban family faced significant problems during this period. Debt plagued the families, and indentured and wage labor were their best economic prospects. By the middle decades of the eighteenth century, they seemed to have no success at all, and they demonstrated a penchant for fleeing from the substantial problems they confronted in the community. Only Rachel Waban, daughter of Capt. Thomas Waban, left children who can be traced beyond mid-century.

The commodification of social relations did intrude on Indian lifeways. Landholdings fragmented, families dispersed, and economic possibilities were constrained. Despite this evidence of hardship, the documents do not bear out the myth of Indian extinction. Although the Wabans were devastated, like the Speen family, some of them endured. Some Speen lineages are traceable through the written record, and other lines certainly continued even though they cannot be completely documented. Despite their struggles, at least four of the six Speen lineages can be documented into the late eighteenth century: those of Abraham, Josiah, Moses, and James. Isaac and John Speen seem to have had no direct heirs, yet even these proprietors left collateral descendants.

C. *Marriage, gender, and land*

From the beginning, English missionaries targeted Indian household structure, marriage, gender roles, and family life for transformation according to their own notions of order. The English "colonized the family" by mandating marriage form and regulating behavior within families, although throughout southeastern New England (and possibly in Natick), Indians continued also to practice customary marriage and at times retained Native marriage rituals and ideals.[77]

As is evident in the life histories of the Speens and Wabans, the stress of changes that followed from intensified entanglement in the market economy carried stark implications for Indian families. So, too, did the structural realignment of property relations affect marriage patterns, family forms, and gender

---

[76] MCP #23396, Hezekiah Waban, Admin., 1752. Muzzy presented an elaborate narrative detailing his experiences with Jabez Waban. The administrator's expenses included an inquest on the body of Jabez, and on the body of his brother Solomon, though no explanation for Solomon's death is offered.

[77] Plane, "Colonizing the Family," 407–8.

roles, although Indians responded in diverse ways to the shifting social, cultural, and economic cirumstances in Natick.

The marriage choices and family forms displayed by the Awassamugs, Abrahams, and Thomases illustrate many aspects of cultural change in Natick. Marriage choices and alternate family forms give insight into the ways that Indians selectively participated in and resisted the market economy. Although some Indians married locally, others wed Indian men with no apparent connection to Natick, which helps account for some Indian influx into the community. For these men, marrying into proprietary families may have been the only access they had to land rights. Some of these families went on to build English-style farms, which demonstrates their dynamic understanding of cultural identity. This conception of identity, together with a fluid notion of community, enabled the proprietary families to redefine and thus perpetuate their lineages.

Stories from these three lineages also highlight the complex impact of the realignment of economic roles on gender relations in Natick. Some Indian families accepted, at least to some extent, English cultural ideals that defined agriculture as men's work. For some Indian women, becoming more like their English counterparts left them "divorced from the land" and impoverished when their husbands died or left them.[78] When Eunice Brooks, in 1762, complained of having "submitted to the most pinching want that any one could conceive a person of Estate could Submit to," she sounded a common theme among the female descendants of the proprietors.[79] Because they no longer farmed the land, when they found themselves alone they were unable to use it to make a living except by selling it.

Other family histories suggest that some Indian men resisted English prescriptions for gender roles. The periodic or permanent absence of men from their families is striking in many life stories, especially in the Awassamug lineage. Financial ruin drove some Indian men to abandon their families along with the legal consequences of their woes, but some enlisted repeatedly in military campaigns, which resulted in lengthy stints away from their families. These short- or long-term absences permitted Indian men to resist English notions about men's work, and at least in the case of military participation and seafaring, to reformulate Indian ideas about mobile male economic roles.[80] But the new shape of male Indian mobility, even more dramatically in the case of men who abandoned their families, now had the effect of undermining household economic sufficiency and creating wants instead of alleviating them because

---

[78] Jean M. O'Brien, "Divorced from the Land: Accommodation Strategies of Indian Women in Eighteenth-Century New England," in *Gender, Kinship, and Power*, ed. Mary Jo Maynes, Ann Waltner, Brigette Soland, and Ulrike Strasser (New York: Routledge, 1996).

[79] MA 33:204–5, 1762. She was allowed to sell only twelve.

[80] See Richard R. Johnson, "The Search for a Usable Indian: An Aspect of the Defense of Colonial New England," *Journal of American History* 63 (1977): 623–51; and Daniel Vickers, "The First Whalemen of Nantucket," *William and Mary Quarterly* 3d ser., 40 (1983): 560–83.

men left behind women and children to struggle for themselves. It also seems that even some landowning Awassamug men resisted English ideals by not farming their holdings, in contrast to husbands of Thomas women who embraced the idea of male agriculture, perhaps leaving this customarily female task to the women. Male landowners who did not farm their land rejected English notions about how the market economy should structure gender roles. The experiences of the Awassamugs, Abrahams, and Thomases point to important gender dynamics at work in eighteenth-century Natick as well as to the difficulties faced even by once-prominent Indian families.

Like the Speen families, John Awassamug held claims to prominence that predated the settlement of Natick. A proprietary right had been awarded to his heirs in 1719, probably because of his prestige and the family's customary right to lands around Natick. His father, John, had sold several large parcels of land near Natick in the 1680s, and his marriage to Yawata, daughter of the Pawtucket sachem Nanapeshamet, represented the merging of two high-status Indian families.[81] Neither John nor his four (or possibly five) brothers survived to witness codification of the proprietary system, but the community acknowledged their importance by awarding a common right to the heirs.

John Brooks, an Indian whose exact origins are unknown, parlayed his marriage to Hannah Awassamug Pelemy, daughter of proprietor John Awassamug, into a comfortable English-style life. It gave him the opportunity to leave a "good Farm . . . & some moveables" at his death in 1745.[82] Farm implements inventoried at that time included hoes, axes, a pitchfork, shovel, scythe, meat tub, churn, cheese tub, and cheese press. He also owned livestock: a horse, three cows, a bull, a steer, a heifer, and three swine. His home was furnished with a bed and bedstead, earthenware, knives, forks, baskets, and "Barks," presumably meaning Indian-crafted containers.[83]

Beneficiaries of John Brooks's estate were his second wife, Elizabeth Peegun Brooks (of Barnstable), their two sons, Joseph (b. 1743) and Joshua (b. 1744), and John and Hannah's three daughters, Elizabeth (b. c. 1725), Eunice (b. 1731), and Anna (b. c. 1734). The land brought to the marriage by Hannah, who died in 1737, was kept separate and, in keeping with English practice, was settled solely upon the offspring of the first marriage. The three daughters received about twenty acres of land each. All five of John Brooks's children were placed under the guardianship of Englishmen. The lands of at least two of them (Eunice and Anna) were leased out by their guardians.[84]

---

[81] See Chapter 3; and Temple, *History of Framingham*, 39–40. Temple described John Awassamug Sr. as the nephew of the Nipmuck chief sachem Wuttawushan.

[82] Rev. Oliver Peabody included a note in Brooks's probate file that this farm "came by his first wife." MCP #2845, John Brooks, Admin., 1745.

[83] Ibid.

[84] Ibid; and *NVR*. Eunice's guardian, Hezekiah Allen of Dedham, used proceeds from her lands to purchase clothing, "Sunderys," boarding, and medicine. The only financial

The children failed to duplicate the success of their parents. Elizabeth Brooks Lawrence petitioned the General Court in 1753 for a land sale, reciting a litany of misfortune. Five years before, her husband had become ill in Mendon and accumulated a large sum in debts. The debts mounted when he got sick again in Natick. In about 1755 "her husband went away and left her, and has been absent ever since," leaving Elizabeth and her small children in "very great Straights and difficultys." Her troubles were exacerbated by debts amassed for the illness and funeral of her sister Anna, for which Elizabeth took responsibility. Elizabeth's husband brought no estate to the marriage, and she wanted to sell twenty acres of "unimproved, & unprofitable land four miles from the meeting house" that belonged to her, keeping the more profitable and convenient land that had belonged to Anna.[85] Elizabeth's husband apparently never returned, and she married Stepney Senah of Medway in 1758. Two years later, their son Joseph was born, described in the Natick Church Records as "negro."[86]

Eunice Brooks petitioned to sell part of her legacy in the mid-1750s as well. Eunice Brooks had married Thomas Spywood at about age twenty-eight, and they had two sons, Thomas and John.[87] She had much in common with her sister Elizabeth. Describing herself as "being of a feeble constitution [who] . . . can neither Support her Self in time of health, nor pay her charges arising in time of sickness," Eunice also complained that her shelter was unsafe "and uncomfortable because Leakey." Eunice moved to sell twelve acres, which she argued could be done without damaging the value of her home lot. So determined was she to retain her property that she "never yet Sold any, chusing rather to undergo hardship than to dispose of any of her land."[88]

Her second petition, filed in 1762, pleaded that her "Husband Some Years Ago Absconded and left her in very distressing Circumstances, and he having never returned." Her weak constitution had prevented her from laboring to support herself and her children, who were now all deceased. Having land already laid out as well as a common right, Eunice moved to sell twenty acres. Despite Eunice's claims of infirmity, she lived until 1785.[89]

Elizabeth and Eunice were abandoned by their husbands, mired in difficult economic circumstances and left to fend for themselves and their children. Though it is impossible to measure precisely the magnitude of the problem, scattered references to men absconding from Natick do suggest that Elizabeth and Eunice Brooks were not alone. This practice certainly contributed to a decline in the male population of Natick from at least the 1750s onward.[90]

---

benefit Anna garnered from her holdings, managed by Joseph Chickering of Dedham, seems to have been expenses arising from her "last sickness" in 1753. The balance of her income was expended for building a stone wall on her property. MCP #2847, Eunice and Joseph Brooks, Gdn., 1745; and MCP #2846, Anna and Joshua Brooks, Gdn., 1745.

[85] MA 32:440, 1753. [86] NCR.
[87] *NVR.* [88] MA 32:749, 1756.
[89] *NVR.*
[90] The shifting sex ratios of the population throughout the eighteenth century are discussed in Chapter 6.

Military service also helped to account for temporary absences of Natick men, and sometimes for their demise. Indian participation in colonial wars had begun as early as King Philip's War in 1675–76. Thomas Awassamug explained that he had been "repeatedly called out in the Countrys Service," and had returned suffering from "Weakness and Indispasitions."[91] He wanted to sell land for relief and necessities. Four years later, he elaborated:

> Your Petitioner hath been in his Majesties Service by the Space of Thirty years Successively; And by his hardships sustained therein, by Scouting &c is at length, and has been for Sundry years, rendred unable to labour by reason of the Gout, and other ails . . . But after-all has Estate of whereby he could Support himself.[92]

Infirmity and injury resulting from military service posed a severe problem for many Indian families. Repeated service by some individuals drew them away from the community for extended periods, and must have badly handicapped efforts at building an economic livelihood within Natick.[93]

Thomas Awassamug was just one of a number of Natick Indians who were landowners, but who seem to have eschewed farming. Perhaps he continued to view agriculture as women's work. By the 1750s, Thomas Awassamug had been reduced to a state of poverty despite owning land in Natick. Two of his daughters suffered as well, one of whom appeared frequently in the documentary record after 1763 as a pauper. Both of them married, however: Thankful Awassamug married William Feggins in Natick in 1763, and Submit married Solomon Wamsquan in Hopkinton in 1781.[94]

In some senses, involvement in the military just added another dimension of mobility to the lives of Thomas Awassamug and his family. The births of five children of Thomas and his wife, Deborah Abraham Awassamug, were recorded in Natick, Needham, and Medfield. Deborah, a Natick church member, was from Hassanamisco, adding another location to which this family had ties.[95] Thomas's son also married outside of Natick, first to Hannah Pegan Quitticus of Dudley in 1758, then to Jerusha Simons of Stoughton in 1772.[96] A petition to the General Court indicates that Submit was living in Holliston in 1774, destitute and resident in an English household where she was boarded and nursed.[97]

---

[91] MA 31:663, 1749. Thomas Awassamug's precise relationship to the proprietor is unclear. Two men by this name represented the proprietary right in meetings about the final division of common lands in 1763, which suggests they were direct heirs of the proprietor despite the absence of conclusive vital record links.

[92] MA 32:703, 1754.   [93] See Chapter 6.

[94] See Chapter 6. On Thankful Feggins and poor relief, see, for example, JH 44:20, 3 June 1767; and JH 45:162, 5 July 1769.

[95] *NVR*; and *Vital Records of Hopkinton, Massachusetts to the Year 1850* (Boston: New England Historical and Genealogical Society, 1911).

[96] *Vital Records of Dudley, Massachusetts to the end of the Year 1849* (Worcester, MA: Published by Franklin P. Rice, 1908); and *NVR*.

[97] MA 33:597, 1774.

Although the Awassamugs were among the most prominent Indians that originally settled in Natick, all of the descendants of the original family seemed to face severe constraints by the 1750s. Hardship and dispersal characterized the lifeways of these individuals and families. But just as Speen lineages continued, so too was the Awassamug family perpetuated beyond midcentury.

The experiences of the Abraham lineage underscore the shifts in fortune faced by different generations of families in Natick. When proprietor Samuel Abraham's son and namesake married Hannah Nehemiah, the family had two proprietary rights that they could draw upon. Whether access to two separate common rights guided their marriage choice is not clear, but Samuel Abraham Jr. did leave a much larger estate than his father had, nearly half of it "which came by his first wife," Hannah, through the proprietary right of her father, Thomas Nehemiah. He owned twenty acres plus one-half of a dwelling house on a fourteen-acre home lot. She left seventy-nine acres to be divided among five children, who received land ranging from eight to twenty-five acres. Samuel's second wife, Rachel, received one-third of the estate Samuel owned separate from the lands Hannah had brought to the marriage, just under seven acres of land with half a dwelling house. It was necessary to sell only five acres to discharge debts against the estate.[98]

Although Samuel and Hannah's children received inheritances, none of them used his or her bequests to duplicate Samuel's lifeways. Two of the younger Samuel Abraham's children had their estates probated. No real estate was listed in Joseph Abraham's 1759 inventory. His possessions consisted primarily of wearing apparel, including a "Beaverett hatt," deerskin breeches, "Old Indian Stockings," and "1 Old Wigg," plus shoemaking tools, and various other items. He also owned a Bible, spelling book, and brass ink pot. Some of his estate was sold to pay his debts.[99] Only an account is contained in the probate docket of Hosea Abraham. Included as credits were wages, which the administrator traveled to Boston to retrieve, and money received "for his Moveables Sold at Lake Geo[rge]."[100] Joseph Abraham seems to have followed a culturally mixed lifestyle. His brother Hosea engaged in pursuits indicating enmeshment in the English economy (wage labor) as well as activities with an older Indian cultural meaning (the military).

Samuel Abraham the proprietor clearly had held views sympathetic to the cultural modification that his son carried forth.[101] He strove to modify his lifeways in accordance with a future in which the lives of Indians and English settlers would be intertwined. He sold land in 1726 in order to build an English-style dwelling

[98] MCP #69, Samuel Abraham, Admin., 1747.
[99] MCP #66, Joseph Abraham, Admin., 1759.
[100] MCP #65, Hosea Abraham, Admin., 1757. He died in the military. Myron O. Stachiw, ed., *Massachusetts Officers and Soldiers, 1723–1743; Dummer's War to the War of Jenkins' Ear* (Boston: Society of Colonial Wars, 1979).
[101] I have found little information about other children of the proprietor.

house. Merged in his motivations were practical considerations and a vision of the changes occurring in the community. Having "a great desire to continue . . . under the Gospel" he also wanted "to Live more like my Christian English neighbours." At the same time he explained that he was "weary of Living in a Wigwam, it being also very difficult getting materials any where near us, where-with to build Wigwams, so often as we are obliged to do." He saw Natick "sur-rounded with English towns." Selling some of his "vacant land" would serve several purposes: provide him with a durable and comfortable house in exchange for land he did not intend to use, and provide encouragement for the Rev. Oliv-er Peabody, who (as we have seen) wanted an English neighbor.[102] At his death, he left forty-nine acres in wood lots, meadow, and pasture, in addition to his home lot and one-half of a dwelling house, a variety of husbandry tools, a horse, furniture, and household goods. Debts, however, rendered the estate insolvent.[103]

The three daughters of proprietor Solomon Thomas (d. 1727) and his wife, Sarah (d. 1741), all married Indian men who built English-style farms.[104] Judith married Joseph Ephraim Jr., son of a prominent Natick resident who was active in purchasing Indian land.[105] Sarah married Ammi Printer, a proprietor at Has-sanamisco. The Printers farmed an estate there of more than 300 acres with orchards and a furnished dwelling house. Ammi Printer's 1741 will left his interest income to his widow, his lands and future rights to his two sons, and 100-pound bequests to each of his four daughters.[106]

Leah married Jacob Chalcom, an Indian with unknown connections to the community who participated aggressively in the Natick land market. Together they produced nine children, at least four of whom died young. Two more failed to reach the age of eighteen; one, Benoni, died in 1755 in the Crown Point expedition in the Seven Years' War.[107] Only two Chalcom children seem to have survived to adulthood and married: daughters Esther (b. 1732, m. Oliver Sooduck of Dedham, 1753) and Hepzibah (b. 1735, m. Jonathan Peegun of Dudley, 1758). Leah Thomas Chalcom also had a son before her marriage: Daniel Thomas (1728–1778), who left a well-equipped English-style farm at his death.[108] When Daniel Thomas died in 1778 he owned a dwelling house fur-nished with pewter, brass, a bed, chests, tables, chairs, and a looking glass, plus thirty acres of land and a barn to shelter his livestock. His widow, Mary Tray

---

[102] MA 31:136–7, 1726. Six other proprietors and Peabody endorsed his petition.
[103] MCP #67, Samuel Abraham, Admin., 1746.
[104] They also had two sons, Solomon and Paul, who both survived to adulthood and married.
[105] MCP #22412, Solomon Thomas, Admin., 1736.
[106] MCP #7006, Joseph Ephraim Jr., Admin., 1743; and Worcester County Court, Probate Records (hereafter cited as WCP), #48045, Ammi Printer, Will, 1741. There are no birth records for any of these children.
[107] Robert E. Mackay, ed., *Massachusetts Soldiers in the French and Indian Wars, 1744–55* (Boston: New England Genealogical and Historical Society, 1978).
[108] *NVR*; and MCP #22397, Daniel Thomas, Admin., 1778.

Thomas, acted as administrator of his estate. [109] When she died in 1784, an even more impressive inventory was produced by their educated daughter, Hannah.[110]

The Chalcom women were raised according to English expectations for economic behavior, instead of traditional Indian practices that classified agriculture as women's work. In 1758, after Jacob Chalcom's death, Leah, Esther, and Hepzibah filed a joint petition with the General Court to sell the forty-six acres and common rights they owned, particularly since they had been "brought up to Household business, [and] are incapable of improving Said lands." They requested that the proceeds be invested so they could draw the interest for their support.[111]

The ties between the women remained strong throughout life. When Leah died in 1761, she left a will with bequests to each of her daughters, Esther and Hepzibah, and to Hepzibah's daughter, and Bethiah Peegun. Her estate was very small. The daughters endorsed a notation on the inventory stating that: "Being desirous that the wearing apparel and Furniture of our Said mother Should not be sold and Enjoyed by Strangers [we] have divided the same between us."[112] The daughters viewed their mother's property as something more than assets within an estate.

The transformation of property relations, which intensified after land became commodified in Natick, bore importantly on Indian marriage, family form, and gender relations. Access to land resources, diverse Indian views about men's and women's work, and gendered dimensions of Indian mobility as reformulated under colonialism all affected Indian families through marriage choice and family formation among the persisting Awassamug, Abraham, and Thomas lineages. Yet the diverse experiences of Indian lineages suggest that cultural tensions surrounded marriage, gender, and property relations. Awassamug family experiences suggest that proprietary land rights drew into the community landless Indian men who wanted to engage in agriculture, and that some Indian women were abandoned by husbands and left to struggle on their own. The absence of men from their families, including for military service and seafaring, reformulated Indian ideas about male mobility, but instead of contributing to household needs, the newer mobility often exacerbated them. Men's views toward performing agriculture, too, may have guided women's decisions about marriage choice. Although women from the Thomas lineage accepted English ideas that agriculture constituted men's work, some men, evidenced by Thomas Awassamug, seem to have rejected this cultural prescription. The cultural tensions surrounding gender roles produced diverse patterns.

[109] MCP #22397, Daniel Thomas, Admin., 1778. She was the daughter of proprietor Benjamin Tray.
[110] MCP #22397, Daniel Thomas, Admin., 1778; and MCP #22407, Mary Thomas, Will, 1784.
[111] MA 33:106–7, 1758.   [112] MCP #4125, Leah Chalcom, Will, 1761.

D. *Indians and the land market*

As is clear in all of the life histories of proprietary lineages, the individualization of landownership that made a land market possible constituted the most significant structural alteration in the Indian community in the eighteenth century. Indian families approached the emergence of the market in Natick lands in very different ways, but none of them remained unaffected. Even if individuals wanted to stand aloof from the new status of their property as a commodity, English institutions could now intrude and compel Indian land transactions to cover relations of debt.

Some Indians, however, began to look at land differently, and turned to the market as a way of negotiating cultural change and their identity as Indians. Like the Ephraim families, they drew upon their proprietary privileges, amassed land, then bought and sold it in order to acquire items of English material culture and, often, to build English-style farms. Or like Jacob Chalcom, a newcomer, they married women with proprietary rights and entered the market with a view toward expanding their holdings. Many also assisted their children, hoping to help them replicate their own choices and ensure the future of Indian landownership in Natick. Using the land market to accumulate more land than one could use suggests a radically different pattern of property relations than had operated within Native usufruct principles. Yet the imperative of giving land to their children to be farmed in English ways seems to have been a central premise behind Indian participation in the land market. Given the new status of land as a commodity with ownership backed by the English legal system, some individuals seem to have concluded that only by working through these mechanisms could they meet the objective of perpetuating Indian landownership into the future.

Some Indians tried to resist participation in the land market. Proprietor Thomas Peegun wanted to retain his landholdings intact to pass onto the next generation, but his children's debts and some of his own forced him to liquidate much of what he owned. Thus, although he participated in the land market, he did so largely involuntarily. Others, such as the Rumneymarsh and Tray families, though they bought and sold Natick land, seemed to try to draw boundaries between the Indian community and English neighbors by confining most of their land dealings to other Indians. Despite the fact that some of these Indians had adopted aspects of English material culture, the shape of their land market involvement signaled their wariness of English neighbors, and suggests that while they may have accepted the notion of individual landownership, they also wanted to use the English legal system to protect Indian ownership of Natick.

Leah Thomas's husband, Jacob Chalcom, bought land eight times from seven different Indian landowners, sold land four times to Indians, and exchanged land three times.[113] He also sold land fourteen times in separate transactions to eight

---

[113] NPB2, 15, 1731, 30 acres from Isaac Waban; MCG 27:516, from John Pittimee, 1728/1728, 30 acres; MCG 46:98, from Samuel Abraham Jr., 1731/1746, 20 acres; MCG

different Englishmen.[114] Chalcom's twenty-nine separate transactions involving nearly five hundred acres of Natick land made him a key player in the turnover of Natick lands.[115]

Jacob and Leah Chalcom struggled throughout their twenty-six-year marriage to establish and upgrade their English-style farm and provide for their children. They became involved in the local land market to raise capital for building their farm, providing dowers for their daughters, and coping with financial setbacks. In 1753 Jacob Chalcom described their achievements:

> Your Petitioner by his labour and industry hath purchased rights in the Propriety at Said Natick . . . and hath built a good dwelling-house and barn, and lives in English fashion, and having but One Son, and Two daughters, hath learned them to Read & Write; And your Petitioner having occasion to keep a yoak of oxen to carry on his husbandry business, hath here to fore bought oxen, and paid for them, and paid his other Dues with ease.[116]

On this occasion, Chalcom owed money to several individuals, and wanted to provide his recently married daughter, Esther, fifty pounds in furniture as a dowry.

When Jacob Chalcom's estate was inventoried three years later, his home lot of thirty acres and "Buildings thereon" were appraised at 240 pounds. He also owned land "within Battle's," "beyond Richardson's," (both Englishmen), and a common right. He owned an assortment of household goods and husbandry

---

49:172, from John Peegun, 1738/1750, 20 acres; MCG 51:93, from Isaac Waban, 1730/1753, 30 acres; MCG 49:173, from Peter Ephraim, 1741/1750, 1/2 acre; MCG 53:250, from Jeremiah Comecho, 1750/1755, 130 rods; and MCG 53:251, from Joseph Comecho, 1754/1755, 6 acres and rights. Leah's inheritance: NPB2, 95, 1744, 36 1/2 acres. To Indians: MCG 40:357, to Benjamin Tray, 1739/1739, 22 1/2 acres; MCG 46:271, to Joseph Ephraim Jr., 1739/1747, 22 1/2 acres; MCG 47:145, to Andrew Abraham, 1737/1747, 11 acres; and MCG 47:49 to Jonas Obscow, 1742/1747, 5 1/2 acres. Exchanges: MCG 45:156, with Isaac Comecho, 1742/1745, 10 acres and 7 pounds for 10 acres; MCG 46:88, with Thomas Sooduck, 1742/1746, 20 acres for 13 acres; and MCG 49:283, with Thomas Awassamug, 1742/1750, 10 acres for 10 acres.

[114] NPB2, 15, 1731, 26 1/2 acres to Samuel Perry; NPB2, 16, 1731, 3 1/2 acres to Samuel Perry; NPB2, 31, 1733, 1 3/4 acres to Hezekiah Broad; MCG 36:545, to Nathaniel Battle, 1730/1735, 32 acres; MCG 39:533, to David Morse, 1731/1738, 6 acres; MCG 40:129, to Samuel Perry, 1731/1739, 32 acres; MCG 40:356, to Hezekiah Broad, 1738/1739, 22 1/2 acres; MCG 51:47, to Hezekiah Broad, 1740/1752, 17 1/3 acres; MCG 45:148, to Abraham Belknap, 1745/1745, 36 1/2 acres; MCG 45:157, to Nathaniel Battle, 1742/1745, 23 acres; MCG 48:35, to Oliver Death, 1745/1748, 10 acres; MCG 48:36, to Oliver Death, 1745/1748, 6 1/2 acres; MCG 49:377, to Oliver Peabody, 1748/1752, 1/2 acres; and MCG 63:100, to James Whitney, 1748/1765, 6 1/2 acres.

[115] Surviving proprietors' records and deeds for Chalcom document that he acquired 168 acres of Natick land, and sold just over 286, suggesting the records for his transactions are incomplete. Chalcom may have acquired additional Indian lands through informal mechanisms.

[116] MA 32:417–8, 1753.

tools, a horse and cow, and books as well. The inventory masked the many shifts in fortune and real estate transactions Chalcom had engaged in while trying to build an estate. Despite his efforts, by the time of his death his debts amounted to more than one-third of his real and personal estate. Land, livestock, and implements were sold to cover the costs, and the account includes an entry for "Moveables sold before Inventory taken" amounting to just under two pounds. This left fifty-two acres to be divided among his widow, Leah, and their daughters, Esther Sooduck and Hepzibah Chalcom.[117]

Joseph Ephraim was the brother of Simon Ephraim, who was designated a proprietor in 1719.[118] Ephraim inherited his brother's common right and over the course of his eighty-six years, he vigorously pursued an English lifestyle in Natick. He was elected a deacon in the church when it was gathered under Rev. Oliver Peabody in 1729.[119] The Natick church records include the adult baptisms of five of his children in 1728. Five of his children joined Joseph in attaining full communion in the church, two of them on the same day as their father.[120]

Joseph Ephraim was born about the time King Philip's War was being waged in New England. He came of age during the resettlement process of the community in the 1680s, and became an integral part of Natick. Joseph Ephraim survived at least two wives, and nine children of his have been identified: six sons and three daughters.[121] At least seven of Ephraim's children married, producing at least twenty-eight grandchildren, an average of four surviving children each.[122]

Joseph's aspirations thoroughly reflected English cultural values. Symbolized by the importance of the church to Joseph and his family, this orientation was visible in his economic lifeways as well. Joseph reported that,

> in his younger years he was able by the blessing of God on his Labour to suport himself and family very comfortably [and] lived in a Convenient dwelling-house of his own procuring, kept a Teem, and a Stock of Cattle, carried on Husbandry business, and gave his Children where with to Set up for themselves.[123]

Joseph Ephraim apparently achieved the transformation that the missionization process was designed to effect.

---

[117] MCP #4124, Jacob Chalcom, Admin., 1756. His daughters may have been educated, but they placed their marks on the division agreement, not signatures. Jacob Chalcom was literate and signed several documents. Jacob or his son Jacob died in the military. NCR.

[118] It is not clear what happened to Simon Ephraim. I have uncovered only two references to him: his proprietary grant in the Natick proprietors book, and the reference his brothers Joseph, Andrew, and John Ephraim made to him in petitioning to sell land in AR 10:225, Appen. 5, Chap. 190, 16 Nov. 1722/3.

[119] NCR.   [120] NCR.

[121] NVR. In a General Court petition, Joseph claimed to have had nine sons. MA 32:401–4, 1749.

[122] NVR.   [123] MA 32:614–5, 1755.

Ephraim became thoroughly involved in the Natick land market. He received a sixty-acre freehold in 1719, inherited sixty acres from his brother Andrew plus his brother Simon's sixty-acre plot and his proprietary right; he added 92¾ acres more by drawing upon these land privileges eleven times.[124] He also bought land from proprietors Israel Rumneymarsh and Samuel Abraham, his son John Ephraim, and Indian Samuel Paugenit. He sold land to Indians eight times,[125] and exchanged four acres for two acres belonging to Abraham Speen.[126] At least twelve more parcels went to English purchasers.[127] Ephraim accumulated at least 332½ acres, sold 94½ acres to Indians, somewhere between 95 and 130 acres to English buyers, and gave 173 acres to his sons Peter, Ebenezer, Joseph, and Isaac, and to daughters Sarah and Deborah.[128] When he sold land, he earmarked proceeds for frame houses for himself and his children, a barn, livestock, and agricultural implements.[129]

---

[124] MCG 56:131, from Andrew Ephraim, 1734/1758, 60 acres; NPB2, 24, 38, 43, 51, 57, 58, 58, 59, 59, 128, and 128.

[125] NPB2, 44, 1737, 20 acres from Israel Rumneymarsh; NPB2, 44, 1737, 3 acres from Samuel Abraham; NPB2, 29, 1733, 2 acres from James Coochuck; and NPB2, 52, 1737, 1 acre from James Coochuck; MCG 59:438, from (son?) John Ephraim, 1760/1762, 10 acres; MCG 65:253, from son John Ephraim, 1760/1765, 12 acres; and MCG 67:616, from Samuel Paugenit, 1756/1768, 12 3/4 acres.

[126] NPB2, 29, 1733, 2 acres to James Coochuck; NPB2, 52, 1737, 1 acre to James Coochuck; MCG 45:652, to Jeremiah Comecho, 1747/1747, 3 acres; MCG 48:609, to John Ephraim, 1750/1750, 1 1/2 acres; MCG 49:3, to Benjamin Wiser, 1742/1749, 30 acres; MCG 49:359, to Josiah Speen, 1743/1752, 32 acres; MCG 56:133, to grandson Joseph Ephraim, 1756/1756, 12 acres; MCG 56:133, to grandson Joseph Ephraim, 1756/1758, 13 acres; and MCG 49:376, exchange with Abraham Speen 1739/1752, 2 acres for 4 acres.

[127] NPB2, 93, 1744, 22 acres to Mr. Ward; NPB2, 126, 1744, 10 acres to Edward Ward; MCG 48:610, to Samuel Perry, 1750/1750, 6 acres; MCG 49:345, to Matthew Hastings, 1749/1752, 5 1/2 acres; MCG 56:134, to Moses Fisk, 1756/1758, 12 acres; MCG 59:438, to William Wright, 1760/1762, 10 acres; MCG 63:408, to Thomas Ellis, 1756/1765, 2 acres; MCG 65:257, to John Bacon, 1760/1765, 12 acres; MCG 65:258, to John Bacon, 1760/1765, 4 acres; MCG 65:462, to Stephen Badger, 1754/1765, 4 acres; MCG 67:414, to Timothy Smith, 1754/1768, 6 1/2 acres; and MCG 67:619, to Jason Whitney, 1756/1768, 13 3/4 acres. Four more transactions to English purchasers may have come from Joseph Ephraim, or by his son and namesake: MCG 40:238, to Timothy Bacon, 1739/1739, 6 acres; MCG 40:315, to Edward Ward, 1739/1739, 14 acres; MCG 42:444, to Nathaniel Battle, 1739/1741, 11 acres; and MCG 49:376, to Oliver Peabody, 1739/1752, 4 acres.

[128] As with Jacob Chalcom, the fact that the acreage accumulated does not precisely add up suggests either gaps in the proprietors' books, or additional land acquired through informal mechanisms. MCG 45:568, to Ebenezer Ephraim, 1738/1746, 20 acres; MCG 45:627, to Peter Ephraim, 1737/1746, 20 acres; MCG 46:263, to Joseph Ephraim, 1731/1747, 25 acres; MCG 45:593, to Peter Ephraim, 1737/1746, 20 acres; MCG 39:34, to Isaac Coolidge, 1722/1738, 60 acres; MCG 40:238, to Timothy Bacon, 1739/1739, 6 acres; MCG 40:315, to Edward Ward, 1739/1739, 14 acres; MCG 42:444, to Nathaniel Battle, 1739/1741, 11 acres; MCG 49:376, to Oliver Peabody, 1739/1752, 4 acres; 46:153, to Sarah Comecho, 1746/1746, 8 acres; MCG 48:485, to Isaac Ephraim, 1746?/1749?, 60 acres (part of house lot, with house, barn, orchard, and fences); and MCG 50:534, to Sarah Comecho and Deborah Sooduck, 1746/1752, equal parts in 20 acres, part of house lot.

[129] See, for example, MA 31:219, 1738; and JH 8:359, 24 Oct. 1728.

Ephraim's hopes for his offspring met with mixed results. Five who survived to adulthood died before Joseph did in 1761. His efforts toward setting them up must have been a severe disappointment. Petitioning to sell land in 1753 he lamented:

> Your Petitioner hath had nine Sons, and all of them now dead but Two, and the Youngest of the two, viz Isaac Ephraim having some years ago, been imprudent, and unfortunate, And hath lost a good horse and Considerable Live Stock, and is involved in Debts to ye value of Near L300 Old Tenr, and cannot pay the Same, nor will be ever Able to do it unless by Sale of some of his lands.[130]

Isaac had "humbled himself" to his father and asked assistance, promising "reformation," and making some progress in the preceding year. Joseph endorsed the petition of his son, who asked to sell land in order to sort out his finances, and wanted to sell twenty-five acres of his own to help Isaac. At the age of seventy-eight, he was "uncapable of Labours," and owed money himself for the long illness and funeral of his wife. The proceeds were to be invested "That he may not be Obliged to Suffer for food or Raiment in his old age."[131]

Ephraim sold land on several occasions to build farms for himself and his children. He gave land to all of his children except one.[132] The estate settlements of two of his sons indicate that his assistance met with some success. At his death in 1746, son Ebenezer owned thirty acres of land, a cow and two swine, and basic husbandry tools, all valued at 237 pounds. Debts against the estate, however, required the sale of most of his estate, including his house and lands.[133] Peter Ephraim's 1743 estate consisted of real estate: a house and a total of twenty-six acres in three pieces, valued at 394 pounds. Peter had no personal estate. His holdings were judged to be "incapable of making more than one settlement," and were awarded to Peter's eldest son, Joshua, who was to pay his brothers, Peter and Ebenezer, their shares in cash.[134]

Like his father, the third son, Joseph Ephraim Jr., aggressively accumulated land, entering credit arrangements for the purposes of assembling his landed estate. His activities were not confined to Natick, either. In 1736 he and Indian Andrew Abraham wanted to sell forty-four acres they owned jointly in Grafton.[135] Ephraim wanted to purchase a cart and wheels, tools, and some meadow, as well as a barn "for the better securing his Corn Flax &c . . . and pay some debts contracted for purchasing stock."[136]

---

[130] MA 32:401, 1753.   [131] MA 32:401, 1753.
[132] MA 31:617, 1749.
[133] I have not located any evidence of children of Ebenezer and his wife Mary Awassamug. MCP #7003, Ebenezer Ephraim, Admin., 1746.
[134] MCP #7010, Peter Ephraim, Admin., 1753.
[135] JH 12:258, 16 Jan. 1735.   [136] Ibid.

The younger Joseph Ephraim accumulated 169 acres in Natick even without the benefit of his own proprietary right. He added to the twenty-five-acre parental gift he had received 140 acres that he purchased, and four acres gained through his wife's inherited proprietary privileges. Ephraim bought land totaling 133½ acres, eleven times from Indians in the space of nine years, and he also purchased 6½ acres from Englishman Moses Fisk.[137] He exchanged land with Indians on three occasions, and sold six acres to his brother John Ephraim.[138] His accumulated lands well outbalanced his five sales to English purchasers totaling 72½ acres, assembled through his own hard work and willingness to take on debt to accumulate land.[139]

The estate of Joseph Ephraim Jr. signaled a turn in fortune from his earlier land accumulation efforts; valued at 339 pounds, it included fifty acres of land in five pieces and a very modest personal estate, but no husbandry tools. Virtually all this was consumed by debts. Englishman Richard Sanger of Sherborn was allowed to levy an execution against Joseph Ephraim Jr.'s estate in 1743 because of "necessaries which the Petitioner supplied him and his family with in his sickness."[140] Joseph had been contributing to his father's support, too. A variety of debts were claimed against the estate, including payment for husbandry tools, cloth, "curtain lace," provisions, "5 pair of gloves . . . for Simon's funeral," and taking "oxen to Boston."[141]

Ironically, the one son to whom Joseph offered no assistance managed to attain a measure of success on his own, and by the end of his life Joseph was dependent on this son for his support. John Ephraim was born in Natick around 1711.[142] He married Sarah Quitticus of Dudley in 1740; they had six

[137] NPB2, 24, 1731, 10 acres from Hannah Tabumsug; and NPB2, 47, 1737, 3 acres from Hannah Abraham; MCG 25:722 (with Thomas Awassamug) from Isaac Monequassin, 1727/1727, 30 acres; MCG 46:262, from John Thomas, 1730/1747, 10 acres; MCG 46:263, from Benjamin Tray, 1733/1747, 2 acres; MCG 46:265, from Thomas and Patience Peegun, 1734/1747, 3 acres; MCG 46:266, from Thomas Awassamug, 1738/1747, 16 acres; MCG 46:269, from Samuel Rumneymarsh, 1739/1747, 20 acres; MCG 46:271, from Jacob Chalcom, 1739/1747, 22 1/2 acres; MCG 46:272, from Thomas Peegun, 1739/1747, 7 acres; MCG 47:530, from Solomon Thomas, 1731/1749, 10 acres; and MCG 49:71, from Moses Fisk, 1739/1749, 6 1/2 acres.

[138] MCG 46:268, exchange with Samuel Abraham, 1739/1747, 3 acres for "other land"; MCG 46:274, exchange with Thomas Peegun Jr., 1740/1747, 10 acres for 10 acres; and MCG 46:444, exchange with Thomas Peegun Jr., 1740/1747, 10 acres for 10 acres. The latter two exchanges could be duplicates. MCG 46:270, to John Ephraim, 1739/1746, 6 acres.

[139] MCG 32:511, to Joseph Mills, 1732/1732, 2 acres; MCG 39:539, to David Morse, 1733/1738, 8 acres; MCG 39:540, to Isaac Monequassin's administrator David Morse, 1733/1738, 30 acres; MCG 40:628, to Moses Fisk, 1729/1740, 10 acres; and MCG 40:630, to Moses Fisk, 1739/1740, 22 1/2 acres.

[140] MCP #7006, Joseph Ephraim Jr., Admin., 1743; AR 13:214, Appen. 8, Chap. 210, 7 April 1743; and JH 20:150, 13 Jan. 1742/3.

[141] MCP #7006, Joseph Ephraim Jr., Admin., 1743. Joseph Ephraim Jr. died in military service. NCR. His son served in the military, too, and in 1756 filed a petition complaining that he had been left off a muster roll for the Crown Point expedition. JH, Part 1, 33:31, 2 June 1756.

[142] MA 33:553, 1772. In this petition, he gave his age as 63.

children in Natick between 1741 and 1758.[143] John had purchased the proprietary right of Isaac Speen, and he used his land privileges to emulate his father's strategy.[144] In a 1761 petition he explained that

> having many Years ago, by his hard labour and industry, Purchased a whole Right in the Propriety of Natick, hath also built him a House and barn, keeps a teem, and carys on husbandry business, Supports his family comfortably, And has procured as good an Education for his Children, as his English neighbours . . . and not being altogether free from Debts incurred by his large Purchase, building, Clearing, fencing, buying stock, and Husbandry-Tools: And having the Care of his Aged Father Dean Joseph Ephraim who is more than Ninety Years of Age, All the Said Charges concuring to keep Your Petitioner Involved, and in So great Anxiety of mind as is not easily Expressed.[145]

In underscoring that he had "procured as good an Education for his Children, as his English neighbors," Ephraim defiantly asserted his accomplishments. His effort to retire his debts was cast as the reasonable action of a hardworking, successful, and responsible resident of the community who should be respected on an equal basis with his English neighbors. Illness in his family and the deaths of two of his children represented a setback. He was allowed to sell forty acres.[146] Two years later he was given permission to sell fifty acres with a house and barn because he had another homestead with a barn that he was improving.[147]

At least one of Joseph Ephraim's three daughters married an Indian man who shared her father's economic strategies. Deborah Ephraim's first husband was Thomas Sooduck, who died in 1746 during military service at Cape Breton. The three-year marriage produced two children, Meribah and Ephraim. Deborah's second marriage to Joseph Comecho produced four: Joseph, Samuel, John, and Lucy.[148]

Joseph Comecho had been educated and was literate. His goals and activities were English-influenced: "In his Minority [he] Served an Apprentice-Ship with an English man, and being well instructed in the art or calling of Husbandry, he intended to follow Sd calling."[149] He had land, purchased a team of

---

[143] NVR.

[144] MCG 38:617, from Isaac Speen, 1737/1737, 60 acres and common rights.

[145] MA 33:159, 1761.   [146] Ibid.

[147] AR 17:393, Appen. 12, Chap. 33, 3 June 1763; JH 40:51, 3 June 1763. No records of John Ephraim's estate have survived to document his long-range situation. He did petition to sell land in 1772 and 1783 because of debts. MA 33:553, 1772; and AR 18:774–5, Appen. 13, Chap. 129, 25 Feb. 1774. His father's estate docket is incomplete, too, containing only his will. Joseph continued to depend on John, directing that he take care of his estate and in particular, to "pay all the remaining debts of my son Isaac Ephraim Deceasp." MCP #7009, Joseph Ephraim, Will, 1761.

[148] NVR. No marriage between the two was recorded, but Deborah Comecho was named in Deacon Joseph Ephraim's will as a daughter. MCP #7009, Joseph Ephraim, Will, 1761.

[149] MA 32:86, 1750.

oxen, and had begun to build a barn. During the course of building the barn, he took a bond from an unnamed Indian for some land he wanted to sell. When Comecho called for payment of the bond the Indian refused to pay "altho he had it by him and could have paid it." Comecho sued, but the Indian resold the land and fled before Comecho could receive satisfaction. He was also inconvenienced because he owned no meadow; instead he had to purchase hay and cart it eight miles to his farm. Comecho wanted to sell twenty acres of "unimproved land" to finish his barn, purchase meadow, "and if any thing Remain, to . . . build a small Dwelling house for ye comfort of himself and Family."[150] Comecho's financial woes continued: In 1760, his estate was declared insolvent, and his widow, Deborah, inherited only the widow's thirds, three acres of land on which to live with her two surviving children.[151]

The Ephraim families worked to build farms and participate in a market economy, as was envisioned when Natick was founded. In many ways, cultural change in the community was symbolized by Deacon Joseph Ephraim. Although he seemed to attain some of his goals in the cultural reorientation of his family, even members of his family struggled in Natick in the middle decades of the century.

In contrast to the Ephraim families, proprietor Thomas Peegun strove to keep his land resources intact and tried to avoid participation in the land market. He stressed frugality in his own ways, and he worked to provide a viable economic future for his progeny. In 1742 he explained his strategy and the frustrations he had met in attempting to fulfill his goals:

> altho Your Petitioner has always been desirous to keep out of debt as much as possible, & to preserve his Rights of Land Entire for the benefit of his posterity, Yet So it is That your poor Petitioner (moved thereto by perhaps too Strong an Affection to his Children) has in his Advanced Age Involv'd himself and become obliged to pay Sundrey debts for one & another of them, & Specially for one of them Since gone off to Sea.[152]

Peegun took responsibility for his children's troubles, which compounded his own indebtedness, incurred during a period of illness in his family. He was regularly threatened by writs of attachment, and his debts continued to increase. Peegun asked to sell some of his distant and unused lands to cover the 100 pounds he now owed, as much as "Shall be Sufficient to Satisfie & discharg his debts."[153] He had already been forced to sell twenty acres of his common land in order to free his son John, who had been incarcerated for debts.[154]

Despite the bleak situation he sketched out, the elder Thomas Peegun did retain some property for the four children he and his wife, Elizabeth, had pro-

---

[150] Ibid.   [151] MCP #4847, Joseph Comecho, Admin., 1760.
[152] MA 31:400, 1742.   [153] Ibid.
[154] MA 31:258–9, 1739.

duced, all of whom married and had children of their own.[155] When he died, he left a house and nineteen-acre home lot worth 472 pounds plus an additional twenty-three acres. His personal estate contained a book and "Specticles," a table and chairs, household goods, farming implements, swine, and a horse. Peegun managed to pass land on to his children, but in most cases in parcels so small the land must have held more symbolic value than any real economic worth: his children or their heirs each received a small parcel of land ranging from four to 6½ acres.[156] Son Thomas had received a forty-acre lot during his father's lifetime.[157]

Although no evidence survives that describes proprietor Israel Rumneymarsh's perspective on the land market, his land activities suggest that he resisted its influence. Granted sixty acres in the initial division, Rumneymarsh had no other land laid out in his right until after 1737. A total of just over 220 acres were laid out between 1737 and 1763.[158] During his lifetime, Rumneymarsh sold a total of 8½ acres in three parcels to two Indians, and he exchanged land once with an Englishman. Twenty acres more went to his daughter Sarah and her husband, Jeffrey Henry, for "affection."[159] He and his wife, Esther, had five children who had survived to adulthood (Samuel, James, Bethiah, Sarah, and Mary) but all five had died by the time their father's estate was settled in 1750.[160] Israel Rumneymarsh's grandchildren inherited land after his death in 1745.[161] When the final division of common lands was being negotiated in 1763, the proprietary right of Israel Rumneymarsh was represented alternatively by Sarah Rumneymarsh, Sarah Lawrence (an Indian with unknown connections to the family), and Englishman Samuel Morse.[162]

[155] Thomas, John, Gideon, and Elizabeth. *NVR*; MCP #17105, Thomas Peegun, Admin., 1746. Sorting out the various Thomas Peeguns is difficult. The Natick vital records sometimes make distinctions between father and son, and sometimes list the mother and father in the birth records, but not consistently. Four Peegun children have been left out of my reconstruction of this family for this reason, and because I have found nothing more about them.

[156] MCP #17105, Thomas Peegun, Admin., 1746. A ten-acre woodlot was divided four years later.

[157] Ibid. He received the land in 1729.

[158] NPB2. The average amount of land granted to each proprietor was 197 acres. See Chapter 6. Samuel Rumneymarsh, son of the proprietor, died three years after his father. No personal estate was inventoried for him, either. In 1759, at age eighty, Samuel's widow, Sarah, petitioned to sell this "unimproved" land (ten acres) for her support. MA 33:113–4, 1759.

[159] Jeffrey later married Mary Toss.

[160] MCP #19572, Israel Rumneymarsh, Admin., 1748. The Rumneymarsh family usually used this surname, or Rumbleymarsh, but sometimes used Pumhammon. An Israel Bumhainun appears on a 1702 petition of Natick Indians, and Samuel Rumneymarsh's estate settlement is filed under Pumhammon alias Rumneymarsh. MCP #18264, Samuel Pumhammon, Admin., 1748.

[161] Just under 140 acres valued at 1,282 pounds were inventoried as Israel's estate, including lands laid out in settling the estate. MCP #19572, Israel Rumneymarsh, Admin., 1759.

[162] NPB2, 140 and 141.

Instead of engaging vigorously in the burgeoning land market with the English, as had the Ephraims, or hoping to avoid it altogether, like Thomas Peegun, the Tray family members (like Israel Rumneymarsh) tried to confine their dealings to other Indians. Seven Tray family members engaged in forty-four land transactions in the eighteenth century. Twenty-eight (64 percent) – eight transfers to family members, eight purchases, six sales, and six exchanges – involved other Indians.[163]

Benjamin Tray was active in the land market, but only two of his eighteen transactions involved English neighbors: He gave six acres to Minister Oliver Peabody, and he exchanged seventy-nine acres with Englishman John Goodenow of Needham for forty-two acres, partially fenced, with a house.[164] Tray sold 50½ acres to Indians in five separate parcels, bought ten acres in one lot from an Indian, and exchanged land six times with Indians.[165] Tray also passed on land to his sons: sixty-five acres and his proprietary right to Benjamin and thirty acres to Jonas.[166] Tray confined most of his land activities within the Indian community and usually gave or exchanged land instead of engaging in monetary transactions for land.

By the time he died sometime before 1748, probably in military service, proprietor Benjamin Tray and his wife, Sarah, had produced at least six children.[167] Of three sons, only one seemed inclined to pursue English farming practices. Even the estate of this son, also named Benjamin, was modest when it was inventoried in 1757. Though he owned a forty-two-acre home lot, small shares in two other lots, and a cow, no agricultural implements were enumerated when his estate was settled. Enumerated were a Bible, wearing apparel, a bed and chair, some basic household goods, and two notes of hand from English-

[163] MCG.
[164] He petitioned to sell land in 1728 in order to finish a house, but then apparently decided to exchange land and improvements with Goodenow. JH 12:355, 17 Oct. 1728; JH, 12:360, 24 Oct. 1728; AR 11:458, Appen. 6, Chap. 135, 19 Dec. 1729; and MCG 32:267, Tray and Goodenow exchange, 1730/1731. Tray's request for conveyance to Peabody came in 1740, and was recorded in the proprietors' book in 1742. JH 18:139, 26 Nov. 1740; AR 12:706, Appen. 7, Chap. 91, 5 Sept. 1740; and NPB2, 69.
[165] MCG 39:507, to Samuel Abraham Sr., 1733/1738, 12 acres; MCG 40:357, to Jacob Chalcom, 1739/1739, 22 1/2 acres; MCG 43:470, to James Coochuck, 1735/1743, 4 acres; MCG 45:558, to Samuel Abraham Sr., 1737/1746, 10 acres; MCG 46:263, to Joseph Ephraim Jr., 1733/1747, 2 acres; and MCG 46:428, from Samuel Abraham Sr., 1737/1747, 10 acres. Exchanges: MCG 39:509, with Thomas Peegun, 1733/1738, 10 acres for 10 acres; MCG 39:620, with James Coochuck, 1737/1739, 20 acres for 20 acres; MCG 39:637, with Samuel Abraham Sr., 1731/1738, 10 acres for 10 acres; MCG 39:641, with Nathaniel and Mary Coochuck, 1734/1738, land for 6 acres; MCG 39:642, with William Thomas, 1737/1738, 8 1/4 acres for 8 1/4 acres; and MCG 44:164, with Thomas Sooduck, 1735/1743, 16 acres (Tray) for 20 acres.
[166] To Benjamin Tray: MCG 39:437, 1738/1739, 20 acres; MCG 45:656, 1740/1747, common right; and MCG 54:25, 1740/1755, 45 acres. To Jonas Tray: MCG 47:449, 1740/1749, 20 acres and 10 acres.
[167] NVR. In 1744, Benjamin Tray was among those listed as "feared dead" in the military. NCR.

men. The only tools inventoried were a pail, hatchet, trammel, and shovel. Benjamin's will contained bequests for his mother and all three of his sisters, but his wife was to receive only ten shillings "and no more She Being Eloped and not Living with me to take Care of me in my sickness."[168] The case of his brothers seems more clear. Neither Phillip nor John had personal estate inventoried, though both owned land. Phillip served an apprenticeship, then entered military service and died at Cape Breton.[169]

Two daughters of Benjamin Tray moved more explicitly in the direction of English patterns. Mary Tray lived on an English-style farm during her marriage to Daniel Thomas, son of Leah Chalcom Thomas. Another daughter, Hannah Tray, married Moses Mockheag sometime before 1754.[170] They produced three sons between 1754 and 1759, but then disaster struck. The joint administration of their estate in 1759 was occasioned by the death of the entire family within two months that year, the only documented case of an entire family dying in an epidemic in Natick.[171] No immediate heirs remained to inherit their modest estate, which included six acres of land, two Bibles, three pamphlet sermons, a spinning wheel, and an assortment of personal and household goods. Their estate included no husbandry tools, but did contain a "fire Lock & Armour."[172]

The emergence of the market in Indian land that stemmed from individualization of landownership both transformed the community and allowed for new ways for Indians to transform themselves in relation to the land, as the Ephraim, Peegun, Rumneymarsh, and Tray lineages tell us. Indians participated in different ways in the market, engaging aggressively in buying and selling to the English as well as to Indians in order to accomplish changes in economic and material culture for themselves and their progeny, or drawing boundaries between Indians and the English by restricting the bulk of their transactions within the Indian community. But the new status of land as an individually owned commodity affected even those who would have preferred to maintain their land resources intact for themselves and their children, as Thomas Peegun learned in liquidating much of his land to save himself and his children from relations of debt. Stories about participation in the land market, and the economic strategies it represented, also shed light on the narrative of disappearance. We can find out so much more about Indians who viewed land transactions as a means for adopting aspects of English economic and material culture, and who successfully accumulated property, because their economic activities prompted the generation of documents. Sources about the motivations,

---

[168] MCP #22768, Benjamin Tray, Will, 1757.
[169] MCP #22771, Phillip Tray, Admin., 1746; and MCP #22770, John Tray, 1746.
[170] Established through the probate documents of the Trays.
[171] *NVR.*
[172] MCP #15315, Hannah Mockheag, Admin., 1759; and MCP #15316, Moses Mockheag, Admin., 1759.

aspirations, and activities of Indians who may have rejected English ways scarcely exist, which does not mean those Indians were not present. But whatever ways in which Indians viewed and participated in the land market, as it steadily eroded Indian lands it also erased Indians from the documentary record by eliminating a principal location in which Indian lives and lifeways received confirmation, contributing to Indian invisibility and the myth of disappearance.

E. *Indian notions of "place"*

Collectively, stories about the proprietary families contain a crucial subtext: the persistence of a larger, Indian sense of place that continued to resist the fixity to which the English aspired. Natick Indians found spouses locally, but they also drew upon a regional network of Indian places for marriage partners.[173] Wage labor, seafaring, and participation in the military drew Indians away from Natick for temporary (and sometimes more permanent) absences. Even the intrusion of English institutions contributed to Indian mobility, as when Indians needed to attend to legal proceedings in Cambridge or Boston, when legal prosecution left them imprisoned in Cambridge, or when they absconded to avoid the arm of the law.

For Natick Indians, place as a social and physical construct was variously imagined. Most crucially, marriage outside the community continued kinship patterns that connected individuals and families beyond the bounds of natal villages, and composed a network of places for visiting despite Indian dispossession throughout New England. The nearly wholesale loss of Indian lands throughout the region meant that landless Indians needed to reconfigure the connection between place and securing a livelihood, which Indians often did by becoming wage laborers, indentured servants, soldiers, whalers, and peddlars.

A continuation and reformulation of earlier, mobile Indian ways of life, eighteenth-century Indian ways of placing themselves on the land knit together a network of locations throughout southeastern New England that sustained Indianness within the colonial context.[174] The Tabumsug and Bowman families illustrate some of the ways in which Indians reformulated mobility and their sense of place as the Indian landscape became transformed under the influence of the English presence. These families also highlight a choice made by some Indian individuals in the eighteenth century: abandonment of Natick as a primary place.

Like other Indian men, Nathaniel Coochuck's sense of place drew him from elsewhere to the Indian community of Natick, where he married, acquired

---

[173] Bragdon, "'Another Tongue Brought In,'" 145.
[174] See also Ann McMullen, "What's Wrong with This Picture? Context, Coversion, Survival, and the Development of Regional Native Cultures and Pan-Indianism in Southeastern New England," in *Enduring Traditions: The Native Peoples of New England*, ed. Laurie Weinstein (Westport, CT: Bergin & Garvey, 1994), 123–50.

land, and enthusiastically embraced English economic and material culture. Coochuck married into the Waban family and, after his wife's death, into the Tabumsug family.[175] Access to his wife's proprietary privileges aided Coochuck's vigorous pursuit of English lifeways, which met with successes and failures. He was literate (he signed his petition and owned books), understood the English system, and attempted to operate within it.[176]

Mary and Nathaniel Coochuck drew upon the proprietary right of her mother, Hannah Tabumsug. Mary had been designated executrix of Hannah's will in 1731 despite the fact that Hannah had two sons and another daughter.[177] Nathaniel bought thirty-six acres from Indians and exchanged land with Benjamin Tray to add to the fifteen acres received through Mary's proprietary right. He also sold land seven times to five different Englishmen up to 1740:[178] in 1734, for example, to purchase cattle and husbandry tools,[179] three years later to finish a barn and purchase tools and sheep,[180] and in 1744 to further expand their farming enterprise.[181] Interestingly, in this last petition the Coochucks explained that they had inherited a proprietary right from Mary's father, Joseph Tabumsug. But it was really her mother's privilege that Mary had inherited.

Heirs to the Tabumsug right held broader notions of place that embraced not just Natick, but locations in Worcester County well. The Coochucks seem to have left no children, but other Tabumsug heirs could be found elsewhere. Samuel Tabumsug died sometime prior to 1756. His estate entered probate in that year in Worcester County. Samuel Tabumsug was described as a resident of Westborough, and his estate included not only land in Natick (thirty-six acres in six pieces), but also in Westborough (ten acres), and Hardwich (100 acres).[182] He appeared in the diary of Westborough Minister Ebenezer Parkman from 1737 through 1741 as one of several Indian laborers on Parkman's farm.[183] Tabumsug's lands were sold, and the proceeds were divided among the heirs in three parts, "being the original families." The heirs were Sarah Printer, Leah Chalcom, and Judith Ephraim (all described as "one family," daughters of

---

[175] His first marriage was to Mary Waban, daughter of Capt. Thomas Waban. She died in 1725. Coochuck subsequently married twice. *NVR*.

[176] MA 31:363–4, 1741; and MCP #4958, Nathaniel Coochuck, Admin., 1753.

[177] MCP #22642, Hannah Tabumsug, Will, 1731.

[178] Transactions with Indians: MCG 43:721, from Hannah and Samuel Abraham and Patience Nehemiah, 1728/1744, 36 acres; and MCG 39:641, exchange with Benjamin Tray, 1734/1738, an unspecified quantity of land for 6 acres. Proprietary grants: NPB2, 18, 1732, 7 1/2 acres; and NPB2, 25, 1732, 7 1/2 acres. To English purchasers: NPB2, 22, 1733, 2 acres to John Goodenow; NPB2, 28, 1733, 1 1/2 acres to Benjamin Kendall; NPB2, 34, 1734, 2 1/2 acres to David Morse; NPB2, 43, 1736, 1 1/2 acres to Nehemiah Allen; MCG 36:546, to Nathaniel Battle, 1735/1735, 24 acres; MCG 39:541, to David Morse 1734/1738, 6 acres; and MCG 41:640, to Jonathan Lealand, 1737/1741, 2 acres.

[179] AR 12:66, Appen. 7, Chap. 133, 10 Dec. 1734.

[180] AR 12:438, Appen. 7, Chap. 186, 26 Dec. 1737.   [181] MA 31:471, 1744.

[182] WCP #8953, Samuel Bumso, Admin., 1756.

[183] Francis G. Walett, "The Diary of Ebenezer Parkman, 1729–1738," *Proceedings of the American Antiquarian Society* 71 (1961): 380; and Walett, "The Diary of Ebenezer Parkman,

Solomon and Sarah Thomas, and Natick residents); Elizabeth Comecho and
Mary Ephraim (another "family," relationship unknown, and Natick residents);
and Benjamin Wiser, originally of Natick but by then a resident of Worcester,
the administrator of the estate.[184] The precise connection of these individuals
to one another is not altogether clear, but the fact that they all benefited from
this single estate constitutes formal acknowledgment of their kinship as well as
the larger geography of their kinship connection.

Samuel Tabumsug left Natick early and acquired extensive real estate in two
Worcester County towns to add to his Natick holdings. Benjamin Wiser had
also acquired land in Worcester County on which he made his primary residence. His father, James, was from Natick. Benjamin had left the community by
1743, however, despite receiving thirty acres of land from his father in Natick.[185] He sold these Natick lands at this time, and five years later asked for permission to sell thirty-two acres in Natick in order to build a "Barn on his farm
in Worcester which is of the value of five or six hundred pounds . . . Where
your Petitioner Dwells . . . all which he purchased by his own Industry."[186]
Benjamin successfully established himself in Worcester, married Sarah Printer
in Southborough in 1747, and between 1750 and 1758, they had five children in
Worcester who all lived to adulthood.[187]

Another proprietary family from Natick also included Worcester County in
their notion of Indian place. The heirs of Samuel Bowman petitioned the General Court for the sale of his Natick lands in 1749, two years after his estate
entered probate in Worcester County.[188] The heirs included his widow, Martha,
and six others, including three who were apparently children of Samuel and
Martha (two daughters with spouses, and an unmarried son), and a six-year-old
grandson.[189]

1739–1744," Ibid., 72 (1962): 72–6, 79–80, 88–9, 94–5, 98–101, 105, 108, 121, 133, and
146. In December of 1739, Samuel and an Englishman "bargained with me to clear my
Swamp for 40s per Acre and their Dinners while the work'd." Ibid., 80. Other tasks
included threshing (p. 75), digging potatoes (p. 79), cutting wood (p. 98), and building a
stone wall (p. 100).

[184] Precisely what entitled any of these individuals to a share of Tabumsug's estate remains
unclear, as no relationships to the deceased are detailed. The estate of another Samuel
Tabumsug went to probate in Worcester County in 1777 and was administered by James
Wiser, Benjamin's brother. This estate included "a Small remaining Right in the Com-
mons," and just under five acres near Cochituate Pond in Natick. WCP #5847, Samuel
Tabumsug, Admin., 1777.

[185] MA 31:433, 1743.   [186] MA 31:557–8, 1748.

[187] *Vital Records of Southborough, Massachusetts to the Year 1850* (Boston: New England
Genealogical and Historical Society, 1903); "Worcester Births, Marriages, and Deaths";
Franklin P. Rice, comp., *Vital Records of the Town of Auburn (Formerly Ward), Massachu-
setts, to the Year 1850. With Inscriptions from the Old Burial Grounds* (Worcester, MA: Pub-
lished by the Compiler, 1900); and WCP #66671, Benjamin Wiser, Will, 1775. This
Benjamin Wiser will be discussed further in Chapter 6.

[188] MA 32:6–7, 1749; and WCP #6598, Samuel Bowman, Admin., 1747.

[189] MA 32:6–7, 1749.

The petitioners provide an example of how individuals from even the most prominent Natick families sometimes scattered over the course of the eighteenth century, and a glimpse of how the larger geography of Indian physical and social places operated in New England. They had specific ideas about how their inheritances ought to be used. Martha Bowman was a resident of Worcester and wanted her share invested so she could receive an interest income. Benjamin Wiser, age six and a grandson of Samuel Bowman (relationship to the aforementioned Benjamin Wiser unknown), was living with Zachariah and Betty Equi "in Sturbridge . . . , Dwellers on Land belonging to others." They proposed that Benjamin's share be invested as well, and that the Equi's share be used in ways the General Court thought best "haveing no View of the money Spent Needlessly." Martha and Joseph Peegun were "Settled in Dudly and he has a Freehold Estate of Value and [Live] in English fashion." They wanted either to "furnish their house better," or purchase some cattle. Samuel Bowman, the eldest son, had been "brought up at Husbandry work haveing Served his time with the English." He left it to the General Court to determine how best to use his inheritance.[190]

Samuel Bowman's descendants displayed a range of eighteenth-century Massachusetts Indian lifeways and illustrated the ways in which the colonial encounter had transformed Indian social and physical places: A widow and grandson survived on interest income from a liquidated estate. One daughter and her husband lived an at least nominally English-style lifeway, and another daughter and her spouse must have lived marginally, perhaps tolerated as squatters on lands that had once belonged to their ancestors. His son learned English-style agriculture through serving an indenture.

No members of the Bowman family remained in Natick at the time Samuel's estate was settled. The administrator's account included charges for having his land laid out in Natick.[191] The heirs explained: "their deceased father Lived in Worcester and places adjacent more than Twenty Years before his Death . . . we are all Strangers to Natick [and] are Intirely, if we may be allowed to use the Phrase Naturalized to this part of the Country."[192] Samuel himself had chosen to leave Natick only a decade or so after having been designated a principal proprietor with substantial rights. His abandonment of the community was quite conscious and appeared to be complete. Because of this seemingly broken connection, his heirs thought of themselves as "strangers" to Natick, consciously distanced from the community, and "naturalized" to Worcester. Yet in the same year this petition was filed, the proprietor's son Samuel married, and in 1750, another Samuel Bowman was born. Naturalized to Worcester County they may have been, but when the proprietor's son died sometime before 1759, he died in Natick, still tied to its commodified lands.[193] The proprietor's grandson, a third

---

[190] Ibid.   [191] WCP #6598, Samuel Bowman, Admin., 1747.
[192] MA 32:6–7, 1749.   [193] MCP #2371, Samuel Bowman, Gdn., 1759.

Samuel Bowman, was represented by Englishman Thomas Russell and his English guardian, Micah Whitney of Natick, when the final division of Natick common lands was negotiated in 1763.[194]

F. *Families and the community*

The lineage stories of Natick proprietors tell us much about the political limitations of the New England extinction myth. The sources produced by and for English colonists capture snatches of the Indian experience within the colonial regime, but only by adjusting our focus to incorporate Indian ways of belonging on the land can we really see the complex ways Indians continued to negotiate their identity in relationship to the land. Within the changing circumstances of the New England Indian landscape, Indians perpetuated their lineages, and even under the constraints that English colonialism placed upon Indian families, kinship, and a larger regional community composed of Indian places sustained the Indian truth that you are who your relatives are.

The extinction story, readily sustained if the proof for persistence is to be found only in growing Indian populations in fixed locales, disregards the persistence of Indian difference in colonial New England. Natick Indians shaped, and were shaped by, the colonial experience. Yet despite the illusion of Englishness that can be discerned in aspects of material culture, property relations, family formation, and gender roles some Indians adopted (or were forced to adopt), New England Indians remained distinct from the English who colonized their land and imposed institutions that bore on so many aspects of Indian lives.

Within the colonial relationship, English colonists strove to compel Native peoples to conform to their own notions of social order, with incomplete results. Natick's origins can be found in English ideals about bounding people in towns as ordered places with fixed residency where differential ownership of land as private property would reinforce status arrangements thought of as divinely inspired. But within Natick, individual ownership of land produced widely varying patterns, notions of "order" looked different, and actual Indian mobility resisted English ideals of fixity.

Likewise, English assumptions about properly constituted families, households, and gender relations that helped guide the encounter between peoples from the beginning (which envisioned patriarchal relations of power and male-headed households), failed to shape the Natick Indian experience comprehensively. On the one hand, while some Indians reoriented their lifeways and moved from female to male agricultural labor, for example, others seem to have resisted such transformations. On the other hand, the commodification of Indian lifeways, and in particular the expanding problem of relations of debt for Indian peoples, disrupted Indian family life and household structure. For

---

[194] Ibid.; and NPB2, 140–1.

example, indentured servitude, which by English design had as its principal purpose the training of youths for occupational callings, became for Indians primarily an institutionalized debtor-creditor relationship that also comprehended adults and thus fractured Indian families. Similarly, guardianship arrangements distorted Indian households by scattering Indian children into English households.

Within the colonial regime, the English tried to eliminate earlier Indian ways of belonging on the land by defining it as individually owned property transferable through the workings of the market economy. In Natick, institutionalization of the proprietary system changed the status of Indian landownership in compliance with these English principles, and made possible the development of a market in Natick land. Natick Indians participated variously in this land market, still negotiating their identity in relationship to the land. Some entered the market to accomplish cultural transformations in keeping with English notions; others tried to avoid selling land at all or, if they did sell, to keep land within the Indian community. Even Indians who resisted often were forced to participate in the new market because English colonialism, complete with legal institutions that intruded on the day-to-day lives of Indian people, had created the conditions whereby they must participate. The emergence of the Natick land market, following the dividing of land into individually owned parcels, set the stage for dispossession by degrees that intensified persistent patterns of Indian mobility, and created the conditions whereby the extinction myth would be particularly compelling.

6

"They are so frequently shifting their place of residence"

Natick Indians, 1741–90

That although all possable care was taken by the Genll Court of Sd Province at the first, to give and grant unto us the great Priviledges of Fishing, by ordering our Sittuation so as that Certain Ponds, Convenient and good for Fishing, are included within the Bounds of sd Parish, which Ponds have been of great advantage to us, and Supplyed us with Fish of various Sorts . . . in plenty, whereby our families have been in great measure Supported Yet, notwithstanding the said Ponds are in the lands now in our possession – Ebenezer Feltch and others, English Inhabitants of Sd Parish, (without our consent, and against our wills) have of late so far Trespassed upon our Said priviledges, as to take Possession of our best fishing ground where we sett our [weirs] . . . and have Entered into articles of agreement . . . [We] therefore apply our Selves . . . that our Sd Priveledge may not be taken away, by such persons or means – That so we may Still have our old and Valluable liberty of fishing continued.[1]

A. *Struggles over place*

Angry about the arrogant English flouting of their fishing rights, in 1748 thirteen Indian landowners fired off a petition to the General Court protesting English encroachments. Their complaint revealed important dynamics operating within the Indian community after 1740 as well as a glimpse at festering conflict with English neighbors in Natick. The petitioners asserted that fishing remained central in providing for Indian families, describing it as an "old and Valluable liberty" that at least in part dictated the selection of the Natick site. Their complaint also suggests that Indians consciously protected lands surrounding ponds within the community even after Indians began selling lots to English purchasers; located "in the lands now in our possession," the ponds were regarded as a corporate Indian resource that categorically excluded English residents. Indians defended access to their "old and Valluable liberty" by retaining land adjacent to Cochituate Pond as common property for Indians, not granting it to individual Indians until the final allotment of lands in the 1760s. (See Figure 8.)

---

[1] Massachusetts Archives (hereafter cited as MA), Massachusetts State Archives at Columbia Point, Boston, 31:574, 1748.

Figure 8. Land grants bordering on Cochituate Pond

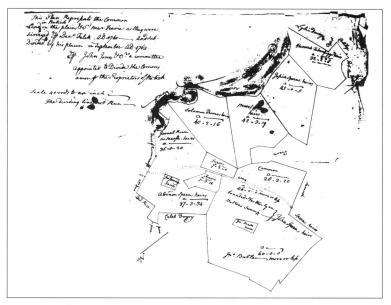

Sources: Various Maps of Property Owned by Natick Residents, 1742–63, Morse Institute Public Library, Natick, MA

Indian-owned lots: Israel Rumneymarsh's heirs, Solomon Thomas's heirs, Moses Speen's heirs, Josiah Speen's heirs, Hannah Tabumsug's heirs. Englishwoman Lydia Drury also appears to have had a lot adjacent to Cochituate Pond. Notice also in this plan the oddly shaped lots, and the three-acre lots of Englishmen Joseph Jennings and Joseph Travis that were carved out of the middle of lands belonging to Abraham Speen's heirs and John Speen's heirs, which suggest that English purchasers searched for the best land they could find, regardless of where it was located.

In continuing corporate ownership, Indians protected these lands from alienation to the English via the market in individually owned land that emerged in the 1720s. Significantly, the protest against English encroachment on an Indian right rooted in a mixed Native economy included the endorsement of several Indians whose own economic lifeways had come to resemble English patterns most fully, notably Deacon Joseph Ephraim, Jacob Chalcom, and Nathaniel Coochuck. The thirteen spokesmen, nine of whom signed their own names to the petition, demonstrated their knowledge of common law with regard to property rights and their determination to use English legal mechanisms to protect Native rights still important to the nearly 100-year-old community.

Still, the conflict over Cochituate and other ponds signifies a dramatic shift in power that occurred within Natick at midcentury. As English neighbors proliferated by steadily acquiring Indian land, they began to flout Indian rights aggressively. The fact that Indians identified Ebenezer Felch as the main culprit in encroaching on their fishing rights suggests the complexity in relations between Indian and English residents. Felch, who acted as surveyor and sometimes as a clerk for the proprietors between 1739 and the final division of lands in 1763, had just four years earlier placed himself in the posture of defending Indian rights to the community's wood supply.[2]

The stories of proprietary lineages suggest the diverse individual life experiences of Indians in Natick, but meshed together and fleshed out with other themes in the community, they compose a larger narrative of a community in crisis by midcentury. The market in land that had emerged in the 1720s laid the groundwork for a radical shift in the population balance and the drastic erosion of Indian power in Natick after 1740. At first mostly animated by Indians who built English-style farms and selectively acquired items of English material culture, land sales to the English accelerated rapidly after 1740, and negative reasons quickly outpaced the more constructive intentions that had informed the early land market. English purchasers avidly acquired Natick land, and the turnover in ownership altered the population of the community. While Indians counted 166 Native people in the Natick community in 1749, only thirty-seven were enumerated in the English-generated census in 1765, along with 450 whites and twenty-four people of African American or mixed descent.[3]

Indian dispossession provoked a reconfiguration of the place of Natick Indians in the community and in the commonwealth more generally. Two broad themes in late eighteenth-century Natick illustrate the changing circumstances of Natick as an Indian place. First, transformation in notions about Indian landownership introduced by the shift to a proprietary system, which dismantled Indian corporate protections and transformed Natick's lands into commodities transferable out of the Indian community, created the conditions for a vigorous land market that attracted English speculators and new English residents into the community. English infiltration into the operation of the proprietary system expanded in the late eighteenth century, and imposition of English forms in the disposition of Indian estates added bureaucracy-generated debt as an actual mechanism for further Indian dispossession.

Second, responding to what became an English majority population in the community, the commonwealth changed the legal status of Natick and categorically excluded Indians from political power. Before it was designated as a parish in 1746, Natick had been regulated as a plantation without the full scope of rights and obligations of legally established New England towns. District status followed in 1761, which, for example, qualified the community to

---

[2] MA 31:485, 1744.

[3] Thaddeus Mason, "A List of the Names of the Indians Old and Young Viz. Parents with the Number of their Children Both Male and Female, which Live in or Belong to Natick; Taken July 16, 1749," *Massachusetts Historical Society Collections* (hereafter cited as *MHSC*), 1st ser., 10 (1792): 134–5; and Michael J. Crawford, *History of Natick, Massachusetts, 1650–1976* (Natick, MA: Natick Historical Commission, 1976), 36.

send delegates to the House of Representatives. When the commonwealth made Natick a parish, it summarily disenfranchised Indians, barring them from voting in local town meetings or holding town office. These alterations were tangled up with a rancorous battle over the location of the meetinghouse, in which English residents manipulated Indians and the actual boundaries of the community in order to add to their own clout and exert power over the religious establishment. Though they failed, reassertion of Indian control over the church came only with the intervention of the General Court, which acknowledged that it was the Indians and the missionary society that provided the financial support.[4] The abrupt seizure of political rights in the town made official the shift in power that had accompanied English inmigration. Beginning in the late 1740s, their numerical dominance emboldened the English to create a separate poor relief system for Indians in Natick and elsewhere. In these actions the English defined Indians as rootless, displacing their own homelessness onto the Native population, and claiming Natick as an English place.

In 1763 Indian proprietors made a final division of their common lands. With this action, virtually every source of Indian power in the town vanished. And in liquidating the common lands, Ebenezer Felch got his way: The very last land allotment recorded gave him 10¼ acres on the edge of Cochituate Pond as payment "for [his] nineteen years Service as their Survyer."[5]

B. *The land market transformed*

Individual Indian land sales to English purchasers, begun in earnest in the 1730s, accelerated so rapidly after 1740 that the General Court took notice. (See Table 2.) A total of forty-eight Indian requests had been filed in the previous two decades; between 1741 and 1763 Indian petitions totaled 115. Indians filed twenty-five more between 1763 and 1790, when little land remained in their hands. In response to the flood of requests, the House of Representatives appointed a committee in 1744 "to project some proper Method to give Relief to the Indigent Indians (Petitioning to Sell land) less expensive to the Province."[6] Three years later, recognizing that Indians "have been often imposed upon by designing and ill-minded men in the dispossessing of their Lands . . . to the great loss & Injury of themselves & Families," the magistrates required that land petitions be reviewed by guardians elected to oversee Indian plantations.[7]

Though acting upon their own bureaucratic problem, the magistrates understood the significant changes that underlay continuing Indian land loss.

---

[4] Michael J. Crawford, "Indians, Yankees, and the Meetinghouse Dispute of Natick, Massachusetts, 1743–1800," *New England Historical and Genealogical Society Register* 132 (1987): 283–4.

[5] Natick Proprietors Book of Record, 1723–1787 (hereafter cited as NPB2), Morse Institute Public Library, Natick, MA, 157, 141.

[6] MA 31:489, 1743.   [7] MA 31:564–4a, 1747; and MA 31:567, 1747.

Table 2. *Indian land sale petitions, by decade*

	Number	/	Percent
	of all petitions		
1720s	16	/	9%
1730s	29	/	15%
1740s	70	/	37%
1750s	41	/	22%
1760s	16	/	9%
1770s	10	/	5%
1780sᵃ	6	/	3%
Totals	188		100%

ᵃ Includes one petition from 1790.

Sources: Massachusetts Archives, Massachusetts State Archives at Columbia Point, Boston, vols. 31–33; Massachusetts General Court, House of Representatives, *Journals of the House of Representatives of Massachusetts, 1715–90*, 55 vols. (Boston: Massachusetts Historical Society, 1919–), vols. 2–53; and Massachusetts General Court, Council, *Acts and Resolves, Public and Private, of the Province of the Massachusetts Bay*, 21 vols. (Boston: Wirth & Potter Printing Co., State Printers, 1895–1922), vol. 12, Appen. 7–vol. 21, Appen. 16, and 1780–90.

After 1740, only 22 percent of petitions cited improvements such as frame houses, barns, additional land, livestock, husbandry tools, and household goods that they needed capital in order to procure. Even Indians who continued to work toward farm building experienced financial pressures: twenty-four of the twenty-eight described debt stemming from everyday needs, financial overextension, illness, injury, and litigation along with more sanguine objectives.[8] After 1755,

[8] MA 31:348–9, 1741 (land, barn, debt: overextension/land); Massachusetts General Court, Council, *Acts and Resolves, Public and Private, of the Province of the Massachusetts Bay* (hereafter cited as AR), 21 vols. (Boston: Wirth & Potter Printing, Co., State Printers, 1895–1922), 13:95, Appen. 8, Chap. 197, 24 Mar. 1741/2 (land in Worcester, house); MA 31:372–4, 1742 (finish house and fencing, husbandry tools, debt: unspecified); MA 31:389–90, 1742 (house, oxen, husbandry tools); MA 31:398, 1742 (house, military disability, debt: overextension/land, sickness); MA 31:403–4, 1742 (barn, debt: unspecified); MA 31:432, 1742 (land, debt: sickness); MA 31:453, 1743 (oxen, chimney, debt: sickness); AR 13:343, Appen. 8, Chap. 268, 7 Mar. 1743/4 (house, debt: unspecified); MA 31:471, 1744 (land, cow, sheep, debt: sued); AR 13:378, Appen. 8, Chap. 44, 20 July 1744 (land); MA 31:488–9, 1744 (house, household goods, debt: sickness, sued); AR 13:468, Appen. 8, Chap. 10, 7 June 1745 (land, debt: sickness); AR 13:411, Appen. 8, Chap. 124, 18 Dec. 1744 (land, husbandry tools, debt: overextension/house and barn); AR 13:500–1, Appen. 8, Chap. 96, 27 Sept. 1745 (improve land, support, debt: injury); AR 13:543–4, Appen. 8, Chap. 209, 31 Jan. 1745/6 (house); AR 13:654, Appen. 8, Chap. 179, 12 Nov. 1746 (moved from town, land, debts: unspecified); MA 31:557–8, 1748 (moved from town, barn, cattle, debts: unspecified); MA 31:617, 1749 (land for son, support); AR 14:341–2, Appen. 9, Chap. 195, 13 Jan. 1749/50 (house, support, debts: unspecified); AR 14:496, Appen. 9, Chap. 222, 15 Feb. 1750/1 (house, finish barn, land, debts: unspecified); MA 32:65, 1750

Table 3. *Factors motivating Indian land sales, 1741–90*[a]

	Number / Percent	
Improvements	28 /	22%
Debt due to financial overextension	12 /	10%
Debt due to lawsuit	17 /	13%
Debt due to sickness or injury	55 /	44%
Debt – unspecified or other	36 /	29%
Needed support or relief	53 /	42%
Military disability	8 /	6%
Moving from the town	11 /	9%

[a] Nearly all requests cited at least two reasons for land sales. These figures represent the frequency of each factor in the 105 of 115 petitions in which reasons can be determined for 1741–63, and 21 of 25 petitions in which reasons can be determined for 1764–90.

Sources: Massachusetts Archives, Massachusetts State Archives at Columbia Point, Boston, vols. 31–33; Massachusetts General Court, House of Representatives, *Journals of the House of Representatives of Massachusetts, 1715–90*, 55 vols. (Boston: Massachusetts Historical Society, 1919–), vols. 18–53; and Massachusetts General Court, Council, *Acts and Resolves, Public and Private, of the Province of the Massachusetts Bay*, 21 vols. (Boston: Wirth & Potter Printing Co., State Printers, 1895–1922), vol. 12, Appen. 7–vol. 21, Appen. 16, and 1780–90.

not a single Indian mentioned improvements, and the only one who did not cite debt had abandoned the town.[9] He joined five others who had liquidated their Natick lands and moved on. (Reasons for land sales are detailed in Table 3.)

Financial disasters stemming from several causes began to overwhelm Natick Indians. Of Indian petitions, 10 percent came from Indians who had overextended themselves financially in the process of farm building. In one sense, their predicaments resulted from optimism about their future in the town. But taking on debt to acquire livestock, additional or more conveniently located land, and to build houses often trapped them in untenable financial situations

(house, oxen, barn); MA 32:87, 1751 (land, debt: sickness); MA 32:429–30, 1753 (house, debt: overextension/land); MA 32:479–80, 1754 (oxen, household goods, debt: unspecified); MA 32:580–1, 1754 (house, debt: sickness, overextension/land); MA 32:607–8, 1755 (house, land, cattle, debt: sickness); and MA 32:701–2, 1755 (house, well, cow, debt: sickness, sued).

9 Massachusetts General Court, House of Representatives, *Journals of the House of Representatives of Massachusetts, 1715–90* (hereafter cited as JH), 55 vols. (Boston, MA: Massachusetts Historical Society, 1919–), 49:149, 11 Jan. 1773 (moved). See previous note plus: MA 31:433, 1743 (moved); AR 14:42, Appen. 9, Chap. 101, 27 Aug. 1747 (moved from town, debt: overextension/land and farm building); AR 14:597, Appen. 9, Chap. 154, 27 Jan. 1751/2 (moved); MA 32:618, 1753 (moved); MA 33:348, 1765 (support, moved from the town); MA 33:366, 1766 (moved from the town, debt: overextension/house, sickness); MA 33:420–1, 1768 (moved from the town, debt: sued); and AR 18:774–5, Appen. 13, Chap. 129, 25 Feb. 1774 (support, moved from town, debt: sickness).

that worsened when family members became ill or disabled and sometimes required the care of English physicians.[10]

English legal prosecution of Indians formed one aspect of the persistent conflict that characterized relations within Natick after 1740. Financial overextension carried the threat of lawsuits, which English creditors pressed when they knew Indians owned land. They may have extended credit and services to Indians in order to pry parcels of land away from them. English neighbors occasionally intervened in the legal troubles of Indians, most likely knowing their land would serve as security against their investments.[11] Of petitions filed between 1741 and 1790, 13 percent came from Indians forced to sell land to satisfy legal judgments against them. At least two Indians composed their petitions from Cambridge gaol. Several absconded. Others, such as Leah Chalcom and her daughters, sold land because they feared that "the whole of their Estate will speedily be exhausted by frequent Law-Suits."[12]

But after 1741, sickness and injury composed the most commonly cited reasons for Indian debt. Overall, 44 percent of petitions narrated financial disasters that resulted from illness, lameness, and military disabilities suffered by family members. Recurring health problems destroyed the economic prospects of families and forced them to sell land as a last resort. Petitioners cited caretaking, medicine, fees from English physicians, and expenses for English-style burials.[13]

[10] See previous note plus: MA 31:449, 1743 (debt: overextension/land); MA 32:417–18, 1753 (debt: overextension/oxen, sickness, unspecified); AR 16:6, Appen. 11, Chap. 155, 31 Aug. 1757 (debt: overextension/land, sickness, unspecified); MA 33:53–4, 1758 (debt: overextension/land, sickness, unspecified); MA 33:106–7, 1759 (support, debt: overextension/land); and AR 17:393, Appen. 12, Chap. 33, 3 June 1763 (support, debt: overextension/second farm with buildings).

In several instances, the cause of debt is unspecified or not entirely clear: MA 31:312–3, 1741 (debt: related to an indenture); AR 13:180, Appen. 8, Chap. 121, 8 Dec. 1742 (debt: unspecified); HR 22:168, 25 Jan. 1745/6 (debt: unspecified); MA 32:16, 1750 (debt: unspecified); MA 32:403, 1753 (debt: unspecified); MA 32:742, 1756 (debt: unspecified); AR (1782–3):691, Chap. 32, 23 June 1783 (debt: unspecified); and AR (1782–83):740, Chap. 8, 2 Oct. 1783 (debt: unspecified).

[11] See previous notes plus: AR 13:76, Appen. 8, Chap. 145, 7 Jan. 1741/2 (debt: sued. Absconded. Filed by English creditor who wants lands attached); MA 31:336, 1741 (debt: sued. Absconded. English creditor wants attached lands sold); AR 13:106, Appen. 8, Chap. 222, 7 Apr. 1742 (debt: sued. Absconded. Filed by English creditor who wants land attached); MA 31:400, 1742 (debt: sued, unspecified); MA 31:425–6, 1742 (debt: sued); AR 13:179, Appen. 8, Chap. 118, 8 Dec. 1742 (support, debt: sued, sickness); AR 13:214, Appen. 8, Chap. 210, 7 Apr. 1743 (debt: sued, sickness. Filed by English creditor who wants land attached); MA 31:459–60, 1743 (debt: sued/wants writs of execution stayed, sickness); AR 13:535, Appen. 8, Chap. 183, 28 Jan. 1745/6 (debt: sued); MA 31:661, 1749 (debt: sued, unspecified); MA 32:354, 1753 (debt: sued/in Cambridge gaol); MA 32:692–3, 1755 (debt: sued); and MA 32:740–1, 1756 (debt: sued/in Cambridge gaol).

[12] MA 33:106–7, 1759.

[13] See previous notes plus: MA 31:352–3, 1741 (support, debt: injury); MA 31:391, 1742 (support, debt: sickness); MA 31:385, 1742 (support, debt: sickness); MA 31:378–9, 1742 (debt: sickness); MA 31:419–20, 1743 (debt: sickness); MA 31:440–1, 1743 (support, debt: sickness); MA 31:469–70, 1743 (debt: lameness); AR 13:481, Appen. 8, Chap. 45, 29 June

Inability to work because of illness, debility, or old age exacerbated the financial woes of many Indians. Overall, 42 percent of petitioners wanted to devote the proceeds from land sales to present or future relief. Between 1741 and 1763, 37 percent of petitions cast their pleas in this manner; after 1764, 67 percent did so.[14] Two petitions were filed by English guardians caring for Indian orphans.[15] The memorials continued a now-familiar theme, similar to the story recited in the petition of Deborah and Sarah Comecho: "That they have, one of em, been in needy Circumstances many years, the other for Some Time past, and both infirm and their labour is greatly abated by Thrumatick disorders . . . and being Justly indebted . . . [they are] in need of some present relief."[16] The Comecho sisters asked to sell their land and have the proceeds "improved in the most frugal manner toward their future support and comfort."[17] This approach toward landholdings, present in the preceding decades, dominated after 1763, and signaled a spirit of resignation that came to prevail among Indians.

1745 (support, debt: sickness, disability); AR 13:481, Appen. 8, Chap. 46, 29 June 1745 (support, debt: sickness); AR 13:491, Appen. 8, Chap. 66, 26 July, 1745 (support, debt: infirm); AR 14:39, Appen. 9, Chap. 92, 22 Aug. 1747 (debt: sickness); AR 14:39, Appen. 9, Chap. 93, 22 Aug. 1747 (debt: sickness); MA 31:529, 1747 (support, debt: infirm); MA 31:656, 1749 (military disability, debt: sickness); MA 32:66–7, 1750 (support, debt: injury); MA 32:296, 1752 (support, debt: sickness); MA 32:401, 1753 (support, debt: sickness); MA 32:440, 1753 (debt: sickness, unspecified); MA 32:474, 1754 (support, debt: sickness); MA 32:614–5, 1755 (support, debt: sickness); MA 32:620, 1755 (debt: sickness); MA 32:694, 1755 (support, debt: nursing); MA 32:749, 1756 (debt: sickness); MA 33:59–60, 1758 (support, debt: sickness); MA 33:104–5, 1759 (support, military disability, debt: crippled); MA 33:113–4, 1759 (support, infirm); MA 33:124–5, 1760 (debt: sickness); MA 33:159, 1761 (support, debt: sickness); MA 33:188, 1762 (support, debt: sickness); MA 33:204–5, 1762 (support, debt: sickness, infirm); MA 33:300, 1764 (support, debt: sickness); MA 33:317–8, 1765 (support, debt: sickness); MA 33:409, 1767 (support, debt: crippled); MA 33:553, 1772 (debt: injury); MA 33:555, 1772 (support, debt: infirm); MA 33:559–60, 1772 (debt: sickness); and AR 18:731, Appen. 13, Chap. 47, 25 June 1773 (support, debt: disabled).

[14] See previous notes plus: MA 31:402, 1741 (support, debt: unspecified); AR 13:346, Appen. 8, Chap. 277, 13 Mar. 1743/4 (support, debt: unspecified); HR 22:242–3, 24 Apr. 1746 (support, debt: unspecified); Peeguns: HR 24:84, 26 June 1747 (support, debt: unspecified); Coochuck: HR 24:84, 26 June 1747 (support, debt: unspecified); MA 31:662, 1749 (support, military disability, debt: unspecified); MA 31:663, 1750 (support, military disability); MA 32:345–7, 1753 (support); AR 15:142, Appen. 10, Chap. 333, 10 Apr. 1754 (support); AR 15:354, Appen. 10, Chap. 65, 16 June 1755 (support, military disability, debt: unspecified); MA 32:703, 1754 (support, military disability, debt: unspecified); MA 32:748, 1756 (support, debt: unspecified); MA 32:708–9, 1756 (support, military disability, debt: unspecified); MA 33:36–7, 1758 (support); MA 33:191–3, 1761 (support); AR 17:441, Appen. 12, Chap. 145, 30 Dec. 1763 (support); MA 33:338, 1765 (support); AR 18:732, Appen. 13, Chap. 49, 25 June 1773 (support); AR (1784–5):208, Chap. 11, 7 June 1784 (support, debt: unspecified); AR (1784–5):337–8, Chap. 37, 7 Feb. 1785 (support, debt: unspecified); AR (1788–9):332–3, Chap. 4, 31 Oct. 1788 (support for heir); and AR (1790–1):112, Chap. 32, 14 June 1790 (support, debt: unspecified).

[15] Martha Peegun: MA 33:317–8, 1765; and Hezekiah Comecho: MA 33:338, 1765.

[16] MA 33:555, 1772.   [17] Ibid.

Figure 9. Number of land transctions by type, 1740–90[a]

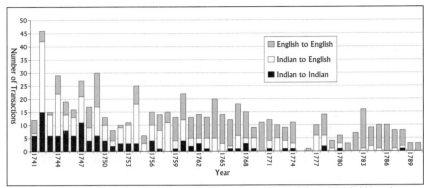

Sources: Natick Proprietors Book of Record, 1723–87, Morse Institute Public Library, Natick, MA; and Middlesex County Court, Grantee and Grantors Records, Cambridge, MA.

[a] One English-to-Indian transaction is not reflected in these figures.

Until the 1760s, Indians remained reluctant to part with more land than was necessary. Nearly 60 percent of petitioners requested to sell twenty or fewer acres from 1741 through 1763.[18] But after 1763, of the twenty-two petitions that indicated amounts of land to be sold, three sought total liquidation, and five specified more than thirty acres. Five other requests failed to state the size of parcels to be sold; instead, they phrased their memorials similarly to that of Abigail Moheag. She wanted "to Sell So much of her Real Estate as the Guardians Shall think of real necessity for the Purposes above Mentioned."[19]

Prior to the final division of common lands to Indian proprietors in 1763, the Indian-to-Indian component of the Natick land market retained vitality in some years. (See Figures 9 and 10.) The number of such transactions equaled or exceeded Indian-to-English sales in 1741, 1745, 1747, 1751, and 1762, but never again. Similarly, acres transferred between Indians eclipsed those passing out of Indian hands six times between 1741 and 1756 and for the final time in 1762.

Continuing Indian dispossession transformed the market in Natick land between 1764 and 1790. Between 1741 and 1763, ninety-nine sales between Indians had transferred ownership of 916 acres, and 174 Indian-to-English deeds transferred a fraction less than 1,574 acres. After 1763, Indian-to-Indian transactions virtually ceased: Only 165 acres changed hands between Indians, in thirteen transactions. Indians sold more than four times as much land (just over 697 acres) to English purchasers in fifty-two transactions. In terms of acreage, sales between English parties dwarfed both of these segments of the

[18] O'Brien, "Community Dynamics in the Indian-English Town of Natick, Massachusetts, 1650–1790" (Ph.D. diss., University of Chicago, 1990), 358.
[19] MA 33:300, 1764.

Figure 10. Acreage sold by type, 1740–90[a]

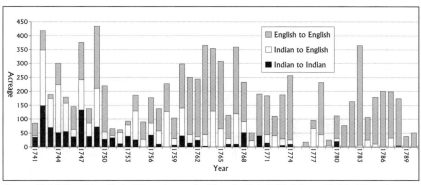

Sources: Natick Proprietors Book of Record, 1723–87, Morse Institute Public Library, Natick, MA; and Middlesex County Court, Grantee and Grantors Records, Cambridge, MA.

[a]Several deeds do not specify acreage: Indian-to-Indian, one in 1749, and two in 1778. Indian-to-English, one each in 1741, 1752, and 1753. English-to-English, one each in 1751, 1755, and 1768.

land market in both periods. One hundred and thirty English-to-English deeds shifted ownership of almost 2,290 acres from 1741 to 1763. Between 1763 and 1790, 188 property transfers turned over ownership of a little more than 3,519 acres, more than half the total acreage of the town, between non-Indians.[20]

The dramatic takeoff in the English-to-English element of the Natick land market beginning in the 1760s reflected at least two important trends. First, transactions between Indians and the English almost always flowed one way: The 1753 deed from an Englishman to an Indian was one of only two such transactions in the entire eighteenth century.[21] The Indian-to-Indian market thus became less viable in direct proportion to the growth of the Indian-to-English market. Second, non–Indians who bought land often purchased small tracts, assembled viable parcels, then turned around and sold them to other English buyers. These actions underscore the speculative impulse that underlay much of the Natick land market. (See Figure 11.) Tracts smaller than ten acres continued to comprise about two-thirds of transactions (64 percent between 1720 and 1740, and 61 percent between 1741 and 1790). But only one of the 151 land sales between 1741 and 1763 involved an English-to-English transfer larger than thirty acres; after 1763 and up through 1790, there were fifty-six (out of 647 overall). Seventeen more transactions of this size involved Indian sellers and English buyers, but only five occurred among Indians.

---

[20] These transactions are only some unknown portion of the non–Indian land market. See Chapter 4 for an explanation of my methodology.

[21] Middlesex County Court, Grantee and Grantor Records (hereafter cited as MCG), Cambridge, MA, 85:442, Nathaniel Smith to Daniel Thomas, 1753/1784, 20 acres; and MCG 49:71, Moses Fisk to Joseph Ephraim Jr., 1739/1749, 6 1/2 acres.

Figure 11. Size of parcels transferred by type, 1740–90[a]

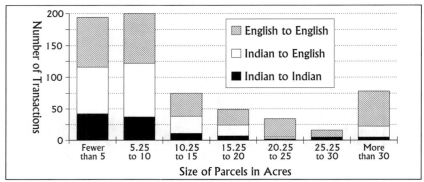

Sources: Natick Proprietors Book of Record, 1723–87, Morse Institute Public Library, Natick, MA; and Middlesex County Court, Grantee and Grantors Records, Cambridge, MA.

[a] Several deeds do not specify acreage: Indian-to-Indian, one in 1749, and two in 1778. Indian-to-English, one each in 1742, 1752, and 1753. English-to-English, one each in 1751, 1755, and 1768.

Participation in the Indian land market was broad; 142 individuals bought land from an Indian at least once, including four women and five African-Americans.[22] At least 194 more bought Natick land from English sellers. Engaging in 336 separate transactions with Indians in the 1720s through the 1780s, the 142 people who bought land from Indians averaged 2.4 transactions per person.[23] Some individuals were far more active in buying Indian land than others. Eighteen Englishmen were involved in five or more Indian transactions. They averaged 7.55 transactions apiece, and their cumulative acquisition of 1,298¼ acres of Indian land placed them in a different category from the rest. Only 13 percent of Indian land buyers, their purchases represented 45 percent of all land bought from Indian sellers.[24]

[22] I use the label "English," even though (interestingly) African Americans also bought Indian land, because it was the English colonial regime that brought African Americans to Natick. In fact, one African American buyer was Oliver Peabody's "servant." He bought 10 acres from Indian Caesar Ferrit without General Court license, then later successfully gained confirmation of his title by petitioning the General Court, pleading ignorance of the law. MCG 62:441, 1758/1765; and MA 32:238, 1755.

[23] This analysis differs somewhat from my other discussions of the Natick land market. It includes individuals who bought land from administrators of estates; these transactions are not included in land market analyses. Excluded are: corporate transactions by proprietors, including transactions to minister Stephen Badger, who received several parcels of land as part of his ministerial settlement; transfers resulting from legal judgments; leases; and exchanges. The magnitude of this market seems astonishing, considering that fewer than 500 non-Indians resided in the town in 1765.

[24] Twelve transactions: Samuel Perry (118½ acres); Joseph Travis (72½ acres); eleven transactions: Moses Fisk (145 acres); Jonathan Lealand (80¾ acres); nine transactions: John Bacon (90¾ acres); Abel Perry (54¼ acres); eight transactions: David Morse (85 acres); Jonathan Richardson (33¼ acres); seven transactions: Oliver Bacon (55½ acres); John

Like those who purchased Natick Indian land in general, most of the eighteen Englishmen who purchased Indian land actively came from towns that surrounded Natick: Sherborn, Framingham, Needham, Dedham, and Medway.[25] Joseph Travis of Sherborn started acquiring Indian land in 1730, when he bought 5½ acres Josiah Speen sold to raise capital for a house. By 1742 Travis had moved to Natick. He bought land from Indians at least thirteen times, which allowed him to give seventy acres to his son Daniel in 1770 and twenty acres to his son Asa in 1772.[26] In 1757 twenty-one-year-old Abel Perry married Kezia Morse of Sherborn in Sherborn. His son Abel was born three months later, and he bought his first parcel of Natick land from Indian Benjamin Tray two months after that. Perry acquired 168¾ acres from English and African American sellers in thirteen transactions in addition to the 83½ acres he bought from Indians.[27] His land activities likely provided Perry the social mobility that permitted him to describe himself as a gentleman by the 1780s.[28]

Goodenow (62 acres); six transactions: Nathaniel Battle (129 acres); Benjamin Kendall (33¾ acres); five transactions: Nehemiah Allen (42¾ acres); Daniel Biglow (34¾ acres); John Drury (72¼ acres); Joseph Perry (57 acres); Samuel Welles (91¼ acres); and John Winn (40¼ acres). This analysis excludes minister Stephen Badger (who received land as part of his ministerial settlement), and includes only transactions counted in my land market analysis, in order to make the figures comparable. Sources: NPB2; and MCG.

[25] This meshes with the findings of John W. Adams and Alice Bee Kasakoff who, based on an analysis of genealogies, found that between 1700 and 1749, 66 percent of migration occurred within 16 miles (median 6.8 miles), and between 1750 and 1799, 49 percent occurred within that distance (median 16.3 miles). Adams and Kasakoff, "Migration and the Family in Colonial New England: The View from the Genealogies," *Journal of Family History* 9 (1984): 24–43. Deeds from 123 of the 142 identify a residential location: Natick (44/36%), Sherborn (24/20%), Needham (13/11%), Framingham (13/11%), Dedham (11/9%), Sudbury (4/3%), Medway (3/2%), Dover (2/2%), Boston (2/2%), Medfield (1/–), Weston (1/–), Hopkinton (1/–), Charlestown (1/–), Andover (1/–), Bradford (1/–), and Brookline (1/–).

[26] From Indians: NPB2, 73, 1742, 4 acres from Mary Coochuck; NPB2, 90, 1744, 19 1/2 acres from Mary Coochuck; NPB2, 101, 1746, 2 1/4 acres from Nathaniel Coochuck; NPB2, 134, 1758, 5 acres in right of Hannah Tabumsug; MCG 38:540, from Josiah Speen, 1730/1737, 5 1/2 acres; MCG 43:11, from Mary and Nathaniel Coochuck, 1744/1744, 4 acres; MCG 43:725, from Hannah Speen, 1742/1744, 6 3/4 acres; MCG 43:727, from Thomas Peegun, 1742/1744, 3 acres; MCG 43:728, from Mary and Nathaniel Coochuck, 1744/1744, 10 acres; MCG 49:49, from Nathaniel Coochuck, 2 1/2 acres; MCG 62:5, from Samuel Bowman's heirs, 1754/1763, 5 acres; MCG 62:6, from Natick Proprietors, 1754/1763, 5 1/2 acres; and MCG 62:7, from Benjamin Wiser, 1758/1763, 5 acres. To Sons: MCG 73:351, to Daniel Travis, 1770/1772, 70 acres; and MCG 73:346, to Asa Travis, 1772/1772, 20 acres.

[27] From Indians: NPB2, 17, 1750s, 1/4 acre from Natick Proprietors; MCG 56:66, from Benjamin Tray, 1757/1757, 2 3/4 acres; MCG 58:48, from Solomon Wamsquan's administrator, 1759/1760, 3 acres; MCG 59:33, from Daniel Thomas, 1761/1761, 7 acres; MCG 64:151, from Natick Proprietors, 1759/1765, 17 1/4 acres; MCG 64:152, from Caesar Ferrit, 1763/1765, 2 3/4 acres; MCG 68:94, from Caesar Ferrit, 1767/1768, 12 acres; MCG 69:252, from Daniel Thomas, 1769/1769, 1/2 acre; MCG 69:252, from Jonas Obscow, 1778/1779, 12 acres; MCG 90:334, judgment against John Ephraim, 1786/1787, 6 acres; MCG 96:417, from Abial Senah, 1787/1787, 7 acres; and MCG 96:527, from Abial Senah, 1788/1788, 7 1/4 acres.

[28] MCG 85:22, with Thomas Drury from Samuel Stratton, 1783/1783, 50 acres and buildings.

Some of these eighteen men, such as David Morse, became integrated into the town before 1740. At age thirty-four, Morse acquired his first piece of Natick land, eight acres purchased from the Rev. Oliver Peabody in 1730.[29] He supplemented eight purchases from Indians with four additional acquisitions from English sellers, which included several mills in Natick.[30] Morse set up sons William, Pelatiah, and Joseph with lands in Natick and Holliston in 1761.[31] An early-comer, Morse held town office, entered full communion in the church, raised five children, married his second wife, and died in Natick in 1773 at the age of seventy-seven. Like Morse, John Winn also established himself in the town; he bought 40¼ acres from five different Indians, married and raised a family, and held office in Natick. A housewright, Winn probably benefited from Indian demands for frame houses.[32]

In their geographic mobility, some English purchasers of Indian land resembled the Indian population of Natick; they came from elsewhere, lived in Natick for several years, then moved on. Not all English purchasers became integrated into Natick as Morse, Travis, and Perry did. Blacksmith Jonathan Richardson of Medway bought nineteen acres the Natick proprietors sold to raise capital for their school in 1737.[33] He was in Natick by 1742, described himself as a gentleman by 1750, then sold his Natick holdings beginning in 1763 and moved to Brookfield by 1766.[34] Nathaniel Battle was described as a husbandman or yeoman from Dedham from 1730 through 1769 and a gentleman from Sherborn in 1784. He listed his residence as Natick when he passed his Natick lands on to his son, Nathaniel, and daughters Tabitha Jones, Silence Perry, and Martha Homer in 1778. Nathaniel Jr. and Tabitha resided in Dedham, Silence in Holden, and Martha in Hopkinton.[35] Some Indian land buyers, among them

---

[29] MCG 30:528, from Oliver Peabody, 1730/1730, 8 acres.

[30] From Indians: NPB2, 34, 1735, 2 3/4 acres, seller not clear; MCG 39:532, from Samuel Abraham, 1731/1738, 10 acres; MCG 39:533, from Jacob Chalcom, 1731/1738, 6 acres; MCG 39:539, from Joseph Ephraim Jr., 1733/1738, 8 acres; MCG 39:540, from Joseph Ephraim Jr., 1733/1738, 30 acres; MCG 39:541, from Mary and Nathaniel Coochuck, 1734/1738, 6 acres; MCG 39:542, from William Thomas, 1737/1738, 4¼ acres; and MCG 50:497, from William Thomas, 1749/1752, 18 acres.

[31] MCG 66:176, to William Morse, 1761/1767, 65 3/4 acres in Natick and land in Holliston; MCG 66:177, to Pelatiah Morse, 1761/1767, 49 3/4 in Natick, and one quarter of his land in Holliston; and MCG 77:423, to Joseph Morse, 1761/1777, 59 acres in Natick.

[32] From Indians: MCG 39:508, from Samuel Abraham Sr., 1733/1738, 12 acres; MCG 39:510, from Thomas Peegun, 1733/1738, 10 acres; MCG 49:284, from Benjamin Wiser, 1748/1750, 6 1/2 acres; MCG 49:284, from Thomas Awassamug, 1750/1750, 9½ acres; and MCG 54:443, from Jonas Obscow's administrator, 1744/1756, 2¼ acres.

[33] MCG 39:243, from Natick Proprietors, 1737/1738, 10 and 9 acres.

[34] MCG 47:7, from John George, 1742/1747, 2 acres (from Natick); MCG 61:605, from Peter Ephraim, 1750/1763, 1 acre (gentleman); MCG 62:64, to Samuel Welles, 1763/1763, 70 3/4 acres in six parcels; and MCG 67:417, to Timothy Smith, 1766/1768, 3 acres in Natick (Jonathan Richardson of Brookfield).

[35] MCG 36:545, from Jacob Chalcom, 1730/1735, 32 acres (husbandman from Dedham); MCG 81:593, to William Biglow, 1784/1786, 12 acres (gentleman of Sherborn); MCG 79:334, to Nathaniel Battle Jr., 1778/1778, 7 acres; and MCG 79:332, to Tabitha Jones of

Daniel Biglow of Framingham, bought Indian land repeatedly but apparently never resided in the town.[36] Others, such as Jonathan Lealand, lived on the border between Sherborn and Natick.[37] He may have added to his landholdings through opportunistic purchases of contiguous land.

Few people rivaled the Natick land activities of Englishman Samuel Welles Jr. He not only bought land from Indians five times, but also extended mortgages to Englishmen who secured their loans with Natick land.[38] Welles engaged in twenty-three transactions with Englishmen, exchanged land with an Indian once, and sued Indian John Ephraim and six Englishmen for debts. Welles entered the Natick land market in 1764 as a Boston resident, lived in Natick beginning in 1765, and moved back to Boston by 1787. His daughter Abigail was baptized in Natick in 1776.[39] Even though Welles may have resided in the town on at least a part-time basis for more than twenty years, his involvement there had more to do with financial interests than a long-term commitment to the community.

C. The land market transforms the community

The carving up of Natick and the influx of English residents facilitated by the land market carried stark implications for Indian economic prospects. Obviously, land loss reduced agricultural opportunities for Indians. Some land-sale petitions included descriptions of English-style farms complete with frame structures, broken and fenced land, livestock, draft animals, and husbandry tools; other Indians probably gardened using Native techniques. But a great many engaged in indentured and wage labor, fishing in local ponds, seafaring,

Dedham, Silence Perry of Holden, and Martha Homer of Hopkinton, 1778/1778, 60, 60, and 40 acres.

[36] Biglow consistently listed himself as a Framingham resident in his thirteen deeds with Indians and non-Indians.

[37] When Lealand passed on half of his farm to his son in 1770, it was described as lying in Natick and Sherborn. MCG 71:36, to Jonathan Lealand, Jr., 1770/1772, half of his farm and buildings in Sherborn and Natick.

[38] See, for example, MCG 66:202, mortgage with John Gay for L96.10.6, secured with 49 and 2¾ and 7¾ acres of Natick land, 1765/1766; MCG 66:175, mortgage with William Cary, L31.4.1 secured with 7 acres of Natick land, 1768/1768; MCG 95:14, mortgage with Joseph Bacon for L27.10.6, secured with 24 acres of Natick land, 1787/1787; and MCG 96:198, mortgage with Isaac Morrill, L27.17, secured with 1 acre of Natick land, 1787/1787. From Indians: MCG 64:109, from Nathaniel Hill, 1764/1765, 15½ acres; MCG 64:109, from Martha Peegun's guardian, 1765/1765, 2 acres; MCG 67:174, from Samuel and Zurviah Ompany's attorney, 1767/1767, 71 1/4 acres (clarified in MCG 101:288, 1773/1789); MCG 67:582, from Abial Senah's administrator, 1768/1768, 9½ acres; MCG 64:109, from Martha Peegun's guardian, 1765/1765, ¼ acre; and MCG 90:394, recovered judgment from John Ephraim, 1787, 15 acres.

[39] MCG 63:107, from William White, 1764/1765, 56 acres (of Boston); MCG 64:110, from Philip Vardner, 1765/1765, ¼ acre; (of Natick); MCG 95:14, to Joseph Bacon, 1787/1787 (of Boston); and Peabody and Badger Records, Church of Natick, 1725–95 (hereafter cited as NCR), Typescript copy, Massachusett Historical Society, Boston, MA.

military service, and town service. The English considered the market for laborers saturated by 1757. In that year, the Sherborn selectmen joined a committee from Natick in asking that they be excused from incorporating Seven Years' War refugees from Nova Scotia because "of the many poor People and Indians who live among them, and depend upon their Day-Labour for their Support," using racial categories to underscore their separatist attitudes.[40]

With the rapid influx of English residents, the lands in Natick became a patchwork, with adjacent parcels alternately owned and used by Indians and their English neighbors. Division of lands through inheritance carved up the landscape into smaller parcels. These two factors discouraged some Indians from using the land they did own. Hannah Speen and Daniel Thomas had inherited land from Benjamin Tray. In 1761 she moved to sell the land because

> [the] lands are Situate in Such a mannar As that they Can be of but Little advantage to your Petitioner being Intirely surrounded by Lands of the English, & No Way [to get] from Said Land but by Trespassing on Others, And it is Apprehended that it will be Very Difficult if Not impracticable, to make An Equal Division, in Quantity & Quality . . . and that A Division Will Very much Obstruct the Sale and Lessen the Value of the Whole.[41]

The Natick experience prefigured the disastrous "checkerboarding" and inheritance complications that resulted from Indian dispossession under the Indian allotment policy between 1887 and 1934 that individualized reservation lands as a mechanism to dismantle Indian tribes and, in theory, assimilate Indians into society as individuals.

In another striking parallel to allotment policy, guardians also leased out Indian lands to English neighbors beginning at least in the 1740s. In 1758 the General Court specifically directed Indian guardians to "take into their hands the said Indians Lands" and allot them to the Indians to be "improved." The rest of the land was to be leased to "suitable persons" for limited terms. The income produced "shall be applied for the Support of Such of the Proprietors in their respective Plantations as may be . . . unable to support them selves & Families, & for the payment of their Just debts at the discretion of their said Guardians."[42] Under the same act, Indian-to-Indian land transactions, including sales and leases, were subjected to the consent of the guardians. And continuing concerns over English manipulation of Indian debts prompted the court to bar any legal actions from being brought against Indians for any sum unless they were first "examined and allowed" by the Court of General Sessions of the Peace or by the Indian guardians.[43] But at the same time the court espoused

[40] JH, Part 1, 34:156, 30 Nov. 1757.   [41] MA 33:192–3, 1761–62.
[42] MA 33:64, 1758.
[43] Yasuhide Kawashima, *Puritan Justice and the Indian: White Man's Law in Massachusetts, 1630–1763* (Middletown, CT: Wesleyan University Press, 1986).

the goal of protecting Indian interests, it legitimated a subordinate status for Indians by granting English farmers official approval to let "creatures run upon the said Indians unimproved lands" lying contiguous to other towns. Although just whose definition of "improved lands" would govern these provisions remained entirely unstated, this provision suggests that the English continued to have trouble recognizing Indian land-use patterns.[44]

Some leases included provisions for maintaining the property and clearing and fencing the land in addition to cash rents.[45] English renters sometimes competed for land leases: "Coochuck Land – Drury to have the Preference. Stratton bids for it, Stratton offers 25ll for Coochuck Place for one Year."[46] Others suggest leases were subject to approval of the Indian community. In 1753 Jonathan Richardson arranged a lease with Eunice Brooks, but Indian Daniel Thomas challenged the agreement, claiming a right to use the land "by virtue of a deed and lease that he had of the Said Eunice." Richardson relented, explaining that

> the Indians are generally disturbed at my hireing the Same . . . altho
> I want the pasture; Yet having had the advice of Majr Jones, this
> day, he thinks best for me not to Insist upon Improving the Sd pas-
> ture; for the Said Daniel having a Stock of his own cattle, has
> turned them into the feed.[47]

In this instance, Indian uses were given priority, and the climate of Indian opinion was taken into account by Richardson and Indian guardian John Jones. Similar leasing arrangements between Indians may have been common, but are largely invisible in the documentary record because transactions between Indians were not subject to commonwealth oversight until 1758.[48]

D. *Liquidation of the commons*

The pattern of proprietary grants confirms the dramatic transformation in Indian land holdings that followed individualization of Natick's lands. After the systematic 1719 allotment of lands to Indian proprietors, land divisions in Natick were made on a piecemeal basis. In a 1744 meeting, proprietors voted that the land records be regularized and steps be taken to see that lands were fully

---

[44] MA 33:64, 1758.

[45] The few surviving documents regarding guardianship of the Natick Indians detail eighteen leasing arrangements dating from 1747 to 1753. These leases are surely only a portion of agreements actually consummated. For requirements placed upon renters see, for example, John Sawin's lease of five acres from Huldah Niar in 1747; Joseph Perry's lease of 2½ acres of orchard and swampland belonging to Moses Speen's estate, 1750; Matthew Hasting's lease of Deacon Joseph Ephraim's pasture and four acres of "Plowland." Middlesex County Court, Probate Records (hereafter cited as MCP), Cambridge, MA, #12363, Natick Indians, Gdn., 1835.

[46] Ibid.   [47] Ibid.

[48] MA 33:64, 1758.

recorded.[49] Five years later, proprietors agreed that each of them should have 150 acres.[50] Proprietors referred to all grants dating from 1720 to 1762 as the second division.[51] In 1760 they met and decided to petition the General Court for permission to sell what remained, because it consisted of "about forty pieces and to[o] intermeet with the English settlements that they are like to be of but little advantage to them."[52] Instead, in 1763, the remaining commons were laid out to heirs of each of the nineteen proprietary rights.[53]

Table 4 summarizes land grants made from 1719 through the final division in 1763 according to time periods.[54] Grants to each proprietor ranged from just over 154 acres to the right of Samuel Ompetowin to about 220 to the right of Israel Rumneymarsh. Each of the proprietors received an average of just over 193 acres in Natick.[55] Some proprietors drew on their land resources earlier than others. Benjamin Tray, for example, received 74 percent of his land by 1740, while Israel Rumneymarsh was granted 73 percent of his land after 1741. More typical in this regard was the proprietary right of Samuel Ompetowin. Half the land granted in his right was allotted in the twenty-two year period before 1741, and half between 1741 and 1763. Overall, proprietors allotted 30 percent of the land they received in the initial 1719 division, and 17 percent between 1720 and 1740. Between 1741 and 1762, land grants constituted 36 percent of all grants, leaving 18 percent of land to be granted to Natick Indians in the final 1763 division.

The pattern of land grants illustrates the dramatic transformation the proprietary system had wrought. These figures show that less than half of land ever granted to Natick Indians was allotted during the first twenty-one years of the codified proprietary system (47 percent), and 53 percent in the last twenty-two years. Although this breakdown suggests relatively consistent granting of land, it is important to bear in mind that Natick had been bounded for seven decades prior to formalization of the land system. Considering the figures from this angle casts a much different light on developments in the town. During the first ninety years, less than half of the common land was allotted, and in the subsequent twenty-two years more than half was divided. Individualization decimated Indian landownership that corporate agreements had quite successfully protected prior to 1719.

When Natick was granted to Indians under the direction of John Eliot in 1650, the plantation was estimated to contain six thousand acres. Proprietors jointly granted 1,252¼ acres to various individuals to acquire public goods and

[49] NPB2, 94.   [50] NPB2, 110–11.
[51] NPB2, 135.   [52] NPB2, 136.
[53] NPB2, 139.
[54] Gaps in the record books make precise calculation of how much land was allotted to each proprietary right impossible. These records must be relatively complete, however, judging from acreage totals that can be determined.
[55] The rights of both Samuel Will and Thomas Nehemiah are included in this calculation.

Table 4. *Divisions of land to proprietors, 1719–63*

1719 Proprietors	1719 Acres	1721–40 Acres	1741–62 Acres	Final division	1741–63 Acres	Total grants
Abraham Speen	60	14	77.5	37.75	115.25	189.25
James Speen	60	12	99	40.75	139.75	211.75
Moses Speen	60	0	77.25	42.75	120	180
Josiah Speen	60	39	40.5	45	85.5	184.5
Isaac Speen	60	42	46.5	25.75	72.25	174.25
John Speen	60	29.75	80.5	46	126.5	216.25
Thomas Waban	60	69	3	46.25	49.25	178.25
Thomas Peegun	60	66.5	45	20.5	65.5	192
Simon Ephraim	60	76	40.08	23.25	63.33	199.33
Benjamin Tray	60	86	30.75	21.25	52	198
Samuel Bowman	60	57	48.75	43.5	92.25	209.25
Samuel Will	60	15.75	104.25	0	104.25	180
Isaac Monequassin	60	0	90.75	21.75	112.5	172.5
John Awassamug	60	51.5	52	22.5	74.5	186
Samuel Ompetowin	60	17	28.5	49	77.5	154.5
Hannah Tabumsug	60	7.5	102.5	37.25	139.75	207.25
Solomon Thomas	60	20	82.75	40.5	123.25	203.25
Israel Rumneymarsh	60	0	130.25	30	160.25	220.25
Samuel Abraham	60	41	48.75	43.25	92	193
Thomas Nehemiah	0	13	140	51.75	191.75	204.75
Total acreage	1,140	657	1,368.58	688.75	2,057.33	3,674.33[a]
Average acreage per proprietary right[b]	60	32.85	68.42	36.25	108.28	193.38
Percent	30%	17%	36%	18%	53%	

[a] Excludes Samuel Will's 180 right; his 180 acres were forfeited back to the proprietors.

[b] Totals for 1719, Final division, and Total grants were divided by 19; Totals for 1721–40, and 1741–62 were divided by 20. These calculations reflect the overlapping Will and Nehemiah rights. Even though Nehemiah replaced Will as a proprietor, both of them received land between 1721–62.

Sources: Land Grants to Proprietors, Freeholders, and Inhabitants of the Town of Natick, 1719; and Natick Proprietors Book of Record, 1723–87, Morse Institute Public Library, Natick, MA.

Table 5. *Disposition of the 6,000-acre plantation of Natick, 1683–1763*

Land grants to Indians, 1719–63	3,674.33	64 %
Corporate grants for goods and services, 1683–1730	1,252.75	22 %
Land sold prior to implementation of the proprietary system	588	10 %
Ministerial settlement, Oliver Peabody	211.5[a]	4 %
Total	5,726.58	

[a] Peabody's total divisions add up to this amount in the index to the proprietors' records. I located only 130.75 acres in grants to Peabody, but the book is missing some of the first several pages.

Sources: Land Grants to Proprietors, Freeholders, Inhabitants of the Town of Natick, 1719; Natick Proprietors Book of Record, 1723–1787, Morse Institute Public Library, Natick, MA; and Middlesex County Court, Grantee and Grantor Records, Cambridge, MA.

services such as mills, meetinghouse repairs, and a school. They lost 588 acres through land sales prior to implementation of the proprietary system, and granted Oliver Peabody 211½ acres as part of his ministerial privilege. Together with divisions to proprietors between 1719 and 1763, which accounted for 3,674⅓ acres, just over 5,726½ acres of Natick land had been granted out by 1763. Land sales to non–Indians totaled 600¾ acres between 1720 and 1740, plus nearly 1,574 between 1741 and 1763, so that in 1763, 1,499½ acres remained in Indian hands (about 24 percent of the plantation). (See Table 5.)

By 1763, Natick was an Indian place in only the most nominal sense. The proprietary system was symbolic of how Indians had been marginalized in their own community. Though Indians retained control over the land base in an official sense, English individuals had infiltrated every aspect of the operation of the land system, serving as clerks, committee members, and surveyors. In fact, the proprietary system created an entire administrative structure that permitted covert appropriation of Indian power at the same time it validated overt land transactions. The four separate meetings held to negotiate the final division underscores the extent to which conditions had changed since the advent of the proprietary system. (See Table 6.) Two proprietary rights, Abraham's and John Speen's, were not represented at all during these meetings. An additional six were represented exclusively by Englishmen. Only in the case of nine proprietary rights did Indians appear exclusively to participate in negotiations for their inherited rights. Absence of Indian spokesmen did not reflect extinction of family lines, either. As discussed earlier, heirs to each of the proprietors except Samuel Will had been identified prior to the final division.

Instead, extensive involvement of Englishmen in these negotiations reflects fundamental changes in the nature of the Indian town, visible in identification

Table 6. *Representatives of Natick proprietary rights, 1763*

1719 Proprietors	May 30, 1763 Meeting	July 4, 1763 Meeting	Sept. 5, 1763 Meeting	Sept. 12, 1763 Meeting
Abraham Speen				
James Speen	Joseph Graves		Abigail Moheag	
Moses Speen	Mary Speen	Mary Speen[a]	Esther Speen	
Josiah Speen	Lydia Speen	Lydia Speen	Sarah Ahauton[b]	Lydia Speen
Isaac Speen	John Ephraim	John Ephraim	John Ephraim	John Ephraim
John Speen				
Thomas Waban	Mary Waban	Mary Waban	Mary Waban	
Thomas Peegun	Samuel Morse		Samuel Morse	Samuel Morse
Simon Ephraim	John Ephraim	John Ephraim	Deborah Comecho	Deborah Comecho
Benjamin Tray		Thomas Russell	Thomas Russell	Thomas Russell
Samuel Bowman	Micah Whitney	Micah Whitney	Micah Whitney	Thomas Russell
Samuel Will				
Isaac Monequassin	Nathaniel Hill	Nathaniel Hill	Nathaniel Hill	Nathaniel Hill
John Awassamug	Thos. Awass. Jr.	Thos. Awass.[c]	Thos Awass. Jr.[d]	
Samuel Ompetowin	Jona. Richardson			Jona. Richardson
Hannah Tabumsug	Esther Sooduck	Esther Sooduck	Benjamin Wiser	Benjamin Wiser
Solomon Thomas			Esther Sooduck	Esther Sooduck
Israel Rumneymarsh	Sarah Rumneymarsh		Samuel Morse	Sarah Lawrence
Samuel Abraham	John Jones	John Jones	John Jones	
Thomas Nehemiah		John Jones	John Jones[e]	Samuel Morse

[a] And Esther Speen.

[b] And Lydia Speen.

[c] And Thomas Awassamug Jr. and Eunice Spywood.

[d] And Thomas Awassamug Jr.

[e] And Samuel Morse.

Source: Natick Proprietors Book of Record, 1723–1787, Morse Institute Public Library, Natick, MA.

of at least some of the relationships between the English spokesmen and the Indian heirs. (See Table 6.) Joseph Graves again made an appearance in connection with the Speen family, for example, acting for the right of James Speen. His extensive involvement with this family included acting as caretaker of James's widow, Abigail, until she died in 1759, and as representive of James Speen's right even though his daughter Abigail Speen Moheag survived as an heir. Samuel Morse acted for the right of Thomas Peegun, and had been the administrator of Thomas Peegun Jr.'s insolvent estate. Thomas Russell spoke for Benjamin Tray's right, and had also administered his estate. Micah Whitney represented Samuel Bowman's right, probably because he had been designated

Table 7. *Items listed in Indian inventories, 1741–90*[a]

Item	Number / Percent 1741–63	Number / Percent 1763–90
Land	46 / 88%	8 / 73%
Dwelling house	16 / 31%	3 / 27%
Barn	2 / 4%	2 / 18%
Husbandry tools	14 / 27%	4 / 36%
Livestock	9 / 17%	2 / 18%
Spinning wheel/weaver's loom	8 / 15%	1 / 9%
Notes/bonds	12 / 23%	3 / 27%
Household goods (general)	23 / 44%	4 / 36%
Household goods (furniture)	20 / 38%	3 / 27%
Apparel	19 / 37%	4 / 36%
Books	17 / 33%	4 / 36%
Gun	6 / 12%	1 / 9%

[a] Total number of inventories: 52 of 64 estates, 1741–63; 11 of 13 estates, 1764–90.

Source: Middlesex County Court, Probate Records, Cambridge, MA.

guardian of the proprietor's grandchild. And Jonathan Richardson acted for Jeffrey and Mary Henry, who had chosen him as a local representative after they moved to Providence in the 1750s.

E. *Bureaucratic mechanisms of dispossession*

English neighbors also assumed a more prominent role in the extension of formal probate procedures over Indian estates after 1740. Only eight had been probated before 1740; thirty-five were settled in the 1740s alone. In addition, while Indian relatives acted as administrators on five of eight estates probated prior to 1740, Indians handled only five of seventy-seven afterward.

Judging from the absence of husbandry tools and livestock from the majority of inventories, Indian landowners either used Native tools that appraisers did not acknowledge as containing value, or many Indians did not farm their land. (See Table 7.) Fewer than 40 percent of inventories listed husbandry tools, and fewer than one-fifth recorded livestock. Barns appeared in only four of the sixty-three enumerations. But virtually all Indians were referred to as "planters" in the probate dockets, with no finer distinctions made as was typical in English probate dockets.[56]

[56] Kathleen J. Bragdon, "Probate Records as a Source for Algonquian Ethnohistory," in *Papers of the Tenth Algonquian Conference*, ed. William Cowen (Ottawa, Canada: Carlton

One Indian was described as a "laborer."[57] Other economic pursuits are suggested by the inclusion of shoemaker's, carpenter's, and surgeon's tools.[58] Nine estates included spinning wheels, presumably used by Indian women.

Even dwelling houses were rare (only enumerated in nineteen of fifty-two estates), and most of them were sparsely furnished. More than one family may have shared enumerated structures, but as many as two-thirds of Indians may have used tents or wigwams for shelter. Only 58 percent (thirty of fifty-two) of inventories included both real and personal estate, although it is possible that heirs divided possessions among themselves before estate administrators intervened.

Extension of probate proceedings accelerated the dissipation of Indian estates by heaping bureaucracy-generated debt onto Indians who already stood obligated to creditors. English administrators carefully detailed their expenses for reimbursement. Charges might include filing fees in probate court and for gaining licenses to sell land from the General Court; expenses for journeys to the General Court and the county courthouse for probate appearances, registering land, and petitioning the court; excursions elsewhere to track down debts and credits; pay to appraisers and land surveyors; and the time and "trouble" of the administrator and appraisers.[59]

Indian estates thus both reflected the process of dispossession in Natick and became another wedge into their remaining landholdings. Only fifty-four of the sixty-three surviving inventories listed land between 1741 and 1790. Of these, 88 percent included from six to 144 acres of land between 1741 and 1763. Indian landownership declined relatively and absolutely after the final division of the commons; landholding fell to 73 percent in the eleven estates inventoried, and they owned from five to 73 acres. Administration costs, added to outstanding debt, prompted administrators to sell at least some land in 72 percent of estates containing real estate (thirty-nine of fifty-four).

F. Struggles over institutions, struggles over place

Two episodes of devastating mortality contributed to the shifting racial balance of the town that the process of Indian dispossession had initiated. Unidentified epidemics claimed the lives of fifty-one Indians in 1745–6, and twenty-three in 1759. In 1749 an Indian-endorsed census listed 166 Indians by household and location in the town, which meant that approximately 200 must have lived there

University, 1979), 137. The estates of Nantucket Indians were much more elaborate than those of Natick Indians. Elizabeth Little, "Probate Records of Nantucket Indians," *Nantucket Algonquian Studies*, Paper #2 (1980): 1–63.

[57] MCP #20862, Thomas Sooduck, Admin., 1748.

[58] MCP #66, Joseph Abraham, Admin., 1759; MCP #4958, Nathaniel Coochuck, Admin., 1753; MCP #21034, Josiah Speen, Admin., 1749; MCP #2490, Peter Brand, Admin., 1754; and MCP #13133, Eleazer Paugenit, Admin., 1741.

[59] See, for example, MCP #23691, Solomon Wamsquan, Admin., 1755.

in the mid-1740s. The epidemic of 1745–6 reduced the Indian population by approximately one-quarter. Assuming that their numbers remained relatively constant, the 1759 epidemic diminished their numbers by an additional 15 percent or so.[60]

Even before the first epidemic, English residents manipulated town boundaries as well as some Indian landowners so they could claim Natick as principally an English place, a strategy they used to try to gain control over local institutions.[61] Ironically, geographically rooted English factions battled doggedly over the location of the meetinghouse, which was supported by the New England Company for the Indians. English inhabitants of northern and western Natick, led by the surveyor Ebenezer Felch (who Indians later claimed encroached on Indian fishing rights), pressed their agenda in 1743 by jointly petitioning the General Court for annexation to Natick of a 1,700-acre area known as Needham Leg. Originally part of Dedham, it had been added to Needham when that town was founded in 1711. (See Figure 2 on page 35.) The petitioners argued that they wanted to attend the much closer Natick meetinghouse, which some Needham residents had been permitted to do since Peabody's arrival in the community, but their Natick allies hoped to gain support in the town meeting to pass a vote to move the meetinghouse from south Natick to the center of the town. The petitioners attempted to add weight to their request by presenting an endorsement of twenty-five Indians, five of whom later claimed that they had been misled. An additional twenty Indians disputed annexation, fearing it would jeopardize the meetinghouse site. In spite of Indian protests, the General Court allowed annexation of Needham Leg in 1744.[62]

The epidemic of 1745–6 exacerbated the population imbalance that annexation had been designed to accomplish, and prompted the General Court to respond by altering the legal basis of Natick. They designated Natick a parish, and barred Indians from voting or holding office in the town. For the rest of the century, different factions of the English population struggled for power in the town meeting and were equipped with legal justification for excluding Indians from local governance.[63]

The General Court understood that Natick's new political status left Indians vulnerable to English manipulation of the meetinghouse location, and thus required the town to gain its approval for any plan to move it. Free to raise taxes on English inhabitants to build its own meetinghouse and hire its own minister because of General Court-granted parish status, instead English residents from the western and northern parts of the town focused their energies on getting the New England Company-supported Indian meetinghouse moved to a location

---

[60] O'Brien, "Community Dynamics," 375.
[61] My discussion of the struggle over the meetinghouse and the changes in Natick's legal status relies heavily on Crawford's excellent analysis of factionalism in Natick. Crawford, "Indians, Yankees, and the Meetinghouse Dispute."
[62] Ibid., 283.   [63] Ibid., 283–4.

more convenient for them. They worked further to alter the population balance of the town by changing its boundaries, insisted most Indians would be better served by a more centrally placed meeting site, and by arguing that Natick was primarily an English place anyway.[64]

In 1747, in a meeting dominated by the Natick-Needham Leg allies, they voted to relocate at the center of the town and began procedures to gain General Court approval. English residents in south Natick preferred the existing arrangements. Their leader, David Morse, acted as an attorney for twenty Indians who wanted to build a meetinghouse on the old site.[65] His opponents questioned the legitimacy of the petition he produced. They charged that "some[,] while they pretend to take care of the Indians[,] only look to their own good and the good of their children,"[66] an accusation to which they were just as vulnerable. But the General Court-appointed committee that looked into the dispute found moving the site "to be against the General Mind of the Indians; & in Opposition to the Commissioners, who settled, & for more than twenty six years past have almost wholly maintained a learned orthodox minister among said People with very little assistance from the English inhabitants."[67] The General Court rejected the central location and instead suggested a compromise, setting the building midway between the current and proposed locations, which the Natick-Needham Leg allies refused. Morse and others from south Natick complied with a different court-proposed compromise the next year. In exchange for assisting the New England Company in erecting the new, larger meetinghouse in south Natick, they were exempted from ministerial taxes.[68]

When the minister of the newly formed religious society, Oliver Peabody, died in February of 1752, the controversy was renewed. In a call for unity under a new minister, the faction that favored the central site again tried, unsuccessfully, to have the meetinghouse moved. In 1753 Stephen Badger was selected by the New England Company to replace Peabody; he was fully aware of the divided nature of the ministry he was to fill. The controversy was silenced temporarily when Needham successfully petitioned the General Court in 1760 for the return of Needham Leg on the grounds that its inhabitants had attempted to move the meetinghouse, contrary to its own stipulations, and that they failed to attend meetings at Natick anyway, which was the ostensible motivation for annexation in the first place.[69] Two years later, the parish voted to unite in support of Badger, which the parish did until it renewed the controversy in 1778. Confirming the decision, the General Court also voted to upgrade Natick to district status, and retained its control over the meetinghouse location.[70]

[64] Ibid., 284–9.   [65] Ibid., 284.
[66] Ibid., 285.   [67] AR 14:294, Appen. 9, Chap. 84, 11 Aug. 1749.
[68] Crawford, "Indians, Yankees, and the Meetinghouse Dispute," 287–8.
[69] Most of Needham Leg was returned to Natick in 1797. Ibid., 291.
[70] Ibid., 287.

The battle over the location of the meetinghouse amounted to a struggle over whose place Natick was, and both sides constructed their arguments using information about the racial composition of the town. In insisting upon monitoring the meetinghouse location, the magistrates had reasoned that

> whereas the great Part of the Inhabitants of Natick are Indians, and the Minister there is in a great Measure supported by charitable Donations or Funds for propagating The Gospel among said Indians; and it is reasonable that the House for publick Worship should always be placed convenient for them.[71]

Advocates of the central site rejected such logic, and added, "we think it might have been as well pleaded that the Town house in Boston ought to Stand where it would accommodate the Indians, because this Province was formerly an Indian place, and there is many Indians living in it now."[72] Embedded in their sarcastic retort was a claim that Indians now occupied a marginal and deteriorating position in Natick, just as they suggested that New England in general was a "formerly . . . Indian place." Following up on the issue of numbers, in 1747 the faction favoring relocation counted eleven Indian families who owned 406 acres near the meetinghouse and twenty-six who owned 981 acres more centrally located. In 1748 they claimed Natick contained fifty-nine English and perhaps twenty Indian families. Surveyor Samuel Livermore drew a map in 1749 that identified fifty-three English houses and twenty-three Indian wigwams and houses. Indians countered with a census that identified 166 Indian individuals, 148 of whom were well served by existing arrangements.

More than a numbers game, the battles of the 1740s represented a two-fold struggle over place: whose place Natick would be, and what place Natick Indians would occupy in the community. Given the century-old missionization emphasis toward Indians and the financial support of religion in Natick by the New England Company, magistrates felt compelled to defend the Indians of Natick vis-à-vis the meetinghouse. But excluding Indians from local governance once English residents could plausibly argue for their numerical dominance laid bare mid-eighteenth-century notions about the role of Indians in political institutions: They would have no political place in local units where they were outnumbered by the English.

Around the same time, English town and commonwealth officials engaged in a further reconfiguring between place as a physical location and the place of Natick Indians in the colonial social order more generally. In the mid-seventeenth century, they could be "Praying Indians" fixed in bounded places, provided they listened to missionaries and considered altering their cultural practices. After King Philip's War, they could be recognized as "Friend Indians"

---

[71] JH 22:241, 24 Apr. 1746.
[72] As quoted in Crawford, "Indians, Yankees, and the Meetinghouse Dispute," 288.

who had earned protection but at the same time needed to be bounded, settled, and controlled. In working out these arrangements, they had identified Natick as one Indian place that symbolized the position of Indians within the dominant society, and emphasized the importance of Indian fixity there. By the mid-eighteenth century, a further redefinition of the place of Natick Indians in Massachusetts had occurred, which can be seen most graphically in the creation of a separate system of poor relief for Indians, which involved the problem of defining "proper inhabitance" in New England towns and revisted the thorny tension between English fixity and Indian mobility in structuring social order. English solutions to this problem both responded to and completed the process of dispossession.

The process of redefinition had begun by the 1750s. Indian Elizabeth Wedges broke her leg in 1748 and required medical care, which the selectmen refused to provide.[73] The General Court ordered Englishman Jeremiah Gay, with whom Elizabeth was living, to arrange for her care. The court approved payment of charges incurred, but then learned Elizabeth owned four acres of land in Natick and instead compelled her to sell it to cover the costs. Landless and still infirm, Elizabeth Wedges now posed a different problem for the town. Physician John Allen presented accounts for her care to the commonwealth in 1751, explaining that Natick selectmen refused to care for her under the provisions of the poor laws, which held towns of origin responsible for poor relief, "not deeming her an inhabitant of the said town." He understood the commonwealth was responsible for such indigent persons.[74] The Natick selectmen did not regard Wedges a "proper inhabitant" of Natick even though she had been a landowner and had attained full communion in the church.[75]

The issue of proper inhabitance received an even fuller hearing during a protracted debate over responsibility for the debts of the impoverished Indian widow Sarah Wamsquan. In 1767 she petitioned to sell land to provide money for her support.[76] Three years later, she was brought to the home of Stephen Badger "in a destitute State & in great measure helpless."[77] Another Indian widow, Eunice Spywood, took Sarah in and cared for her. Badger argued that the court ought to pay Spywood's charges in boarding and nursing Wamsquan, particularly since the account of an Englishwoman submitted earlier on behalf of Wamsquan had already been paid by the court.

In 1770 Indian guardian John Jones provided Sarah's life history to the General Court:

> The parents and grandparents of the said Sarah dwelt at Billerica in
> the County of Middlesex . . . her Grand-parents were Sachems and

[73] MA 32:66–7, 1750.   [74] MA 32:147, 1751.
[75] NCR.   [76] MA 33:409, 1767.
[77] MA 33:515–7, 1770.

owned that Town and Lands adjacent . . . her parents came occasionally to Natick when her mother was pregnant with Said Sarah,
and tarrying a few days she was born there. (At that time Natick was
not incorporated, nor an English family in it) . . . the Said Sarah was
carried to Woodstock or Pomfret [Connecticut], and kept there till
she was seven years old – Then bound to Deacon Braddish of Cambridge, who she served till she was eighteen. [She] then went to service with Doctor Dalhone of Boston 2 or 3 years . . . and then
married . . . an Indian of Cape Cod whose name was Lawrence – he
dying she married to Solomon Wampsquan of Natick, who has
been dead near 20 years.[78]

Sarah had deep roots in Natick, even though she also lived elsewhere from
time to time. She was born in Natick around 1702, though her parents were
sachems near Billerica. She lived in Connecticut until about 1709, and then in
Boston until 1723 or so. She had at least two children in Natick by her first
husband, Thomas Lawrence, who died in 1730, then married Solomon
Wamsquan in Natick in 1732. Together, Solomon and Sarah had six children
in Natick between 1734 and 1744.[79] Solomon was neither a proprietor nor a
freeholder in Natick, but he did own thirty acres of land, ten of which he
inherited from his brother John and twenty of which he probably purchased.[80]
Of the four children who we know survived Sarah, three stayed in Natick.[81]
Sarah was born, married, bore children, owned land, and died in Natick,
though her story was not so simply contained by her deep roots in Natick. But
despite her clear connections to the community, Badger and others came to the
conclusion that "it cannot be made to appear that she is properly an Inhabitant
of Natick or indeed of any other Town since she was freed from bond Service
in Cambridge at the usual Age of Life,"[82] and a petition that bore her mark
asserted that she had "no Pretentions to a legal Residence" anywhere, never
living in one place for the twelve months required under poor relief laws.[83]
This petition made an argument that attended to the niceties of English regulations about poor relief, entirely invalidated Indian patterns of mobility, and
emphatically denied that Sarah Wamsquan had any real place in Natick. Given
her circumstances and the colonial relations of power, even though she made
her mark on the petition it is impossible to know what she really thought about
her "proper inhabitance."

In making the case that the province should assume responsibility for Sarah
Wamsquan's care, Indian guardian John Jones testified to stark racial divisions
in Natick that were expressed even in ideas about charity:

---

[78] MA 33:513, 1770.
[79] Thomas W. Baldwin, comp., *Vital Records of Natick, Massachusetts to the Year 1850* (hereafter cited as *NVR*) (Boston: Stanhope Press, 1910).
[80] NPB2, 32, 1731.   [81] *NVR*.
[82] MA 33:515, 1770.   [83] MA 33:409, 1767.

upon the whole, the Indians are not able to support her – nor themselves, – and the English of Natick are already Over-Stocked with
their own poor, Some of whom I know suffer for want: This poor
woman has been supported by this Province – Pray Let Something
be done that Shall Speedily relieve the poor person that has her – or
they will perish together – I have no expectation that the District of
Natick will pay Eunice Spywood's acct for the time past or take
Care of the Said Sarah Wampsquan for the future.[84]

In Natick, Indians cared for Indians, and English for the English. Jones had no
faith the district would comply with commonwealth directives about poor relief
for Indians. He then got to the heart of the matter by asserting that if they held
Natick responsible in this case, "[it] will prove an inlet to as many other Indians
to come, as shall hear of it – And towns that shall have an Indian in them will be
likely to send him when he shall want relief."[85] As Jones made clear, Natick's
English residents feared that providing relief for Indians would act as a magnet
for other Indians. They had special reason to worry about the consequences in
Natick, given the fact that it had always been an Indian place. The General
Court obliged the parties when it ordered payment out of the public treasury,
declaring that Wamsquan was not "an Inhabitant of any particular Town or
District in this Province."[86]

Unwilling to set the threatening precedent of subsuming Indian poor relief
under the English system in Massachusetts (which Rhode Island had done),
towns, guardians, and individuals carefully kept track of charges incurred in
providing charity for Indians, then submitted them to the commonwealth for
payment.[87] Magistrates made general appropriations for impoverished Indians
beginning in the 1760s. In 1767 Natick guardians inquired about the possibility
of establishing a fund "for support of diverse poor Indians in Natick."[88] Rev.
Stephen Badger, by dint of his position as a minister still paid largely through
the missionary society, found himself at the center of the Indian poverty problem. The court allowed him six pounds in 1767 "for the charge he has been at
or may be at in supporting any of the poor Indians of Natick."[89] The next year
the court appointed a committee "to consider the distressed State of the poor
Indians in this Province."[90] In 1769 Badger asked the court to make arrangements "for the future support of the said Indians, and such others as may be
under the like circumstances."[91] In 1770 the court ordered payment for Natick

[84] MA 33:513–4, 1770.
[85] Ibid.   [86] MA 33:517, 1770.
[87] See, for example, AR 18:339, Appen. 13, Chap. 14, 6 June 1768; AR 18:383, Appen. 13,
Chap. 17, 1 July 1769; MA 31:255, 1738; MA 33:164, 1761; MA 33:597, 1774; JH
42:227–8, 28 Jan. 1766; and JH 44:95, 5 Jan. 1768. I would like to thank Ruth Wallis Herndon for sharing her portion of an unpublished paper cowritten with Ella Sekatau that looks
in part at Indian poor relief in Rhode Island, and for several illuminating conversations.
[88] JH 34:36, 9 June 1767.   [89] AR 18:240, Appen. 13, Chap. 30, 12 June 1767.
[90] JH, 45:29, 3 June 1768.   [91] AR 18:383, Appen. 13, Chap. 17, 1 July 1769.

physician William Deming's account for "medicine & attendance to diverse poor Indians of Natick."[92] By 1789 the court was reviewing batches of accounts submitted by individuals and towns for supporting Indians throughout the commonwealth.[93]

The problem of providing charity for Natick Indians was met by the commonwealth by erecting a parallel system of poor relief based upon a complicated accounting system that categorically denied that Indians could claim "proper inhabitance" in any particular English-dominated place. The system had several dimensions and evolved over time. In the case of Natick Indians, any landholdings of the individual were liquidated first in order to pay their debts. Then, remaining proceeds were placed in the hands of the guardians, who invested them and extended relief to or paid the individual's debts as they arose.[94] By thus liquidating Indian landownership, the commonwealth could even more forcefully argue that Indians had no "legal inhabitance."

Other Indian places maintained at least some corporately owned lands, and trust funds had been created for most of them through periodic sale of their lands to the English.[95] In these cases, the commonwealth approved expenditures from trust funds to which individual Indians were connected when they evaluated claims for Indian poverty relief.[96] Indians in Natick had been so thoroughly individualized that no such corporate fund existed, but descent and intermarriage linked Natick Indians to support systems in Dudley and Hassanamisco, too, which suggests that English creditors themselves identified or encouraged Indians to identify entitlements wherever they could make a claim to them, and that officials also tried to use these assets until they had been exhausted.[97] For example, Sally Ephraim sent a note by messenger from

92 JH, 46:170, 19 April 1770.
93 AR (1788–9):386–91, Chap. 161, 17 Feb. 1789; and AR (1789–90):249–57, Chap. 176, 11 Mar. 1791.
94 See, for example, AR (1784–5):932–3, Chap. 172, 23 Mar. 1786; AR (1794–5): 296–7, Chap. 116, 28 Feb. 1795; and MA 33:533, 1771
95 See, for example, Hassanamisco accounts in MA 31:292, 1740; MA 31:525, 1746/7; MA 32:4, 1750; MA 33:42, 1758; and MA 33:206, 1762. Dudley accounts in MA 33:463, 1767; MA 33:518, 1768; and MA 33:552, 1772. Mashpee accounts in 32:129, 1749. Punkapoag accounts in MA 31:221–4, 1738; and MA 31:551–5, 1747.
96 See, for example, Punkapoag: AR 17:452, Appen. 12, Chap. 173, 12 Jan. 1764; MA 32:122, 1751; MA 32:630, 1755; and Hassanamisco: MA 32:592, 1755.
97 Natick recepients of funds in Dudley: Thomas and Hannah Awassamug, and John and Sarah Ephraim, MA 33:518–20, 1768. Both of these Natick men had married Indian women from Dudley. The Ephraims had six children, all of whom were born in Natick. NVR. Natick recepients of funds in Hassanamisco: Sarah Printer Lawrence, daughter of Hassanamisco proprietor Moses Printer. She and her sister Mary Printer Tom had inherited Natick land from their uncle, probably proprietor Israel Rumneymarsh, but she lived in Grafton. Hassanamisco Trustees Accounts, 1718–1857, John Milton Earle Papers, American Antiquarian Society, Worcester, MA, 15 (1731), 17 (1733) and throughout. Mary Printer Tom, wife of Zachariah. They lived in Natick. Hassanamisco Trustees, 25 (1737), 26 (1738), 41 (1746), 44 (1746/7), 46 (1748), and throughout. Their daughter Mary Tom Comecho, wife of Job, Hassanamisco Trustees, 90 (1763) and throughout. Sisters Submit

Grafton to Natick guardian Jonathan Maynard asking for money to pay for "two summers sickness" in 1799. The selectmen of Mendon sent a message to the same guardian in 1804 noting that Deborah Comecho, "needy," claimed property in Natick, and they asked him to dispense with it. Comecho endorsed a note of the bottom to send "so much Money as you shall think necessary for me at this time."[98]

Finally, the province itself became a source of relief in the last resort only after all other sources of Indian capital had been exhausted. This practice was well established, though rather informal. Individuals and selectmen from the towns made direct pleas to the General Court for reimbursement whenever they expended money for Indian poor relief. Individual Indians did, too. This practice served to shift the burden from towns to the commonwealth, and spread the responsibility of a mounting problem more broadly. Towns thus protected themselves from providing poor relief for Indians, and erected a barrier to prevent needy Indians from congregating in particular places.

Poor relief for Natick Indians took one more amazing turn in the early nineteenth century. In 1828 the General Court empowered Natick guardian Samuel Fiske to sell the last piece of land owned by a deceased Natick Indian, Hannah Thomas, "in all things as the law provides in case of the Sale of the real estate of persons non comp mentis."[99] The proceeds were used to establish a fund for poor relief for Natick Indians to be administered by English overseers of the poor in Natick.[100] This action had the effect of restoring a corporate dimension to Natick lands, and recognizing the existence of the group "Natick Indians" after nearly all of them had been dispersed from the town.

The commonwealth, using sleight of hand to create this separate Indian poor relief system, declared that Indians were not really residents of any town, despite instances where very clear connections can be established. They even regarded as rootless those Indians who had been born and married in a single town and had owned land there. The 1759 petition of Natick Indian Joshua Ephraim recited the assumption succinctly and ironically: "the Indians, *Native* of this Province, are not accounted the proper burthen of any one Town."[101]

and Hannah Awassamug, daughters of Thomas Awassamug and Deborah Abraham Awassamug. Deborah's father was Hassanamisco proprietor Andrew Abraham. Hassanamisco Trustees, 94 (1766), 96 (1767), 98 (1768), and throughout. The Hassanamisco monies came from annual interest paid out to original proprietors and their heirs from the proceeds of land sold to the town of Grafton in 1728. These arrangements resembled an annuity system.

98 Indian Woman's Letter, 1799; and Letter Regarding One of the Last Natick Indians, 1804, both from Vault Materials, Morse Institute Public Library, Natick, MA.

99 MCP #12363, Natick Indians, Gdn., 1835; and William S. Simmons, *Spirit of the New England Tribes: Indian History and Folklore, 1620–1984* (Hanover, NH: University Press of New England, 1986), 16.

100 John Milton Earle, *Report to the Governor and Council concerning the Indians of the Commonwealth, Under the Act of April 16, 1859* (Boston: William White, Printer to the State, 1861), 72–3.

101 Emphasis added. MA 33:104, 1759.

Ephraim's commentary may or may not have been deliberately sarcastic in underscoring the fundamental tension in the claim that aboriginal people had no legal claim to particular places in the province. But what is clear is that as Indian dispossession from Natick proceeded, the English, almost none of whom had been there before 1740, apparently saw no contradiction in behaving as if Natick had never been an Indian place at all. Their official actions thus confirmed in practice their emerging stereotype of Indians as aimless wanderers without geographic origins, which reconfigured assumptions English colonists brought with them in the seventeenth century, and justified their displacement of the Native population. "Wandering Indians" in the eighteenth century differed from their seventeenth-century counterparts in that the colonial encounter divorced their "wandering" from actual Indian possession of their lands rather than reflecting English misunderstanding of Indian mobile economies. By the end of the eighteenth century, the English had done more than give up on the larger colonial project of culturally transforming Indians: They defined them as entirely extraneous to the social order.

G. *Dispossession, displacement, and dispersal*

No wonder Indians wandered. Dispossession increased mobility between places where Indians persisted, and it badly distorted Indian patterns of mobility. It also helped fuel crucial transformations within Natick after midcentury, and gender dynamics figured prominently as Indians were separated from their land. From the 1720s through the 1750s, men and couples submitted a solid majority of land-sale petitions, suggesting a relatively balanced Indian population committed to the community. But after 1760, petitions declined dramatically, and those from women and orphans dominated General Court Indian land business in Natick. (See Table 8.) Single women, widows, and orphans were more likely to stay in the town, drawing on their few remaining resources, wage labor, craft production, and charity for support, and skewing the population toward increasing dependence. The Indian-generated census of 1749 also helps plot the demographic changes in the community. Of eighty-two adult Indians, forty-eight were women (59 percent), and thirty-four were men (41 percent). At least ten of the women were widows. The Indians cautioned that "perhaps we have not thought of every one, and we hope some may be alive who have been soldiers or at sea not here named."[102]

As the census takers suggested, the increasingly skewed sex ratios in Natick are partly explained by the systematic participation of Indian men in the military.[103] The incomplete Indian death register enumerated fifty-nine female and sixty-four male deaths between 1740 and 1769 (after which no Indian deaths

[102] Mason, "List of Names," 136.
[103] Richard R. Johnson, "The Search for a Usable Indian: An Aspect of the Defense of Colonial New England," *Journal of American History* 64 (1977): 623–51.

Table 8. *Indian land sale petitioners by decade*

	Men and Couples	Women and Orphans
1720–29	15 / 94%	1 / 6%
1730–39	28 / 97%	1 / 3%
1740–49[a]	67 / 96%	4 / 6%
1750–59	29 / 71%	12 / 29%
1760–69	5 / 31%	11 / 69%
1770–79	4 / 40%	6 / 60%
1780–89[b]	1 / 17%	5 / 83%

[a] Includes one joint petition by a widow and her brother, which is counted twice.
[b] Includes one petition from 1790.

Sources: Massachusetts Archives, Massachusetts State Archives at Columbia Point, Boston, vols. 31–33; Massachusetts General Court, House of Representatives, *Journals of the House of Representatives of Massachusetts, 1715-1790*, 55 vols. (Boston: Massachusetts Historical Society, 1919–), vols. 2–53; and Massachusetts General Court, Council, *Acts and Resolves, Public and Private, of the Province of the Massachusetts Bay*, 21 vols. (Boston: Wirth & Potter Printing Co., State Printers, 1895–1922), vol. 12, Appen. 7–vol. 21, Appen. 16, and 1780–1790.

were recorded), but Oliver Peabody included an additional twenty-two military deaths and noted there were others.[104] At least fifteen Natick men served in the military in the first four decades of the eighteenth century; at least fifty-nine more did so after 1740. Twenty-two of these fought in the American Revolution, including Natick's most famous participant, Crispus Attucks, who was killed in the 1770 Boston massacre.[105] Contemporary accounts describe him as a "mulatto" and servant of a Framingham resident. His surname may be a shortened form of the Indian name Aquitticus or Quitticus.[106] Disabilities the Indians suffered in military service rendered individuals such as Joseph Paugenit and Benjamin Tray unable to support themselves or their families, adding to the hardship of their absence.

Some Indians chose to leave before the process of dispossession was played out in situ. Although Indians Caesar and Naomi Ferrit, who were originally

[104] NCR. Children's names are rarely noted, so I omitted them in compiling figures on deaths.
[105] O'Brien, "Community Dynamics," 406. For an overview on Indian participation in the American Revolution, see Colin G. Calloway, "New England Algonkians in the American Revolution," in *Algonkians of New England: Past and Present*, ed. Peter Benes, The Dublin Seminar for New England Folklife Annual Proceedings (Boston: Boston University, 1993), 51–62; and Calloway, *The American Revolution in Indian Country: Crisis and Diversity in Native American Communities* (New York: Cambridge University Press, 1995).
[106] J. B. Fisher, "Who was Crispus Attucks?" *American Historical Record* 1 (1872): 531–3; John Fiske, "Crispus Attucks," *Negro History Bulletin* 33 (1970): 58–68; and Janette Harris, "Crispus Attucks," *Negro History Bulletin* 33 (1970): 69.

from Milton, came to the town in the 1750s because he had "a desire to dwell at Natick among his Own Nation the aboriginal natives,"[107] they were more than counterbalanced by those who left. Aside from sporadic accounts of husbands "absconding" or going "to sea," men and couples left to get a fresh start elsewhere. Among these were Benjamin Wiser, and Jeffrey and Mary Henry. Still resident in Worcester and continuing in his capacity as executor of Samuel Tabumsug's estate, Benjamin Wiser moved to sell 36½ acres, the "Remaining . . . Tract of Land in Natick that is not Sold."[108] The lands in question were the 37¼ acres laid out in the right of Hannah Tabumsug in the last division. Wiser and many other heirs to the Tabumsug right had been long absent from the town, and getting more land from the final division did not persuade them to return.[109] Wiser sold 32½ acres the same year to Andrew Dewing.[110] Four more acres that came from Hannah Tabumsug were sold in 1785 to pay the debts of two female heirs, sisters Dinah Speen and Sarah Pero, who had stuck around.[111] Elizabeth Fay of Rhode Island wanted to sell her Natick lands in 1773, though it is unclear how she came to possess them in the first place.[112] In 1765 Samuel and Zurviah Ompany, who now lived and owned land on Martha's Vineyard, asked to sell thirteen separate parcels of land totaling about 100 unimproved acres, "Mostly being the last Division in the Common and undivided Lands."[113] The land came from Zurviah's parents, Rachel and Samuel Abraham.[114] Rhoda Wamsquan, who married in Natick, followed her husband to New Haven and stayed there after he died in 1766. She liquidated Natick lands inherited from her father, Jonathan Babesuck, who was originally from Woodstock, Connecticut.[115]

Indian kin connections spanned widely beyond Natick. Before 1767, between 27 and 40 percent of Natick Indians married outside the community; after 1767 the percentage climbed to 82 percent, and women married out more frequently than men.[116] Hundreds of Indian marriages appear in the vital records of at least seventy-three Massachusetts towns throughout the colonial period, although making precise linkages for individuals is very often impos-

---

[107] MA 32:429, 1753.   [108] MA 33:420–1, 1768.

[109] NPB2, 143.

[110] MCG 71:145, Samuel Tabumsug's administrator, Benjamin Wiser, to Andrew Dewing, 1768/1771, 32 1/2 acres.

[111] MCG 92:103, to Elijah Stone, 1785/1785, 4 acres.

[112] JH 49:149, 11 Jan. 1773.   [113] MA 33:448–9, 1765.

[114] MCG 85:491, Samuel and Zurviah Abraham, quitclaim to Stephen Badger, 1760/1784, 14 acres.

[115] He bought the lands in four separate transactions from three different Indian proprietors between 1740 and 1743. MA 33:366, 1766; MCP #580, Jonathan Babesuck, Will, 1746; and MCP #23690, Rhoda Wamsquan, Admin., 1769.

[116] Based on Kathleen Bragdon's analysis of the Natick vital records. Overall, she found that 34 percent of Indians married outside of the town, compared with 44 percent for the English. [Quoting from Philip J. Greven, Jr., *Four Generations: Population, Land, and Family in Colonial Andover, Massachusetts* (Ithaca: Cornell University Press, 1970), 211.] Bragdon, "'Another Tongue Brought In': An Ethnohistorical Study of Native Writings in Massachusett" (Ph.D. diss., Brown University, 1981), 145.

sible, lacking complete birth and death records.[117] Just taking nine distinctive surnames of Natick Indian proprietors, twenty of these towns include at least one vital record.[118] The twenty towns are in seven different counties: Worcester (seven towns), Middlesex (six towns), Plymouth (three towns), Barnstable, Bristol, Dukes, and Suffolk (one town each). Connections existed to towns in Connecticut and Rhode Island as well.[119]

Some Indians found African American spouses by the mid-eighteenth century, which further blurred the vision of those who searched for Indians using categories of racial purity. Indian women with African American husbands seem to have been more common, which seems logical given the apparent decline in the male Indian population, coupled with the demography of African American slavery in New England, which skewed the sex ratios toward more males than females.[120] New surnames emerged as a result, adding credence to the erroneous notion that Natick families became extinct. Local folklore recognized the mixed heritage of the population.[121] One nineteenth-century history of neighboring

[117] This includes only Massachusetts towns for which published vital records are available.

[118] Abraham, Awassamug, Bowman, Ephraim, Peegun, Rumneymarsh, Speen, Tray, and Waban. The surnames Bowman and Tray could be English. I counted towns with these surnames only if the record included the notation "Indian" or "colored." Three proprietary surnames show up nowhere that I have located: Monequassin (although the shortened form "Quasson" or "Quassont" does), Ompetowin, and Tabumsug. This list could be greatly expanded if other Natick names with strong connection were included. This figure is presented to provide a sense and conservative estimate of the complex network of Indian places into which Natick Indians were connected.

[119] Worcester County: Barre, Dudley, Grafton, Lancaster, Sturbridge, Webster, and Worcester; Middlesex County: Cambridge, Groton, Hopkinton, Lexington, Sherborn, and Weston; Plymouth County: Bridgewater, Kingston, and Rochester; Barnstable County: Barnstable; Bristol County: Dartmouth; Dukes County: Chilmark; and Suffolk County: Boston; *Vital Records of Woodstock, Connecticut, 1686–1854*, Vital Records of Connecticut, Ser. 1, Towns 3 (Hartford: The Case, Lockwood, and Brainerd Co., 1914); *Vital Records of New Haven, Connecticut, 1649–1850*, 3 vols. (Hartford: Connecticut Society of the Order of the Founders and Patriots of America, 1917); and James N. Arnold, *Vital Records of Rhode Island, 1636–1850*, First Series: Births, Marriages, and Deaths, A Family Register for the People, vol. 2, Providence County (Providence: Narragansett Historical Publishing Company, 1892).

[120] Ann Marie Plane, "Colonizing the Family: Marriage, Household and Racial Boundaries in Southeastern New England to 1730" (Ph.D. diss., Brandeis University, 1994), 22 and 263; and Ira Berlin, "Time, Space, and the Evolution of Afro-American Society on British Mainland North America," *American Historical Review* 85 (1980): 44–75.

[121] Determining the degree of intermarriage between Indians, African-Americans, and English is difficult, lacking vital records that systematically note the race of the individuals, and is problematic, given the underlying assumptions about race and purity. Even when race is designated in vital records, labels such as "colored" and "mulatto" indicate only that intermarriage had occurred sometime in the past. Clerks did not necessarily use these labels consistently, either. Certainly intermarriage had been occurring between Indians and African Americans over the course of the eighteenth century, and marriage between Indians and the English was not banned until 1786. See Jack D. Forbes, "Mulattoes and People of Color in Anglo-North America: Implications for Black-Indian Relations," *Journal of Ethnic Studies* 12 (1984): 17–62; Forbes, *Africans and Native Americans: The Lan-*

Needham noted that there was "a colony of negroes, with more or less Indian blood, dwelling along the south shore of Bullard's Pond (Lake Waban)."[122]

Because of extensive marriage to Indians associated with other places as well as with African Americans, the identity of Indians connected with Natick bewildered many observers. The Massachusetts Commissioner for Indian Affairs collected the following account of one Indian family at Hassanamisco in 1859:

> There is a family residing here, Elbridge Gigger the father, is of Indian blood, and married to a negro wife with four children[.] his mother [is] of the Hatchaco[uah?] tribe – (I don't give the right name) was named Lucinda Brown – his father Josiah Gigger was half African & half Portuguese. his grandmother was named Hannah Cumachee[.] She married an Indian named Andrew Brown – they had no permanent dwelling place – usually lived in Westborough in a hut through the winter – and through the warm Season near a pond in Waltham where they encamped – and sold Baskets in the [lower?] towns – she wore her hair long[,] wore a Red Blanket & a [?] Hat, and had property in Real Estate.[123]

Josiah Gigger was a son of Beulah and Nichodemus Gigger. Born in 1743, Beulah was a granddaughter of Natick proprietor Josiah Speen. Nichodemus, who was warned back from Natick to Marblehead in the same year he married his first wife in Lynn, was Beulah's third husband. Beulah's first husband, Saul Rodgers, was an African-American servant from Boston. The second was Moses Waban of Natick. In 1804 Josiah Gigger married Lucinda Brown of Princeton in Natick. She was the daughter of Andrew Brown of Grafton and Hannah Comecho of Natick. Two of Josiah and Lucinda's children were married in Gardner in the nineteenth century. Josiah's brother, Daniel Speen Gigger, married in Natick in 1797, then perhaps again in Shirley in 1826.[124]

---

guage of Race and the Evolution of Red-Black Peoples (Urbana: University of Illinois Press, 1993); and Kawashima, *Puritan Justice*, 98–9. I have been unable to confirm a single instance of intermarriage with the English, however. The only confirmation of Indian-English intermixture I have discovered is a notation in the probate docket of Capt. Thomas Waban. Francis Foxcroft, the judge of probate, noted with chagrin that the widow "brot a child in her armes af abt 18 moth old it looking of mixt blood [I] asked her whose it was[.] They all said its father were an Englishman by a daughter of this Testates." MCP #23401, Thomas Waban, Will, 1725. See also David D. Smits, "'We Are Not To Grow Wild': Seventeenth-Century New England's Repudiation of Anglo-Indian Intermarriage," *American Indian Culture and Research Journal* 11 (1987): 1–32.

[122] George Kuhn Clarke, *History of Needham, Massachusetts, 1711–1911* (Cambridge, MA: University Press, Privately Printed, 1912), 558.

[123] S. H. Lyman to John Milton Earle, July 30, 1859, John Milton Earle Papers, American Antiquarian Society, Worcester, MA, Box 2, Folder 5. He is listed as a Hassanamisco Indian.

[124] *NVR*, plus Nichodemus Gigger's first marriage: *Vital Records of Lynn, Massachusetts, to the End of the Year 1849* (Salem, MA: The Essex Institute, 1905–6); Nichodemus Gigger warned back to Marblehead: First Book of Records for the Parish of Natick, 1745–1803, Morse Institute Public Library, Natick, MA, 82. Beulah Speen's marriage to Saul

The commissioner's account of the family jumbled together assumptions about racial purity, place, and culture in struggling to explain who the Giggers were. He used the categories "Indian blood," "negro," "half African," and "half Portuguese" in addition to a tribal affiliation "Hatchaco[uah]" that he realized was mythological. But even though he used these categories, at some level he acknowledged the Indianness of the Giggers by recording their story. He also allows us to add Westborough and Waltham to Natick, Hassanamisco, Marblehead, Lynn, Boston, Princeton, Grafton, Gardner, and Shirley as places of significance to Gigger relatives, and pointed out the mobility through which Josiah and Lucinda made a living in Indian ways despite the fact that they owned land.

Amid the permeating poverty that Indians clearly confronted by the end of the colonial era was at least one story of diaspora as a strategy that secured an economic livelihood the English could recognize as legitimate. Benjamin Wiser liquidated his Natick holdings beginning in 1743 to seek his future elsewhere. Wiser left a sizable estate when he died in 1775. His administrators valued his Worcester farm, including land and buildings, at 186 pounds. His livestock included a horse, two cows and a calf, a bull, four pigs, two swine, and eight sheep. He owned a full stock of implements with which to farm, including two plows plus scythes, hoes, rakes, axes, a grindstone, and a spinning wheel and spindle. His home was comfortably furnished. Besides owning three beds and bedsteads and "other furniture," Wiser counted among his belongings pewter platters, plates, basins, and spoons as well as other flatware, towels and tablecloths, a looking glass, spectacles, and books. At least for that year his farm had produced well. Enumerated were twenty pounds of wool, thirty-three pounds of flax and several yards of finished cloth, as well as Indian meal and pork. His whole estate valued at over 226 pounds, Wiser had accomplished what must have seemed unlikely to him had he stayed in Natick.[125]

Benjamin Wiser was survived by his widow, Sarah, whom he designated as his executrix, and five children who had been born in Worcester, all of them under the age of twenty-one. Sarah died in 1794 at the age of seventy-seven in Auburn, her life memorialized by an inscribed headstone in the Center Burial Ground:

> She was kind and faithfull[. In] her[,] the poor have
> lost a benefit, the sick a skillful assistant, her
> acquaintances a very great friend, her family

Rodgers: *Boston Marriages From 1700* (Boston: Municipal Printing Office, 1898); Hannah Comecho's marriage to Andrew Brown: *Vital Records of Grafton, Massachusetts to the end of the Year 1849* (Worcester, MA: Published by Franklin P. Rice, 1908); Gigger children's marriages: *Vital Records of Gardner, Massachusetts, to the end of the Year 1849* (Worcester, MA: Published by Franklin P. Rice, 1907); Daniel and Josiah are described as sons and heirs of Beulah Speen in an 1803 petition to the General Court: AR (1802–1803):444–5, Chap. 148, 7 Mar. 1803; and Daniel Speen Gigger's marriage to Almira Travis: *Vital Records of Shirley, Massachusetts, to the Year 1850* (Boston: Published by the New England Historical and Genealogical Society, 1918).
[125] Worcester County Court, Probate Records, #66671, Benjamin Wiser, Will, 1775.

> blesseth her.
> Her life was much desir'd
> Lamented when she expired.[126]

In all, eight Wisers were memorialized by inscribed headstones in the Auburn Center Burial Ground, two with religious inscriptions. A degree of economic success appeared to provide this family a respected place in society, but not in Natick.

H. *Dispossession by degrees*

In 1797 the Rev. Stephen Badger answered an inquiry about the history of the missionary work among the Indians at Natick. His response offered his impressions of what happened in Natick, but few concrete facts. Badger claimed that conclusive documents scarcely existed from which to reconstruct their history. He based his account on his memory of forty-five years as minister in the town. Nonetheless, in the acuity of its vision, Badger's account is instructive. Much of what he sensed about Natick's history can be corroborated in the documentary record, though the prejudices and attitudes of his day permeated his observations and prevented him from fully analyzing what he saw.[127]

Badger noted that "the number of Indians in this place, as well as others, especially where the white people have been either intermixed with them, or have been settled in their vicinity" had greatly declined.[128] He did not emphasize a single factor to account for "this strange and melancholy effect."[129] He contended that adapting to a way of life so drastically different from the Native way posed grave difficulties for Indians. Badger asserted that customary usages were tenacious, that adaptation had had a detrimental effect on "their health and constitution, and of course had a tendency to shorten their lives."[130] Discussing Indian missionization in general, he observed that Christianity and "civil government" constituted a radical change, particularly as they had "to counteract . . . principles and habits of indolence and laziness, roughness and ferocity of manners, and an irregular and improvident disposition and practice."[131] Consequently, the struggle for Indians had been tremendous, and the success of missionary work had been meager and fleeting. In describing Indians in this way, he echoed stereotypes that had become chiseled in stone.

---

[126] Franklin P. Rice, comp., *Vital Records of the Town of Auburn (Formerly Ward), Massachusetts to the Year 1850: With Inscriptions from the Old Burial Grounds* (Worcester, MA: Published by the Compiler, 1900).

[127] Stephen Badger, "Historical and Characteristic Traits of the American Indians in General, and Those of Natick in Particular; in a Letter from the Rev. Stephen Badger, of Natick, to the Corresponding Secretary," *MHSC*, 1st ser., 5 (1790): 32–45.

[128] Ibid., 34.   [129] Ibid.

[130] Ibid., 35.   [131] Ibid., 36.

Despite perpetuating those stereotypes, Badger did recognize the discriminatory attitudes that informed the English treatment of Christianized Indians and crushed the Indians' spirit:

> [Indians] are generally considered by white people, and placed, as if by common consent, in an inferior and degraded situation, and treated accordingly. Of that they themselves seem to be not a little sensible. This sinks and cramps their spirits, and prevents those manly exertions which an equal rank with others has a tendency to call forth.[132]

His analysis of the implications of racism, which he analyzed as gendered and did not name as such, included recognition of its devastating psychological consequences.

Badger succinctly disclosed the mechanisms English neighbors used to dispossess Indians:

> If [Indians] have landed property, as has generally been the case, and are intermixed with white people; if these last are settled near their borders . . . [the English] have been under temptations to encourage their Indian neighbours in idleness, intemperance, and needless expenses, and thereby to involve them in debt for the sake of preparing the way for the sale and purchase of their lands, which, it is probable, under such circumstances, have generally been sold at a very low rate, in order to have their debts discharged; and the game, undoubtedly from the same motives, may have been continued and repeated, by which they have been impoverished and disheartened.[133]

Badger saw this as a general pattern, and that such methods had been employed in Natick "cannot be denied."

In Badger's estimation, the dismal circumstances in the town had developed not long before. At the outset of the eighteenth century, Indians had succeeded in establishing a civil and religious society based on English principles: "They then held up their heads; considered themselves of some importance, and were for some time stimulated to continue both in the profession of the christian religion, which they had embraced, and in some measures to conform to the manners of their English neighbours."[134] Conditions deteriorated, however, which Badger attributed to the bad example of English neighbors and the "strange propensity" of Indians to "excess." Gradually, the English gained a foothold in the town, joining Indians in conducting town affairs.[135]

Badger held a low opinion of the English who arrived. Reversing the usual stereotype, he characterized the infiltration of English residents into the town that occurred after Indians began to admit them into town affairs this way:

---

[132] Ibid., 38.   [133] Ibid.
[134] Ibid.   [135] Ibid., 39.

> After this, some English, from neighboring towns, some of whom, through indolence and excess, had neglected the cultivation of their own farms, and were necessitated to sell, purchased small tracts of the Indians, and became settlers, and, by degrees, obtained possession of more; the Indians were dispirited, and adopted some of the vicious manners of which they had too many examples before their eyes; [they] became more indolent and remiss in their attention to the improvement of their lands, to which they had before been encouraged, and in some degree lost their credit.[136]

Unlike other English observers, who feared that proximity with Indians would result in English declension, Badger argued that the vicious example of English who arrived in Natick destroyed the thriving Indian community. After they "by degrees, obtained possession" of Indian lands, the English displaced Indians from local governance. English residents became more numerous, and some, he concluded, "took every advantage of them that they could, under colour of legal authority, without incurring its censure, to dishearten and depress them."[137] Badger even remarks on how the laws, ostensibly imposed on land to "civilize" Indians, cloaked the questionable techniques English designed to displace Indians and make Natick their own.

In spite of examples of cooperation between the two peoples, Badger regarded separation as the predominant characteristic of the town. Distinctions were made in death as in life. He cited the burying ground that had been assigned to the English, and explained that Indians made exclusive use of their own two burying grounds. Those African Americans who were "unconnected with them" were buried in the English cemetery. He claimed no knowledge of any venture entered into cooperatively by the two peoples that had endured very long, and his primary example hit very close to home: the religious establishment. Although the church consisted of Indian and English members when he arrived to begin his ministry and Indians continued to join for a while, Indian communicants soon began to decline. Clearly embittered by the meetinghouse dispute that continued to fester even while he wrote, Badger charged that the English sought to alienate Indians from the church, discouraged church attendance, and manipulated Indians to their own advantage. He claimed that during his first few years there he had baptized and married more Indians than English, though the church records contradict him.[138]

---

[136] Ibid. The more typical point of view in this regard is well expressed in the following passage from Badger's biography: "As a younger contemporary put it, a large portion of the white inhabitants adopted Indian ways, became half civilized, and treated Badger accordingly." "Stephen Badger," *Biographical Sketches of Graduates of Harvard University, In Cambridge, Massachusetts*, ed. John Langdon Sibley (Cambridge, MA: C. W. Sever, 1873–1975): 12:106.

[137] Badger, "Historical and Characteristic Traits," 39.   [138] Ibid., 40 and 44.

Badger also focused on Indian transiency, which left him perplexed even though he understood its patterns:

> Indians are . . . strangely disposed and addicted to wander from place to place, and to make excursions into various parts of the country, and sometimes at no small distance from their proper homes, without any thing on hand for their support . . . for this, they depend, with unanxious concern, upon the charity and compassion of others. Some of them, after an absence of near twenty years, have returned to their native home. The most trifling and uninteresting causes have been assigned, by some of them, for their travelling thirty, forty, fifty miles, and more; . . . They have not infrequently taken infant and other children with them in their journies, which they generally perform very leisurely; many times [they] take shelter in barns, and in some old, impaired, and uninhabited building, and sometimes sleep on the ground . . . While in this vagrant state, they scarcely ever have any regular meals . . . They are generally not very well furnished with clothing; most of what they have, they beg, or purchase, with a little temporary labour.[139]

Even though he had precisely narrated the dynamics that accomplished Indian dispossession, he failed to make the connection between that process and Indians "wander[ing] from place to place." He could still conclude that transiency was a "strangely" Indian trait.

Badger provided one of the few contemporary estimates of the total Natick Indian population that survived:

> It is difficult to ascertain the complete number of those that are not here, or that belong to this place, as they are so frequently shifting their place of residence, and are intermarried with blacks, and some with whites; and the various shades between those, and those descended from them, make it almost impossible to come to any determination about them. I suppose there are near twenty clear blooded, that are now in this place, and that belong to it.[140]

As Badger unwittingly suggests, the story of Natick Indians is not a simple tale of extinction, but a complicated narrative of dispossession, displacement, and dispersal. Although his enumeration of twenty "clear blooded" Indians left in Natick sums up a story of extinction, his remarks upon the difficulty of counting Indians who "belong to this place" tells a different story, one that acknowledges a larger Indian sense of place that transcended Natick's physical bounds. Badger's confusion in coming "to any determination about them" both embraced and rejected ideas about racial purity as a criterion of Indianness as well as Indian ways of placing themselves on their land which importantly included wandering that had been transformed by the colonial encounter. Even

---

[139] Ibid., 39–40.   [140] Ibid., 43.

though in Badger's view an unknown number of Indians belonged to Natick, in the strict English legal sense, that place no longer belonged to Indians.

When the final common lands were divided, for all practical purposes Natick ceased to be an Indian place in anything but memory. In fact, Indian control had begun to unravel by the 1740s. Visions of estate building that frequently had been cited became rare after that time. Instead, increasingly marginalized in Natick, Indians set their sights on objectives of very basic subsistence in some degree of comfort. And as had always been the case, many simply left, either seeking better opportunities elsewhere with capital mustered from liquidation of their Natick landholdings, or filling social places that were permitted them as soldiers, whalers, laborers, indentured servants, basket and broom makers and sellers, utterly dispossessed of land. The hopes for estate building were replaced by anger over aggressive English trespass on Indian fishing grounds and manipulation in the meetinghouse affair, and finally, hopelessness that any future remained for them in Natick.

Conflict accompanied the arrival of larger numbers of English residents, whose aggressive attitudes signaled the shift in relations of power. The meetinghouse battle constituted the most obvious and blatant English manipulation of Indians. The English used a myriad of devices to insist that Natick was principally an English place. Other actions attested to their presumptions about whose place Natick was. Their attempted seizure of customary Indian fishing grounds said much; their denial that Elizabeth Wedges was a "proper inhabitant" of the town said more.

The development of the poor-relief system for Indians represented an amazing culmination in the history of Indians in Massachusetts. In the earliest stages of colonization, the English acquired enormous tracts of land through dubious methods in order to legitimize their settlements. Natick was established in 1650 by an insidiously paradoxical grant that returned a 6,000-acre tract to Indians in their own homeland on the condition that they conform their lifeways to English models and expectations. Acquisition of title to land remaining in Indian hands continued apace in the 1680s as English magistrates acquired additional extensive tracts through corporate transactions, and as towns scrambled to gain quitclaims to land they had already occupied. In the eighteenth century, Natick's landholdings were individualized, and Indians gradually sold what few holdings remained in their possession in small tracts on a piecemeal basis, many of them initially out of a desire to build English-style farms. Increasingly, sales occurred out of dire need as enmeshment in the colonial society led almost inevitably to financial failure. Elaboration of the poor-relief system provided the means to squeeze every last convertible asset out of Indians who remained in Massachusetts, carrying to its absolute logical conclusion the transformation of human relations into transactions in a ledger. The story that this ledger tells in Natick is the dispossession of its Indian population.

By 1763, Natick Indians had lost virtually everything they had once been grudgingly allowed as converts. Much of their land had been whittled away in hundreds of small parcels; any influence they had in proprietary matters became obsolete with the final division of lands in 1763. And the power to govern their town had been pried loose from them when magistrates stepped in to mediate the meetinghouse dispute. The one institution in which they retained even nominal control was the church. Even here, however, they did not go unchallenged. Indians emerged victorious in that battle only because of the intervention of the General Court and missionary society. These structural changes in the town were accompanied by the infiltration of English neighbors in Indian affairs in every conceivable area of their lives, as employers, masters, guardians, caretakers, clerks, surveyors of their land, and administrators of their estates. When Hannah Speen argued she was "Intirely surrounded by Lands of the English," she left a great deal unspoken.

In effect, the English, who as colonists were rootless people by definition, displaced their own dislocation onto Indians. This occurred first, by a gradual dispossession, and then by the creation of various political institutions and administrative mechanisms for poor relief that equated this dispossession with a lack of geographic origin or place. In contrast to the missionary venture, which was premised on fixing Indians in a bounded location, the establishment of a separate social welfare system for Indians entailed a complete discount of the Indians' place. The maneuver disclosed deep ironies of a project that began by imposing a construction of place as property and fixity upon Indians, and then dispossessing Indians of their property and defining them as rootless in order to establish themselves in their place. The transformation is quite explicit in the successively worked out (and sometimes overlapping) categories of "Praying Indian," "Friend Indian," and "Wandering Indian" which the English deployed to assign Indians to their place in the colonial social order.

As official recognition of changes that had occurred, in 1781 Natick was finally extended the status of a town.[141] All legal powers, privileges, and immunities accompanying that designation were extended to the community. In authorizing this change, the court ordered Natick to honor its agreement with the Rev. Stephen Badger. The court did, however, lift its restriction against moving the meetinghouse without its approval. With this act, the General Court removed the final remaining source of power reserved to Indians in the town. One hundred and thirty-one years after being bounded as an Indian place, Natick had been transformed into an English town.

[141] AR (1780–1781):26, Chap. 13, 19 Feb. 1781.

Conclusion

In 1861 John Milton Earle, a commissioner appointed to inquire into the conditions of the Indians in Massachusetts, described the difficulties involved in enumerating the Native population of the commonwealth:

> Situate as most of them are, near the seaboard, in the immediate vicinity of our fishing and commericial ports, the temptation to a race naturally inclined to a roving and unsettled life, are too great to be resisted, and nearly all of the males, first or last, engage in seafaring as an occupation. Thus, the men are drawn away from home, and are often absent for years at a time, frequently without their friends knowing where they are. The women, left behind, seek employment wherever it can be had, usually in the neighboring towns and cities . . . . After thus leaving home, they frequently remove from place to place, keeping up no correspondence or communication with those who have left; till at last their place of residence ceases to be known by their friends, and all trace of them is lost.[1]

Earle went on to describe the Natick Indians as "scattered about the state, and comingled with other tribes, particularly the Hassanamiscoes."[2]

Earle's characterization of Massachusetts Indians as inveterate wanderers provides an important clue for understanding Indian history in New England. Though he appears to be perpetuating a familiar racist stereotype, Earle had in fact grasped the basic pattern Indian peoples had followed in order to survive the catastrophe of English conquest. Indeed, it was his ironically accurate perception of the migratory nature of Indian societies that enabled him to identify nearly twice as many Indians as were enumerated in a similar survey reported in 1849.[3] Earle did not bother to investigate analytically the "roving and unsettled life" of the Indians, but his insights help us understand the seeming invisibility of Native peoples in New England since the earliest stages of conquest.

In fact, the Indian presence in New England is well documented throughout the eighteenth century. As long as Indians owned land, voluminous documentation was produced. Much can be learned about their lifeways for the very simple reason that the English craved that land, and had a propensity for excruciating

---

[1] John Milton Earle, *Report to the Governor and Council concerning the Indians of the Commonwealth, Under the Act of April 16, 1859* (Boston: William White, Printer to the State, 1861), 6–7.

[2] Ibid., 71.

[3] F. W. Bird, Whiting Griswold, and Cyrus Weekes, *Report of the Commissioners Relating to the Condition of the Indians in Massachusetts* (Boston: Commonwealth of Massachusetts, 1849). Earle counted 1,610 Indians in his 1861 report, but this report enumerated 857, not including Naticks.

attention to legal detail in acquiring virtually every acre that Indians grudgingly were allowed to possess as converts to English Calvinism.

There is another dimension to land and visibility. For the English, land was central to identity and place in society. Most families strove to own land, and family farms were the basic unit of society outside commercial ports like Boston. Landownership was thought to be essential for independence and membership in a community, and property ownership bestowed a political voice on male heads of household. The English bounded land as a commodity, and owning this particular commodity conferred place in society in an essential way.

For Indians, land was something much more essential. Land also signified identity for Indians, but in a fundamentally different way than it did for the English. For Indians, land meant homeland, which conferred identity in a corporate and religious sense, and it contained the crucial kinship networks that inscribed their relationships on the land.[4] As English colonization proceeded, land also became a commodity for Indians. Eventually, it became a source of social welfare, which completed the process of dispossession in Natick. But even though Natick Indians lost the legal tenure the English had imposed on their homelands, they remained in their ancestral territory, migratory and occupying marginal places that the colonizers permitted them as indentured servants, wage laborers, soldiers, mariners, and itinerant sellers of baskets and brooms. From the English perspective, Indians without fixed residences and individually owned land could not begin to claim a full place in the English cultural world.

In Massachusetts, the connection between individual ownership of land and full membership in society as it affected Indians became an acute problem during the era of the Civil War. Between 1849 and 1869, the anomaly of African American citizenship in Massachusetts and the state's vociferous role in the cause of abolition rendered their treatment of Indians as separate peoples without citizenship a political embarrassment. The census produced by John Milton Earle fit into debates over how to resolve this issue. Indian groups at Natick, Hassanamisco, and Punkapoag (all of which originated as Praying Towns under John Eliot's auspices), as well as Dudley, Gay Head, Mashpee, Herring Pond, Chappaquiddick, Christiantown, and Fall River in Massachusetts had retained at least some corporately owned land or corporate funds, and recognition of their separate identity as wards in a guardianship relationship to the state. In 1869, after twenty years of complicated debates about, and within, Indian groups in Massachusetts, the state enfranchised Indians and removed restrictions on Indian land alienation, which paved the way for more Indian struggles over land and identity that persist into the present.[5] But eight years before the extension of citizenship to Indians, Massachusetts terminated the guardianship status of Natick Indians that

---

[4] See Constance A. Crosby, "From Myth To History, or Why King Philip's Ghost Walks Abroad," in *The Recovery of Meaning: Historical Archaeology in the Eastern United States*, ed. Mark P. Leone and Parker B. Potter (Washington: Smithsonian Institution Press, 1988), 183–209.

stemmed from the creation of a poor-relief fund in 1828 on Earle's recommendation when few Indians remained in that formerly Indian place.[6]

Earle's description of Indian transiency meshed with the one provided by
Stephen Badger. These descriptions reveal that the English preoccupation with
Indian mobility, which imposition of their colonial regime grossly distorted, had
endured clear past the colonial period. During the initial stages of English invasion, Indian mobility figured centrally in the development of an English ideology
of conquest that justified dispossession on the basis of "proper" land use. The
missionary overtures the English extended to Indians were predicated on the
notion that Indians could have a place in the social order as converts to English
Calvinism fixed and bounded in Praying Towns. By imposing English notions of
landownership on Indians, they created a system that accomplished Indian dispossession by degrees and transformed their scheduled mobility into "wandering."

Prior to English invasion, Indian mobility had a great deal to do with reaping
the seasonally abundant resources of New England. But there was more to Indian mobility than that. Indian notions of community had always been larger than
the village itself. Long before the English arrived, Indians visited other villages
to maintain kinship ties, form military alliances, and engage in social and ceremonial activities. Neither colonization nor the imported diseases that fractured
families and communities deterred Indians from continuing this essential network. Given the continued ill health of the population, the web may well have
expanded even wider as Indians sought spouses to maintain their numbers.

Indian communities had become minority clusters dotted throughout southeastern New England after the English extended domination throughout the
region. Though conquered militarily and subjugated politically, New England
Indians persisted virtually everywhere in New England in clusters of a small
size (which contributed to their invisibility) although they were almost entirely
proscribed from meaningful place in the social order. Discriminatory attitudes
served to strengthen their identity as a separate people as well as the ties
between Indian enclaves that persisted. Indian societies adapted, probably
widening the geographic scope of their communities, and certainly incorporating African Americans.

By the end of the eighteenth century, Indian ownership of the vastly
restricted land base of Natick as a bounded place had entirely evaporated, and
English people had rooted themselves firmly in that formerly Indian place.
Indians left Natick because they had no reason to stay. The arrival of a growing
and disdainful English population reduced the Indian incentive to remain there

[5] Ann Marie Plane and Gregory Button, "The Massachusetts Indian Enfranchisement Act:
Ethnic Contest in Historical Context, 1849–1869," *Ethnohistory* 40 (1993): 587–618; Jack
Campisi, *The Mashpee Indians: Tribe on Trial* (Syracuse: Syracuse University Press, 1991);
and James Clifford, "Identity in Mashpee," in *The Predicament of Culture: Twentieth-Century Ethnography, Literature, and Art* (Cambridge: Harvard University Press, 1988),
277–346.

[6] Earle, *Report to the Governor*, xli and 71–3.

to the vanishing point, and eventually they left Natick out of their geographically broad itineraries that continued to inscribe their social order on the land.
In the case of Natick, and New England more generally, what had vanished was
not Indian people, but instead, Indian power to define the terms for possessing
the land. At least on this final score, observers should not have been so sur-
prised about vagrancy, since they were attempting to cope with an accelerating
"strolling poor" problem quite apart from the "wandering Indian." Even the
creation of these two similar categories articulates a stark racial separation that
governed English ideas about Indians.

Over the course of 140 years, Natick Indians had continually redefined their
vision of the future in creatively resisting erasure by the English colonial order.
Recognizing their precarious position after the permanent arrival of the English, they considered English Calvinism in order to secure some of their lands
within the imposed English system that dictated procedures with regard to the
legal tenure of land. They used their connection to the English religion as well
as their military alliance with the English during King Philip's War to make
claims for special treatment within the colonial relationship. When rapid proliferation of English colonists undermined Indian economies, they selectively
adopted and shaped English ways, and when they struggled demographically,
they intermarried with African Americans, which sustained their numbers.
Natick Indians responded to the shifting relations of power and changing colonial circumstances by negotiating cultural transformations that did not negate
their identity as Indians, but rather represented resistance to erasure that
ensured their survival as Indians even though the newcomers failed to grasp
Indian change as persistence. European (and Euro-American) assumptions
about Indian cultures as static and race as indelible, coupled with their notions
that Indians are Indians only when their autonomy is secured through diplomatic relations with colonial powers and a recognized and unbroken land base,
blinded them to Indian survival in New England.

For seven decades prior to the formalization of a proprietary system in 1719,
Natick Indians had kept their land base largely intact. Even many seventeenth-
century English encroachments had been turned back. A market in individually
owned land that emerged in the 1720s included an Indian-to-Indian component
that surpassed the Indian-to-English segment. But Indian land loss in these
years prefigured later developments. After the 1740s, Indian dispossession
erased earlier optimism. Once Indians began dividing and selling their land,
opportunistic English neighbors aggressively sought more. By the 1760s, Natick ceased to provide the essential things that had drawn Indians there in the
first place: An Indian-dominated community on an Indian-owned land base.
Indians were overcome by debts, illness, and injuries, which, together with
repeated military service, caused social and economic disruption.

The fact that Natick Indians struggled through epidemic illness and chronic
poor health, which threatened their survival and helped fuel their dispossession,

contains a profound irony: Though Indians in the town faced a land crisis by the third and fourth generations, just as English residents did in their towns, Indians might have averted the land scarcity that occurred in English towns precisely because their numbers very likely were not increasing. Had Indians retained their land base intact, it may well have been sufficient to support the Indian population. Communal ownership and usage of the land would very likely have provided the flexibility to respond to individual needs and periodic crises as it seems to have before 1719 when little land passed out of Indian hands. Instead, by 1763 Natick Indians no longer faced a viable future in the town.

Indian physical and psychological abandonment of Natick occurred in proportion to English enchantment with the town. Ironically, it was the reestablishment of the church (the first and last source of Indian institutional power) with an English minister that drew many English people from surrounding towns to make a commitment to Natick. Oliver Peabody argued for English neighbors in the 1720s, and his presence was critical in luring them there. The English ministry, Indian willingness to allow the English a part in town governance, and steady accumulation of Indian land made living in Natick thinkable for English people from surrounding land-strapped towns, especially Sherborn, Framingham, and Natick's old nemesis, Dedham. But the accelerating presence of often contentious English neighbors made living in Natick unthinkable for most Indians; those who were not harried out by land loss through debts or by English threats of legal prosecution liquidated what remained of their holdings and moved on. They left behind Indian women and orphans dependent on vastly reduced landholdings, craft work, a complicated charity system that treated them differently from English neighbors, and the English impression that Indians were disappearing into thin air.

As has been noted by scholars William Simmons, Yasuhide Kawashima, and others, much of what occurred in relations between Indians and English colonizers prefigured later developments in U.S. Indian policy.[7] Euro-Americans discovered little that was new. Reservations, removal, and allotment (ironically engineered by Massachusetts Senator Henry Dawes), and at least the semblance of the notion of a trust relationship all can be found in one form or another in colonial Massachusetts. The ideological underpinnings of missionary programs, too, involved ideas about education, a sedentary agricultural economy supplemented by spinning and weaving by women, rigid organization of time and space, redefinitions of family structure, and the thoroughgoing alteration of gender roles that changed little into the twentieth century. John Eliot and others envisioned widespread Indian landownership, organized according to English notions, as part and parcel of religious conversion.

---

7 William S. Simmons, *Spirit of the New England Tribes: Indian History and Folklore, 1620–1984* (Hanover, NH: University Press of New England, 1986); and Yasuhide Kawashima, "Legal Origins of the Indian Reservation in Colonial Massachusetts," *American Journal of Legal History* 13 (1969): 42–56.

The rhetoric of Indian declension and inevitable extinction, another parallel between Natick's Indian history and later U.S. policy, has misunderstood changing Indian identity in Natick and elsewhere as well, and reinforced ideas about Indian societies as rigidly bounded and Indian cultures as static and fixed in the past. In 1650 the establishment of Natick drew individuals and families from several separate Indian groups to a particular place where they could dynamically shape their present and future. Natick was a refugee town, and "Natick Indians" were a created group that had a kind of separate existence for nearly a century and a half. But Natick was never a closed community. A larger regional structure endured throughout the existence of the Indian town. It is within this context that one can understand what eventually happened to the group. Natick Indians came together, then they came apart. But they did not become extinct.[8]

Families and individuals moved into and out of Natick continually until Indian landownership there evaporated. By the end of the eighteenth century, most Indians had omitted Natick from their itinerary and instead moved on to other places within the familiar New England Indian network. The movements of individual Indians and families throughout the region appeared random to those who noticed them at all, offering further confirmation of the stereotype of the wandering, vanishing Indian. Natick Indians may indeed have been difficult to find in nineteenth-century Massachusetts, but that does not mean they were not there. Descendants of the colonized population persisted in connection with other Indian places. The term "Natick Indians" was artificial to begin with, created to describe the population of that town in 1650.[9] Beyond this exceedingly narrow and restricted usage, the term carries the weight of relatively arbitrary and ultimately irrelevant cultural assumptions about residence, stability, wandering, and vagrancy. Ironically, John Milton Earle's 1861 description of "a race naturally inclined to a roving and unsettled life" contains more than a grain of truth.

Just as we might suppose from Earle's description of the dynamics of Indian lifeways in the nineteenth century, New England Indians lived a rich and traceable history in the colonial period. With a different, geographically larger notion of community, and an Indian way of relating to the land as more than just a commodity, Indians persisted in a way not easily grasped by contemporary observers. By tracing families and individuals through the available documentary record, the uniqueness and viability of this regional community becomes manifest. Insights provided by Earle and other observers help us to understand how New England Indians have managed to survive to the present, despite the persistent narrative of impending extinction.

[8] For similar processes see, for example, James H. Merrell, *The Indians' New World: Catawbas and their Neighbors from European Contact through the Era of Removal* (New York: Norton, 1989); and William C. Sturtevant, "Creek into Seminole," in *North American Indians in Historical Perspective*, ed. Eleanor Burke Leacock and Nancy Oestreich Lurie (Prospect Heights, IL: Reissued by Waveland Press, Inc., 1988), 92–128.

[9] Lemuel Shattuck, *A History of the Town of Concord* (Boston: Russell, Odiorne, and Co., 1835), 24n.

Index

Index